JUST SEX

JUST SEX

Students Rewrite the Rules on Sex, Violence, Activism, and Equality

edited by
Jodi Gold and Susan Villari

ROWMAN & LITTLEFIELD PUBLISHERS, INC.
Lanham • Boulder • New York • Oxford

ROWMAN & LITTLEFIELD PUBLISHERS, INC.

Published in the United States of America
by Rowman & Littlefield Publishers, Inc.
4720 Boston Way, Lanham, Maryland 20706
http://www.rowmanlittlefield.com
12 Hid's Copse Road
Cumnor Hill, Oxford OX2 9JJ, England

British Library Cataloguing in Publication Information Available

Library of Congress Cataloging-in-Publication Data

Just sex : students rewrite the rules on sex, violence, activism, and
  equality / edited by Jodi Gold and Susan Villari.
      p.   cm.
  Includes bibliographical references and index.
  ISBN 0-8476-9333-3 (cl. : alk. paper). — ISBN 0-8476-9332-5 (pbk.
  : alk. paper)
    1. Sex.   2. Sex customs.   3. Sex differences (Psychology)
  4. Students—Sexual behavior.   5. Sex discrimination.   I. Gold,
  Jodi.   II. Villari, Susan, 1957–   .
  HQ21.J87   2000
  306.7—DC21   99-35070
                                                              CIP

Printed in the United States of America

To our families . . .
For their love and endless support in helping us achieve our goal.

Bob, Rochelle, Stephanie, and Tom

Sam, Eileen, Nanny, Steven, Antje, Chance, and Alivia

CONTENTS

FOREWORD

Andrea Dworkin

This book is more than just interesting or intelligent or filled with challenges to little-recognized but commonplace assumptions; this book represents the work and thought of a series of college generations for whom
stopping rape has the same import that ending legal race-based segregation and stopping the Vietnam War had on college campuses in the sixties. Had these students been hurling Molotov cocktails, they would have
had the front pages of every major newspaper for the last decade. Or had
they been taking out rapists, quietly, underground, no bragging rights, the
body politic might consider rape an urgent problem: Victimizing males,
even or especially guilty ones, brings out the empathy in everyone from
soccer moms to a current U.S. head of state himself accused of rape. Instead, what we have here is a new generation of feminists, female and
male, who work hard to try to stop rape: to get in the way of male entitlement over women's bodies; to educate men and women on the ways
in which sex roles function to legitimize the rights of rapists over the rights
of women; to try to intervene in the forced solitude of the rape victim, a
loneliness with no parallel; to serve and to educate. They are, in fact, doing national service, out of uniform, with no medals for bravery, no hierarchy of command or humiliation; like most workers against rape, they
are literate about sexual abuse and respectful of those assaulted, while at
the same time enraged with the rapists. But they have added a crucial new
dimension to the work against rape that they do: They want to stop rape
from happening altogether; they want to intervene before the injury; they
want to pull apart the rape culture with its constituent subcultures: the
rape-legitimized heaven of the male athlete or the rock star or the professor, protected by tenure, age, and, of course, a lot of practice.

When women my age (now in their fifties and sixties) were trying to
figure out what rape was and what rape was not, there was no commu-

nity in which stories of rape had any cogency. The politically progressive folk on the one hand saw rape as a joke and on the other saw it as an inevitably false accusation with a racist agenda: black rapist, white victim. The political right saw rape as a heinous, if rare, crime, an expression of a deviancy that ranged from being a black male to being a sociopath, essentially a continuum with no middle: This was in fact the black and white of it: Black-on-white rape has its roots in blackness per se, and if white, the rapist was born bad. In terms of who was left out, that would be all the black women raped by men of any color; all the white women raped by white men; and all the white men who raped. Brown, red, and yellow women were left to fend for themselves: as were all the brown, yellow, and red rapists. All the political Little Evas—white, innocent, incapable of evil—wanted under no circumstance to make a charge of rape against a black man: even when raped; even when brutalized or battered or threatened with a knife or gun as part of the force used to accomplish the rape. The hurt, the shame, the broken pieces inside where no one sees were the rape victim's alone: her burden to bear; her flesh-and-blood contribution to standing against the legal jeopardy in which so many black men found themselves—for being black, not for raping.

My generation changed the moral algebra of that equation. Anyone who rapes is a rapist and belongs in jail; neither black men nor white women deserve their special places in the U.S. mythic rape scenario; black women were also raped, and this fact required political recognition, moral outrage, and legal remedy—none of which have been forthcoming. Once one started asking real questions about rape, especially to the victims of it, there were new facts, virtually unbelievable to both the rape-is-heinous boys and the rape-is-a-joke boys. Rape was a crime of proximity, which is why most rape was intraracial—in a racially segregated society, men raped the women closest to them. Rape was indeed committed by really nasty strangers, but more frequently it was committed by apparently pleasant acquaintances, dates, neighbors, teachers, an uncle or stepfather: Girls and women were in more danger at home or in the neighborhood or playing with friends than hitchhiking or talking to strangers. Girls and women were most often raped by men and boys they knew. This was, in essence, the worst of all possible worlds: Girls and women were still held responsible for stranger rape—if she had not been there (wherever) he could not have raped her. If she had not worn x or gone to y (after dark no less) or been alone, the bad deed would not have happened, at least not to her. At the same time, home was supposed to be a safe place, a refuge from the conflict and indignity of the egregious insults and assaults that happened outside the house.

At colleges there was a different rape ambience: It was not home exactly and the rapists were not strangers exactly; suddenly young women

were "pussy," and valued as such: which is to say, boys hunted, sometimes in packs, for women to fuck. The strategies they used to get the results they wanted had the advantage of being tried-and-true: get her
drunk or stoned, get her physically isolated, get her afraid of what will
happen to her if she leaves: just get her body prone by any means necessary and get inside her. Some girls were asking for love, some for friendship, some for sexual affection; college relationships have the peculiar
quality of being both transient and forever. Rape, too, is both transient and
forever. It starts, it stops, it never ends.

Rape has been very hard for women to understand. Each woman, after all, sees herself as a person with qualities and talents and problems
and ambitions and a great curiosity about life: What will happen? What
will I become? Will I be able to do what I want, to make my ambitions
real and concrete, not just a dream in my mind? Then a rapist intervenes.
In acquaintance and date rape, the woman's idea of herself or any hard-
won self-knowledge is pissed on. She's opened up and, through an internal assault, a man says to her: You're nothing and no one. Rape is intensely
expressive; the message is inscribed on the unwilling body. And if he can
do this, anyone can. Women in general, especially young women, want
to live in a harmonious world, one in which kindness and generosity
matter, a world in which empathy is the main dynamic of friendship. How
does one live in a world in which anyone one knows, gendered male,
might well rape? Add into the mix the social requirement that women be
nice: receptive, caring for others, not pushy or rude, always assuming the
best, never the worst. Is it really true that having a cup of coffee with a
man or inviting him into where you live (if he is not already there) or
going out after dark is an invitation to rape? Each time a woman has a
conversation with a man, is she supposed to be able to get him to establish with some certainty that he is not a rapist? Since most rapes are not
stranger rapes, what kind of rap sheet would her science teacher or her
brother's best friend or, for that matter, her brother have? Suppose a
woman wants to live in the world as a fully enfranchised person? Yes, she
wants to go to the mall and to the library. She's also allowed to have a
drink or two or three alone in a bar; she has every right to take a walk
after dark; she can sit on a park bench in broad daylight to read a newspaper or book; she has a presence, physical or intellectual or creative, that
demands attention; she loves life and has a vitality that is equal parts
appetite and engagement; she is friendly; she enjoys male company and
believes in her own equality with men (although that is a shockingly low
standard to meet); she likes sex or not and is articulate about the presence
or absence of her own desire; but above all, she cannot live in a nightmare
world in which every contact with a male may turn into a rape for which
she will be held responsible. Yet that is the world she lives in, acknowl-

edged or not. Kafka could not have told the story of one day in the life of a woman in a rape culture.

The pedagogy of being a successful female is a pedagogy of victimhood and stupidity, each preparing the way for rape. Women stand up to men—just verbally—at a price; men are taught that to lie in pursuit of sex is acceptable, part of the art of seduction. A woman who deconstructs the lies—just verbally—will be stigmatized as a ball buster or man-hater or prude or lesbian. Another way of saying this is that in standing up for one's integrity one becomes a Victorian lesbian. What's wrong with that?

The know-nothingness of successful femininity means that women live a perpetual lie and that the lie itself has to make her seem stupid so that he will seem smart. Virginia Woolf talks about a woman being a mirror in which a man can see himself as twice his size. Gloria Steinem recollects the femininity of her generation as the girl saying to the boy, Oh, my God, aren't you wonderful, you can tell time! I think of my struggle in elementary school to understand why my mother, who taught me not to lie, insisted that I had to lose when playing checkers with a boy. I did try so hard to understand why this lie was necessary and other lies were wrong. My mother's answer was emblematic of her time: Boys won't like you if you win. So then, said I, they must not be the right boys, if you have to lie to them. Just do it, said mom. Now, of course, it is very hard to lose at checkers consistently, even to boys; and I personally regard the several years of finding new ways to lose as rigorous training in military strategy; the problem is that one has to commit one's intellect to losing, which hurts the heart. This same commitment also causes girls to develop contempt for boys—those fools who think they're winning because they're smart. This contempt is very much a part of femininity: After all, femininity is based on deception and manipulation. Are there really men who believe that women do not have hair on their legs or under their armpits? Patterns of hair density are in part racial: For instance, Asian and Native American men and women have significantly less body hair than whites or blacks. That having been said: Does seeing shaved legs and shaved armpits over a series of decades ultimately persuade that females are born, grow up, and die hairless? Since the female body seems to be the sole signifier of a woman's life, why not use it to taunt and tease men, who appear to be genuinely stupid enough to respond? As a basis for self-esteem there is nothing promising here. As a basis for an ethical life, there is nothing here at all. And contempt-based manipulation is always trumped by violence or force, which is how boys win the games that matter.

Rape affects everything big in life and everything small: Who am I, what will I be, what am I worth, it was my fault, where is there a safe place for me, why doesn't anyone seem to care, why does the legal system protect him and not me, why do my friends shun me, why don't his friends shun him: Why don't my friends shun him? I need milk, the stores are still open, can I risk going out to get it; I want to go to that movie, I'm in the mood, dare I risk it, are all the windows locked, maybe I shouldn't wear this dress, I don't want to be touched, I can't sleep, I have night-mares, I have physical pain still, everything has changed: I don't live here, in my own life, anymore. From the sublime to the ridiculous, every de-tail of life changes. Why? Why for rape? What is so special about rape?

Rape is often confused with assault or with battery. Because under the old rape laws a woman had to fight virtually to the death to prove that she had not consented, the perception that rape is real depends on inju-ries that may accompany but are not rape. Legal assault does not require physical touching or brutalization; so that, for instance, if a woman is es-corted by an armed state trooper to the hotel suite of a governor of a U.S. state and that governor drops his pants and says "kiss it" while the armed state trooper is guarding the door, this series of acts, none of which in-volve touching the victim, constitute assault. Battery is beating, biting, inflicting pain, bondage, torture, restraining someone by physical force: Bites on the lip, for instance, constitute battery; so do skin-breaking bites on a woman's back. A good rape, according to women who work in rape crisis centers, is one in which the woman does not know the man and is hurt so viciously that no one could possibly believe she consented—which is to say, that a good rape, meaning a provable rape, convinces a jury on the basis of how severe the battery was. What, then, is rape? Rape is an internal battery. Rape itself is neither proved nor disproved by swollen lips, black eyes, bites on the back: especially in the defense-lawyer/por-nographer constructed era of rough sex: Hey, she liked it rough; she wanted him to beat her; she liked the bites that broke the skin on her back. Rapists are acquitted so often (and indicted so rarely) because of a pur-poseful confusion in the legal forum, where the rules of evidence oper-ate in favor of the rapist, not the victim, this injustice legitimated by end-less phalanxes of lawyers on television, the nature of which was changed by the broadcast trial and acquittal of O. J. Simpson for murdering the wife he had repeatedly battered and raped and her acquaintance, Ron Goldman, a young man in the wrong place at the wrong time: a young man, I believe, who lost his life trying to help Nicole Simpson (rather than running). The internal battery of rape is wrong, illegal, and still not un-derstood as a stealth crime choreographed by someone determined to do internal, irrevocable harm to a chosen victim.

The question of how one proves rape has to be superseded by the ques-tion, What is rape? A woman is raped; her best friend asks: But did he hurt you? The friend means what she says: Did he hurt you such that we can see injuries; did he really hurt you; show me where it hurts. There are many wrong reasons that states anathematize forced penile penetration into the vagina as rape; but there is one right reason: the unwelcomed penile penetration is the crime of rape.

Just Sex goes right to the heart of what differentiates sex from rape, what differentiates a human engaging in sex from an object used for sexual release; what makes sex intimate instead of annihilating. This is a book my generation of feminists (who were, before that, sexual liberationists) could not have imagined, because this current generation of assault-and-rape prevention advocates are engaged in the process of making both sex and intimacy a whole-body, whole-mind experience. They are doing work that thirty years ago could not have been comprehended. My generation closed down de jure segregation and the Vietnam War (without erasing racism, including de facto segregation, and without stopping war); this generation will close down the kinds of rape now taken for granted as normal, natural, inevitable; and "But did he hurt you?" will be an ignorant, unspeakable insult. They will change the ways in which rape is understood with or without media recognition, with or without a thank-you from the ideologically opposed women they have helped through their work, with or without public knowledge that rape-prevention programs on campuses now include men who do repudiate rape, that repudiation being part of a new male identity, less arrogant, more equality driven. What an honor for my generation of feminists: to have cleared away enough legal and cultural garbage such that new generations of young adults on college campuses have taken up stopping rape with concrete commitment, new activist strategies, a brilliant sense of possibility, and an equality-based ethic of right and wrong. I'm sure glad I was around to see it.

Andrea Dworkin

PREFACE

They Never Burned Their Bras

Hook-up, mash, fool around, or shag—isn't it all just sex? Sex is no big deal, right? But what if it isn't consensual? Then it is not just sex. Then it is acquaintance rape. In 1989, when I became an antirape educator, I expected to fight rape. I believed that all rape was violence. Rape was not sex. What I found out later was that, yes, rape is violence—but acquaintance rape is also about sex. When I joined the anti–sexual violence movement, I found women and men like myself trying to navigate the confusing sexual landscape of the late twentieth century. As a result, I spent more time during college talking about sex than having it.

Our movement began before we did. Our mothers' generation of feminists broke ground by creating a strong foundation of gender equality. My generation has used these building blocks to create our own world with new rules and opportunities. Hampering our recognition of our own feminist activism have been the misconceptions created by the media and blindly accepted about the movement. For example, many in my generation believe in the bra-burning myth. Unfortunately, not many Generation-Xers know that it was a newspaper headline, and not an actual incident, that produced the supposed phenomenon. "Bra burning" was a play on words that referred to the burning of draft cards. The fallacy of bra burning is only one example of how the women's liberation movement was misrepresented to its daughters and sons. Student educators and activists of the 1990s have attempted to learn from both the successes and missteps of previous movements. The myth of bra burning is just one of many reasons that we undertook the formidable task of creating *Just Sex*.

Growing up in Memphis, Tennessee, I had heard all about bra burners and radical activists from the 1970s, but I was much too young to have any firsthand memories of the actual events. Radical political action was not something I encountered regularly in my sheltered suburban life. My

most radical decision was to leave the South to pursue a college education at the University of Pennsylvania.

It was at Penn that I met Susan Villari, the coeditor of this anthology.
She was a radical activist not only in the 1970s, but also in the 1980s and
1990s. She opened my eyes to the realities of sexism and sexual violence
that I had seen without seeing. Through my relationship with Susan, I
gained an appreciation for the feminist legacy bestowed upon my generation. She reminded me that we were neither the first nor the last to fight
sexual violence. Yet when I discounted my own voice as young and inex-
perienced, she urged me to trust my passion and idealism. Our collaboration combined a respectful regard for the past with a hopeful vision for
a future without sexual violence.

For some, passion comes quickly, but a political consciousness always
takes time. Talk to most activists and they will tell you about one moment
or one experience that galvanized them and started them on their path.
For me it began with a peppy voice at an otherwise somnolent sorority
meeting. The voice belonged to Anne, an outspoken southern belle from
San Antonio. She said the phrase "date rape" in a loud, clear voice, and I
woke up. Anne and her roommate, Erica, were organizing a peer education group called Students Together Against Acquaintance Rape, STAAR.
Today everyone knows by junior high school about date or acquaintance
rape, but in 1989 we had no name for it. I was shocked when I learned
about it, but I never dreamed that I would spend the next ten years of my
life trying to make it stop.

I had heard stories. I just never knew it was rape. Many of my friends
described unwanted sexual encounters. They had said *no*. They had not
consented. In retrospect, it seems obvious, but I had not previously connected my friends' experiences with rape. It was a startling realization that
rapists were not evil men lurking in the bushes, but my neighbors, classmates, friends, and lovers. The anti–sexual violence movement was fighting a war at home, not abroad. If sexual violence was so close to home,
then the solution could not be limited to stiffer jail sentences. We had to
examine and challenge our own communities, which explicitly tolerated
sexual violence by not holding perpetrators accountable for their actions
and, thus, blaming the victim. As a woman, I was held accountable for
every comment I made, outfit I selected, or action I took. By contrast, many
men were not held responsible even for rape. The solution had to be political because it was necessary to challenge existing power structures that
embraced and protected the status quo.

At age nineteen, I was a living legacy of what the women's liberation
movement had accomplished. I was a single, young woman at a prestigious college who regarded her future as unlimited. I just didn't regard
myself as a feminist. When I accepted my role as a STAAR educator, I had

no idea that I would be trading in my sheltered Ivy League world for a feminist political consciousness about violence and oppression. On campus I had become known as the "rape girl." Men no longer approached me with flirtatious eyes; instead, they told tales of women who didn't say yes, but didn't say no. With everything I heard and everything I learned, my eyes were further opened to the prevalence of date rape, sexual assault, harassment, and male sexual entitlement that allowed some men to assume a right to sex at all costs. There was no turning back.

"Feminism" and "activism" were two words that were not supposed to be a part of my "Generation X" experience. But I could no longer deny my feminist, activist, or political identity. To my surprise I was not asked to sign an agenda or take off my pearls and panty hose in order to be a feminist. I was not required to lead a "sit-in" or get arrested to be an activist. Every time I led a workshop or discussed current events over dinner with my friends, I was attempting to peel away another rape myth or sexist and racist attitude.

One of the greatest aspects of modern student activism is that if you are clever, you can challenge the institution and be funded by it at the same time. STAAR was housed in the strategically neutral Office of Health Education (as opposed to the Women's Center) and was advised by a professional health educator, Susan Villari, now the coeditor of this anthology and Director of Health Education at the University of Pennsylvania. At the time, she was a recently hired health educator with an enthusiasm to change minds, attitudes, and, even if on just one issue, the world. Susan's entrée into activism was through the women's health movement in the late 1970s. Armed with her flashlight, speculum, and recently published *Our Bodies, Ourselves*, she became politicized by viewing her own cervix and teaching other women about their own bodies. In her current role, she is a grown-up student activist who is paid to be radical.

Susan fostered the metamorphosis of well-intentioned freshmen into sophisticated radical activists. With her support, I became a feminist activist who believed in both radical and collaborative political action. Susan taught me that "radical" meant challenging the status quo, not blowing up buildings. I had seen radical activists and politicians ignite the dialogue, but coalition and collaboration were always essential for meaningful social change. Susan introduced me to the basic tenets of student activism and helped me to believe in the process of peer education. In Susan I trusted someone over thirty, and she still remembered what it felt like to be twenty-one.

Susan made critical observations about the student movement against sexual violence. She was impressed by the number of men in the student anti–sexual violence movement, the unlikely coalitions, and the changing sexual climate on campus. Not everyone agrees on a single method or ideology, but everyone deplores violence. At Penn it was commonplace to see religious group members, gay and lesbian student leaders, and football players join together with more "traditional" feminists to fight sexual violence. Susan and I both agreed that women should lead feminist movements, but men's involvement is integral to ending rape. I saw these motley crews of men and women as effective and assumed them to be normal because it was all that I knew. On the contrary, Susan recognized the uniqueness of these powerful alliances as a new era in the feminist movement.

As a body image and sexuality educator, Susan recognized the changing sexual landscape early on. The current student generation was ushering in a new, revised, but true sexual revolution. College women were expecting equality in the classroom and in the bedroom. Men and women were beginning to grapple with an evolving sexual paradigm that focused on consensual sex and kept up with changing sexual roles and expectations.

During my college years I learned how intimately political it is to advocate for a woman's right to be sexual. In theory I had already examined the politics of women's sexuality. But I fully understood the deeply rooted obstacles to sexual liberation at the most unlikely of places, in a late-night drinking game called "I Never." In this highly evolved game of "Truth or Dare," the object is to trap the participants into revealing embarrassing, typically sexual, escapades. Each participant takes a turn creating an "I never" statement such as "I never had sex in a car." Only those in the group who have had sex in a car are required to drink. Gathered around the beer cans and ashtrays were twelve bright women who would soon be taking Wall Street, law school, and medical school by storm. Well into the game, one friend raised her glass and laughingly said, "I have never masturbated." An embarrassed silence was followed by a revealing conversation of how little we knew about our own bodies. There wasn't a sober woman in the circle. We had drunk to all sorts of sexual encounters, but we couldn't have found our "G-spot" to save our lives.

A few years after the "I Never" game, I led an all-women workshop entitled "Masturbation 101" at the University of California in Davis and at the State University of New York in Buffalo. Far from a "how-to" session, the workshop was devoted to the role of sexuality education within the antirape movement. During the "I Never" game, we realized that our lovers knew our bodies better than we did. The workshop participants recognized that they had a right know about their own bodies. They had a right to be sexual without shame. They had a right to say yes loudly and clearly. Allowing women to be comfortable with own their bodies and sexuality is a crucial component to ending rape and converting self-consciousness to self-empowerment.

By my senior year in college, STAAR was an established program and we were consulting nationwide with schools that were attempting to develop anti–sexual violence programs. At that time we did not connect peer educators and antirape groups to the larger social change movement; however, as we spoke to more student leaders, we began to realize the importance and magnitude of student organizing. In the now inconceivable pre-Internet era, it was difficult to network with other schools, and many students on hostile campuses worked in isolation. A local sexual violence workshop that we planned turned into a North American conference that grew into fifteen individual conferences, including three in Canada to date. As the movement grew, conference organizers recognized the need for a national student organization to coordinate the conferences, and SpeakOut: The North American Student Coalition against Sexual Violence was born. When STAAR organized the first conference, students facilitated all workshops with the support of a few activist staff from the University of Pennsylvania. We employed a model of peer education that has come to epitomize modern-day student activism. We were the experts in this new movement, and our professors became colleagues who worked with us to find solutions. Through our tears and laughter we created a national dialogue on sex, violence, and activism that has yet to be completely understood or recognized as newsworthy by mainstream government and media.

Py Bateman, a civil rights and feminist self-defense activist who attended the first conference, commented that she had not seen student organizing of such magnitude since the 1960s. Although she compared the size and accomplishments of our movement to leftist campus movements of the 1960s, she observed one critical distinction. She explained that while the free speech movement leaders were always debating and writing position papers, radical grassroots feminists and antirape activists of the 1970s had neither the resources nor the time to document their work. Consequently, feminist activists received little credit for their accomplishments, and some of their work was lost or misrepresented. Until someone with Py's perspectives proffered this observation, we had not considered the historical significance of our movement or the value of memorializing the politicizing process of becoming an anti–sexual violence activist. *Just Sex* is an attempt to heed Py's warning.

Energized by the success of the First Annual North American Student Conference on Sexual Violence, Susan and I decided to apply for a grant from the Frost Foundation to network campuses and develop a national database. While writing the grant application, we began researching the movement to see what others had written. We simply assumed that others had recognized the impact of this unprecedented student movement, so we naively went to the library to check out books. It was 1992, and we could not find one book on the student antisexual violence movement. We ran a Lexis search and found a plethora of articles on the current scandals involving William Kennedy Smith and Clarence Thomas, but not one title on student efforts to create a new sexual revolution without violence. Py was right. If we did not write down the tenets and events of the student movement, then it would likely be lost or misconstrued. If grassroots activism is not documented, then it historically ceases to exist.

Anyone who was awake in the 1990s knows that sexual violence has become a part of mainstream dialogue as well as fodder for supermarket tabloids. The debates began with the Clarence Thomas confirmation, the Mike Tyson conviction, the Kennedy-Smith acquittal, and soon afterward the O. J. Simpson trial. Despite the excessive airtime given to celebrity trials, the media rarely unearthed the fact that students had been debating sexual harassment, acquaintance rape, and dating violence since the early eighties. Instead, most media attention was focused on a few twenty-something self-proclaimed "antifeminists" who made a name for themselves by belittling antiviolence peer educators and activists. These women, like myself, had grown up with the privilege of a feminist legacy yet irresponsibly criticized their peers who continued to fight for gender equity. These "antifeminists" or "postfeminists" received prestigious publishing contracts, while the students actually doing the work went virtually unnoticed. The proverbial naysayers sat in their dorm rooms or Upper Westside apartments and accused Take Back the Night march organizers of victimizing women, and sexual violence policies of legislating sex. Susan and I were more interested in the truth about the courageous survivors, educators, and activists. We did not want the student movement to be misrepresented as "Victorian," or "antisex" in the same way the second wave of feminists were inappropriately dubbed "bra burners" by the popular press.

Just Sex is what my college history professors would call a historical and living primary document. With all our varied experiences over the past ten years, Susan and I felt as if we could have written every chapter ourselves, but we resisted the temptation to define the herstory of the antisexual violence movement as only our stories. We resisted the temptation to define with analytic artifices. Instead, we have tried to let the movement speak for itself through the voices of many of the students who created it.

Skilled academicians will certainly be able to apply theory and to dissect this movement, but their critiques are infinitely more powerful in combination with firsthand experience. *Just Sex* is about the movement and created *by* the movement. Susan and I edited this book with scarce resources and evolving research skills. We are not professional writers or editors, nor are most of the contributors. Together we are all grassroots activists. We lobbied, educated, researched, and wrote in between living our lives. This book has never been our full-time job. As I write this preface, Susan is due to deliver her first baby. I am sitting at a desk cluttered with *Just Sex* notes and study guides for my looming medical licensing exam. Although the majority of contributors wrote during or immediately following college, many have become parents, professors, lawyers, and writers in the long, arduous years it has taken to bring this book to publication. This project merely reflects the movement at a fixed point in time, whereas the movement and its participants have continued to progress.

After all of these years Susan and I naturally questioned our ability to reflect the diversity of the movement and its relevancy for students entering college in the twenty-first century. During my first year of college, I learned that no one is "asking for it" when she or he is raped, and that rapists are not "men who jump out of the bushes." Today the analysis of sexual violence has traveled miles beyond the date rape debates of the early nineties. Students grapple with homophobia, racism, body image, sexual harassment, dating violence, high school serial killings, hate crimes, Internet violence, and pornography. Fault us for our omissions or lack of sophistication if you choose, but there is no denying the success of the student anti–sexual violence movement. From the earlier debates came campus blue-lights, survivor speakouts, and the acceptance that rape is not regrettable sex. Today colleges are required by law to have campus sexual violence policies. Students learn about acquaintance rape in junior high school, on mainstream television, or on the Internet. We view *Just Sex* as the working papers of a movement whose full-blown impact is unknown and unlimited.

The nineties will be remembered as a national chat room on sex, violence, equality, and power. Random and gender-based violence seem to be spiraling out of control, while our constantly evolving sexual rules and mores are no less confusing. No matter what the final implication of the president's affair with a White House intern will be, for better or worse, it forced the American public to talk about sex and power. The Supreme Court has broadened the dialogue by holding an elementary school liable for the sexual harassment of a grade school student by her classmate. Ally McBeal, Felicity, and Bridget Jones ferret out the contradictions and superficiality of "The Rules" for independent, professional young women and men. The student anti–sexual violence movement, along with the gay rights, civil rights, and women's health movements, has ushered in a sexual revolution. It may be more cautious, but it is finally consensual and inclusive of women, gays, lesbians, bisexuals, and transgenders.

Susan and I have been brought face-to-face with a real sexual revolution and a new form of student activism that emphasizes peer education, and the politics of coalition and collaboration. We compiled this book because we saw a unique feminist student movement with growing numbers of men, a phenomenon that few academics, politicians, or journalists have noticed. By documenting the movement and introducing you to a few prominent survivors, educators, and activists, we hope to validate the work of existing students and staff. We encourage more men and women from all backgrounds to examine the tenets of, and join, a movement that believes in *Just Sex*—consensual, responsible, equitable, inclusive, and free of sexual violence.

Jodi Gold

I would like to thank Susan Villari for believing in the student movement and for trusting me to write our preface.

ACKNOWLEDGMENTS

A project of this magnitude requires the collective work of many people. We are deeply grateful to the hundreds of friends and colleagues who contributed to this anthology.

To the founders of *SpeakOut: The North American Student Coalition Against Sexual Violence*—for your friendship, encouragement, and tireless organizing efforts in creating a forum for national student dialogue. We will always cherish our debates and adventures in D.C., Philadelphia, San Francisco, Davis, Buffalo, and Durham: Nate Daun Barnett, Jennifer Beeman, Anne DePrince, Kristen Gremmell, Jack Gorman, Selden Holt, Ellen Plummer, and Jason Schultz—with special thanks to Nate for his work on the book's appendix.

To the crew at the University of Pennsylvania, including those staff past and present of the Office of Health Education: Kurt Conklin, Janet Zinser-Arey, Mary Webster, Mimi Collins, Ellie Dilapi, and Ben Schein. Much heartfelt thanks for your support, editorial comments, and creative ideas and for never doubting our resolve to finish this book, or at least keeping those doubts quiet.

To Erica Gutman Strohl and Anne Siegle Yaz for their bravery and ingenuity in founding Students Together Against Acquaintance Rape (STAAR) at Penn. We would not be here without you. And to the other charter members of STAAR: Nick King, April O'Malley, and Tristan Svare, who built STAAR's foundation, and the others who participated in the First Annual North American Student Conference on Campus Sexual Violence in 1992: Rob Amir, Michael Brody, Derek Goodman, Beth Kaplan, Caryn Karmatz, Nick King, Deborah Levine, Paul Kostyak, Zachary Liff, Beth Lundy, Lynn Pinkus, Jeremy Rossen, Manish Shaw, Nichole Shaw, and Will Van Deveer.

To our feminist colleagues and social justice mentors who helped frame our analysis and remind us of our past: Bernice Sandler, Lesley Rimmel, Py Bateman, Joani Unger, Richard Orton, Michael Kimmel, Charlotte Pierce-Baker, John Stoltenberg, Andrea Dworkin, Marty Langelan, and Namoi Sachs.

To the folks who helped make the book a reality: the Frost Foundation in Santa Fe, New Mexico, for providing funds to start the project; Peggy Reeves Sanday for introducing our work to agent Geri Thoma at Gloria Steinem's sixtieth birthday celebration; Geri Thoma and the Elaine Markson Literary Agency for believing a student movement existed and persevering to find a publisher; Jessie Minier, Steve Devlin, and Larry Moneta for helping us develop and publish our national survey; and to the staff at Rowman & Littlefield Publishers—Dean Birkenkamp, Jill Rothenberg, and Mary C. Hack—for your direction and patience in producing this anthology. Special thanks also to Alan McEroy and the Safe Schools Coalition for their support of the student movement.

For our friends, lovers, and supporters who inspired our work and bravely asked "How is the book going?" year after year: Lise Anderson, Lonnie and Michael Beer, Jon Caroulis, Jeannine Coyne, Meg Duarte, Lisa Fox, Andy Goodman, Jen Goodman-Feldman, Mike Green, Chris Haines, Sandi Herman, Deni Kasrel, Sharon Kershbaum, Liz Landrigan, Andrea Lazarini, Jim Ryan, Cathy Schwartz, Shari Silverman-Minsky, Greg Spiritosanto, Roger Wolfgram, Mark Woodruff, and the late Kate Webster.

And finally, to the women and men who have survived the degradation of sexual violence, and to the healers, activists, and educators who courageously fight this war against humanity every day.

JUST SEX

INTRODUCTION

THE NEW SEXUAL REVOLUTION

We are often asked why those involved in a movement to end rape spend so much time talking about sex. Didn't the early antirape feminists teach us that rape is about power and not about sex? Fortunately, they did—and in doing so put a name to a crime against women that at the time most people believed was perpetrated by sociopaths, not their husbands, lovers, and acquaintances. Twenty-five years later, despite tremendous legal and social reform, society still has trouble distinguishing between sex and violence. Efforts to clarify the distinction are labeled as puritanical, radical, and revolutionary.

Start by asking someone the definition of acquaintance rape, and invariably part of the response will include a reference to the infamous gray area, where sexual definitions, rules, and roles are ill defined or never defined. Follow it up with a question about whose responsibility it is to prevent acquaintance rape, and you are barraged with codes of conduct based on gender or the infamous *he said, she said*. The schism between *he said, she said* also defaults to gray, a place where there is still a hesitancy to assign blame or responsibility. It is as if the gray area is a misty fog that descends upon you and impairs your vision and reason. When caught in the gray, you cannot see far in the distance. The fog may be so dense that two rational and intelligent people experience the same event with an opposite understanding of it. The gray area is powerful enough to jam communication channels during a sexual encounter, causing one person to refuse sex while the other person assumes consent. This gray area seeps into our offices and under our bedroom doors. It invades computer monitors and TV screens. The gray area is enlisted when one person's harassment is another person's joke, or when the same photograph is simultaneously defended as free speech and condemned as a hate crime against women.

The search to clear up the gray area has exposed the mainstream of American society to the controversial connection between sex and violence. The late twentieth century may well be remembered for our heated national debates over sexual harassment, acquaintance rape, interpersonal violence, and pornography in both private conversations and in the public arena. From the Clarence Thomas confirmation hearings to the William Kennedy Smith rape trial to Tailhook to Paula Jones's allegations against President Clinton, the relationship between sex and violence has increasingly been framed as an issue of civil rights and equal protection under the law.

Nowhere have the debates been stronger and the voices louder than on college campuses. Since the mid-1980s a campus social movement has been stirring that, at its core, rejects the belief that forced sex is an acceptable rite of passage for women. Outraged by the high incidence of acquaintance rape, students have begun to dismantle the gray by publicly debating issues of sexual consent, social constructions of gender, and equal protection. Using new as well as recycled tactics, students' efforts to rewrite the rules on sex, violence, and gender relations may well be their generation's chief contribution to social change, much like advocating for peace had been for previous generations.[1]

Women and men who came of age in the 1980s and 1990s were the first generation to be weaned on feminism, civil rights, and the so-called sexual revolution. For the first time women acquired degrees at the same rate as their male counterparts.[2] For many of these women college not only represented greater academic and career opportunities but seemed to afford the same rights as men to experiment both socially and sexually. Unfortunately, the illusion of sexual freedom smacked up against the reality of acquaintance rape, bringing them face-to-face with deeply rooted sexism. In case after case, when women brought charges against the men who raped them, their cases were dismissed as a relationship problem, or they were chastised for daring to enjoy the same freedoms as their male peers.

In her essay *The Perfect Rape Victim*, contributor Katie Koestner describes why she decided to go public in a case that landed her on the cover of *Time* magazine in 1991: "My activism did not emerge from the physical rape alone, but from the whole of the experience. . . . There was the dean, who told me after having found my rapist guilty of violating the conduct code, that we made a nice couple and should try to get back together again."

Although a dramatic shift in public awareness has helped dispel myths about rape, too many people still believe that women provoke and encourage men to rape them by the way they dress and act. Similarly, men are told they are unable to separate their desires from their actions. Once sexually aroused, or so the story goes, men must pursue sex even if it is forced or coerced. So-called sexual liberation has done very little to change the rule that men are still encouraged to be sexual aggressors and women are assigned as gatekeepers to sex. Following this logic, it is not surprising that women are still held accountable for men's sexually aggressive behavior and ultimately for the prevention of rape.

Asking women to "be aware" or assuming that all men are potential rapists is not the answer. At the heart of the student movement is the collective belief that sexual violence is neither inevitable nor inherent. On campuses across the country, students are calling into question traditional notions of masculinity and femininity, particularly because these beliefs often dictate what is considered acceptable behavior, both socially and sexually, for men and women. Listen closely to most conversations about acquaintance rape, and you will more fully understand our deeply entrenched gender and sexual roles. *What did she expect? She had been drinking and she was in his dorm room at two A.M. How can you blame him? He is just like any other red-blooded American male.*

Rigid gender roles hinder women's ability to say yes to sex and men's ability to say or hear no. Men are told that seduction means pushing verbally or physically until you get a yes, or believing that no really means yes. Consequently, verbally coercive sex and legally defined rape are protected under the guise of seduction. Challenging this accepted behavior, campus activists promote consent, not coercion, as sexy. In what many believe to be a *new sexual revolution*, they lend their passion and power to the continuing struggle for gender and sexual equality.

THE OLD, THE NEW, AND THE RECYCLED

This anthology provides an overview of the people, strategies, and issues that have shaped the student movement to end sexual violence. Borrowing techniques from previous generations' efforts to raise awareness about sexual violence, today's activists organize Take Back the Night marches, survivor speak-outs, and self-defense workshops. They challenge campus policies and advocate for increased resources for prevention programs and support services. Traditional forms of antirape activism often serve as the catalyst for the institutionalization of programs and services, but much of today's social change efforts include service projects, peer education, and working within the system. In our separate essay, "Peer Education: Student Activism of the Nineties," we argue that this style of student activism is specific to this generation and in many ways serves the same function as consciousness-raising (CR) groups did for women in the sixties and seventies. By viewing students as the experts, groups like Students against Violence against Women (SAVAW) at Ithaca College, and

Auburn Working for Acquaintance Rape Education (AWARE) provide educational workshops where information and statistics on acquaintance rape are disseminated. More important, these workshops provide a safe place for students to demystify the gray area by exploring how rigid gender roles and power inequities are connected to acquaintance rape. Simple statements such as "Men and women are equally responsible for the prevention of rape," or "It is possible to give nonverbal consent to sex" prompt lively debates on the unwritten rules for "hooking up" and the nonverbal language of sex. Male facilitators will ask other men if it is possible to separate desire from action. Often men genuinely ask, "How can I be sure that I am not raping someone?" Female facilitators will shatter myths about female sexuality and physicality by openly discussing masturbation, orgasm, and how to fight back when in danger. These types of questions and ensuing discussions reveal how disparate socialization is for men and women in this society. Student educators respond by encouraging both men and women to stop and confirm consent if they are receiving mixed messages. In the age of HIV and AIDS students no longer believe that sex must be mysterious and unspoken. More women and men are having sex in college than ever before, but they want it to be fun, safe, and consensual.[3]

RAPE AS A POLITICAL ISSUE

For anyone to appreciate fully the current wave of antirape activism, it's critical to understand the movement's historical foundations. Kate Millet articulated the first feminist analysis of rape in her 1969 book, *Sexual Politics*. The opening lines of her theory of sexual politics begins:

> Coitus can scarcely be said to take place in a vacuum; although of itself it appears a biological and physical activity, it is set so deeply within the larger context of human affairs that it serves as a charged microcosm of the variety of attitudes and values to which culture subscribes.[4]

For Millet politics is defined as "power over," and patriarchy means men's power over women. Therefore, sex is always political in a patriarchy because it reflects the societal inequality between women and men. All sex is not rape, but the power that men have over women and the socialization of men as aggressor and women as passive cannot be excluded from the bedroom. Following this logic, rape is not aberrant behavior, but a natural extension of a system that must maintain male dominance.

It was acquaintance rape that ignited the rumblings on college campuses in the mid-eighties, but acquaintance rape was not a new phenomenon. Harry Kalven Jr. and Hans Zeisel conducted a study of three thousand trials in the 1960s and found that 40 percent of rapes going to trial involved acquaintances.[5] Menachem Amir examined police files between 1958 and 1960. He concluded that rapists are generally "normal" men. About half of all rapes were committed by men who knew their victims, and not all the victims resisted loudly.[6] It was the radical feminists of the women's liberation movement who recognized the political importance of acquaintance rape. The central revelation of the first speak-out and conference on rape held in 1971 by the New York Radical Feminists was:

> The violent rapist and boyfriend/husband are one. . . . The act of rape is the logical expression of the essential relationship between men and women. It is a matter to be dealt with in feminist terms for feminist liberation.[7]

Susan Brownmiller, in her 1975 *Against Our Will*, was the first to use the phrase "date rape." She documents the history of rape and examines the cultural forces that maintain women as passive and men as aggressive.[8] At the time of publication many believed that a women could not be raped "against her will," that certainly a woman would fight to the death.

Brownmiller and other radical feminists acknowledged the existence of and political nature of acquaintance rape, but Diana Russell took it one step further in her first book, *The Politics of Rape*, published in 1974. She interviewed ninety rape survivors and one rapist, who was interviewed by a male colleague. Not all the women were raped by acquaintances, but the rapists included lovers, best friends, fathers, and husbands. The goal of her book was to "emphatically contradict the prevalent view of male authors, clinicians, and doctors, that women enjoy being raped."[9] In 1978 Russell conducted a study of acquaintance rape with 930 randomly selected women. She used the California definition of rape, and she excluded those who "felt" raped but were not "forced." Contrary to the Kalven and Zeisel and Amir findings, she discovered that the vast majority of rapes were perpetrated by acquaintances.[10]

Stranger rape was the easiest and most visible issue of the seventies antirape movement. However, radical feminists had been saying all along that the boyfriend and rapist were one. They pursued three avenues of social change: rape prevention, service reform, and legal advocacy. The first rape crisis center in the world was founded by the Bay Area Women against Rape in 1970 in response to the rape of a Berkeley high school student.[11] Within a few months the D.C. Rape Crisis Center was founded, followed by centers in Philadelphia, Ann Arbor, New York, and Pittsburgh. By 1976 there were four hundred autonomous rape crisis centers. The early rape crisis centers were based on feminist organizing principles of working outside the system, disregard for academic "credentials," attention to process, and a commitment to self-help. They saw themselves as alternatives to the criminal justice system, which generally blamed women for being raped. The predominantly women-only volunteers served as escorts for rape victims during encounters with the law enforcement, medical, and legal systems. They demanded respect for women from emergency room personnel and police and supported victims through a self-help form of recovery. Rape crisis center volunteers were committed to social change in the community and on the campus. The first forms of campus antirape activism occurred in concert with the broader rape crisis movement.

THE EARLY CAMPUS CONNECTION

Antirape activism on the college campus is not new. Community rape crisis centers often worked closely with college campuses providing advocacy, support services, self-defense workshops, and an avenue for campus antirape activists. In 1972 a group of residential advisors at the University of Maryland campus responded to a series of gang rapes and abductions by forming one of the first campus-based rape crisis centers.[12] On April 3, 1973, women at the University of Pennsylvania staged a four-day sit-in in reaction to a series of six rapes and the gang rape of two student nurses. They achieved all their demands, which included a women's center whose primary mission was to provide rape crisis services, a women's studies program, and improved security measures on campus.[13] A campus rape at the University of California at Berkeley led to the adoption of sexual assault programming throughout the entire University of California system in 1976. A committee of students and staff at Berkeley argued that the university was "obligated to create as safe an environment as possible" for women and that rape education was missing from the curricula. Remnants of the University of California sexual assault education program still exist today.[14]

Throughout the 1980s the nation witnessed a surge in antirape activism and research. In 1981 Claire Walsh founded Sexual Assault Recovery Services (SARS) at the University of Florida. The following year she and students formed Campus Organized against Rape (COARS), a peer education group that became one of the earliest nationally recognized antirape peer education programs.[15] A 1982 *Ms.* magazine article entitled "Date Rape: A Campus Epidemic," is credited as the first instance of date rape hitting the mainstream media,[16] and research by Dr. Mary Koss would further prove that the biggest threat on campus was not the crazed stranger, but the trusted friend.

Koss began her landmark research at Kent State University in Ohio the same year that Russell conducted her study in California. Koss believed the logical next step after *Against Our Will* was to conduct a comprehensive epidemiological study of acquaintance rape.[17] She started her work at Kent State with a study of college students' experiences with forced sex. Her results were so intriguing that she replicated the study in 1985 with the help of the National Institute of Mental Health and the *Ms.* Foundation. She surveyed 6,159 students at thirty-two campuses. Koss's findings were later translated for a lay audience by journalist Robin Warshaw in her popular book, *I Never Called It Rape.* Koss documented the increased vulnerability of college-age women to acquaintance rape. The research showed that one out of four women in college today are victims of rape or attempted rape, and 84 percent are assaulted by men whom they know. The average age at the time of the rape was 18 1/2 years old for both the perpetrator and victim/survivor.[18]

The most disturbing yet controversial finding was the reluctance of men and women to define their experiences with forced sex as rape. Only one-quarter of the women surveyed whose experience met the legal definition of rape identified their experience as rape. One in twelve men surveyed reported sexually violent behavior, but the majority did not define their behavior as rape. This phenomenon confirmed what radical feminists had been saying all along—that violence against women is so insidious, it has been framed as part of normative sexual behavior.

Prior to 1985 a limited number of schools had policies or programs addressing sexual assault.[19] By the mid-1980s to the early 1990s, a strong catalyst for institutional reform can be attributed to courageous students going public with their assault stories. Our national survey of college campuses demonstrates that 35 percent of policies enacted by 1993 resulted from a high-profile assault case and/or student activism.[20]

For example, in 1983 several Ohio State basketball players were accused of gang rape. By a twist of fate the NCAA basketball tournament was taking place in Columbus that year. With national media attention protesters picketed outside the stadium, and the university president was quick to respond by funding a rape prevention program that continues to be a national leader. The program was founded with a feminist agenda charged with the task of developing culturally specific curricula. Ohio State is one of the rare schools that actually pay graduate students forty dollars an hour to present workshops to the sixty-thousand-student body.[21]

Student protests at the University of Michigan (1985)[22] and the University of Minnesota (1986)[23] resulted in comprehensive campus sexual assault services. In 1987 a landmark case at Carleton College, a prestigious liberal arts school, launched a national debate when four female students sued their college for not protecting them against the men whom the college knew to be repeat rapists. The women testified that the school was aware of the previous assaults by their rapists and did nothing to prevent these men from attacking them.[24]

During the late 1980s activism not only sparked the development of institutional policies and procedures, but also tested the limits and enforcement of those policies. At Princeton University, in October 1987, protest and outrage at the lack of enforcement of the sexual harassment policy prompted immediate university action. During an annual Take Back the Night event, several march participants were harassed by fellow Princeton students. One man screamed "We can rape whoever we want," while others dropped their trousers and hurled beer at marchers. The protest that followed this event led to the hiring of a sexual assault director, Myra Hindus, whose job was to oversee the university's sexual assault/harassment policies and procedures.[25]

During this time public opinion was also being shaped by the media and entertainment industries. The topic of acquaintance rape was introduced into television and movies via talk-show hosts, daytime soaps, and drama shows. In 1988 Jodie Foster won an academy award for her role as a "bad girl" rape survivor in the film *The Accused*, which was based on a New Bedford, Connecticut, gang rape trial.

WHY HAS THIS ISSUE MOBILIZED COLLEGE STUDENTS TODAY?

Several important factors appear to have set the stage for the current student movement to end sexual and gender-based violence. In addition to the influence of previous social movements on this generation, and a different sense of entitlement, the contemporary campus is a virtual microcosm of a rape-supportive culture. First-year college students of traditional age represent the highest risk group for being involved in a sexual assault either as perpetrators or victim/survivors.[26] Koss's research found that the use of alcohol and other drugs were involved in a majority of rape cases—70 percent of the men involved and 55 percent of the women involved reported drinking or taking drugs prior to the assault.[27] The use of alcohol and other drugs is perceived as a social lubricant and an easy way to de-stress from academic pressure.

The campus environment is also influenced by powerful male-dominated institutions, such as fraternities, whose rituals encourage hypermasculinity and excessive alcohol use, further adding to the fertile ground for rape to take root in. In 1985 Erhart and Sandler conducted groundbreaking research on the propensity of all-male groups to rape, identifying fraternity culture as conducive to sexual violence.[28] In *Fraternity Gang Rape: Sex, Brotherhood, and Privilege on Campus*, author Peggy Sanday describes what is called "a train"—a sexual ritual in which a number of fraternity men line up to take turns "having sex" with an intoxicated and unwilling female victim. The behavior is described by the participants as normal, "something that you see and hear about all the time."[29] Sanday describes this all-male behavior as homoerotic, and argues that pornography coupled with fraternity culture teaches young men about sex. Athletes who participate in aggressive sports are also at a higher risk for perpetrating sexual violence.[30] It is important to note that *most* athletes and fraternity members do not commit rape. Rather, the odds are greatly increased when excessive alcohol use is coupled with hypermasculine all-male environments whose groups have privilege on campus.

Finally, the work of previous antirape activists and recent legislation has helped to institutionalize sexual assault prevention and support services. The staff who coordinate sexual violence programs, that is, women's center directors and health educators, often got their start in the first and second wave of the women's movement. Students are often greeted by a generation of sixties and seventies activists firmly rooted in positions of power ready to serve as willing allies. This provides a unique partnership for current student activism. Activist faculty and staff teach students how to organize effectively and also give them access to resources. On the other hand, student activists can push the envelope without fearing loss of employment.

The North American Student Conferences on Campus Sexual Violence, which began in 1992 in Philadelphia, exemplify this unique and effective partnership.[31] Organized by and for students, with significant support from key administrators, the conferences bring together student educators and activists from around the continent. The first conference was originally planned as a regional event, but students were so eager to network and share resources that registrations came in from schools as far away as Oregon, Hawaii, and Alberta, Canada. Py Bateman, feminist self-defense activist and founder of Alternatives to Fear, remarked after her keynote address at this 1992 student conference:

> College students are perfectly placed for social change. They're young and in position to put pressure on university administration; open to new ideas; and in training for leadership. *The First National Student Conference on Campus Sexual Assault* is a perfect example of the power of students. I have not seen anything like this since the organizing in the 60s.[32]

THE NEW FACE OF STUDENT ACTIVISM

Despite the stereotype that today's college students are apolitical and disengaged, a recent study by Jeanette S. Cureton and Arthur Levine finds that current undergraduates are the most socially active since the 1930s.[33]

Social-change efforts on campuses today are often overlooked or misrepresented because twenty-somethings have developed their own style of activism, a style that on the surface sharply contradicts the popular image of a student activist. According to Paul Loeb, author of *Generation at the Crossroads: Apathy and Action on the American Campus:*

> Students have been looking for different ways to voice social concern. They want to act. They want to help. They don't want to deal with complicated issues and factions or the messy contention of politics. Instead they have revived approaches to involvement that focus on individual service . . . yet, the same approaches often lead them back toward larger social change.[34]

By the early 1990s peer education programs addressing sexual violence were being implemented all across the country. Generally, peer educators are trained volunteers, with very few receiving academic or monetary compensation. By 1995, 56 percent of schools surveyed had students facilitating workshops on sexual violence—with one-third of those students being men.[35] Program names such as CORE (Creating a Rape Free Environment), POWER (People out Working Together to End Rape), and STAAR (Students Together Against Acquaintance Rape) reflect the belief that if men and women work together, sexual violence can be prevented. Sharing only a commitment to end sexual violence, educators and activists find themselves in coalitions with people they normally might not associate with. For example, it is not uncommon to see a fraternity brother facilitating a workshop with a self-identified "radical" feminist or an openly gay man working with the president of the campus Republicans. The common experience of sexual violence and its profound impact on a community cross gender, racial, ethnic, and sexual orientation boundaries. This diversity is what strengthens the activists' ability to infiltrate a large cross section of campus. Groups educate in dorm rooms, classrooms, bars, and locker rooms.

Students become involved in antirape work for a variety of reasons. The most common motivation is being or knowing a survivor of sexual assault. Men frequently become involved because a girlfriend discloses being raped. These men focus their anger and accompanying sense of powerlessness into educating other men.

Groups such as Men Acting for Change (Duke University), Men against Rape and Sexism (Iowa State University), and Black Men for the Eradication of Sexism (Morehouse College) often feel equally constrained by rigid gender roles and resent the perception that all men are potential rapists. Omar Freilla, founder of Black Men for the Eradication of Rape and Sexism, comments: "We have discussion groups and talk about what it is, what it means to be a man, and how we were brought up. We are really trying to de-program ourselves."[36]

The issue of deconstructing masculinity is addressed not only in small discussion groups but also in large-scale campus events. Responding to a comment made by journalist Anna Climlin that the "good guys have to stand up and speak out," Rutgers University launched the Real Men of Rutgers campaign in the spring of 1994. Appealing to men's role in ending sexual violence, Ruth Koenick, coordinator of Sexual Assault Services, and student educators designed a poster that featured photos and quotes from twelve male student leaders nominated by the campus. Each man chosen contributed his opinion on how violence could be prevented within his own student community. Posters hung prominently in all major offices and buildings on campus.[37]

At Ohio State University, contributor Michael Scarce, then coordinator of the Rape Education and Prevention Program, placed placards above men's urinals on campus that read, "In your hands, you hold the power to stop rape."[38]

SEXUAL POLITICS ROCK THE NATION

According to educator and author Michael Kimmel, the early 1990s may well be remembered as the "decade in which America took a crash course on male sexuality,"[39] with the media not only highlighting high-profile celebrity cases but also bringing national attention to activist strategies happening locally on campuses. Responding to the national attention directed toward Brown University in 1990, contributor Jesselyn Brown writes "you know something has touched a nerve when it manages to get lambasted by feminists, antifeminists, and establishment organs alike." Frustrated by a judicial system that continually dismissed sexual assault cases, women at Brown used their speech to protect their fellow students. To have their speech heard, four Brown women generated a conversation on a centrally located women's bathroom stall, which eventually became known on campus as the "rape list." This simple act caused an uproar across the nation, with administrators denouncing the list as "anti-male" and referring to the women as "Magic Marker terrorists." Jesselyn Brown argues that when women were sexually assaulted on her campus, the cases were dismissed as trivial; yet when women wrote names of men who assaulted them, using their freedom of speech, it was immediately viewed as an infringement of the men's rights.

During the same time period the issue of how to negotiate consensual sex brought national media attention to the campus of Antioch College. Initiated by activist students, the now infamous Sexual Offense Policy at Antioch College requires "willing and verbal" consent for each sexual act. Despite the fact that this policy was supported by the majority of students, it was criticized by outsiders as "sexual correctness" and "courtship management," and it even ended up being spoofed on an episode of *Saturday Night Live*. Contributor Andy Abrams, who has been humorously referred to as the Antioch poster boy, believes that asking for consent is not only sexy, but smart. "If you don't talk, then all you got is guesswork."

As we watched in horror the interrogation of Anita Hill, Congress was busy debating antirape legislation. The early 1990s would see the passage of the Campus Security Bill and the Student Right to Know Act, the Ramstead Amendment and the introduction of the Violence against Women Bill (see appendixes 7 and 8).

LAPTOPS, CELL PHONES, AND THE INTERNET

The use of new technology such as the Internet and E-mail not only helped effectively organize students involved in the movement to end sexual violence but also contributed to a new round of debates over free speech.

In 1995, when Cornell male students E-mailed over the Internet "Top 75 Reasons Women (Bitches) Should Not Have Freedom of Speech," angry students from across the country flooded Cornell's E-mail system, eventually causing it to shut down temporarily.[40]

During the planning stages for the First Canadian Student Conference on Campus Sexual Violence at the University of Alberta in Edmonton in 1998, the Canadian Post Office went on strike. Amber Dean, student coordinator of the conference, quickly turned to electronic means to organize the conference, effectively using E-mail to communicate with conference participants and register students on-line.

As we move into the twenty-first century, the impact of this campus movement remains to be seen. The student movement continues to be strong and vibrant, with the North American Student Conferences on Campus Sexual Violence and its sponsoring organization, SpeakOut, looking forward to hosting their eighth year of annual conferences in the year 2000.

Our hope as editors is that you will applaud the courage of college students who came of age in the 1980s and 1990s in their collective efforts to dismantle the "gray" and redefine consensual sexual relationships and perhaps more importantly appreciate their significant historical role in the broader social movement for gender equality.

ORGANIZATION OF THE BOOK

We feel especially pleased to introduce you to several of the key activists involved in the student movement. Most of them are new writers, but some are experienced. This book includes their personal stories; their analysis on the issues being debated; strategies employed to effect change; and the subsequent impact on institutions and groups.

Part I, "Putting a Face to the Name: From Rape Survivor to Activist," opens with an overview of the variety of styles of activism present in the movement, from campuswide events to peer education to scholarship. Selden Holt examines why survivors and those affected by sexual violence chose to do this work, including the obstacles they must overcome. The remainder of the section includes essays by four writers who share the common experience of being raped by someone they trusted in their own communities. In their attempt to heal, they have become survivors. In their attempt to seek redress, they became activists. Their experiences as survivors have significantly shaped their personal lives and professional paths.

Part II, "The Issues That Divide and Conquer: Free Speech, Pornography, and a 'Gentler, Kinder Feminism,'" explores some of the most challenging issues confronting this social-change movement, including free speech, equal rights, and backlash from feminists who criticize the movement for further victimizing women. In theory everyone has access to free speech as a constitutional right. In reality gender, race, and class determine power in our society. Jesselyn Brown and Krista Jacob demonstrate how free speech and hate speech are used indiscriminately to silence women and protect men's constitutional rights. Kathy Miriam examines how "postfeminists divide and conquer by separating the good (unthreatening) feminists from the bad and angry feminists"—antirape feminists. She compares this phenomenon to broader conservative backlash politics in the late twentieth century.

Part III, "Rewriting the Rules," includes writings from three activists who helped shape our understanding of the meaning of affirmative sexual consent and healthy sexual relationships. Both Andy Abrams and Kristine Herman played instrumental roles in the development of the now infamous Antioch College Sexual Offense Policy. Both also became national spokespersons, enduring numerous media appearances in an attempt to tell the truth about this precedent-setting policy. Jason Schultz, one of the founding members of Men Acting for Change (MAC) at Duke University, outlines his own set of dating and sexual "rules" for men.

Part IV, "Revolutionary Strategies," highlights some of the old and new strategies used to educate and effect change. Although protest, sit-ins, and "in your face" activism are still used in this wave of antirape work, the current movement has also introduced some styles specific to this generation, such as peer education and service activism. We argue that this style is often overlooked because on the surface it contradicts the popular image of a student activist. In reality it is quite effective in challenging the cultural and attitudinal norms that help sustain sexual violence. Similarly, Martha McCaughey believes that too often self-defense is overlooked as a way to end violence against women. She believes that physical feminism truly transforms rape culture by actively challenging body politics, gender, and aggression. Drawing from experience as a campus activist, Janelle White describes the internal backlash present when activists resist the connection between racism, classism, heterosexism, and sexism. She believes, like many race and feminist theorists, that oppression cannot be placed in a hierarchy. This part concludes with Stephen Montagna's response to the often asked question, "What do men really talk about in male-only rape prevention workshops?" He discusses the controversy over and necessity of male-only spaces in rape prevention.

Part V, "Institutional Change," examines change within the media, sports culture, and the legal system. Journalist Elizabethe Holland argues that the media should move beyond the controversial debate of whether to print victims' names. Instead, she encourages a more thoughtful examination of how sexual violence is portrayed in the media and the development of new standards for covering such stories—in effect, giving the victims "faces" instead of just "names."

In *Training Camps: Lessons in Masculinity* contributor Nate Daun Barnett, former athlete and host of the Fourth North American Student Conference on Campus Sexual Violence, tackles the dynamics of locker room culture as it relates to sexual violence. Using his own personal experience as well as that of other male athletes, Barnett examines masculinity as it is defined through athletic competition, the ensuing sense of entitlement, and the role coaches play in teaching and perpetuating sexist attitudes and assaultive behaviors.

Finally, Brett Sokolow, founder of Sexual Assault Risk Management Programs at Campus Outreach Services, Inc., educates and walks the reader through significant recent legal reforms that have affected not only how we define sexual violence but also how cases are adjudicated.

PART I
PUTTING A FACE TO THE NAME:
FROM RAPE SURVIVOR TO ACTIVIST

I

SURVIVOR-ACTIVISTS IN THE MOVEMENT AGAINST SEXUAL VIOLENCE

Selden Holt

> When I was a freshman dealing with people my age, it was probably the hardest year for me to be addressing these issues. I didn't know how much respect I'd get from my peers and I started to be known as the rape girl. People would say, "You did that rape program last year." I could really only smile because I knew people had ideas about my history, but I knew they had no clue. I didn't mind being known as the rape girl because by assuming that role I was demonstrating a lot of strength. I've just been lucky I haven't cared more what people thought of me. I know that those who do reach out are doing it out of respect and sensitivity.

The student quoted here is a campus activist against sexual violence. In addition to standing out as one of the academic and social shining stars of her campus community—involved with the peer education group, community internships, exciting in-classroom work—she came to campus with a history of sexual violence, as her statement subtly implies. The combination of unwanted experience and social commitment summarized by the label "survivor-activist" is not unusual in the campus movement against sexual violence. Students bring a range of experiences to their activist work. Some may be survivors of heinous violence. Some have come to the work because someone they care about relied on them for support in the wake of an assault. Other activists get their motivation from faith or an ideology. Some may have lived perfectly safe, unexamined lives, but came away from their first march or prevention education program forever changed. Whatever the motivation, these students engage in activism to respond to a very powerful, life-altering occurrence. For many the work they do against sexual violence will complicate and enrich their college experience. Through insight gained from interviews with student activists, this essay will explore who the activists are, what they do, and how the challenges that activism poses can strengthen and heal those who get involved.

The terms "survivor" and "victim" will be used in this writing, both with reservation. The term "victim" refers to someone who has had a crime perpetrated against her or him. (Notice the lack of agency in the term. Neither the victim's decisions and acts of resistance, nor the perpetrator's actions and ultimate responsibility, are indicated.) Recent social commentators on the left and the right have added to the word's negative connotations by using it to decry people they consider undeserving whiners of all varieties. The term "survivor" has more positive and active connotations, implying the individual's initial survival and long-term progress toward healing. Both "survivor" and "victim" as sole identifiers suggest that an experience of violence makes an individual unique. Sadly, though, violence links survivors to millions of others. No one should be defined or labeled only by his or her experience of violence. Although the wordier "someone who has experienced sexual assault" might be preferable in theory, the currently accepted "survivor" will be the term of choice for this essay. For a great analysis of these issues, see the article by Kelly et al., entitled "Beyond Victim or Survivor: Sexual Violence, Identity, and Feminist Theory and Practice."[1]

SEXUAL VIOLENCE ACTIVISM DEFINED

Broadly speaking, activists in this field undertake the monumental task of eliminating sexual violence. On a day-to-day basis, they work to change how people understand sexual violence, because if enough people understand its true nature, they will be able to determine how to stop it and how to help survivors face their histories of violence.

Students participate in a wide range of activities that can be defined as sexual violence activism or service. Whether the individual chooses to think of that work as activism or service is largely irrelevant. Service—work with individuals or groups in their current situation—is certainly part of activism, which has the larger, perhaps more ambitious, goal of social change. The different kinds of work—special events, peer education, direct service, policy advocacy, scholarship, and individual case-oriented action—appeal to the varied personalities of those who decide to participate. Each activity requires certain skills and perspectives, as well as self-confidence and courage. How these common forms of campus activism can affect individual and social change is summarized in this section.

Many campuses hold Take Back the Night marches in the tradition begun in the 1970s, to empower women in general, and survivors of sexual violence as well. Students create similar large-scale programming, such as sexual assault awareness weeks, visual outreach projects like the White Ribbon Campaign in Canada, the Clothesline Project in the United States, and countless others. When they include a speak-out or a free expression board, organizers raise awareness of the impact and prevalence of the problem in the specific community while giving survivors a venue for expression. The dual healing and education components make these events very effective by involving large numbers of participants in dramatic, empowering activity. Although they may not think of themselves as activists, the individuals who take part in the collective action by marching, speaking out, painting a shirt, or tying a ribbon (activities that often involve disclosing a personal experience of violence) are important to the success of this kind of event.

> [Take Back the Night] was inspiring both on a personal level—all these folks were out here because of something I did, something I organized—but also on the level of dealing with the issue of rape. These folks were willing to come stand in the cold and try to light candles in the wind. That . . . show[s] you you're not alone in this struggle. The other thing that was really rewarding was the Survivor Speak-Out afterward. As depressing and heartbreaking as that is, it could also be really energizing because you're helping to play a part in the recovery of survivors. I've always gone to the Speak-Out afterward because it reminds me why I'm involved with this stuff at all.

On a smaller scale, student activists use interactive theater and other forms of peer education to introduce sexual violence topics to their campuses. This work requires significant time and planning and can be very meaningful for the writers, actors, presenters, and facilitators. Confronting an audience of peers can be a momentous experience and an opportunity for healing for the presenters.

> Writing the skit was overwhelming in the sense of how many issues I wanted to address in a short time and having to decide which were most important and to which this audience would be most receptive. It is essential to try to understand your audience, and what becomes difficult for me is I want to push them harder than I think they are willing to grapple with these issues. You're in your own learning process and recovery process, and you want people to jump to where you are, but you have to remember they don't even know the basics.

Peer educators also learn to balance the impact of their presentation on their audience; the uninformed need to understand the devastation of sexual violence, while survivors need messages of hope.

> The first [challenge] is breaking down barriers, stereotypes, myths, and false images, which is particularly hard on our campus because it's so conservative. The second is more of a presenter's problem . . . how to present the

information, the program, in such a way that will keep the audience from getting defensive and will in some way open up discussion. It's more interactive than just a boring lecture. [You are] hoping to . . . let [survivors] know they're not alone, helping the healing . . . helping to convince guys that it's a negative thing and they shouldn't rape.

Some students work directly to let survivors know they are not alone by providing crisis intervention services. They may not call this activism, preferring instead to think of it as community service. Students staff on-campus crisis response services and community rape crisis centers, where their duties may include providing response by phone and accompanying victims to local hospitals, police stations, and magistrates' offices. This work requires specific training and skills in active listening and crisis intervention and requires a student to put aside personal issues to be able to interact in a calm, focused manner with the survivors who need support.

> There's nothing better than watching the relief on someone's face when they tell you their story and not only do you believe them, but you tell them it took an incredible amount of courage to come here to the Sexual Assault Center. That's the reward, but it's also really draining to realize how much it affects people's lives to their core and how, once an assault has happened to someone, it's not something that anyone can take away.

Seen from the other side of the equation, every student who chooses to seek help from a counselor, health care provider, judicial officer, or dean affords a new lesson, or at least a refresher course, for that service provider. Because so few professional programs offer practical courses on sexual violence response, service providers get their most valuable training on the job. Every time a student seeks assistance, she or he expands the knowledge and, ideally, the sensitivity of the service provider, increasing the likelihood that the next student who needs help will be met by an informed, believing individual.

In their book *Sexual Assault on Campus*,[2] Carol Bohmer and Andrea Parrot describe a group of students who reach out to service providers and, in the process of getting their needs met, create policy change in their campus environment. These unintentional pioneers may not understand the political consequences of their actions, but they change campus culture nevertheless. The first student to bring a complaint of sexual assault through a school's judicial process may be forcing administrators to consider and write protocols they never addressed, hoping they would never need them. The students who feel that they were mistreated or that their case was severely mismanaged sometimes go public with their experience or sue the school, ensuring that more attention will be paid to these procedures in the future. People who seek redress from the criminal courts do the same thing; by refusing to be silenced by an imposing, unfriendly system, they clear the path for future cases.

As the university's "customers"—that is, the ones who suffer when services are not offered or coordinated well—students can be the squeaky wheels, urging change in campus policy. A university that needs to work on its protocols should include students in the process, although this puts a burden on the student leaders, who, either consciously or unconsciously, are expected to represent every student or survivor. As students become acquainted with the complexities of university politics, they may find themselves moderating their former demands as short-term solutions elude them. This, plus the lack of concern that fellow students exhibit about the issues, can be a rude but important awakening for the students who envision themselves as change agents on the policy front.

> Both policy work and lower-scale programming and education efforts have always been a lot harder for me because I can't get people to the damn meetings [laughing]. It's hard to raise enthusiasm partly because it's not experiential.

Policy-oriented activism extends to the work students do beyond campus. Students serve on the boards of community rape crisis centers and get involved with organizations at all levels, such as statewide sexual assault coalitions, SpeakOut (North American Student Coalition against Sexual Violence), and NCASA (National Coalition against Sexual Assault). Activists lobby county officials for matching funds for rape crisis centers, work with state legislators to sponsor victims'-rights legislation, and provide information to Congress regarding the continuing need for legislation such as the Violence against Women Act. Elected officials at all levels influence both the laws and funding affecting sexual violence work; they always need additional education and assistance on these issues; and, as lobbyists or staffers, students can help provide it.

Scholarship is another example of the macro-level work that affects the ability of activists across the country to work effectively. Rarely do students think of scholarship as activism, but the student who stays in the library rather than joining the protest outside can play a crucial role in the struggle. As understanding of these topics grows, theorists, researchers, and writers bring this knowledge into popular consciousness. This includes the campus newspaper as well as the professional journals that administrators, scholars, and other decision makers turn to for assessment of the issues. Although writing a senior thesis may take a student away from the more visible activist circuit for a while, it can also give her a depth of knowledge that will provide a solid foundation for further activist work. Researching and writing on sexual violence can give students broader perspective, reduce their sense of isolation, and strengthen their intellectual comprehension of the problem.

Regardless of the nature of their activism, student activists all have the common task of developing a stance, a framework with which to evaluate new data and the sometimes painful information that a heightened awareness of sexual violence may present to them. Good activists employ a continually evolving theory to undergird their work, and by striving for a flexible consistency, they continue to learn. For example, a campus activist might ponder the following questions: How do I deal with one of my friends telling me that a mutual friend, somebody I liked and also would have trusted, raped her? How do I reconcile the fact that some (but not all) sexually violent people were abused physically or sexually as children? How should I, as a student leader, respond to a man who is a great presenter but is dating his way through the peer education group, jeopardizing the ability of group members to work together effectively? These dilemmas would challenge a simple model, so activists strive to develop increasingly complex and more realistic ways—personal, experiential, and intellectual—to understand the violent world and to guide their efforts to change it.

MOTIVATION AND IDENTITY

Students take on the challenging work of sexual violence activism for a variety of reasons. Exciting academic work engages some, most often through the disciplines of psychology, sociology, or women's studies, although sexual violence can be approached from any academic perspective. Others come to activism through programming presented at their college or through the media. Another group looks for a means of putting their sense of purpose into action, motivated by feminism, faith, a strong community ethic, a curiosity about social work or nonprofit organizations, or any number of other factors.

> It's about my feminism. I strongly believe in working with and for women, and I think sexual violence work in particular is an area of huge need. Women need to be giving women strength around issues of violence.
>
> Rape crisis or anti-sexual-violence work has helped me really understand connections between the personal and theory. Had I not done some kind of crisis advocacy, that connection would not have happened in the way it has for me. There's something that happens when you get a call, or get trained to get a call or are in a safe room. . . . I don't think I would be where I am on a personal level, made the gut connection. I guess my heart's in it.

Campus skeptics try to dismiss student activists because they think students get involved for superficial reasons. One student expressed her frustration at these attitudes:

> I feel really good about identifying as a non-survivor, but also feel very committed. I wish there were some forum where I could say that. It would

have the same impact as a straight man talking about gay rights or a white person talking about race. I wish it could happen more while not silencing survivors. I just wish it could be acknowledged that there are lots of people doing this because it's important.

People sometimes come to activism because of a first- or secondhand experience. The next section will address survivors-activists more specifically. "Secondary survivor" refers to someone who interacts with and is affected by someone who has experienced sexual violence. Most people, and particularly men, are reared with the idea that they should be able to take control and fix things when something goes wrong; however, taking control away from survivors will not help them heal. Activism, and particularly preventative work, can be a great outlet for secondary survivors who want to "do something!" about this plague that has changed the life of someone they love.

> The other motivation is being able to learn more about—I guess forcing myself to learn more about—things I've dealt with or am dealing with, whether it's secondary survivor and codependency issues, or presenting on relationship violence, that being directly applicable to friends.

Men who choose to get involved with sexual violence activism, as the minority gender in the ranks of activists, face challenges from within and without the movement. Although they participate in smaller numbers than do women, their actions receive great scrutiny and accolades, both undeserved at times. Other men may see them as gender traitors, and women may question their motives. Male activists have to work to avoid reproducing the relationships of power and privilege within the activist community that are so ingrained in day-to-day gender relations. Members of the activist community also need to realize the equally important roles people of all genders can play in eradicating sexual violence.

Similar to men's critiques of other men in the movement, students who belong to a strongly identified racial, class, or ethnic group may be accused of forgetting about the plight of their community if they become involved in activism not historically identified with their group. They may feel pressure to defend the actions of individuals from their community for the sake of community cohesion. Imagine the internal and external pressure on the African American woman working at the battered women's shelter who believed O. J. Simpson did murder his former wife. Students who are not of the majority often feel as if they are assigned one main aspect of who they are and must organize their interests accordingly. They feel that family and friends may judge them if they choose to work on an issue thought to be unrelated to that single factor of their identity, or which reveals information about their community that would seem to give ammunition to bigots.

There's another piece that's totally involved with culture and how [my parents'] background leads them to react to my work and some of my interests. . . . My father, his comments are very disturbing. He didn't respect what I was doing. Afterward I discussed it with him. A lot of it is language barrier, English not being his first language, and his vocabulary is limited compared to mine, so because I realize that, I've been able to be more understanding of what he says, and it's been easier. That's not to say there aren't still cultural barriers, two different schools of knowledge, thought processes about issues, ideas. . . .

Whether or not activists decide to share their status as survivors, or their motivations, people make assumptions that may or may not be correct. Activists in the sexual violence movement get labeled with negative, sometimes hurtful, words (radical, liberal, antisex, neo-Victorian, feminist, man hating, femi-nazi, bitch), just like anyone else who has the courage to stand up for an ideal. Men doing this work often get insulted with derogatory female or homosexual slurs. While some activists are gay, lesbian, or bisexual, people tend to use these identifiers as epithets rather than as affirmations of identity or signs of respect.

I think in a lot of ways they are unsure of what to do with me. I think I come across to most people, especially people who don't know me real well, as kind of a traditional, conservative, I hope fairly masculine twenty-some-year-old guy. As soon as I begin to challenge that, I get labeled a flamer, really kind of criticized for any feminist attitudes I have, I mean to the point that people have asked my girlfriend whether or not I'm gay, which is really kind of uneducated, close-minded. I mean, they weren't even educated enough to ask if I was bi. People aren't really sure what to do with me.

Whatever their motivation, those who respond to the need for education and service on this issue face a worthy task. Regarding identity, activists learn not to worry too much about the assumptions and labels that others, including those closest to them, pin on them in order to keep their own fears at bay. They begin to use the encounters over their identities and motivations as teaching moments, helping others understand the many sides of who they are and the many reasons why people get involved in activist work against sexual violence.

SURVIVORS IN THE MOVEMENT AGAINST SEXUAL VIOLENCE

Most people working against sexual violence operate under the assumption that although not all activists have experienced a sexual assault, at least a significant minority have. How extensively survivors populate the ranks of sexual violence activists hasn't been thoroughly researched, for several reasons. First, the activist's survivor status doesn't really matter unless it hinders her or his ability to work in a thoughtful and focused way. Second, being a fairly dynamic, swiftly changing population, student activists are challenging to track. Knowledge about the student activist community consists primarily of anecdotal evidence from those who have been working in the movement—the activists themselves and the professional staff people who work with them.

Not all survivors, and probably not the majority of survivors, choose to get involved with sexual violence activism. From the activist perspective, however, many colleagues seem to be survivors. It is hard to know if this work attracts survivors or if the activist community merely reflects the relative frequency of survivors in the rest of the population, but with a key difference. Because of the increased awareness and support available among activists, survivors may be more willing to share their histories, which would make them seem more prevalent than they are in general. People committed to these issues know the level of ignorance and outright denial in our society regarding sexual violence, which keeps general knowledge of survivors limited. Sexual violence activists struggle against that silence every day.

Every survivor-activist decides whether to disclose her or his history of trauma while doing this work. This personal decision also can be a strategic one. Most of the direct service providers in the field choose not to disclose their status when working one-on-one with someone. They feel it takes the focus off the client and draws attention to the service provider. Others remain silent because people in our culture tend to discount the experience of, and ignore the work done by, survivors in the movement against sexual violence, for a variety of reasons. Because their knowledge is informed by experience, critics claim it is impossible for survivor-activists to be objective. The idea that "because she was raped, she thinks all men are rapists" expresses the defensive posture that many men and women take toward prevention programming in which the presenter discloses her own history of abuse.

On the other hand, a well-contexted disclosure, particularly one that focuses on the long-term issues of healing rather than on, or in addition to, the details of an assault, can be extremely moving and educational. Before presenters share their stories with a group, they should be comfortable having their life experiences become common knowledge. Disclosing presenters should be able to talk about their experience without minimizing the trauma or sending the survivors in the audience into a tailspin of anxiety or fear. Usually their courage and strength, exhibited by addressing these issues directly and standing up to tell their story, inspires rather than disempowers their audience, particularly the audience members who know from experience how much courage it really takes. Survivor-activists demonstrate the possibilities to grow and move beyond the violence.

ACTIVISM AND HEALING

Many people get involved with activism because of the stimulating challenge and sense of esteem they get from it. A positive learning experience for anyone, it can also be part of someone's healing process. From all accounts, healing happens in stages, varying from person to person, influenced by the resources and experiences unique to each individual. The work that a person does externally, like volunteer service or a job, by its experiential nature, can reinforce work that she or he may be doing internally—intellectually, emotionally, and spiritually.

One of the most basic tools that activism provides survivors is help in naming their experience. People know when something bad is happening to them, but they often fail to express the horrible magnitude of its impact to others or to themselves. They feel afraid or depressed, but initially feel powerless or reluctant to articulate how deeply changed by their experience they are. Survivor-activists who work with the issues surrounding sexual violence find that their work helps them assess and understand their own experiences of violence.

> Being a feminist activist is really important to me because of my own experiences of being victimized by men. It's, like, when I started doing that work, I started to see it in every aspect of my life and every other woman's life. It was something I'd been blind to before. . . . It can be extremely validating to know that so many other women have experienced violence, and that's motivation to do something constructive about it, whatever form it takes. With me it's taken the form of being an advocate for women.

For survivors, activism can also reduce isolation. Fear of the perpetrator and fear of being socially labeled and judged as a victim, with all the unfortunate and inaccurate connotations that can convey, keep people silent, sometimes for years. People hide their histories out of the emotional need to control the trauma. For this reason most people are unlikely to be aware of the survivor status of the people around them. Rape crisis hotlines and support groups try to address this issue, but many survivors, for cultural or personal reasons, fear using them. Getting involved with sexual violence activism provides an avenue of reconnection through contact with people who are willing to talk about this scary issue and provide informal support. The support necessary to undertake sustainable activism on sexual violence, which should be available to all activists, is particularly useful to survivor-activists.

> One of the things that makes this work easy or better to do is being in a supportive environment with people who have similar ideologies and who really validate the work. Since I've started doing it, I've found refuge, I guess, in my colleagues that I don't get even from my family, friends, and

my partner. If it wasn't for [colleagues] validating me, then it would be almost impossible to do, because I would start to feel like I was crazy, since that's the message I often get from others in my life, significant others.

Activism does not function as a healing tool for everyone; in fact, for some their involvement is detrimental. A person may go through training to be a direct service volunteer, only to find she cannot handle the fear and grief she feels with each new disclosure. Some cannot face the lack of control they feel when interacting with an audience of unpredictable peers. Emotional wounds that have not been fully healed can open afresh, uncovering new memories, triggering nightmares, hyperarousal, scanning, flashbacks, and other physical and behavioral symptoms indicative of post-traumatic stress disorder (PTSD), commonly suffered by people who have experienced trauma. If not addressed, this response can intrude in the survivor-activist's daily life.

There's no way sexual violence work doesn't affect you. One thing I've realized is how careful you have to be in doing it, the violence that's affected me by taking it in. The violence doesn't just happen . . . to the victim, who becomes a survivor, but to everyone who comes in contact with [the victim], whether they know about it or not. I'm realizing how hard it is for me emotionally, and that I feel very physical manifestations.

Survivors in crisis do not always manage to set limits for the sake of their well-being, or to maintain other boundaries. Sometimes they turn to friends who are good listeners instead of finding therapists for deeper help in dealing with their anxiety, depression, or histories of abuse. Part of the theoretical understanding with which activists, and particularly survivor-activists, grapple is how gender, sex, sexuality, and violence all relate, which involves critically evaluating relationships, expectations, and needs.

An example of poor boundary maintenance is the student who, out of devotion to activism, fails to pay attention to the emotional issues the work evokes. The feeling of competence that some activists get from their work may keep them from acknowledging and addressing how out of control and afraid they really are. Some survivors use their busy activist schedule as an excuse not to engage in the draining, time-consuming, sometimes disruptive but crucial process of facing their trauma.

I also see folks who use the activism as a way to distance their own feelings and emotions from the issue. They're able to both focus on other people and ignore themselves. They convince themselves that they're dealing with the emotional stuff, the personal stuff that they need to get a handle on, even though they're not. I think their brains and emotions had a lot going on that needed to be dealt with in some way, but because they were able to neglect it, their problems actually got worse.

Despite the challenges for many survivor-activists, sexual violence activism functions as an acknowledgment of their history and an act of resistance against their perpetrators. It can be a declaration of their ability to manage the fear that remains long after a physical assault. By doing prevention education, crisis intervention, scholarship, or institutional advocacy, survivor-activists exercise control not just in the face of a perpetrator or a hostile audience but also against society's sometimes cruel and clueless institutions. Few survivors choose to use the criminal courts to punish a perpetrator. Not very efficient or user friendly, the trial system can disrupt the healing process because so much is out of the control of the survivor. For the many people who wanted to take action but didn't have "a good case," who weren't "a good victim," or whom the system failed despite their efforts, getting involved with activism can give them the satisfaction of working to fix the institutions that are broken or in need of adjustment. Working to change the plight of other survivors, a step beyond a personal tragedy, can feel like a reinvestment in our flawed but invaluable world.

Reconnection is a third function crucial to long-term survival. Every time a survivor-educator explains the dynamics of sexual violence, and every time a service provider helps another survivor regain a sense of equilibrium, it can feel as if another hurdle has been cleared on the path toward healing.

CONCLUSION

Clearly an activist need not be a survivor to work against sexual violence or to benefit from the insights gained by doing so. Everyone needs an understanding of sexual violence because of its prevalence—not just an awareness of the issue, but a personal perspective on it. Many college students start a relationship with those issues during the first prevention program, speak-out, Take Back the Night march, or disclosure they hear. As members of what many have dubbed a rape culture, activists and nonactivists alike need to evaluate their risks in this dangerous world.

Survivor-activists in the movement against sexual violence serve as educators for the whole community, and they serve as role models for other activists and survivors who learn from their successes. They accomplish this by their actions even if they choose not to disclose their survivor status. The work is replete with challenges for them and for anyone who does it, but for those at the right stage in addressing their trauma, activism and healing can be mutually reinforcing activities. Survivor-activists engage the world despite their experiences of abuse, personifying the struggle for personal and social change that constitutes the movement to end sexual violence.

> If I weren't an activist every day of my life, I don't think I'd be happy. I definitely think of this work as activism. I think of my day-to-day inter-action with my family, in the classroom, as activism. If I weren't fighting—not the right word—promoting, advocating, just speaking my mind, I feel I'd be abandoning who I am and what's most important to me. I guess each struggle awakens a strength in me that allows me to be proud of myself and assert who I am, out of self-respect. I guess I feel if I didn't keep stand-ing up for these issues, I'd be letting my past overtake me, and I would also be abandoning those who need these issues to be heard.

2

THE PERFECT RAPE VICTIM

Katie Koestner

Seven years, hundreds of local and national newspaper stories, the cover of *Time* magazine, an HBO docudrama, a dozen talk shows, scores of local and national news programs, and more than six hundred speeches at universities, colleges, high schools, and military institutions ago, I was raped. I was an eighteen-year-old virgin in the third week of her first year of college, on a date with Mr. Tall-Dark-and-Handsome, Prince Charming. The night ended in miscommunication, a misunderstanding, or just "bad sex," according to some. I say it ended in rape.

We met during orientation. We were taking the same chemistry class. We studied together, hung out, and saw each other often over the next ten days. When he asked me out on a formal date, I accepted. After dinner at a fancy restaurant, we went back to my dorm room. My roommate was out of town for the weekend, and I was hoping he and I could spend the evening together dancing, talking, and, yes, fooling around. I really liked him, and I wanted to be intimate with him, to a certain extent. He knew my limits. I had told him that I was a virgin and wanted to remain so until I was married. I gave him my reasons, and he led me to understand that he was willing to respect my values.

But after our date, back in my room, he was not interested in my values or my lack of willingness to have sexual intercourse. More than a dozen times I said no and fended off his more and more insistent advances. I cried, yelled, tried to make him understand. The more I reasoned with him, the less rational he became. Finally, sometime after two o'clock in the morning, realizing that I wasn't going to give him what he wanted, he blew up at me in frustration and then decided to go to sleep. His room was far across campus, so he decided to sleep in my room. I wanted to ask him to leave, but I was afraid of his temper. I made the worst judgment call of my life. (I am not apologizing for my decision, or saying that it was my fault; I'm just expressing the lingering regret that I was raped. The pain never quite disappears entirely.) I decided to just let him stay in my room. I thought he would go to sleep, wake up in the morning, and leave. Later, I could call him and break off the relationship and never see him again.

I curled up in the corner across the room from where he slept. I was exhausted and my stomach was upset as I sat vigil and waited for him to wake and leave. Sometime around five o'clock in the morning, the sun started to come up. He awoke and spotted me in the corner. Realizing I had stayed awake all night, he apologized for his behavior and promised me that it would never happen again. He sounded truly apologetic. I wanted to like him. I wanted him to be sorry. He hadn't hit me; it could have been worse. I convinced myself that his passion had just gotten out of hand, and that he was back in control.

Exhausted, I crawled into bed and began to fall asleep. Half-awake, I realized he had begun his advances anew. My protests were ignored, and before I could move, he was on top of me. I don't remember how long it took. I don't remember where his hands were, or what it felt like. I remember his weight on me, and tasting blood in my mouth as I bit through my cheek to keep from screaming. He thanked me as he gathered his clothes and left my room.

That's it. It seems so black-and-white, so emotionless on paper. Mechanical. Yet when told onstage to an audience of a thousand plebes at the U.S. Naval Academy or 450 first-year students at Hamilton College during orientation, it is more than real. It is not a script from an actress, it is not glamorous, it is not third person, it is not video on a two-dimensional screen, it is not a docudrama; it is real life pain relived. Many days I wake up in some city and think that I cannot tell it again, because I begin to hate the story more than when it first happened.

Then I am reminded of the woman who told me, after my speech the previous night, that she "could relate" to my story. She has not been able to say the Word, yet. She hasn't told anyone. It was her best friend's boyfriend, and she got pregnant and had an abortion. And she was very drunk, so maybe it was her fault—at least a little bit—so why make a big deal? But she said she felt better telling me, telling someone.

Or I remember the night before that, when the guy told me that on prom night last year he raped his girlfriend. He was the last one of his friends to be a virgin, so they helped him get her drunk, until she passed out, and then watched to make sure he did it. He said he was sorry. He's never told her that. Or I think about the boy who told me that on his thirteenth birthday, his father and his father's best friend took him to a strip club to "make him a man." They gave him a lot to drink; he wasn't used to the alcohol. He wound up in the bathroom stall throwing up, and his dad's best friend followed him in. He thought the man was going to help him, but he raped him in the stall. The guy has a wife and three kids, the boy said. He said that he's hated his birthdays ever since, and no one knows why.

I remember the guy at one college who said he had to leave my speech early for a science lab. When he got to class, he found out it had been canceled. He decided to return to my speech. On the way back, he was walking along a poorly lit path behind a woman. He suddenly realized that she might be afraid, that she might feel crowded and nervous because he was a man. *Just* because he was a man. So he purposely dropped his keys to give her more space but, picking them up again, realized that she will probably always be afraid, always need more space. It wasn't fair, he told me. What could he do to eliminate her fear, he asked?

So I decide that I will tell my story again. Because it will connect; it will make a difference, a small miracle.

My activism did not emerge from the physical rape alone, but from the whole of the experience, the night and the days that followed and continue to follow. I told my roommate and resident advisor (RA) of the "incident" the day after it happened. In seeking assistance and support, I met with a nurse who gave me sleeping pills instead of a PERK (physical evidence recovery kit), even though I was at the college health center within seventy-two hours after the assault. There was the dean who told me, after having found my rapist guilty of violating the conduct code and giving him nothing more serious than probation, that we made a nice couple and should try to get back together again. The commonwealth's attorney (DA) told me that I had a 15 percent chance of winning a criminal case, and he wouldn't play those odds. My hallmates rejected my story in favor of keeping their friendships with my rapist or felt that any "misunderstanding" could be resolved between us by "talking things out."

Thus, it was out of frustration with a system that had failed and my desire to make that system change that I called the local newspapers. At first I was an anonymous coed. Rape victims were never named in the papers, I found out. I was only one more number for a statistic. There was no tangible victim, just another "somebody else," not a friend, daughter, or sister. As I read more studies and research on rape and sexual assault, I became convinced that I should reveal my name and break the silence. Rape victims should not have to feel ashamed. The next article used my name and picture. I felt stronger, somehow empowered by seeing my own face staring out of a photograph under the headline.

Eventually the entire campus knew, along with everyone who watched *NBC Nightly News*, read a national newspaper, or saw the cover of *Time* magazine on June 3, 1991. I didn't have to make any more phone calls to the media. The story was out and the press was calling me. Of course, I must acknowledge that white skin, virginity, Christianity, a prestigious college (William and Mary), good grades (I did eventually graduate magna cum laude and Phi Beta Kappa), an upper-middle-class socioeconomic status, heterosexuality, an alcohol-free date (almost—he persuaded me to have two sips of champagne), youth, and innocence had something to do with the fact that it was a "perfect victim" image, rather than some otherwise equally "qualified" victim, on the cover of *Time*.

Thus, it was the media that paved the way to my soapbox. I decided to use my spokesperson status to take my message from the sets of talk shows to the stages of college campuses (where I wouldn't have to do sound-bite battle with the woman who is marrying her rapist after twenty-plus years and living happily ever after, the attorney who defends rapists in court, or the likes of Katie Roiphe and other nonfeminist feminists). Sharing my story with students took me to over a dozen colleges by the time I graduated, and I have decided to continue this crusade. I intend to go to graduate school eventually, when my "peer educator" status expires. Currently, I work from campus to campus (college, high school, and military) not only as an educator, but as a catalyst for change. My goal has never been to show up for a couple of hours, speak, and leave, but rather to reach as many people as possible, leaving ideas, enthusiasm, and inspiration behind.

Change means going beyond awareness, moving from theory to practice. My most basic goal is to help students understand that rape is no longer a crime of force alone, but also one of consent. Though state laws still vary in their definitions of sexual assault, I believe we are moving toward this more respectful interpretation: that the burden is on the initiator of a sexual interaction to obtain some clear form of consent, before proceeding.

Is this an attempt to challenge biological destiny? That is the question I ask myself as I have traveled from school to school speaking to men about rape. Men seem to disagree on the answer. I was told at one school that, "Well, no means no, up to a certain point. Let's call it the point of no return. Then she can start kicking and screaming, but it doesn't matter because she's taken me that far, now it's too late." Or another man: "If she teases me and then says no, I'd jerk off all over her," quickly followed by, "Katie, you're trying to change biological destiny—you know Darwin, survival of the fittest—men just have to spread their seed around."

Fortunately, comments like these seem to be getting slightly less common as I continue my activism (thank God). Is this real progress, or are men just more savvy about keeping their comments between themselves and "the boys"? The real question is, Do fewer comments translate into fewer sexual assaults? Theory to practice. On occasion a high-schooler will state that, "Guys can always control themselves; it doesn't hurt that bad."

Or another admits that he can tell "when a girl has had enough" (somewhat less encouraging), or a rare brave individual will challenge a roomful of his peers about sexism or harassment.

Ultimately, I am not challenging biological fact, but rather social stereotype and traditional gender roles. For hundreds of years women have been expected to resist sex, and to protest so as not to appear too eager. Men have been taught to read these signals as "maybe" and thus to proceed with whatever convincing it takes to change a woman's mind. As a result, some women are playing by these rules and some women are playing by the new rules that obligate a yes to mean yes, a no to mean no, and maybe to mean maybe. Every day that I speak, I see confusion over the current rules under which the dating game is being played. Male students are afraid to ask permission out of fear of rejection. They are unsure how they should go about communicating. Some men are worried that they will be accused by a vengeful woman even if they do everything "right." Women still feel trapped by the no-win labels of "slut/tease/prude."

By far the most dramatic changes in attitudes have come from my "He Said—She Said" program. I tell my story first, and Brett Sokolow, my cofacilitator, speaks on alcohol, responsibility, and communication. After the lecture portion we divide the entire audience into single-sex groups and facilitate discussion around various realistic scenarios of student sexual interactions. The scenarios are challenging enough that they require more than a simple analysis, which engages the audience and heightens the level of debate.

The students begin their discussion by framing comments and opinions in terms of "Todd" and "Amy," the characters from the scenarios (yes, this is heterosexist), but move on to "I" statements rapidly. I believe this transition produces the self-examination that leads to behavior change. I hear the strongest endorsement of clear verbal communication and respect toward women from the men after these programs. Meanwhile the women benefit from a forum of empowerment and a chance to voice their differing opinions on "risk reduction." After the breakout sessions we invite students to a coed postprogram forum where they talk to each other.

Analyzing the assumptions made about levels of sexual interaction and how one arrives at each enables the students to dispel rape myths. I recall a male student who finally understood that one level of sexual interaction does not necessarily translate into a green light for the next level. At the beginning of the program he said that he could not understand why a woman who was bold enough to perform oral sex on a guy when he asked for sex would not therefore be able or likely to voice her discomfort with vaginal penetration. By the end of the workshop he stated that he would get verbal clarification from future partners.

Sometimes I think that it is one thing to teach students the definition of rape, but entirely another to get them to understand what that definition means. That is the advantage of the breakout sessions, as opposed to the lecture format. For example, you can tell students that having sex with someone who is incapacitated because of alcohol or drugs is against the law, and they will nod in agreement. However, when you then ask them who is responsible if both parties are incapacitated, or how drunk is "incapacitated"—there are a hundred different responses. Other points of contention are the difference between "seduction" and "coercion," or "How much of a threat is a threat?"

To illustrate, I will often tell the story of a high school tenth-grader who said, "I asked her nineteen times, and every time she said no, but the twentieth time she said, 'Fine, get it over with.' Is that rape?" Even after hearing my story (during which I explain that I was asked and said no at least a dozen times), some students will say that the twentieth time she gave consent. Only upon further discussion am I able to show them that consent needs to be a freely given agreement and mutually understandable to both parties, and that context matters.

Changing the attitudes of students is only half of my mission. I also work with the administrators, staff, and faculty at schools that will permit me to meet with them. Having now visited nearly every state, I have found a wide range of approaches to the problem at different schools. In my opinion there is no perfect school. There is no school without rape, no matter how Catholic or Mormon, no matter how liberal or conservative, no matter how rural, no matter how few students are enrolled.

There is also no one school that is doing everything possible to stop sexual violence from happening or to deal with it when it does. Some schools have good policies in their handbooks. Some have good resources in the form of rape crisis centers in their communities for rape victims. Some have great orientation programs and dedicated peer educators who even get work study or academic credit for their endeavors. Some have well-trained, extrasensitive police forces or security. Some have great proactive people in high administrative places. Some have dozens of bluelights, safety walks, low hedges, well-lit walkways, and doors that are never propped open. Some have campuswide sexual assault response protocols, sexual assault response coordinators, and sexual assault task forces—with members who *all* attend on a *regular* basis. And so on . . . Some have a combination of the above. No one is perfect.

Our knowledge about the issue is rapidly developing, and lawsuits and criminal cases are producing new precedents for risk management guidelines. Those schools that think they are doing "everything possible" are as vulnerable as the woman who thinks that she is smart and responsible and will never be raped.

I visit some schools that fall into that top echelon of proactive approaches, who still do not have their "Sexual Assault at XYZ University" materials written in a "victim-friendly" manner. Rarely is there enough information on why paper bags should be used to take clothing worn at the time of the assault to the hospital for a rape kit, how much the kit costs, how to get transportation to the hospital, and who might come along as a support person. That's just one example. Many campus "What to Do If . . ." brochures do not list the hours when you can call resource phone numbers, or whether or not those resources are confidential. Sometimes the schools have only the brochure, and little or no information in the handbook itself. But the handbook, in many ways, is the "safest" place for a victim to turn, because she doesn't have to go asking for the "SEXUAL ASSAULT BROCHURE," and most students already have a copy of the handbook. If she is seen reading it by her roommate or a friend, it doesn't automatically mean that she was raped. These are just a few of the ideas on victim sensitivity I try to share with college administrators.

Fortunately, if nothing else, there are mandatory federal guidelines for the bare-bones approach to sexual assault on campus. The Campus Security Act of 1990 and the Sexual Assault Victims Bill of Rights were both passed in the last ten years and give some minimal direction to schools.

Yet are all the colleges even complying with these basic minimum rules? No. I visited one university last year where the school used to have a sexual assault policy, and then it was taken out. Why? Because, as the vice president (who informed me that he had been in higher education for longer than I had been alive) said, he has seen handbooks grow thicker and thicker over the last thirty years, and the incidence of sexual assault has not decreased in the least. I asked him if he thought that we should discard our state laws on murder and other crimes as well, since those crime rates hadn't significantly decreased. At another school I encountered an administrator who believes that the solution to the sexual assault problem on college campuses today is to make sure that there is a chair in every single dorm room, because sex never happens on chairs. Another dean said that there is no sexual assault at his institution—in fact, "There isn't any sex here period—this is a Catholic institution." Denial and cover-up.

Are most schools like this? I can't speak for "most," because I haven't been to most. There are certainly too many, though. As with the students, my goal is also to inspire administrators to change their views on this issue. I recognize that I cannot change everyone. I cannot assume that because an administrator is a man, he will not be receptive, or because she is a woman that she will be sympathetic. In fact, in my experience often the older female administrators are more difficult to work with than the men. I imagine that they have won difficult battles in what has been traditionally, and still is for the most part, a male-dominated profession. I am sure some women perceive addressing the issue of sexual assault as addressing a "women's issue," and if they become known as supportive of "women's issues," they will not be taken seriously by their male colleagues on other issues.

The good news is that many of the schools that I work with do change. I find out months after my program that they have developed a Men Against Rape group, or that the administration has incorporated my suggestions on consent, or ideas from my book, into their college policy. Sometimes I hear that the school has created a sexual assault response coordinator position and started development of a protocol checklist system for the members of a campus sexual assault response network. Most change results from student activism and actual incidents of sexual assault (and sometimes the lawsuits that come out of the incidents); more than the federal guidelines, these things are what seem to propel the not-so-proactive college administrators along. Sometimes I encounter students or staff who are lower in the "chain of command" and are needing that extra push from an outsider to get the attention of the "decision makers" at their campus. They know that by bringing me to campus, their voices and efforts will be validated by someone with "authority" from the outside.

High schools, mainly private boarding schools, and especially private boarding schools that used to be all male, concern me the most. I have visited about two hundred high schools, and most of them are private schools. Many public high schools refuse to discuss sexual assault, including my own alma mater. High schools do not have to follow any federal regulations regarding the rights of sexual assault victims. High schools rarely focus on more than sexual harassment issues, if that, despite the occurrence of sexual assault. There are fewer lawsuits against private high schools for sexual assault issues. The students, because they are young, often do not have the support or the understanding of the issue necessary to try to make changes. Private schools are even more vulnerable than many colleges to public scandal, because they are smaller and have insufficient resources to weather the storm of a "big" rape case. One woman student told me that one night she was drinking with some other students in a dorm room in the boys' hall. She thinks something was slipped into her drink. When she came to, she remembers that there were about a dozen boys in the room surrounding her, and that she didn't have any clothes on. She vaguely remembers being carried to another room, but also remembers different guys on top of her. What was done about the incident when she reported it to the head of the school? She and one of the boys were suspended for a couple weeks for violation of the alcohol policy. When I confronted the administration, I met with a wall of denial.

So are attitudes really changing? Is there less rape? Some studies purport that peer education on sexual assault issues is having little to no effect on long-term attitudes and behaviors. If I believed these findings, I would quit my mission. I believe in change. I believe in going beyond awareness to the emotional, sensitive root of the issue. I believe in small miracles, one at a time. Like when the members of a fraternity at one school—whose five brothers had yelled "Hey ho, hey ho!" and "What do we want, lots more date rape!" at the women who passed by fraternity row during their Take Back the Night march—came to my speech and then stayed afterward to speak with me and the women whom they had offended and angered. I explained to the president of the house that although their harassing comments did not necessarily mean they were rapists, they fell squarely on the "continuum of sexual violence." This concept, although familiar to those of us who have ever taken a women's studies class or read any of the literature on sexual violence, was not one that made any sense to him, until I explained it. I believe that hearing my story of rape, representing one end of the continuum, enabled him to be willing to understand the relationship between what happened to me and the comments that were made from his fraternity porch. Unfortunately, I think most of the time it is the personal story of one person, not the horrific statistics, that compels students to look for the relevance of my message in their own lives.

Another small miracle was the letter of intense apology and remorse written to a woman by her rapist. He had realized from my speech that what he had done was indeed rape and decided to write to her in an attempt to bring her some healing and closure. He did not expect to "make up" with her, or to get anything in return.

Every day that I tell my story is one less day that "he" has power over me. It is one more day that other survivors can see there is someone else out there who will not wear her rape like a scarlet R on her chest for others to scorn. It is one more day that I will hear stories of rape and renew my hatred of statistics because of the faces behind them. It is one more day that college administrators will be asked to reexamine their policies and protocols, and question whether they are doing everything possible on this issue. It is another day that a survivor's voice will shatter silence. It is one more day toward a day without rape.

3

MALE-ON-MALE RAPE

Michael Scarce

In the autumn of 1989 my friend Tom and I returned from summer break
to begin our sophomore year at Ohio State University. We unpacked our
belongings and settled into room 332 on the third floor of Bradley Hall,
an undergraduate residence hall in the south area of campus. Each of the
four floors of Bradley Hall was divided into two wings—one for women
and one for men. Eve Wing had its own bathroom shared by the thirty-
some residents living there. The rooms were not air-conditioned, and the
dining hall food was less than stellar, but we were glad to be back on campus. The majority of the thirty-two men sharing our wing were first-year
students, and they were equally as excited to be out on their own for the
first time in their lives.

The return of students to campus ushered in a flurry of activity as
Welcome Week programs and parties abounded around us. Tom and I had
been elected president and vice president, respectively, of the Gay and
Lesbian Alliance, our campus gay and lesbian organization. We held
weekly meetings and organized events while striving to increase membership and politicize the organization's activities. As GALA became more
visible throughout autumn quarter, the organization and its officers frequently appeared in the local media, promoting GALA and challenging
homophobia on campus. As our visibility increased, so did our Bradley
Hall floormates' recognition that their two neighbors in room 332 were
gay.

The stares and sneers from our thirty floormates began early in the
academic year and slowly escalated to verbal abuse, menacing, and death
threats. Messages were left on our answering machine, death threat notes
were mailed to us, signs saying "Die Faggots" were posted on our door,
and as the intensity of the intimidation increased, so did the frequency.
Eventually the third-floor men's wing became so dangerous for Tom and

me that the university was forced to evacuate everyone, relocating the male students and splitting them up across campus before someone was bashed or killed.

Tom and I were moved to a nearby Ramada Hotel, where we lived in adjoining rooms for the last few weeks of spring quarter. Both of us were escorted around campus by an armed security guard hired by the university to protect us in the midst of hostility. A protest of more than three hundred students erupted on campus soon thereafter. Some students applauded the university's relocation decision while others criticized campus officials for "pandering" to gay activists. Still others blamed the university administration for allowing the situation to escalate to a level that necessitated such drastic action. The third-floor men's wing of Bradley Hall remained vacant, sealed, and empty for the remainder of the academic year. A media frenzy ensued, with coverage from CNN to the *New York Times*. This year was devastating for me as I struggled to survive in such an environment of hostility, humiliation, and degradation. I lived in constant fear and frustration while the weight of the events took its toll on my academic performance, my relationships with family and friends, and my health.

However, the pain and violation I experienced during those months before the relocation exceeded the incidents of homophobic harassment. During winter quarter of that academic year, Tom went home for a weekend visit and I was left alone. I was nervous about what could happen to me, what those men could do to hurt and punish me. It was a weekend in February and I decided to go dancing at a gay bar downtown to get out from under the suffocating weight of it all. I went alone, expecting to meet up with friends. The music was great, the bar was hopping, and I was having a wonderful time. As I danced, I noticed a handsome man standing at the edge of the dance floor. He watched me for the duration of several songs and smiled when I returned his stares. Later we talked and I learned he was from out of town, visiting Columbus on business. After an hour of conversation and heavy flirting, I invited him to return with me to my residence hall to escape the loud music, crowd, and cigarette smoke.

On returning to my room and continuing our conversation, we grew more physically intimate with each other. We were on my bed and began to kiss. Slowly he attempted to unzip my pants, and when I resisted, he became surprisingly rough. The more I pushed his hands away, the more aggressive he became until finally he used force. I asked him to stop but was too embarrassed to raise my voice for fear that others next door or outside in the hallway would hear what was happening. I was afraid the men who hated me for being gay would use this situation as one more excuse to bash me. After several attempts to unfasten my jeans, he finally succeeded and yanked down my pants and underwear. What happened next is somewhat of a blur. I remember he forced me to lie on my stomach and climbed on top of me. He shoved his penis into me, without lubricant and without a condom. He held me down as I squirmed and fought, suppressing the urge to vomit. The physical pain of the anal penetration worsened as he continued, and I began to cry. Soon thereafter I stopped moving in hopes he would just finish and get off me. Eventually he did stop, pulled up his pants, and left without saying a word.

The walls in Bradley Hall were very thin. The air vents in the doors were so large you could hear practically everything through those wide cracks, and many of my neighbors were home that night. One yell, one shout would have attracted the attention I needed to stop what was happening, but I could not bring myself to cry out. What would my floormates think? They already hated me for being queer, so how might they react if they responded to my cries for help and burst in on that lovely scene—a man on top of me, penetrating me? There was nothing I could do except lie there and go numb.

After he left, I took a long shower, standing under the water and crying. The smell of him was on my body, his semen was between my legs, and I washed with soap over and over—lathering and rinsing continuously. I endured some minor rectal bleeding for the next day, and remained sore for many more. I did not contact the police or visit the hospital emergency room. I did not seek counseling or formal support, nor did I confide in any of my friends for several years. I was ashamed and embarrassed by what had happened, identifying the experience as a form of bad, regretted sex.

It was not until a year later that I began to make more sense of my experience. Through my academic course work in OSU's Department of Women's Studies, I took an internship with the university's Rape Education and Prevention Program, where I conducted library research on rape and sexual violence. Gradually I came to terms with the fact that I had physically and mentally resisted that night a year ago in Bradley Hall and that I had been, in fact, raped. I now blame those thirty floormates for my rape as much as I blame the man who assaulted me. They created and shaped a space, both actively and through negligence, in which I was gagged, effectively silenced, and unable to resist. Their intimidation weakened my spirit, lowered my self-worth, and forced me to appropriate a victim mentality that impeded me from regaining control of my life.

So very little has been published on the rape of adult males. As I began to search for documentation that resonated with my own assault, I was dismayed at being unable to locate many scholarly articles or even popular, first-person accounts of this form of sexual violence. Slowly, over the last few years, I have collected what scarce writing and research have been published about men raping men. Although I was raped by a gay male acquaintance, I discovered multiple other forms of same-sex rape between men—rape in prison institutions, assault by strangers, gang rape, and more.

As my knowledge and understanding of the subject has grown, so has my interest in speaking and educating others about this form of sexual violence. When I speak publicly and conduct sensitivity trainings on male rape, I relate to others the story of my own assault, for it serves as a highly useful illumination of the ways in which homophobia and other forms of oppression create climates that foster and perpetuate rape behavior. My rape in Bradley Hall was simply a microcosm of the broader rape culture we all live in, a culture that encourages and condones sexual violence wielded as a tool for the subordination and control of those with less power in our society. Scores of male survivors have approached me after speaking engagements or contacted me later to share their own rape stories with me.

As I gradually became more involved in antirape work on campus, I began facilitating sexual assault workshops for the Rape Education and Prevention Program in classrooms, residence halls, student organizations, fraternities, and sororities. My involvement continued through graduate school, and after receiving my master's degree I was hired as the full-time coordinator of the program. My transformation from helpless victim to empowered survivor has refashioned my sense of self and purpose in life. The atrocities I have experienced provide a lens through which I am better able to see the complexity of injustices around me, and I have learned to harness the resulting anger in positive and productive ways that fuel my drive for social change. I wonder if the man who raped me realizes what he has created.

An estimated 5 to 10 percent of rapes committed in the United States involve male victims.[1] The Bureau of Justice's National Crime Victimization Survey found that, of the rapes reported to the survey in 1994, the most recent year for which data are available, 5 percent of rape victims aged twelve years and older were males.[2] These and similar data necessarily reflect only an estimation of the rape of men in the United States because of the vast underreporting of rape in general, and because of the fact that fewer men than women seem willing to report being raped.[3]

DEFINING THE TERM

The term "male rape" is frequently used in reference to the same-sex rape of men. Unless carefully defined, the term may be semantically confusing because many people remain unsure whether the "male" in "male rape" is an indicator of the rapist, the victim, or both. The use of "homosexual rape" to connote men raping men is also problematic. The (homo)-

sexual terminology perpetuates the stereotypical notions that all gay men are sexual predators or that gay men rape other men. On the contrary, the majority of men who rape other men are identified as heterosexual.[4]

Emphasis on the root word "sex" in "homosexual rape" also conflates consensual sex with rape behavior. Fortunately, feminist social movements since the 1970s have laid much of the groundwork for an understanding of rape as an act of power rather than of sex. Until now most research on male rape has concluded, as has research on opposite-sex rape, that the rape of men is not sexually motivated.[5] Instead, it is a form of violent power and control exercised over others. Although opposite-sex rape can be seen as a violent expression of power related to gender inequality, same-sex rape can involve other power dynamics related to physical strength, weapon use, influence of alcohol and other drugs, political strength, economic power, social power, and more.

One attempt to delineate the different kinds of male rape involves an examination of the sexual identity of both the rapist and the survivor. Viewing same-sex rape as an act of power through this lens is especially poignant, considering the controversy surrounding the dichotomization of rape and sex employed by feminist movements of the last twenty-five years. For example, the rape of gay men (or men perceived to be gay) by heterosexual men is often accompanied by misogynist verbal epithets in which the rapist degrades his victim with such language as "bitch," "girl," and so on.[6]

When same-sex rape is employed as a hate crime against gay men, usually as part of gay bashing, social inequality between heterosexual and gay men is clear evidence of a propensity to commit acts of violence. Rigidly traditional forms of hegemonic masculinity portray gay men as weak, feminine, and fit only for punishment and humiliation in the most dehumanizing way possible. "The victim may symbolize what they (the rapists) want to control, punish, and/or destroy, something they want to conquer and defeat. The assault is an act of retaliation, an expression of power, and an assertion of their strength and manhood"[7] Sexual violence within gay male relationships or between gay male acquaintances is also a serious problem, just as it is for heterosexual people and lesbian women.[8]

Same-sex rape of heterosexual men carries the stigma and shame associated with homosexuality in our culture; if the general population equates sex and rape to some degree, a man who has been raped by another man is, by implication, a homosexual. These categories could be further differentiated on the basis of whether the assault was stranger or acquaintance rape, interracial or intraracial, familial or nonfamilial, involved individual or multiple assailants, and so on. All of these factors can influence the rape experience, the dynamics of power involved, and the devastating aftermath faced by the male survivor.

DENIAL OF THE SIGNIFICANCE OF MALE RAPE

Discussions of adult male rape are frequently absent in campus rape education and prevention programs because the general public and popular culture have traditionally viewed rape in a context of violence against women. Although women statistically constitute the majority of rape victims, assessments in medicine, law, and education continue to deny, dismiss, or diminish the significant number of men who are sexually assaulted. Male survivors of sexual assault may be less likely to report or seek treatment for their assault, in part because these men view rape crisis centers and hotlines as having been established to serve only women.[9]

At many colleges and universities the rape of men by other men has only recently begun to generate responses from campus communities. Many sexual assault programs and organizations across the country are implementing minor initiatives to include and accommodate males in rape-related work, but the growing pains of such developments quickly become apparent.

A primary example is the dilemma of college rape education and prevention programs, often housed within campus women's centers and organizations that provide services and funding to male survivors. Many of these programs have mission statements that define their priority as the improvement of the campus climate for women while empowering them to overcome obstacles of sexism.

Is it, then, appropriate for these organizations to use resources that have been allocated for women's benefit to acts of violence that occur against and between men? If not, then where should such services originate, and who should be held responsible for primary and secondary male rape prevention programs? How can we change existing systems to confront and deal with the phenomenon of male rape without compromising or damaging the successful sexual assault education and prevention services we have fought so hard to develop? Even an acknowledgment that men can be victims (or perpetrators) of same-sex rape may introduce a gender contradiction into the women-centered missions, objectives, and goals of some sexual assault prevention programs, disrupting the fundamental structure and philosophy upon which they may have been built.

RECOMMENDATIONS

Concrete suggestions for the infusion of male rape programmatic content and services into general prevention education and crisis services are numerous. Here are six areas that campus health professionals should consider in evaluating how prepared they are to meet the needs of male rape survivors.

Prepare Resources and Referrals for Male Survivors

Are campus sexual assault centers prepared for male survivors' needs? Adequate referrals for support groups, counselors, hotlines, medical attention, financial assistance, and academic support should be at hand. Male-specific or gender-neutral literature and a short reading list should be available to the survivor. These resources should be compiled before a survivor contacts the office, not as the result of a last-minute search on behalf of a survivor in need of immediate crisis assistance.

Provide Training to Campus Health Clinic and Emergency Room Staff

Are campus health clinics and local hospital emergency rooms trained in the care of adult male survivors of rape? Many rape advocates and medical professionals never receive any such formal training. Not all hospital and statewide protocols for the forensic collection of evidence in rape cases include male-specific content. Adequate training for the examination of men's bodies is crucial, as are procedures for the identification and interpretation of physical findings.

Determine and Address the Legal Implications of Same-Sex Rape

Do law enforcement officials receive sexual assault sensitivity training? If so, is the occurrence of male rape addressed? State and local legal statutes may strongly influence the campus climate for male rape survivors. How is male-on-male rape defined by state and local laws? In many states, rape laws are gender specific, rendering the rape of men a legal impossibility.

Ensure That Campus Policies Apply to Same-Sex Sexual Violence

Do campus policies relating to rape and sexual harassment, codes of student conduct, and nondiscrimination policies allow for the possibility of same-sex sexual violence?

Conduct Prevention and Education Work in Addition to Treatment

Is any form of proactive education and prevention work being done on campus? Reacting to the rape of men is essential, but it is not enough. Absence of attention to male rape denies the reality of same-sex rape and subsequently renders male survivors invisible. Infusion of male rape content into general rape education programming can be effective, not only for the provision of information but also for signifying that the organization or office is receptive and prepared to work with male survivors. Even a basic informational handout can be effective in heightening awareness that rape of men happens in campus communities, not solely in prison populations.

Provide Culturally Competent Programs

Has population-specific awareness and programming been considered? When the entire college rape prevention programming is based on heterosexual models, the sexual assault of gay men, as part of gay bashing or acquaintance rape, is overlooked. Race, class, and other socioeconomic factors could influence the assault characteristics and impact. Single-sex campus environments, such as athletic teams, ROTC, all-male residence halls, and fraternities may also be at a higher risk for male rapes, given the hierarchical structure such environments tend to rely on and the internal power struggles that often manifest as physical violence.[10] Outreach to these communities is essential.

These suggestions are not all inclusive. The diversity of higher-education institutions will dictate the development of additional programs and differing approaches to meet the particular needs of students. More extensive research on the same-sex rape of men is needed to draw further conclusions and closer estimations of this form of violence. As the knowledge and visibility of male rape increase nationally, so will the call for expertise in prevention, education, and treatment related to same-sex rape in campus communities.

4

CREATING A SACRED SPACE OF OUR OWN

Aishah Shahidah Simmons

I start with the recognition that we are at war, and that war is not simply
a hot debate between the capitalist camp and the socialist camp over which
economic/political/social arrangement will have hegemony in the world.
It's not just the battle over turf and who has the right to utilize resources
for whomsoever's benefit. The war is also being fought over the truth: What
is the truth about human nature, about the human potential? My responsibility to myself, my neighbors, my family and the human family is to try
to tell the truth. That ain't easy. . . . We have rarely been encouraged and
equipped to appreciate the fact that the truth works and it releases the Spirit
and that it is a joyous thing. We live in a part of the world, for example,
that equates criticism with assault, that equates social responsibility with
naive idealism, that defines the unrelenting pursuit of knowledge and wis-
dom as fanaticism.

—Toni Cade Bambara

I come from a long line of women who probably would not have used
the word "feminist" or "womanist" to describe themselves; however, these
women, Rhoda Bell Temple-Robinson-Hudson-Douglas (my maternal
great-grandmother), Rebecca White-Simmons-Chapman and Juanita
Cranford-Robinson-Waston (my paternal and maternal grandmothers),
Jessie Neal Hudson and Mattie Simmons-Brown (two of my maternal and
paternal great-aunts), in their own ways, throughout their lives, fought
against racism and sexism. They were hardworking family women, Baptist
and AME church-going women, union women, voting women. . . . When
it came to the horrific reality of rape and sexual assault, some of these
women believed that if saying no didn't work, they had the right to defend themselves by any means necessary. In spite of the blatant and gro-
tesque racist, sexist, and classist barriers that existed in their lifetimes,

these women carried themselves with dignity, pride, and self-respect, and they persevered in everything that they set out to accomplish.

My grandmothers and aunts raised my mother, Gwendolyn Delores Robinson/Zoharah Simmons, and my father, Michael W. Simmons, to respect themselves and those around them, and to speak out against injustice—even if they were the only ones speaking—among many other things. I know that my parents' upbringings created the solid foundation that helped to shape them into the lifelong activists that they are today.

All of my life I heard about and participated in struggle. I literally grew up accompanying both of my divorced parents to meetings on Black liberation, women's rights/liberation, U.S. foreign policy in the third world, socialism and communism, union organizing—anything left of center that was about the liberation of oppressed people throughout the world. I participated in marches, rallies, and demonstrations in Philadelphia; Washington, D.C.; New York City; and other parts of the United States.

When it came to rape and sexual assault, both of my parents consistently told me "Aishah, a woman has the right to say no." When I was a child, my mother shared with me her personal experiences of violent attempted rapes committed against her when she was a student in Spelman College, and when she was involved with the Student Nonviolent Coordinating Committee (SNCC) in the 1960s. When she reported one of her attacks, which occurred during an SNCC orientation, to her superiors in SNCC, the resounding sentiment was "We don't have time for this. Why the hell didn't you just give him some?" She talked about the irony of having to fight against sexual harassment and attempted rape at the hands of some of her male comrades while simultaneously working with them, under the serious threat of death, to fight against racial injustice in the United States. When my mother became the SNCC director of the Laurel Mississippi Summer Project, she instituted, among many things, a sexual harassment policy to protect the female volunteers on the project. Based on her enforced policy, she developed the reputation of being an "Amazon"—which meant "she didn't take any shit, especially off of men!" Because of her reputation the Laurel Project was referred to as "The Amazon Project." Throughout her life my mother, like most Black women living in America, has walked and still walks the thin line of simultaneously fighting against both racial and gender oppression.

My father has always taught me that I am in charge of my body and that I have the right to say no and/or change my mind at any point, including during the act of sexual intercourse. He taught my brother, Tyree Cinque Simmons, that if a woman says no even after she says yes, he, my brother, has an obligation to stop and/or not try to coerce the woman to have sex. During the Mike Tyson rape trial in 1992, my father told me and Tyree that men are not animals who cannot control their sexual desires.

Tyree and I have heard our father, on numerous occasions, publicly speak out against the rape and sexual assault of women. Our father's position has always been that just as white people must take up the issue of racism with other white people, men must take up the issue of misogyny, domestic violence, rape, sexual assault, and other forms of violence against women with other men.

> We can learn to work and speak when we are afraid in the same way we have learned to work and speak when we are tired. For we have been socialized to respect fear more than our own needs for language and definition and while we wait in silence for that final luxury of fearlessness, the weight of that silence will choke us.
>
> —Audre Lorde, *Sister Outsider*

The writings of Black lesbian, feminist, mother, warrior, poet Audre Lorde saved my life in 1990. Her written words taught me that my silence will not protect me, and that silence is not golden. Lorde's words tapped into my inner power, my inner strength, to say, "I, Aishah Shahidah Simmons, am a Black feminist lesbian who is a physical, emotional, and spiritual survivor of sexual abuse. A rape that could have resulted in my unplanned pregnancy, from which I was fortunate to have a safe and legal abortion." To own these aspects of my identity is my act of self-revelation, my way of not allowing the pain and, in some instances, the horror, fester inside of me and eat away at my organs like a deadly virus. I know I am not alone. Unfortunately, too many women suffer alone because either they think they are alone, or they are afraid to break their silence and tell their truth for fear of various forms of societal and cultural retaliation, and for other reasons.

I believe in the power of the spoken and written word as well as the power of the image on the screen. One of the reasons that I am a Black feminist lesbian cultural worker and activist is because I want to continue to break the silences that Black women have kept secret for far too long: incest, rape, sexual abuse, and domestic violence.

During the Mike Tyson rape trial in 1992, as I watched and listened to many of the so-called Black male leaders—the very same ones who in 1989 defended Tawana Brawley when she alleged that she had been raped and sodomized by four white men—accuse Desiree Washington of betraying the Black community, I began thinking about making what has now become *NO!*

NO! will be a ninety-minute experimental documentary exposing the collective silence in the Black community when Black women and girls are raped or sexually assaulted by Black men and boys. *NO!* will create a sacred space within which Black women and men, outraged about intraracial rape and sexual assault, challenge the Black community to look inward and confront this issue, through their testimonies and art. *NO!* will initiate the healing of the political, psychic, and cultural scars of rape and/or sexual assault within the Black community. Through narrative, interviews, archival footage, music, poetry, and dance, *NO!* will delve into how the act of raping or sexually assaulting, physically and/or verbally, Black women and girls is a race, gender, class, and sexual orientation issue.

As one can imagine, this is a tremendous undertaking. It is one that I dare not do alone. Tamara L. Xavier, the coproducer, and I have been working on *NO!* since our very first preproduction meeting in October 1994. We've created and mailed out *NO!* fliers and brochures to various community organizations, colleges, universities, and rape crisis centers across the country. We have applied and continue to apply to foundations for funds toward the making of the documentary. We've contacted and continue to contact potential individual donors who have the financial resources to give a sizable donation toward the making of *NO!* We've used and continue to use the Internet to inform people about the making of *NO!* and to encourage them to get involved creatively and financially.

Making *NO!* is literally the hardest thing I have ever had to do in my life. It is a tedious and difficult journey to raise the necessary funds to make this documentary a reality. Tamara and I have received many rejection letters from foundations and individuals. Many white foundations believe I am limiting my audience by focusing on the rape and sexual assault of only Black women and girls. While I know that intraracial rape and sexual assault occur in every community worldwide, I specifically want to examine the impact of rape and sexual assault in the Black community.

I've received questions from Black people like "Since you are a lesbian, what's your ax to grind with *NO!?*" My response was and is "Though Black women are 7 percent of the U.S. population, we are 27 percent of the rape and sexual assault victims. I want rape and sexual assault to end, don't you?"[1]

In 1996 a Black *progressive* foundation had the audacity to share its sexist and misogynist reasons for not giving any of the requested thirty-five-thousand-dollar funds toward *NO!*'s research and development budget. The initial comments in the rejection letter were: "Strong point of view and the concept is good; however, the example of Mike Tyson's case and the indifference from the community might be due, in part, to the moral point of view that one does not go to a man's room in the early morning; that opinion cannot be ignored."

I could not believe that, given the racism and sexism in Black women's *herstory* in the United States, a Black progressive foundation would use the question of Black women's morality as a legitimate reason for not funding a documentary that will expose the rape of Black women and girls in the Black community. I was so outraged by this foundation's stated sexist and misogynist reasoning for not giving any of the requested funds, that I wrote a protest letter to the foundation, and I E-mailed and snail-mailed it across the United States and to England.

There have been many other times, as well, when I have literally wanted to throw my hands up in the air and say, "The hell with this, I can't do this any longer!" Then I pause, take a deep breath, and remind myself that every institutional and individual racist, homophobic, and sexist rejection reinforces the need for *NO!* This type of resistance refuels my passionate rage to make this film. I pour libations and call on the Creator, and my blood and my spirit ancestors, to continue to guide Tamara and me on this journey.

In spite of the tremendous resistance, slowly but surely an informal international network of predominantly Black women filmmakers, scholars, and/or cultural workers is being created to help make this documentary a reality. While there are many exceptions, the majority of these women are from the hip-hop generation. Through this informal network the word is spreading about the making of *NO!*, and I am receiving financial, emotional, creative, and spiritual support from women across the United States and in England. I am also receiving requests from *sistahs* to tell their incest stories, their sexual abuse stories, and their rape stories. Contrary to popular myth, these sistahs' perpetrators are not the strange, unidentifiable man lurking in the bushes. No, their perpetrators are their grandfathers, fathers, brothers, uncles, male cousins, husbands, boyfriends, lovers, comrades . . . *men.* Men whom these sistahs trusted; whom these sistahs thought if they said no to would stop; if they said "You're hurting me!" would stop; if they cried, would stop; if they bled, would stop.

> My political obligations? I am a Black woman . . . in a world that defines human as white and male for starters. Everything I do including survival is political.[4]
>
> —Audre Lorde, "What I Do When I Write"

There is a collective understanding among many progressives that the white male heterosexual, imperial, capitalist power structure is the root of all oppression in the United States. However, even in the company of other oppressed people, Black women are still under attack. Black women living in America are caught at the intersection of race and gender. In many instances American society defines Black as male and woman as white. This is most evident in the use of "inclusive" language. Expressions such as "Blacks and women" imply that these two categories are mutually exclusive. Consequently, Black women are rendered invisible.

Black women have herstorically, and continually, been asked to choose between our race, our gender, and, when we are lesbian or bisexual, our sexuality. Asking Black women to choose between our multiple identities when they are bound into one identity is racist, sexist, and homophobic. I have learned to see how damaging this can be, particularly around sexual violence issues. America has "sexually stereotyped Black women as immoral, insatiable, perverse, the initiators in all sexual contacts—abusive or otherwise."[2] Black women have a horrific legacy of rape and sexual abuse in the United States. My sistah and colleague Wanda R. Moore states that "The reason why Black women have been raped and assaulted without question or justice is because we are not white and our womanhood is not considered worthy enough to protect or preserve."

In Julie Dash's critically acclaimed film *Daughters of the Dust*, the character Yella Mary tells the character Eula, "The rape of a colored woman is as common as fish in the sea." This is a powerful moment in the film, and it is one that sends chills up and down my spine every time I see it. (I'm on the fifteenth round.) Yella Mary's statement is definitely said with the covert understanding that Yella Mary is talking about white men raping Black women during the period of enslavement of African people in the Americas. However, because of the impact of both racism *and* sexism on Black women's lives, we are still often unable to speak of our horrific experiences and/or our horrific experiences are rarely acknowledged by our communities and never recognized by society at large.

The Black community has retained the collective memory of this country's bloody history: of the mutilated bodies of Black men—men accused of glancing at a white woman—hanging from trees. The retention of this memory has caused the collective silence on the part of many Black women rather than publicly exposing the abuse that they experience at the hands of Black men. This silence has occurred and continues to occur in spite of the fact that no man, Black or white, has ever been lynched for raping or sexually assaulting a Black woman. This silence has occurred and continues to occur in spite of the fact that Black women not only were lynched and subjected to other forms of racial and sexual violence, but were also (in the specific instances of Ida B. Wells-Barnett and the Anti-Lynching Crusaders) in the forefront of the struggle to eliminate the horror of lynching.[3]

When will Black people, as a nonmonolithic community, stop making excuses for Black men and boys who perpetuate violence against Black women and girls? When do women and girls lose the right to say no? Is it when we agree to go on the date, or when we invite him into our homes or even our bedrooms? Where is the mass mobilization within the Black community when a Black woman experiences any form of violence at the hands of a Black man? Where are the Stop the Violence marches and rallies, in the Black community, geared to addressing sexual violence? How often will we think about rape and sexual assault when the term "Black on Black" crime is used?

Each time Black women are abused by Black men and we go public with our abuse, racism is used in defense of the Black man—as if Black women aren't Black, as if Black women don't experience racism *as well as* sexism; and when we are lesbian or bisexual, our sexuality is used against us to defend the perpetrator who simply wants to "cure us of our disease." I continually ask myself, When will many members of the Black community stop castigating and maligning Black women who speak out on violence against Black women within the Black community? When will atrocities committed against Black women by Black men be viewed as an act of treason against the Black community? When will racism no longer be accepted as an excuse for the abuse that Black women experience at the hands of Black men?

In the white feminist community, white women are usually seen or heard from when a white woman has been raped or sexually assaulted, or if some well-known Black male official, athlete, or musician has been charged with raping or sexually assaulting a woman. Clarence Thomas, O. J. Simpson, Mike Tyson, Tupac Shakur—why are these men household names when discussions about sexual harassment, sexual abuse, sexual assault, rape, and femicide occur? Why is it that when I hear many white feminists speak about ending violence against women, these are the names that I consistently hear as examples of perpetrators? Are these the *only* men who are harassing, abusing, raping, and/or sexually assaulting women? How can we really bring an end to violence against all women and children if white women continue to play into the racist game of portraying Black men as the sole perpetrators? Let's remember President Clinton, William Kennedy-Smith, former senator Bob Packwood, Christian Slater, Tom Capano, and on and on.

In the fall of 1995 a young, white, middle-class woman was raped and murdered in the neighborhood where I live. My neighborhood is a center-city, predominantly white, middle-class community. There was an uproar in the community and throughout the city about this woman's murder. Her story made front-page news in the city's two major dailies. The mayor, who is a white man, had a private meeting with the victim's father, a physician from another major metropolitan city. The mayor, the president of city council—a Black man—and the district attorney—a white woman—attended her funeral. Following the funeral, the front page of the metropolitan section of the Sunday paper featured the question, "Why is the victim's murderer still at large?"

Meanwhile, on the other side of town, at least two thirteen-year-old Latinas have been raped in a working-class Black and Latino community.

When the victims' community called a town meeting, not one police officer, let alone the district attorney, the mayor, or the president of city council, attended the meeting.

There is a serial rapist/murderer still at large in the neighborhood where I grew up and where my parents still live. This neighborhood is a predominantly working-class African American community. In a period of eighteen months at least fifteen Black women have been sexually assaulted and murdered. These atrocious crimes have yet to make the front page of either of the two major dailies. There haven't been any private meetings with any of the victims' families and the mayor. Neither the mayor, the president of city council, nor the district attorney were present at any of the victims' funerals.

Variations of such scenarios happen in every major city in the United States where there are racially diverse populations. The city in which I live isn't unique to valuing white women's lives over Black, Latina, Asian/Pacific Islander, Arab, and Native American women's lives. For example, the rape of the Central Park jogger (a white woman investment banker) in New York City received national media coverage. Multimillionaire Donald Trump even placed a full-page ad in the *New York Times* calling for the reinstatement of the death penalty. During that same time period a working-class Black woman was gang-raped in New York City, thrown down an elevator shaft, and left to die. Her vicious attack did not receive national media coverage.

Where are the voices of white feminists calling for an end to gender-only politics because they are inherently racist and offensive to women of Color? Where is the analysis in the white feminist community of the intersection of gender *and* race and its impact upon women of Color?

Time and time again I ask myself, in the words of Abbey Lincoln, "Who will revere the Black woman?" History and life experiences have consistently taught me that Black women must speak and act in defense of ourselves. Black women must continue to create our own sacred space to deal with racism, all forms of violence in and outside of the home, sexism, classism, homophobia, and ableism. We need this sacred space to address these issues from our extremely diverse perspectives without having to worry about what the responses will be from Black men and/or white women. Far too often, in the name of both racial and gender unity, members from these communities ask us to choose between our identities for their own interests. We must continue to refuse to choose between our race, our gender, and our sexual orientation, with the understanding that any group or community that claims to have our best interests at heart would never ask us to choose.

Sometimes the truth hurts when it is spoken aloud, but it also heals. I am interested in healing the wounds that result in fibroids, high blood pressure, all forms of cancer, AIDS, chronic depression, fatigue, heart disease, alcoholism, drug addiction . . . the list goes on with too many Black women in America. No one can tell me that the fact that Black women's bodies are the intersection of race, gender, class, and sexual orientation doesn't have a profound impact on our health. So while *NO!* has everything to do with rape, it also has everything to do with the wholeness and wellness of Black women's lives, with placing our issues first and foremost, because our issues are the issues of the oppressed, with the acknowledgment of the herstoric and continued survival against the odds. Once completed, *NO!* will be a part of Black women's sacred space. *NO!* will be a testament to Black women's strength, resiliency, and courage.

As Black woman Nobel Laureate, high priestess of writing, Toni Morrison so eloquently wrote,

> I think about us, Black women, a lot. How many of us are battered and how many are champions. . . . I think about the sisters no longer with us, who, in rage or contentment, left us to finish what should never have begun: a gender/racial war in which everybody would lose, if we lost and in which everybody would win, if we won.[4]

In the tradition of acknowledging those who have paved the way and those who stand beside me in struggle, I dedicate this essay to the lives and works of Toni Cade Bambara and Audre Lorde —two Black women cultural workers who consistently challenged the racist, sexist, homophobic, classist, ageist, and ableist status quo in the United States and abroad. I must also acknowledge Michael Simmons, my father-brother-friend and my comrade for teaching me to be a principled person and for challenging me to fight against all forms of oppression. Zoharah Simmons, my mother-sistah-friend and the first feminist I ever knew, for her willingness to tell parts of her herstory in *NO!* and for teaching me, through example, that "It is *never* too late to follow your divine purpose." Tyree "DJ Drama" Simmons, my brother, my friend, and my ninth-birthday present, for consistently supporting my work in various ways. Dr. Clara Whaley-Perkins, my psychologist, who, since 1992, has served as a critical guide to me on this journey called life. Joan Weslie Brannon, coproducer, cowriter, and director of photography of *NO!* and more importantly my beloved partner, sistah, and friend for being there in so many ways. Tamara L. Xavier, coproducer and dance coordinator of *NO!* and my beloved sistahfriend for her long lasting support of this project and her unconditional commitment to bring an end to violence against women. Wanda R. Moore, a sistahfriend, for numerous discussions on the impact of racism and sexism on Black women's lives, and for reading, critiquing, and editing the initial drafts of this essay. Wadia L. Gardiner, a true blue sistahfriend and colleague for being my right arm in Philadelphia. Reanae McNeal, sistah-

diva for helping me to claim my divine purpose and for her uncompromising position on ending violence against women. Bahamadia, another
member of "the 4/22 club" and my homegirl for unconditionally supporting my creative work and for agreeing to create a phat hip-hop track, with
DJ Drama, for *NO!* Tyrone Smith, founder and executive director of Unity,
Inc., my confidante, comrade, and friend for consistently keeping me sane
in an insane world. Robert Brand, founder and president of Solutions for
Progress, Inc., for donating the entire use of his office and supplies to assist in the ongoing journey to make *NO!* a celluoid reality. Louis Massiah,
award-winning documentary filmmaker, for founding and directing Scribe
Video Center, the place where I learned that my stories are worth documenting in video and film.

Making a feature-length film that will expose intraracial rape and
sexual assault in the Black community is an uphill and tedious battle.
There are many, many people who, in one way or another, have worked
and are working diligently to make *NO!* a celebrated celluloid reality. I
believe it is critical to acknowledge some of these people, so that you, the
reader, will understand that progressive revolutionary change does not
occur in a vacuum nor does it occur overnight. It is a collective process
that requires serious time and commitment. The majority of the people
listed here are feminist/womanist and/or lesbian/ bisexual women of
Color who may not see "eye to eye" on a whole host of issues; however,
there is complete agreement that all forms of violence perpetuated against
women must end.

Women Make Movies is the 501c3 Fiscal Sponsor for *NO!* Astraea
National Lesbian Action Foundation was the first foundation that gave
money toward preproduction of *NO!* in 1997. Inelle Cox Bagwell, Sonia
Sanchez, and Loretta Horton/Evangelical Lutheran Church of America
and Robert Brand/Solutions for Progress, Inc., are benefactors of *NO!* The
Union Institute Center for Women named me, on behalf of *NO!*, the 1998
recipient of their Audre Lorde Legacy Award. The funds received from
this award went toward the preproduction of *NO!* In November 1998 I
was the recepient of a major research and development grant from the
Valentine Foundation. The funds received from the Valentine Foundation
enabled me to complete the preproduction phase of *NO!* and begin production in the summer of 1999.

NO! A Work-in-Progress—1997 (The Educational Fund-raising Trailer):
The women and man who shared their personal testimonies and poetry
to make the fund-raising trailer a reality: April Blount, Palesa Beverly
Ditsie, Essex Hemphill, Queen, Zoharah Simmons, and Rosetta Williams.
The crew who either donated their time, resources, or expertise, or worked
at reduced costs: P. Sagwa Chabeda, Charlene Gilbert, Nikki Harmon,
Assitou Kasaundra Cross-Isoke, Denise C. Jones, Barbara Kigozi, Evelyne

Laurent, Gail Lloyd, Kim Mayhorn, Reanae McNeal, Wanda R. Moore, Crystal Morales, Kagendo Murungi, Reynelda Ware-Muse, Hebert Peck, Janine Spruill, Wayman L. Widgins, and Tamara L. Xavier. The people who wrote letters of recommendation for the ongoing grant process: Howard Arnette Jr., Charlotte Pierce-Baker, Alicia Banks, Darwin Beauvais, Diana Onley-Campbell, Fiona Conway, Ashara Ekundayo, Tonya Hegamin, Honoree Jeffers, Denise C. Jones, Chana Kai Lee, LaRaye L. Lyles, Reanae Mcneal, Reynelda Ware-Muse, Michelle Parkerson, Christina E. Sharpe, Denise B. Sneed, Janine Spruill, Skye Ward, Aaronette White, Evelyn C. White, and Janelle L. White.

Through speaking engagements at colleges, universities, community centers, and conferences, Tamara and I have been able to raise funds for both *NO!* and/or awareness about violence against Black women. The following women coordinated these events: Janelle L. White (University of Michigan/1995), Nancy Tart (National Coalition against Sexual Assault/1995), Danista Hunte (Sisterspace: Women of Color Collective/ 1995), Evelyne Laurent (Temple University/1995), Claire Yoo & Nationwide Women's Program (American Friends Service Committee/1996), Patricia Moda Guedes (University of Massachusetts at Amherst/1996), Monica Freeman (National Black Arts Festival/1996), Orianna Lewis (Smith College/1996), Barbara Kigozi (Samuel Adams Independent Film Screening/1997), Sonia Sanchez (Temple University/1997), Janelle L. White (San Francisco Women against Rape/1997), Johanna Bermudez (Antioch University/1997), Christina Elizabeth Sharpe (Hobart and William Smith Colleges/1997, Anuja Mendiratta (Summer Documentary Institute/Antioch University/1997), Mojisola Sonoiki (London Black Lesbian and Gay Centre's Film Screening/1997), Kimberly Coleman (Smith College's Otelia Cromwell Day/1997), Michelle Parkerson (Temple University/ 1997), Mojisola Sonoiki (University of Birmingham [UK]/1998), GiGi Otalvaro (Brown University/1998), ImageWeavers(International House Screening/1998), Ananya Chatterjea and Valerie De Cruz and Kali Nicole Gross (University of Pennsylvania's "Unleashing Legacies: Exploring Third World Feminisms" Conference/1998), Farah Jasmin Griffin and Gayle Ellison (University of Pennsylvania: Afro-American Studies/1998), Joy James and Ashara Ekundayo (Unfinished Liberation Conference/ 1998), Maisha James and Nikki Stewart (DC Rape Crisis Center's Nineteenth Annual Take Back the Night Rally /1998), Kali Nicole Gross (Backyard Talks: Mending the Rift between Activists and Scholars: University of Pennsylvania/ 1998), Ashara Ekundayo and Matema Hadi (Forever Nubian Productions' Through My Sisters' Eyes International Film Festival/1998), Rebecca Helem (Collective Lesbians of African Descent Voices Everywhere/1998), Shari Frilot (Los Angeles Lesbian and Gay Film Festival/1998), Sheila Bhattacharya (Desh Pardesh Conference-Festival/

1998), Kara Lynch (Hampshire College/1998), Sheila Alexander-Reid (Women in the Life/1998), Jonathan Ogle (Westtown School/1999), Charissa King (Outwrite'99), Sam Anderson (Brecht Forum/1999), Clairesa Clay (African American Women Cinema/1999), Joan Weslie Brannon (Twentieth Annual Kentucky Women's Writer's Conference/ 1999), and Farah Jasmine Griffin (Black Women in the Academy II/1999).

In addition to these names, there are many, many women and some men across the United States and in England and France who have given and continue to give financial contributions toward the making of *NO!* For more information on *NO!* please contact: AfroLez® Productions, PO Box 58085, Philadelphia, PA 19102-8085, <AfroLez@aol.com>

5

BREAKING THE SILENCE, MAKING LAUGHTER: TESTIMONY OF AN ASIAN-AMERICAN SISTER

Luoluo Hong

My sexual assault at age eighteen by a white male was a sexist act in which racial humiliation was wielded as the weapon. My sexual assault at age eighteen by a white male was also a racist act in which sexual degradation cut my soul. That night I experienced a total annihilation of my identity both as a woman and as an Asian American. As a result, I regarded both identities as weak, worthless, powerless, dirty, undesirable, and—most important—somehow responsible for my own victimization. In healing I discovered two contrasting elements embedded within my Asian American culture. The first was a tradition of female passivity that increased my vulnerability to the rape. Simultaneously, though, I possessed the tools enabling me to cope with and accept the rape.

My perpetrator was twenty years old and heavily consumed pornography, particularly that involving Asian women. His name was Blake, and he was from Dallas, Texas—a state in which he assured me the "men were bigger and better" than anywhere else in the world. At six foot, two inches tall, and over 200 pounds, he was certainly big to me; I, at a petite five foot, five inches, just under 110 pounds, was no match for him. Blake and I were not dating at the time, merely casual acquaintances—he a sophomore and a member of the Men's Glee Club, and I the accompanist for that group, just finishing my first year at Amherst College. After our performance on Saturday, May 2, 1987, he followed me to my residence hall from the postconcert party and knocked at my door on the pretense of "checking up" on me. I drank six or seven beers at the party, and he was purportedly concerned about whether or not I had made it back to my room safely. He raped me three times that night. I cried; I pummeled my fists against his chest; I sobbed out "no" several times. A conqueror who tramples on another's dignity does not listen or pity, and Blake was no exception.

I went back to visit that room sometime during my sophomore year. When I caught a partial glimpse of the inside through a cracked door, memories overtook all of my senses: the scent of cheap bourbon on his breath and on his neck, the recklessness in his eyes as he ripped off my clothing and pinned down my arms and legs on that night of reckoning. The sweat drenched his body as he shoved his penis in and out of me, not caring that he hurt me. All the while he muttered things to me: "You looked so hot tonight in that dress," "Just relax and you'll like it better," and "I know that you've been wanting this, I could see it in your 'chink' eyes"—each statement further sealing my self-blame in the incident. Then he grunted like an animal when he ejaculated. By this time I was floating somewhere above, gazing down in self-pity and mourning at how help-less my body looked crushed beneath his. Even when he rolled over and fell asleep, I had no peace. He raped me two more times.

The next morning he awoke and got dressed. Kissing me on the cheek and rubbing my hair, he smiled and thanked me, saying he had a good time and that he would see me soon. Then he left to go to church, as nonchalantly as if we had gone on a respectable date. I slept for hours, waking up in the late afternoon to take a long, hot shower in a desperate attempt to wash his stench off my body. I changed the sheets on my bed. Frantically wadding up my clothes from the night before, I shoved them into a hamper, then donned white underwear and a white T-shirt. I didn't think I would ever feel clean again. Devoid of all feeling, I fell asleep again.

Blake returned to my room the following Wednesday at two in the morning. Like a zombie, I let him in the room. I wish I could tell you that I was the wiser for having been burned once. I wish I could tell you that I fought him off with kicks and scratches. I cannot tell you these things, for I no longer had anything to protest. I had no will to fight for myself, for I had no more value in my own eyes. The first rape eradicated my personal and sexual boundaries. I lay there as Blake had his way with me, shell of a person that I was—unfeeling, unresponding, uncaring. I didn't know at the time that my experience is shared by nearly half of all women who survive rape.[1] It would be easy to conclude that having sex again with Blake meant that I wasn't raped in the first place—reflecting the essen-tial irony in rape that the victim is blamed for her victimization. In fact, Catharine MacKinnon argues that until political and social power are re-distributed in our society, all sexual intercourse experienced by women can be contextualized as coercive sex.[2] The first rape was forced sex; the incidents that ensued were coerced sex. By succumbing "willingly" on that second night, I could maintain a false sense of normalcy.

When I haltingly told my boyfriend, who was attending school in Washington, D.C., at the time, that somebody "took advantage" of me, he called me a "slut" and insinuated that I was cheating on him; we promptly ended our year-long relationship. When I met with a psychologist at the campus counseling center to get some help in understanding why I was feeling so depressed, she suggested that I refrain from using sex to rebel against my parents' strictness.

I had no vocabulary back then to describe what happened; "acquaintance rape" was a term that would later pervade the media headlines. Having internalized the stigma that society places on rape, I had yet to develop the awareness to label my experience for what it truly was. Rape was supposed to be something to be ashamed of for any woman, and especially for an Asian woman. Purity and virginity are valued even more earnestly in my culture than in the mainstream one. Denial was the easiest method of coping with my sexual assault.

Blake continued to sexually abuse me about two to three times a week for the next year and a half. Blake used any of a number of means to attain my "consent." He would track me down at parties, where, given my intoxicated state, I was unable to resist him. He might show up at my door at three or four o'clock in the morning, when the confusion of disturbed slumber also made me easy prey. Or he would simply cover my mouth with his hand to silence the protests and throw me against the wall or bed. He frequently wanted to "act out" a scene from a pornographic movie he had just watched.

I experienced sexual intercourse only two other times before Blake raped me. I therefore learned about my sexuality and about sex from him. I learned that it was painful, and that it was dirty. He did not hesitate to restrain me or hit me if I resisted, which was rarely. I never had an orgasm; he always did. I was subjected to sexual contact with him in every way imaginable: vaginal, oral, anal. I never cried out. I just didn't feel anything. Afterward, when he rolled over and fell asleep with loud snores, I would stare quietly into the darkness, trying to fight the feeling of nausea as I felt his semen seep out of me—he had marked me, much as a wolf marks his territory. Sometimes, to preserve my sanity, I would pretend that he and I were actually lovers, that he cared for me deeply.

Throughout the entire period of Blake's assaults, I remember very little about school and other events. I do know that I became very adept at predicting when Blake would come for me, and organized my academic demands accordingly. Sometimes I deliberately provoked his visits on a particular night to ensure a good night's sleep before an important exam— a rational response to an insane situation. I abused alcohol heavily, partially to numb the intense self-hatred I felt, and to alleviate the shame and humiliation of Blake's violation. My eating habits became sporadic. Already thin, I continued to lose more weight and experienced a thyroid disorder during my junior year of college. The inheritance of my mother's mental instability—she battled several bouts of severe depression—stirred within me. At one point in February 1988 I seriously contemplated suicide; a phone call from my sister to inquire about life in general and about mundane details in particular convinced me otherwise.

My victimization did not occur in private. Blake bragged frequently of his sexual conquests among his fraternity brothers and other friends, and many of them approached me to go to bed with them. I usually didn't care whether or not I did; the deciding factor tended to be how intoxicated I was at the time. My emotionless sex with these faceless men, who cared nothing for me, were acts of self-mutilation, of self-deprecation—an attempt to be free of Blake. Blake did not hesitate from "pimping" me, either. He would bet his friends a case of beer that they couldn't get me to go to bed with them; some approached him and offered him a quarter keg for the privilege of "sampling the foreign goods." Incredibly, these men made no qualms about revealing or bragging about these transactions to me.

I sometimes wonder angrily how those who lived around me and with me in the residence halls over the fifteen months that Blake abused me did not realize what was going on; they saw my tearstained face in the early morning. They heard Blake's derogatory accounts; yet they could only conclude that I was a "whore" who didn't know any better. My closest women friends witnessed the struggles that preceded each rape, regarding me with eyes that pitied but showed no mercy; they blamed me in my own plight, my own victimization. Perhaps they were afraid to admit their own vulnerability; perhaps they just didn't know any better. Not until I came out of denial about the abuse did I realize that they, too, were co-opted into the social phenomenon of "rape culture," described by Dianne Herman as a culture in which men's and women's values and beliefs about heterosexual intercourse are molded on a model of forced sexual intercourse.[3] Such a culture renders what happened to me usual and unremarkable.

I wondered often if I had perhaps been aptly nicknamed Jezebel by my abuser—the connotation of that label haunts me still. I doubted my innocence in my own exploitation and wondered if in fact I had consented to those sexual horrors by my very failure to stop them. He would whisper, "Jezebel," with careless ease, wrapping my long black hair around his wrist or neck. I cut off that hair in the spring of 1990—a symbolic rite of passage into my newfound commitment to ardent feminism and female empowerment.

> Chinese-Americans, when you try to understand what things in you are Chinese, how do you separate what is peculiar to childhood, to poverty, insanities, one family, your mother who marked your growing with sto-

ries, from what is Chinese? What is Chinese tradition and what is the movies?

—Maxine Hong Kingston, *The Woman Warrior*

The scripted role of a Chinese daughter is the expectation of demure obedience and lackluster femininity. I conformed to the strict, traditional ways because I had a strong desire to please and to receive approval. Yet my inner self knew that what was being asked of me was not who I really was. The most fervent point of contention between my mother and me centered on dating: I was absolutely not allowed to date until I was twenty years old; parties at friends' houses were also banned. My days were filled with piano practice, reviewing lessons, and diligently completing my homework—all in an effort to maximize my chances of fulfilling the dreams my mother spun for me.

Deprived of typical social experiences, such as attending school dances or going to movies, I quickly learned that it was easier to manipulate my books and homework than to raze the insurmountable walls of protective tradition my mother so vehemently erected. I was socially awkward throughout high school, escaping into my studies. I was sweet and pliant, and all of my teachers liked me, but I had very few friends other than those I might study with, and no close friends. My primary companions were my sister and brother, both younger than I. While we occasionally fought, the friendship and kinship we felt were strengthened and unified both by the gaping emotional distance between us and our parents, and by our constant conflict with them. In the fighting between parents and children, battle lines were drawn not only across generational differences, but across cultural ones as well.

I longed for a strong and doting father figure, longed to be "daddy's little girl." I despised my father's seeming coldness and seeming absorption with what I considered the minutiae of life. He worked hard, tended to the maintenance of our house and our lawn with meticulous devotion, and occasionally graced us with his quick and stormy temper. Silently, we watched as mother and father cycled through stages of threatening divorce, only to succumb again to the ultimate Chinese duty of preserving the family, followed by a period of mutual indifference. Then the pattern repeated itself. We witnessed my father hitting my mother and dragging her down the basement stairs. Instead of abusing alcohol to ease his feelings of helplessness, my father emotionally and physically battered us. My mother destroyed entire dinnerware sets, hurling them at my father or at the floor. She often gathered us to her bosom to share her secret desires. She wished that she had never married and that we were never born to partake of this hell. Feeling unwanted, we vowed to disappoint our mother less often and achieve great things so that she might love us after all.

The feelings of helplessness and frustration I developed were bottled and left to simmer unnoticed throughout my teenage years. Preserving the family's honor and maintaining its harmony were of primary importance; we were taught always to "save face," which meant you did not discuss your problems with others. Each of us learned early on to conceal pain from outsiders. Counselors and psychologists especially were not in our repertoire of acceptable family contacts. We were encouraged to seek only each other's support, no matter how unsoothing it was, or to seek no support at all. In retrospect I see that I had no role model of a healthy relationship, and wonder often if my tolerance for abuse and violence was developing even before I was ever violated.

College bound at the tender age of seventeen, I vaguely comprehended the meaning of what it was to be Chinese American but yearned desperately to be free of those invisible chains and to join the outside world I knew as "American culture." I did not realize when I entered the gates of Amherst College—gates laden with decades of patriarchal tradition and academic excellence —into one of the premier liberal arts campuses in the country, that I would exit four years later with my most valuable lessons acquired not inside the classrooms but outside of them. I commenced my career as an undergraduate with the same hopes of any young adult who enters this stage of life, eager to meet the world, and hopeful that it would accept me and deem me worthy. I chose never to look back, at least not if I could help it.

> Asian-Americans are used as pawns in the power games of racism. We are often held up as model minorities to keep other minorities in line. One outcome of this has been to place Asian-Americans at odds with other people of color who question the legitimacy of our minority status.
> —Jean Kim, "The Limits of Cultural Enlightenment"

As are African American, Hispanic, and Native American women, Asian American women are caught in the double jeopardy of being both women and people of color. We derive our identity and cultural values from both race and gender. As such, we often experience "double jeopardy"—subjected to oppression because of our gender as well as our ethnicity. And, like other women of color, Asian American women for the most part have not participated actively in the U.S. feminist movement, a movement that since its inception has reflected predominantly white, middle-class values.[4] For Asian American and other women of color, participating in such a movement artificially separates gender identity from racial identity—often to the detriment of the latter. As Audre Lorde eloquently stated in her essay "There Is No Hierarchy of Oppressions," "I simply do not believe that one aspect of myself can possibly profit from the oppression of any other part of my identity."

According to Chow, Asian American women must resolve the tension between their Asian ethnic heritage and their adopted American values. This tension falls along four primary dimensions: (1) obedience versus independence; (2) collective (or familial) versus individual interest; (3) fatalism versus change; and (4) self-control versus self-expression or spontaneity. Resolving the dilemma involves creating a bicultural existence that successfully blends elements of both cultural domains.[5] On the one hand, adherence to traditional Asian values fosters submissiveness, passivity, and adaptiveness—characteristics that are not conducive to activism, that may also have increased my vulnerability to rape. On the other hand, acceptance of the American values of mastery of one's environment through change, assertiveness, and emotional expression are consistent with self-empowerment as well as with political activism. At the same time, however, my Chinese upbringing ultimately imbued me with the necessary strength and perseverance for surviving a life event as traumatic as rape—a rape that took place within the context of one of the most rape-prone societies in the modern world by Sanday's definition.[6] There are elements in each culture to keep and to discard.

Given my own experience, I believe it is critical for Asian American women to participate in political and social activism that advances the status of women and of minorities in the United States. We need to alter the traditional roles that Asian women are expected to fulfill in the Asian home and redefine the image of Asian American women that is propagated in the U.S. mainstream culture. These battles are one and the same.

In my cultural heritage sons are inherently more valued than daughters. Financial and social power are transmitted through patriarchal lines in the family, and a woman is merely property of her father, her husband, her brother, or her son. In fact, she exists solely to honor them, by being a dutiful daughter, obedient wife, gracious sister, or sacrificing mother.[7] Some unknowing American males may buy into the myth that the ideal home life consists of a Japanese wife, a Chinese cook, and a Korean maid. The notion that Asian women embody the ultimate definition of femininity—fragile, dependent, pliant, childlike, and erotic—is widely propagated in the mass media, including television shows, mainstream movies, and pornography.[8] U.S. veterans of World War II, the Korean War, and the Vietnam War have brought back and disseminated a similar legacy, either with memories of sexual escapades with "geisha girls" and "China dolls," or with physical proof in the form of biracial children. According to the Coalition against Trafficking in Women—Asia, catalogs such as Lotus Blossom are widely distributed both in the United States and in Western Europe, targeting older middle- to upper-class men who are inclined to having a traditional-minded mate.[9]

In my own life I have had many potential dates—white, black, and Hispanic—say to me some variation of "I've always fantasized about being with an Oriental girl; I hear they treat their men really good." If I ever argued with them, some partners even expressed surprise, confessing that they expected Asian women to be more meek and agreeable.

The eroticization of Asian women's passivity creates several dilemmas. First, we are caught between a dual expectation of pleasure giving and self-restraint. Characterized as the purveyors of Oriental "secrets of lovemaking," Asian women are brought up to believe that we have no sexual identity or urges separate from our husbands; our bodies are for their pleasures only. Otherwise, sex is wrong—a shameful secret to be confined to the realm of wifely duties.

Second, insomuch as Asian women symbolize extreme femininity, we incite fear in men, so much so that they must beat us down, tie us down, hold us down. As Dworkin points out, boys and men will engage in violence against women to renounce whatever they have in common with women so as to experience no commonality with them.[10] Ironically, Asian women's passivity and vulnerability almost incite more violence, more silencing. We are battered; we are raped; we are murdered with very little afterthought. In pornography the most violent acts are perpetrated against Asian women; she is hung, cut, mutilated, defiled, and destroyed. For example, the December 1984 cover of *Penthouse* portrayed Asian girls being hung from trees in lynchlike fashion; this act was imitated when eight-year-old Jean Kar Har was left strangled, raped, and hanging in a tree in North Carolina in February of 1985. Portrayed as enduring any type of trespass or degradation, and vested with less value than a stray dog, the Asian female's personhood is blurred. Warshaw described the ways in which college women in general make ideal victims.[11] Asian women's greater silence makes us especially ideal victims, for we will rarely ever speak out or complain; to do so means "losing face" and shaming the family. Violence and victimization become normalized for the Asian American female. This reality does not touch every Asian woman, but it defined my existence for a very long time.

> Truth is harder to bear than ignorance, and so ignorance is valued more—also because the status quo depends on it; but love depends on self-knowledge, and self-knowledge depends on being able to bear the truth.
> —Andrea Dworkin, *Intercourse*

Blake's transgressions ended in October of 1988 when he was expelled from Amherst College for violating academic probation. I do not know when the abuse would have ended if he had not left. I certainly had not yet reached a sufficient stage of empowerment to leave him. I first came out of denial and found a name for what happened to me after reading *I*

Never Called It Rape by Robin Warshaw, a book about acquaintance rape on campus. That was one of the most cathartic experiences of my life. Reading the book conferred on me the power of naming, the power that "enables men to define experience, to articulate boundaries and values, to designate each thing its realm and qualities, to determine what can and cannot be expressed, to control perception itself." For the first time in my life, I was able to conceive of the notion that what happened was not entirely my fault or of my asking. I name my experience for what it was: rape—not a mistake I made, not "boys will be boys," not a "night to regret."

I asked the one essential question every rape survivor asks: Why me? Until I realized that there was no meaningful answer for this question, I could move no further with my recovery. It was obviously too late to report the assault to police. I searched for another means to reclaim control. Besides, I doubted that the legal system, bereft of objectivity in matters of sexual violence, had the capacity to accommodate my case. My experience would be with me for the rest of my life affecting the way I think, respond, and behave. The wound would heal, but the scars would remain forever—an important reminder of the pain I had experienced and the growth I would come to know.

Early in my recovery, flashbacks and nightmares invaded my consciousness. Every glimpse of khaki pants worn with Dock-Sides shoes and no socks, coupled with clean-cut good looks, would vividly remind me of Blake. Momentarily, my breathing would stop, I would get a choking feeling in my throat, and a wave of nausea would hit my stomach. I also began to have a recurrent nightmare in which I chopped Blake up into hundreds of little pieces with an ax, filling the bathtub with his blood and evil. When the police knocked on the door, I desperately stuffed the evidence of my revenge into plastic garbage bags and buried them in the backyard. I woke up time and time again from this horrifying dream with a constricted feeling in my chest. This dream was most vivid in the beginning of my healing. The intensity abated as I came to terms with the plethora of my emotions. Reading the work of Burgess and Holmstrom, I realized that my reactions and feelings were a natural part of healing from rape.[12]

My shame was overwhelming. Why had I let him do those things to me? Of course, it was years before I realized that I did not "let him" do anything; those things were done to me. At age twenty, I needed to develop a viable language for discussing subjects that were taboo in tradition Asian culture—sex, sexuality, rape, and violence. I also felt guilty, as if I had let my parents down by not being more cautious and careful.

I learned how to feel and express anger. Such emotions were not acceptable in my childhood. For Asians, anger constitutes an imbalance in what should be a predominantly intellectual, analytical mind, as opposed to an emotional, irrational one. As such, any such outpourings were punished. Now I certainly had plenty of opportunity to practice anger.

Music became an outlet for my anger, even as it became a source of my pain. I studied and performed as a pianist for over seventeen years. Blake would watch me play during Glee Club rehearsals and concerts; he attributed to me the magnetism of a mythological siren, like one of those who tempted Odysseus. Music became tainted with the seduction perceived by Blake, even as it was also a source of control and escape—an outlet for communicating my pain and hope—throughout much of the sexual abuse. I could not let Blake take my music away; it was mine. At times the poetry of Chopin or Debussy were the only outlets for voicing the agony and reclamation for which I then had no words. I bought a piano in 1995 before I possessed any other real furniture in my apartment. My playing has become less frequent since graduating from college, but I will listen to recordings of my performances, particularly the one of Chopin's Piano Concerto No. 2 in F Minor—it captures both the anger and the hope that Blake's act engraved on my spirit.

Healing from violence took all of the courage I could muster. To ease the psychological pain that could so suddenly overwhelm me in remembering, I developed an infectious, jaded sense of humor. Humor was sometimes the only way to cope with what I had lost, and laughter was my salvation, for it refurbished the warmth of my inner core. Though I was quiet and reserved as an adolescent, my adult personality began to take shape.

Ironically, being raped conferred upon me a strength and an invaluable insight that I would exchange for nothing. I am no longer ashamed to say, "I am a rape survivor." Having lost so much, I reprioritized my goals, wants, and desires, as well as what I thought was important. I became an activist instead of a reactionist. I sought to reclaim my soul and my existence.

I reevaluated and changed my career goals; turning my back on both medical school and law school, I instead pursued the true calling in my heart: teaching. It was an opportunity to help others and, in so doing, heal myself. I realized that what happened to me wasn't only the fault of one man, but the responsibility of an entire society's cultural norms.

I was hired as a peer health educator two weeks after Blake raped me: Destiny does work in surprising and purposeful ways. This field appealed tremendously to me, even before the full import of why it probably did was revealed. It energized me in a manner that nothing else ever did, including music. It was as if I was desperately trying to reach out to others and help shield them from experiencing the harm that I had experienced. To this day I believe wholeheartedly that I would not have found health education as my chosen profession and lifelong commitment if not for Blake. Through my commitment I take back what he stole. During my senior year of college I publicly revealed my status as a rape survivor and founded a self-help support group for other women on campus who had experienced sexual violence. I lovingly called it H.E.R.S.—Helping and Empowering Rape Survivors. That acronym consumed hours of brain power to generate, I assure you. The response at the first meeting, when it convened in January 1990, was remarkable: Eight women showed up. The group continued to grow over time. Sharing with these other survivors, as well as validating each other's pain and growth, was essential for me in confronting the rape. Our newly forged bond culminated when, bearing a banner that we designed and signed, we marched in Take Back the Night during April 1990.

My recovery was marked by what became almost an obsession with any topic related to sexual assault: culture, media, substance abuse, eating disorders, sex role socialization, and so on. I consumed books, journal articles, movies, news articles, reports, and anything else that addressed rape with a voracious appetite. I wanted to learn everything there was to know about it. I also did things in the hope of reducing rape in our society. I wrote my master's thesis on it. I presented at national conferences. I volunteered and worked at local rape crisis centers both in New Haven, Connecticut, and here in Baton Rouge, Louisiana. I spoke out publicly as a survivor whenever and wherever appropriate. Violence became my area of expertise as a health educator and consultant. I also advise Men against Violence at Louisiana State University, where I now work as a health educator. The first campus organization of its kind, MAV focuses on men's role in fostering cultural change. Working with the group has been immensely healing.

Eminent in my healing was learning to take care of myself again. First, I learned to forgive myself, then accept and love myself again. My self-esteem had to be rebuilt. Being treated badly can become a comfortable habit, and just as difficult to break. After having my will repeatedly thwarted and ignored and trampled on for so long, succumbing to another's will became the default, the path of least resistance—and of least physical harm. My personality exhibits a situational schizophrenia that always fascinates me. Although I am confident and assertive in academic and professional situations, assuming leadership roles with ease and excelling in organizational tasks, I have failed to be so in my relationships with men until very recently. That side of my life was instead beset with crisis after crisis. Setting boundaries, both physical and emotional, is a skill that I must continually and consciously work on.

The reaction of friends and boyfriends when I finally chose to disclose that I was a rape survivor became of importance, as well. I became very adept at picking those whom I could tell. I wanted those close to me to understand that this experience greatly altered my life, but not to perceive me as being somehow vulnerable or weak, "messed up" or unstable, "used" or "dirty." Most were unable to comprehend the sexual abuse in its entirety and found it more comfortable to blithely ignore the subject. Some, of course, blamed me for putting myself in harm's way; a few did not believe me. A key point of contention for many when I share my story is whether or not I had been clear about my nonconsent with Blake. I don't know: I always thought that "no" was pretty clear in every language, even by most "reasonable woman standards." Frankly, the issues were too volatile for most of my friends to handle logically, objectively. Their blaming questions only further implicated me in my own victimization: "Why didn't I go to the police?" "Why didn't I just stop the abuse?"

Only a special few—many of them survivors themselves—regarded my telling as a gift that I bestowed upon them: I shared something of deep magnitude as far as explaining who I was and defining what I wanted to be. My younger sister and brother both know. Someday I hope I will be able to tell my parents, too; the fear of their disownment—maybe unfounded—stops me from doing so thus far.

It was always hardest for me to tell partners. Men seem always to take this sort of thing personally. The white men and the men of color whom I dated exhibited different reactions. White men were generally appalled and disgusted at the horror committed by a fellow male and rushed to separate themselves from those kinds of "pigs." They approached me with the attitude of a carpenter about to repair a broken piece of furniture; they assumed I needed fixing, protecting, and shielding. In other words, the rape was a big deal; they did not like to talk about it or hear the real details, which were too degrading. It was enough to be assured that they were not like my rapist. I have a theory that rape is only too characteristic of white men as a whole, committing innumerable unpunished crimes against women and nonwhites throughout all of history; if I were a white man, I suppose the burden of that guilt would be best left unattended. Black men, however, having survived prejudice and discrimination at the hands of white men since the slavery era, had a more palatable, supportive perspective about sexual violence. Oppression became a bond that we could share. Rape was something that strengthened me; I received their empathy, not pity.

I defied that most basic of Asian tenets that demands "saving face." It is only through the support of those close to me and the help of mental health professionals, as well as through speaking out, that I will be able to continue the lifelong process of healing. Building walls around myself will not shield me from pain or shame; they only confine them within me to fester. As a Chinese proverb cautions, "Dry ground only cracks; nothing will grow there until it has softened."

> Being in this intimate relationship with my young body, I grew to understand and confirm three things: my body belongs exclusively to me, my soul is not at rest when my body is detached, and we (body and soul) must take good care of each other.
> —Pamela R. Fletcher, "Whose Body Is It Anyway?"

My physical self-image suffered tremendously as a result of such long-term sexual abuse. When I looked at myself in the mirror, what stared back was the face of a woman attached to the body of a child. My dark eyes, olive skin, and sensuous, full bottom lip were maturely provocative, but my flat breasts and narrow hips were prepubescent. I was attractive by most standards, and beautiful to some. Historically for me, though, attractiveness conveyed danger: It invited further victimization. I wanted to be sexually desirable, yet I was afraid that it would result in unwanted sexual aggression. In recent years, as I have been better able to accept my sexuality, my physical self-image has improved accordingly. I have allowed the passionate and sensual aspects of my personality to emerge, and I have enjoyed the maturation of my body into more womanly curves. This stage of healing was especially difficult to reach but critical. While feminists stress that rape is a crime of power, not of passion, the act of rape has ramifications on the sexual self.

After coming out of denial about my rape, I confronted the uncomfortable fact of how many men I had slept with during the alcohol-drenched mental haze that characterized the period of my sexual abuse. I had yet to take ownership of my sexuality. At nearly twenty-one years old, I had never experienced an orgasm—didn't even know such a thing existed for women. Inevitably, I went through a period for almost two years, spanning my senior year and into my first year of graduate school, during which the very thought of a man touching me was downright revolting. This was a cleansing period, an opportunity to foster my "second virginity," so to speak. As I ended my first year of graduate work toward a master's of public health at Yale University, I was ready to develop a sexual self defined in my own terms.

I participated in sex that I wanted, that I chose to have. I learned to separate sex from humiliation. At first certain sexual positions and certain smells would cause me to have flashbacks about Blake. As I gradually reconditioned myself to associate sex with pleasure instead of humiliation, these flashbacks waned in frequency. With each additional positive sexual encounter, my feelings of vulnerability dissipated and I began to trust men in sexual situations. I entered a stage of sexual abandon and freedom during which I explored the limits of how my partner and I could make our bodies feel good. I consumed my partners with the voracity of someone who had stumbled upon a full bottle of Thirst Quencher after hours of running under a hot sun.

Ultimately, developing a healthy romantic relationship is an important landmark in recovery. This has been perhaps the greatest challenge for me. For a long time I believed that I didn't deserve happiness with a caring partner because of what happened to me—I was "used goods," tainted and soiled by the rape and sexual abuse. I have stayed in some lousy relationships because of this feeling—sometimes repeating the abusive pattern I experienced with Blake.

The advantage of being in so many unhealthy relationships is that you learn what a healthy one looks and feels like. For me a healthy relationship entails finding the appropriate balance between two contrasting states. On the one hand, to share intimacy with another person means rendering yourself vulnerable; I, however, have many secrets, many of which are still somewhat shameful for me. So the pressure of being able to open myself up completely without fear of being rejected for my past or for my periodic insanity is tremendous and scary. At the same time, a relationship also means being able to assert yourself and set boundaries, so that the interdependence does not become codependent but instead fosters mutual growth. With my history of long-term abuse, this aspect of a relationship is unfamiliar and uncomfortable. Because we are rarely taught the appropriate skills and know-how by our parents, mentors, and other adults, healthy relationships are certainly hard work for anybody. They are especially challenging for a rape survivor. Bad habits must first be unlearned with great reluctance and then rescripted with new, healthy ones.

I now live and work in Baton Rouge, Louisiana. I think I left the North in some vain attempt to escape what happened to me in college. I know now that I will never outrun it. I function in a constant state of vulnerability; being raped doesn't confer some sort of immunity on you, like having the chicken pox, because rape isn't about what the victim does. It is all about what the aggressor wants.

I completed a Ph.D. in educational leadership and research in December 1998. I was promoted in June 1998 and now oversee health education, disability services, and the Women's Center at Louisiana State University. In addition, I volunteer at the local rape crisis center. Most recently, I have been traveling to campuses all over the United States as a speaker and consultant with the agency CAMPUSPEAK. Eventually, I hope to write and lecture on a full-time basis.

After nearly two years of court proceedings, my parents divorced in 1994; both reside in Connecticut. My sister, also a health educator, lives in Chicago, while my brother is about to complete his senior year at the University of Pennsylvania. My sister and I have raised him to respect women, and to respect himself. I live with Toby, a cocker spaniel with a wonderfully affectionate and malleable temperament, and six cats named Mozart, Whitney, Aiwa, Bacchus, Athena, and Puck. I'm entering that decade in life when my closest women friends (whom I treasure) are starting to get married and have babies. I myself have settled comfortably into a tender, stable, and healthy relationship with a Nordic from Wisconsin. Through his acceptance and understanding, he has been a part of my healing. Most important, he has taught me that I am worthy of being loved, and he has allowed my sexuality to be my own. We eloped in February 1998. Married life suits me; I found my soulmate.

I am very compulsive; I hate messy rooms, kitchens, or bathrooms. Sometimes I check whether I've locked the door at night three or four times before I go to bed. I obsess about it when I go out of town. I suppose these are efforts at maintaining control in a world that I know can be so uncontrollable. I love to cook. I love John Grisham novels. I love to dance; there is nothing as freeing as dancing for hours to music with a driving bass beat and then leaving the club drenched with perspiration. These are my hobbies, my home, my family, and friends—you see, I was raped, but I'm still me.

Recovery is forever. In Mandarin Chinese my given name means "happiness"—combined with my family name, ("Hong" means "great" or "abundant") my name means "great joy," or "music." The blessing that my mother gave me has been slow to coalesce. These days I am happy most of the time. I deliberately live life to its fullest because I know how tenuous one's hold on it can be. There are days, sometimes weeks, when I am engulfed by self-pity and mourning for the innocence and health that were stolen from me, for the mistakes that I made but could never change, for the pain that the sexual abuse has caused in my life and in those around me. These periods occur less frequently as the years wane. Usually, though, I am very much in touch with living. Each day that I learn and give and think and plan and look ahead, I am striving to repair all the damage that my rapist wreaked—to take back the control he not only took away but almost destroyed. By breaking the silence, I am reclaiming that which was stolen, and reframing that which was horrible and unspeakable. I will never give Blake the satisfaction that I succumbed to the ugliness and darkness he brought into my life. In fact, I am laughing. I just wonder if Blake would ever get the joke.

PART II
THE ISSUES THAT DIVIDE AND CONQUER: FREE SPEECH, PORNOGRAPHY, AND A "KINDER, GENTLER FEMINISM"

6

THE WRITING ON THE STALL: FREE SPEECH, EQUAL RIGHTS, AND WOMEN'S GRAFFITI

Jesselyn Alicia Brown

In the fall of 1990 Brown University gained notoriety when graffiti naming alleged rapists was found on the stall walls of a central campus bathroom. Though the series of scribbles in the stall was as much a conversation as a collection of names, it came to be known around campus as the "Rape List." It began with a single sentence inscribed inside a stall. There, in a forum that guaranteed a female-only audience and anonymity, a woman had written, "_____ _____ is a rapist." The man she named was a Brown student. Over time other women added other names along with complaints about the university's failure to adequately discipline Brown men who had sexually assaulted female students.

The dialogue on the stall walls continued quietly for months as the list grew to perhaps thirty names. When a late-October opinion piece in the *Brown Daily Herald* alerted the university to the underground list,[1] the campus of sixty-five hundred erupted into controversy over concern that "innocent men" might be targeted. By mid-November the story had been strung to major news organizations, and articles had appeared in the *New York Times*, the *Chicago Tribune*, and *Newsweek*.

What did not make the front-page news was that for years women had tried to bring charges against many of these same men through official channels. In the fall of my sophomore year at Brown, I was sexually assaulted on my way home from a semiformal by three football players. I had not been drinking, but I was doing all of the other "wrong" things: I was walking home alone, at night, wearing a little black dress.

The intoxicated football players started off by following me and making comments about my body. I vaguely knew one of them, Jack Olson, because he lived in the same dormitory. The other two were complete strangers to me; however, because we were all classmates at the same university, we would later be referred to as "acquaintances." The comments

77

escalated to sexual touching: patting my behind, groping at my breasts, and tugging on my dress—asking if they could "get a little." They let up when a car drove by on the empty street.

I returned to my dormitory room to find a fairly detailed rape message on the memo board: "Hi. It's Jack and I have a very big dick and I'm going to fuck you up the ass . . ." and further specifics of what he was going to do to me. The message was signed "Jack Olson" at the bottom. "Fuck you bitch" and "fucking cunt" were written all over the memo board. It made what I thought was a random drunken incident from just minutes earlier seem very deliberate.

I photocopied the memo boards and called Police and Security to register a formal complaint. Police and Security interviewed the men involved, who admitted to their participation in the incident, but said they were just joking around.[2] The police investigation stopped at that point, and the complaint was channeled to the dean of students, David Inman. Dean Inman met with the accused men and later told me that there was no need for a hearing because they had confessed to their involvement in the incident. He then turned the case over to the football coach to mete out punishment: extra laps at practice.

I expressed outrage at the lax disciplinary measures and demanded something more substantial and permanent. This ultimately resulted in a letter of warning to the author of the memo board message—for alcohol policy violation, but not for sexual misconduct—and a polite suggestion that he write me a letter of apology.[3]

As was typical in cases like mine, alcohol became a mitigating rather than an aggravating factor and was used to sidestep the issue of the resulting sexual misconduct. Dean Inman felt that he lacked the authority to punish any offense sexual in nature because, at that point, no explicit provision prohibiting sexual misconduct existed in the Code on Student Conduct (though there were general provisions against harassment and assault).

The next semester I attended a forum held during Sexual Assault Awareness Week. There I met three other women—Lisa Billowitz, Jenn David, and Christin Lahiff—who knew of or had been through experiences similar to mine in dealing with the disciplinary system for sexual misconduct complaints. We attempted to work with administrators during that spring and summer to make the system work better for women. Labeled the "Committee of Four," we wrote detailed memos to deans about the (mis)handling of sexual assault and harassment cases and made concrete suggestions for reforming the system, but our input was continually ignored or dismissed. Therefore, we were very surprised when the exposure of the bathroom graffiti garnered such immediate administrative attention. Sadly, the bathroom wall writing got attention not because women were being raped, but because of the supposed infringement of men's rights.

THE REACTION ON CAMPUS

Free Speech versus Equal Rights Debate

As the "Rape List" controversy brewed at Brown University, campuses nationwide were experiencing upheaval over a broader consciousness-raising movement of "political correctness." This movement was often framed in constitutional terms, even by nonlawyers, as First Amendment rights versus Fourteenth Amendment rights.

Most people have a rudimentary understanding that the First Amendment protects freedom of speech and that the Fourteenth Amendment provides equal protection of the laws. With the advent of campus hate-speech codes, antipornography laws, and hate-crime ordinances around the country, First Amendment "speech rights" were continually being pitted against Fourteenth Amendment "equality rights." This greater societal debate formed the backdrop against which the "Rape List" controversy erupted.

Fourteenth Amendment advocates, from feminist legal scholar Catharine MacKinnon to French thinker Jacques Derrida, place a premium on equality. At the core of the Fourteenth Amendment argument is the idea that things like pornography and hate speech inflict harm not only on the individual, but on all women or minorities in a kind of "collective defamation."[4] The goal of Fourteenth Amendment advocates is to fight phenomena such as hate speech and pornography through laws that would permit victims to seek redress against perpetrators of bigotry or producers of porn by showing how the hateful speech or images have harmed them. Similar arguments for equal protection have been advanced in seeking redress for violence against women.

Fourteenth Amendment advocates view regulation not as a "free speech" issue, but as a question of harm being done to certain groups of people and the need to give subordinated groups protection equal to those in power. Fourteenth Amendment advocates resent the fact that inequality of subordinated individuals is always being framed in terms of the oppressor or offender's "freedom of speech." They feel that what had been judicially understood until recently as acts of discrimination (harassment, bigoted policies and practices, threats, and so on) suddenly became issues of "free speech" during the political correctness debate.[5]

First Amendment advocates, on the other hand, characterize Fourteenth Amendment advocates as missionaries of censorship. With the 1990

Newsweek cover story on "Thought Police," the so-called "PC"—political correctness—debate went mainstream.[6] The alarming title and the derisive term "PC" itself reveal the majority's perspective in the debate. First Amendment advocates who champion free speech, such as George F. Will, fear that Fourteenth Amendment advocates want legal or disciplinary curbs for *all* controversial expression, hateful or not:

> According to the theory behind the proliferation of campus speech codes [and similar regulations], there is this new entitlement: the right of certain groups not to have their sensibilities hurt. So censorship is progressive when it suppresses expression that offends subordinate groups. Such groups include almost everyone except white heterosexual males.[7]

The "Rape List" controversy, however, turned the traditional "free speech versus equal rights" conflict on its head. Men's graffiti is as good an example as any of the traditional paradigm: Many men defend their graffiti as free speech, while many women find it derogatory. The "Rape List" inverted the speech-equality paradigm. *Women* framed the graffiti as a free speech issue: It was their only means of expression in an institution that had systematically silenced their voices. Men complained that *this* speech maligned, slandered, and defamed them. The men claimed, in essence, that the graffiti was a form of hate speech ("man hating") that threatened their status as equal citizens on the Brown campus. The situation became the classic clash of free speech with equality rights—but this time it was *women's* speech that was threatening *men's* equality, not the other way around.

Has free speech really "been on balance an ally of those seeking change?"[8] What happens when the metaphor of speech is stretched to include women's graffiti? Will First Amendment exceptions suddenly be stretched to include words that subordinate men?

The Attack on Brown Women's Speech

Women have been the targets of bathroom wall scribblings for years. So it was not without irony that women students chose the women's restroom walls to list the names of men they said violated them.

Robert Reichley, Brown's executive vice president of university relations, denounced the list as "antimale" and the women who created it as "Magic Marker terrorists."[9] By equating being "antirape" with being "antimale," Reichley appeals to an age-old stereotype that pits men defensively against women in a debate about injuries that men have affirmatively perpetrated against them. He also impliedly equates being "antirape" with being "antisex," making women the embodiment of a New Puritanism hostile to sexuality itself.

Robert Mathiesen, professor of Slavic languages, warned the graffiti writers to beware of witch hunting, comparing them to "notorious 15th-century inquisitors."[10] Historically, witch hunting was sanctioned by the male judicial system, and most of the people who committed the crime of witchcraft were women. The women who were "hunted" as witches were "deviants" who in some way were not seen to fit the role prescribed for women. Often they were in powerful situations, economically or politically, or they were expressive (either verbally or sexually) of their discontent with their role. The practice of witch hunting created a mechanism for hegemonic institutions to constrain women seen as "deviant."[11]

If Mathiesen believed that some of the men listed on the wall were sexual assaulters and some might not be,[12] then in his parallel, were some women witches and others not? Clearly, all "witches" were falsely accused. However, this was by no means clear with the men listed on the bathroom wall.

It is precisely the accusatory tone of *Mathiesen's* argument, coupled with his institutional power as a university professor, that more closely resembles the repressive witch hunt. It is *his* argument that implicitly destabilizes female students' attempts to legitimately express and empower themselves.[13] It is precisely people like *him* to whom Justice Brandeis was referring when he said that "[f]ear of serious injury cannot alone justify suppression of free speech. . . . Men feared witches and burnt women."[14] Fear that men will be dishonored cannot alone justify suppression of women's graffiti. Men fear feminist activists and silence women. Still, the "witch hunt" remained a popular metaphor throughout the graffiti debate.

The dean of the college compared the graffiti writers to Nazis[15] and referred to their actions as "vigilantism."[16] A student soon followed the dean's lead and widely circulated an unsigned flier on so-called feminazis, proclaiming "The Rise of the Fourth Reich."[17] It characterized the Sarah Doyle Women's Center as the "Non-sexual Sarah Doyle Action Party (N.S.D.A.P.)"—N.S.D.A.P is the German abbreviation for the full name of the Nazi party—and the women it served as S.S. troops:

> This report is an update on the activities of the Non-sexual Sarah Doyle Action Party (N.S.D.A.P.), meant to provide a foundation for our program this semester.
>
> A. Update. The previous semester was an excellent example of efficiency, ideological veracity and the further establishment of uncontestable control over the University administration. A total of 44 males were expelled for various sexual offenses, including prolonged eye contact, unauthorized approach and introduction, illegal possession of non-P.C. literature, and courting an intoxicated womyn.
>
> Specifically, Aaron Weinstein and William M. Burroughs were found in their rooms watching a strictly forbidden pornographic videotape depicting a womyn manipulated into sexual encounters for financial benefits. This

was discovered by our crack Security Surveillance (S.S.) 29th Sturmbann Unit, specializing in unauthorized on-campus dormitory searches. These males were brought before the People's Disciplinary Council (or People's Court) and quickly dispatched.

Gauleiter Elizabeth Stone was approached by the male WASP John Crabbings, member of the illegalized terrorist group Delta Tau. He introduced himself without requesting permission and compounded his crime by asking her to accompany him for a drink. Gauleiter Stone immediately immobilized him, and S.S. troops soon arrived to apprehend the culprit. The People's Court sentenced Crabbings to castration and expulsion.

The other crimes were relatively minor, all receiving forced labor in various womyn organizations, time in reeducation camps or some form of University sanction as approved by the N.S.D.A.P.

B. Goals. This semester, the N.S.D.A.P. must become more active in enforcing the cleansing of the male ranks of all who are white and/or heterosexual. These males are a threat to the Party and must be eliminated at all costs. This directive is to affect the S.S. and the People's Court directly.

Unfortunately, a small resistance force has formed which has eluded capture and dismissal until now. To eliminate this threat, it will be necessary for a new branch to be created within the N.S.D.A.P., which will deal with clandestine operations, subversion against non-P.C. institutions, etc. This unit, the General Elimination Squads Through All Political Opponents (GESTAPO), will be an elite, highly specialized clandestine operations group which will use extra-legal methods to obtain incriminating information against target groups (white, heterosexual males).[18]

Like accusations of misandry, "Magic Marker terrorism," and witch hunting, accusations of Nazism continued to be hurled in the debate—despite the fact that three of the four student leaders of the antirape movement were Jewish and one came from a family of Holocaust survivors.

Reichley's press statements continued to illustrate who is a full citizen in the college community and whose injury gets recognized. He explained that "[w]hen you pay the princely sum of $20,000 a year to go to this august institution, you ought to have some reassurance that when you are *defamed* . . . the institution cares about it."[19] It was never discussed whether you ought to have some reassurance that when you are *raped*, the institution cares about it. Nor did Reichley discuss whether, when women are similarly "defamed" on bathroom walls or memo boards, they ought to have the same recourse as men.

If the application of free speech principles is unequal between male and female students, it is even more unequal between students and administrators. University officials can enter the metaphorical "marketplace of ideas" and publicly respond to speech—in this case, graffiti—that they consider hostile to the university's educational mission. Such university expression in support of its substantive policies is consistent with principles of freedom of speech, so long as it does not drown out or suppress other speech. Administrative counterspeech in this case, however, did not move beyond ad hominem attacks.

An academic official—such as Vice President Reichley or Professor Mathiesen—can significantly chill the climate for academic inquiry and intellectual debate by engaging in institutional speech that expresses categorical disapproval of certain political positions. Although such an opinion would be well within the free speech rights of a student or an outside observer, it takes on a different character when voiced by a university official in charge of academic or administrative policy, even if the official never disciplines the proponent of the controversial political position.

In Defense of Brown Men's Equality

Men whose names appeared on the list abandoned any allegiance they had to First Amendment principles and quickly embraced arguments made by those in favor of regulating hate speech (most often women and racial minorities):

> The sort of speech [that the hate speech movement] wishes to restrict falls into two expressive categories that the Supreme Court has previously held (and, the advocates of restrictions argue, correctly held) to be undeserving of First Amendment protection. The categories are those of "fighting words" and group defamation. . . . The "fighting words" or "assaultive speech" paradigm compares [hate] expression to physical assault. . . . The defamation paradigm, by contrast, compares [hate] speech to libel, which is an assault on dignity or reputation. The harm is essentially social; to be defamed is to be defamed in the eyes of other people.[20]

The defamation model drove the Brown debate. The dean of the college, who had in the past opposed campus speech regulations, condemned the graffiti on defamation grounds: "In the case where individual students are named, this action not only constitutes potential *libel* but also *harassment*."[21]

The men continued to invoke the language of defamation, saying that they had been maligned, slandered, and socially damaged.[22] The two recurring themes voiced by those condemning the graffiti were "defamation" and denial of "due process." One man on the list proclaimed:

> I am writing today because I am angry and confused: angry that someone has falsely accused me of a crime that I find despicable and detestable, and confused because I fail to see the point of this list. . . . I am not a rapist. And more generally, the idea of presumed guilt in such a sensitive area is extremely dangerous. . . I find it difficult to view this [list] as an active support network, rather I see it as a mechanism to *malign* people. . . . I resent the fact that from now on there will be women on this campus who fear me.[23]

Another listed man lamented:

> As I understand current laws, an alleged criminal has the right to know the identity of his (or her) accuser, and the type of crime which he (or she) has committed. . . . [I]nstead of being tried, convicted, and hanged in absentia, I would truly appreciate the privilege of knowing who accuses me. . . . When people judge other people without due judicial process, it hurts the credibility of the accusers and *defames* the character of the accused.[24]

Note here the degree to which men appeal to judicial guarantees (innocent until proven guilty, the right to face your accuser, and so on) of the very same legal system that had so failed the women writing on the bathroom walls.

The Brown University judicial board—the University Council on Student Affairs (UCSA) and later the University Disciplinary Council (UDC)—had heard cases ranging from fist fights to embezzlement. It refused, however, to hear cases of sexual harassment or assault. Rather than receiving an outright denial of a hearing, women in such cases were instead steered in the direction of nondisciplinary alternatives like counseling or mediation. If that did not work, they were often blamed for the incident, being told such things as: "'[Y]our rape can be boiled down to a case of bad chemistry,' and 'sometimes he forced you, sometimes he didn't. You can't have it both ways.'"[25] Male students, therefore, got more mileage out of a disciplinary system that had simply not worked for women.

The university immediately set up a grievance procedure for men. David Inman, then dean of students,[26] sent a letter of notification to every man named in the bathroom graffiti.[27] The letter extended an invitation to file a complaint and receive counseling for the injury as well as a guarantee of support from Police and Security. Yet women who wanted to file complaints were rarely directed toward initiating disciplinary action against an assailant, and no case of sexual assault had ever reached a full disciplinary hearing.

By denying knowledge of the graffiti writers' motives, Dean Inman erases the injuries that had been suffered by these women. Over half of the names listed on the wall were of men against whom women at Brown had tried to seek disciplinary action for sexual misconduct.[28] Dean Inman, in his capacity as dean of students, was the administrator in charge of handling such student complaints. When he learned the identity of the men listed in the bathroom, it was not the first time he had heard many of their names in connection with allegations of sexual misconduct. Nor was he unaware of the dissatisfaction of many of the women who had tried to go through the "proper" channels by filing a formal complaint with him, only to be denied any kind of recourse.

The university issued a directive to have all graffiti removed, which in practice translated to all graffiti written by women. Administrators ordered janitors to scrub off the women's room graffiti, only to have the "Rape List" reappear in bathrooms all over campus, from the Science Library to Alumni Hall. Janitors still continued to scrub it off every day. Women began writing in indelible ink. The white bathroom stalls were then repainted black. Women responded by writing in white or metallic "paint" markers on the darkened walls. Meanwhile, misogynistic graffiti that blanketed public areas of campus—library carrels, sidewalks, cafeteria tables—remained untouched. One woman jokingly suggested writing the "Rape List" on top of all the misogynistic graffiti in an attempt to get men's comments to be as aggressively and diligently erased.[29]

Though the university's repeated attempts to remove women's graffiti backfired, so did women's attempts to have the new graffiti removal policy applied equally. The policy was couched in gender-neutral terms: "The route of graffiti and anonymity whether against men or women is not an acceptable substitute for either due process or justice."[30] However, it was clearly instituted to protect men. Slam lists of "Top 10 Campus Sluts," "Women Who Go Down," and "Objects Women Like to Put in Their Vaginas" (including big dicks, knives, bottles, and a blow torch)—graffiti on Rockefeller Library carrels assigned to women—were not seen to be damaging in the same way as a list of "Men Who've Assaulted Me or a Woman I Know."

In December 1990 graffiti criticizing the leaders of the antirape movement appeared in the men's bathroom of the Rockefeller Library, including a "List of Women Who Need to be Raped":

List the accusers—women to avoid
1) _____ _____
2) (she's waiting to snip off your dick)
3) You'll know her by her hairy legs and her explosive chastity belt.
4) _____ _____
Men—don't let them bring us down. Stand up for your penis. Rape a feminist.
I'm "taking my penis back"!![31]

As one of the women named in the graffiti, I tried to file a complaint with Police and Security. I was told that a complaint had already been filed and was asked why I wanted a complaint form.[32] Three female administrators—Associate Dean Carol Cohen, Coordinator of the Women's Center Gigi Dibello, and Assistant Director of Student Activities Kris Renn—told me that Dean Inman was aware that I had been targeted in the disturbing graffiti and that they had reminded him to send me and the other activists similarly attacked a letter like that extended to men listed on the bathroom walls. No such letter was ever sent.[33]

THE REACTION FROM OUTSIDE

The response of the outside world was no more sympathetic to the women's graffiti than was that of the university. Indeed, something has touched a nerve when it manages to get lambasted by feminists, antifeminists, and establishment organs alike.

Nearly three years after its infamous "Thought Police" issue, *Newsweek* produced another cover story on the tyranny of PC, this time entitled "Sexual Correctness." The article begins by discussing the "Rape List" scandal at Brown University:

> The women at Brown University play hardball. Three years ago, fed up with an administration that wasn't hopping into action, they scrawled the names of alleged rapists on the bathroom stalls. Brown woke up, revamped its disciplinary system and instituted mandatory sexual-assault education for freshmen.[34]

In her controversial book *The Morning After: Sex, Fear, and Feminism on Campus*, Katie Roiphe also takes note of the graffiti phenomenon:

> At Wesleyan, the bathroom walls are filled with written conversations about rape and sexual harassment. Some people have named names, and there are comments back and forth. At Carleton College, in the bathroom on the third floor of the library, there is a list of alleged date rapists, popularly referred to as the "castration list." Brown has a similar list. These lists are intended to allow victims to voice their experience in a safe, anonymous space. They enable victims to accuse without confrontation and consequences.[35]

The basic gripe of Roiphe's book and the *Newsweek* article is that, by attempting to regulate sexual violence through codes on student conduct, what they have derisively labeled the "rape-crisis movement" paints women as passive victims who cannot take care of themselves and need protection.[36]

If a generic Harvard graduate and a mainstream weekly are threatened by what they have deemed ironically a "victim mentality," then it is not surprising that a self-proclaimed antifeminist like Camille Paglia would condemn such unconventional actions of college women on similar grounds:

> [Y]oung women have been convinced that they have been the victims of rape. On elite campuses in the Northeast and on the West Coast, they have held consciousness-raising sessions, petitioned administrations, demanded inquests. At Brown University, outraged, panicky "victims" have scrawled the names of alleged attackers on the walls of women's rest rooms.[37]

She too hurls what is becoming the all too familiar "victim accusation" (women are making themselves victims) at the feminist campaign against sexual assault, harassment, and date rape.

The words of a warrior-polemicist like Paglia are not surprising. What does surprise many advocates in the fight against campus sexual violence is the degree to which well-known feminists like Betty Friedan and Naomi Wolf have been just as critical and have just as much misunderstood the debate as their antifeminist counterparts. Laying the foundation for Paglia's militant diatribe, Friedan wrote in the early 1980s: "Obsession with rape, even offering Band-Aids to its victims, is a kind of wallowing in that victim state, that impotent rage, that sterile polarization."[38]

Naomi Wolf's book about female power, *Fire with Fire*, criticizes the work of both Roiphe and Paglia for doing something slick and dangerous with the notion of victimization. Yet Wolf, with her cut-and-dried definition of "victim feminism" and uninformed interpretation of what happened at Brown, does just as much of a disservice to women's activism:

> Over the last twenty years, the old belief in a tolerant assertiveness, a claim to human participation and human rights—power feminism—was embattled by the rise of a set of beliefs that cast women as beleaguered, fragile, intuitive angels: victim feminism. . . . During the backlash years, the following events transpired under the banner of feminism. They were really examples of victim feminism: Brown University undergraduates wrote alleged rapists' names on bathroom walls. . . . You can only hope to whisper about sexual assault in the most feminine of spaces, the ladies' room, where no one gets a fair hearing, rather than shouting to make the investigation of sex crimes really work.[39]

Wolf also buys into the "women are making themselves victims" rhetoric; however, when one reads between the lines, she gets closer to the real problem troubling the likes of *Newsweek*, Roiphe, Paglia, and Friedan: *Men* are not getting a fair hearing.

If women are really acting like passive, helpless, scared "victims," would all of these mainstream journalists and scholars be so defensive?[40] In a 1993 cover story, tellingly entitled "Crying Rape," *New York* magazine's reportage on campus sexual violence most vividly belies the media's claim to "neutrality":

> Without "objective, legalistic" standards, a *man* has little chance of proving he isn't a rapist. In a guerrilla technique pioneered at Brown University a few years ago and now used at other schools, including Columbia, the names of male students accused of being rapists are "stickered" or scrawled on campus walls. No defense is possible, because the accusers never reveal themselves.[41]

Here the heart of the matter becomes clear. The problem is not really that women are making themselves into "victims," but rather that *men* are being made into victims.

In a Yale Law School class on "The Administration of Freedom of Speech," Harvard Law School professor Alan Dershowitz, a famous First Amendment advocate, posed a hypothetical: "What if I'm teaching class and there is a male student who continually makes derogatory and sexist comments every time a woman speaks? He says, 'Women never have anything intelligent to say,' or 'That's just what a dumb woman would say.' As a teacher, taking into account the First Amendment, what is my role here?" He went around the room soliciting student responses until the hypothetical deteriorated, unresolved, into other topics.

Toward the end of class I asked to return to his hypothetical. The previous discussion had focused on how the professor should respond and never seemed to contemplate that the female student(s) might also respond. "Regardless of whether *you* do or do not respond to the sexist male student," I asked, "what would you think if the women students created an anonymous list of 'Sexist Jerks Who Won't Shut Up in Class'?" His response was favorable:

> Oh, like at Brown University! Anonymity under the First Amendment is unresolved; however, at Brown I think it was relevant and fair information. Perhaps the women should have put the names in a more public space rather than on the bathroom wall, so that everyone could participate in the marketplace. But I've never seen a case for censorship that has compelled me.[42]

While Professor Dershowitz supported women's expression consistent with his self-proclaimed free speech absolutism, the fact that his original hypothetical never took into account the possibility that women might actually be the ones to respond is typical.

WOMEN'S GRAFFITI AS SPEECH

"McCarthyite." "Man hater." "Magic Marker terrorist." "Witch hunter." "Feminazi." "Radical." For an institution that was trying to censor *women's* speech, Brown University was certainly not short of words. This taught women an unforgettable lesson about the distribution of power in the college community. And it taught a lesson about the distribution of power in society more generally—where many women are not privileged with access to speech at all. Things look very different when understood in the context of social power than they do when viewed abstractly. Things *sound* different when said on someone else's turf in someone else's language.

Women at Brown and elsewhere are discovering that the same doctrinal principles do not apply to them.

Women need to pay attention to when First Amendment defenses are raised and when they are not. When I came home to a signed rape message on my door that said, in pertinent part, "Hi. It's Jack and I have a very big dick and I'm going to fuck you"—he was allowed to defend that "it was just a joke."[43] Jack Olson's message, although an offensive and injurious utterance, was treated by the university as "only words." He was sent a letter of reprimand that acknowledged sexual harassment but refused to punish it. Dean Inman suggested the usual remedy for instances of sexual harassment or assault: a letter of apology[44] and, in this case, extra laps at football practice.

The university's formulation of *my* injury effectively erased my original complaint. It focused exclusively on an alcohol policy violation—which was not the reason I had filed a report. When I expressed dissatisfaction with the remedy of an apology letter (which, incidentally, I never received), I was told to "drop it."[45]

The university's formulation of *men's* injuries again erased the complaints of women. The university never looked beyond the immediate harm to men to see why women resorted to writing on bathroom walls as their only means to protect one another. The multiple injuries to women, who were not only sexually violated but also denied any sort of recourse when they sought disciplinary action against the perpetrators, were completely ignored.

The university portrayed the list as a tool for purposely hurting men. If officials had actually listened to what the women graffitists had to *say*, they would have realized that the motivation was to protect women in the absence of a judicial board willing to hear complaints of sexual violence.

It was not about hurting men or "women making themselves victims"—as Roiphe, Paglia, Friedan, Wolf, and other critics have suggested. Women were empowering themselves in the face of victimization and the unavailability of institutional remedies. The "Rape List" was an innovative, albeit controversial, self-help strategy.

Little did women know then that there is an unspoken double standard in free speech theory. Women are finding themselves subject to a special First Amendment exemption: speech that makes those in power uncomfortable.[46]

Does the university think the kind of harm men suffer from having *their* names mentioned in a lavatory dialogue outweighs the harm women suffer from being denied institutional recourse when they are harassed or assaulted? Are women less harmed when they are the object of bathroom graffiti?

The last time I checked, the Supreme Court had not exempted graffiti from First Amendment protection. Women have rarely had the power to affect the definition of speech. Women have a sex equality right to speech. There needs to be a recognition of graffiti's status as "speech," and women need to redefine the existing legal conception of harm (from "actual injury" to more esoteric concepts of inequality and subordination) if First Amendment law is to be a promising route to empowerment.

One of the problems in relying on legal principles (like the First Amendment) as a tool for social change is that invoking law usually means having to shoehorn a woman's complaint, understanding of an injury, and notion of a remedy, into the established, male-constructed legal definitions. But the legal definitions have rarely been crafted with women's interests or experiences in mind, and they do not often comport with women's perceptions of the harm (offense, embarrassment, degradation, powerlessness, fear, and so on). There is a need for women's voices to be heard, even if it is through unconventional forms of expression. And these unconventional forms of expression—whether it be performance art or angry songs or graffiti—need to be recognized and protected as speech unless constitutionally exempted. Until then any egalitarian role the First Amendment is to play—that everyone's opinion be given a chance for influence—will not be realized.

The "Rape List" is a classic tale of how historically male strategies are suddenly disavowed when appropriated by women. The problem with the "Rape List" was something far beyond the gates of Brown University, however, implicating greater socio-legal questions of whose speech is really free and whose interests are really protected. It is most instructive to look at this problem in the context of violence against women because this is where the differences are most vivid.

7

ILLUSIONS OF POSTFEMINISM: "VICTIM-FEMINISTS," "WELFARE MOTHERS," AND THE RACE FOR HETEROSEXUALITY

Kathy Miriam

A specter is haunting North American feminist politics—a specter of a feminism without a women's liberation movement, a women's movement without a liberation, and a liberation without a power struggle. Twenty-odd years since the emergence of second-wave feminism, we find ourselves in the postfeminist nineties and therefore incredulous to discover that "A surprising number of clever and powerful feminists share the conviction that American women still live in a patriarchy where men collectively keep women down."[1] Or to put it in academy-speak, "the patriarchal system of domination" is a "phrase [that] has become permanently disabled,"[2] in which case we are poststructuralist as "post-everything"[3]—beyond such categories as oppressor and oppressed, patriarchy, male power. Whether in the popular realm of talk-show circuits or in the high altitudes of academic conferences, we hear signals of "the end of something even though we hardly achieved it in the first place."[4]

As political scientist Carole Pateman points out, doing without the word "patriarchy" "would mean that . . . feminist political theory would then be without the only concept that refers specifically to the subjection of women, that singles out the form of political right that all men exercise by virtue of being men."[5] This is precisely the concept that postfeminists contest.

> Not everyone, including many women who consider themselves feminists, is convinced that contemporary American women live in an oppressive "male hegemony." . . . To rally women to their cause, it is not enough to remind us that many brutal and selfish men harm women. They must convince us that the oppression of women, sustained from generation to generation, is a structural feature of society.[6]

Postfeminists long for a kinder, gentler feminism, or a "Feminism without the threat—no rage at men, no rhetoric about oppression or empowerment."[7] Welcome to a "kinder, gentler" backlash. Rather than outright antifeminism, postfeminists divide and conquer by separating the "good," unthreatening feminists from the "bad" and angry. So, Who Stole Feminism? Postfeminists want to reclaim a "good" feminism "stolen" by "victim feminists," and contender number one for "victim feminist" is the feminist who speaks out against and fights antiwoman violence such as rape, pornography, prostitution, sexual harrassment, battering, and incest. The "victim feminist," in other words, is she who claims that sexual violence is a mechanism of structural male power. A particular focus of my essay is the postfeminist who, claiming to speak for a younger generation of feminists against the old feminist order[8] makes antirape campus activism a special target of her polemic against "victim feminism."

I hope to show that postfeminists want to save a "feminism" that looks awfully like an unreconstructed liberal individualism, in other words, an American dream that any woman can stop acting like a victim and just pull herself up by her bootstraps and get over her so-called "oppression." Postfeminists want to reclaim women's agency—an agency denied (in their estimation) by "victim feminists." However, by "taking up a vocabulary of [female] agency," postfeminists co-opt it "for a conservative agenda aimed at rescuing masculinity and blaming women for male dominance."[9] Postfeminism thus harmonizes with broader trends of conservative backlash politics in the nineties.

This is a decade when, twenty years past the gains of the civil rights and women's movements, "victims have fallen from grace"[10] and victim blaming has come back in style. Women have borne the brunt of this backlash against victims. Witness the recent welfare "reform," an often undisguised attack on poor women and women of color. Welfare reform legislation of 1996 was part of the Republican-initiated and neoliberal condoned "Contract for America." Policy makers relied on popular racist myths about "welfare mothers" to explain women's "dependency" on the state as a failure of individual self-discipline rather than due to a structural problem of poverty. The result is a bipartisan contract on women, particularly women of color and their children, in policy that threatens to further impoverish the poorest segment of the poor.

So what do the postfeminist attack on "rape-crisis feminism"[11] and the conservative backlash attack on "welfare mothers" have in common? In this essay I compare the two forms of backlash to show their shared agenda as a contract on feminism. I look at some of the specific ways that both forms of antifeminism aim at maintaining male dominance, white power, and class privilege through an individualist rhetoric that makes the reality of structural social power disappear. I want to show how this individualism, in both cases of backlash, aims at preserving a myth of "normal" sexual relations between men and women. While most of my argument in the following pages concerns the postfeminist backlash against antirape activism, in the final section of this essay I examine connections between the two forms of backlash.

THE "SEX LIBERAL" BACKLASH AGAINST ANTIRAPE ACTIVISM ANTIFEMINISM AS A BAD GIRL/GOOD GIRL STORY

The postfeminist account of antirape activists as "new Puritans" and "New Victorians"[12] rehashes a narrative first generated in eighties debates over pornography, namely a good girl/bad girl story. The story contends that feminist opposition to sexual violence stems from sexual repression rather than from a critique of male power. Katie Roiphe won media acclaim for her "brave first book,"[13] *The Morning After: Sex, Fear, and Feminism on Campus.* Roiphe excoriated "rape crisis feminists" for their "unfounded" representation of rape as "epidemic." In her view this "feminist hysteria" derives from a "conservative" ideal of female sexuality:

> The image that emerges from feminist preoccupations with rape and sexual harassment is that of women as victims, offended by a professor's dirty joke, verbally pressured into sex by peers. This image of a delicate woman bears a striking resemblance to that fifties ideal my mother and the other women of her generation fought so hard to get away from.[14]

Feminism, according to this sexual liberal,[15] postfeminist position, is a politics of reaction and resentment: "The movement against date rape is a symptom of a more general anxiety about sex."[16] This claim allows those who defend the status quo—for example, men's sexual access to women—to imagine themselves as sexual outlaws vis-à-vis their dowdy, repressed sisters.

The "cat fight" between self-identified feminists such as Roiphe and feminist activists in the movement against sexual violence played well in the mass media. The ultimate patriarchal fear and fantasy was evoked by a woman in public: the "ugly and sexually repressed feminist." Enter "do me feminists"—thus *Esquire* magazine heralded Roiphe and other patriarchal party girls in an article that included such sound bites as, "There are a lot of homely women in women's studies. Preaching these anti-male, anti-sex sermons is just a way for them to compensate for various heartaches—they're just mad at the beautiful girls."[17] Sound familiar? It was radio talk show host Rush Limbaugh who declared that "Feminism was established so as to allow unattractive women easier access to the mainstream of society."[18] The sour-grapes myth of feminism is as old as patriarchy and always used against women who cross the line of their gender role.

Liberalism and Radicalism

The presence of "do-me feminism" at the ideological core of the postfeminist backlash illustrates the essential difference between liberalism and radicalism. Even postfeminists are conscious of this difference. Wendy Kaminer, for example, explains (and approves) Roiphe's "liberal feminist" view of "rape as aberrant, violent behavior," in contrast to "radical feminism [which] presents it as normal sexual behavior in a male-dominated world." The linchpin of this distinction between radicalism and liberalism lies in two incompatible views of heterosexuality: What distinguishes liberal feminists "from their radical sisters" is a "[t]enacious faith in the commonness of benign, consensual heterosexual relations" and, Kaminer adds, "[l]oss of that faith is what Roiphe laments."[19] "Faith" is the operative word here: A leap of faith more precisely describes this liberal view, for it is one that abstracts sexuality from its context in hierarchical social power.

Postfeminists want their benign heterosexuality, which they contrast to a "paranoid" radical feminist "vampire model of male sexuality."[20] This model allegedly "accepts all men as sexual predators and women as chaste prey."[21] I suggest, however, that the postfeminist faith in benign heterosexuality masks the banality of male power as it is normalized through institutionalized heterosexuality.[22] The whole point of the feminist analysis of rape is to expose everyday, banal male power rather than pay further homage to the horror-movie dream made of itself. Radical feminists, in other words, argue that rape is "an extension of normative male behavior, the result of conformity or overconformity to the values and prerogatives which define the traditional male sex role."[23]

With the concepts of "date rape" and "marital rape," for example, feminists demystified men's "sex right," meaning their right of access to women's bodies, resources, work, and sexuality—what Adrienne Rich explained as "compulsory heterosexuality."[24] More specifically, by naming and resisting date rape and marital rape as rape, feminists pushed into public view a classic catch-22: First, most rapes are acquaintance rapes rather than stranger rapes.[25] Yet, second, the fact of the victim's acquaintanceship or (worse) prior intimacy with the rapist works against the possibility of winning a conviction against him in court.[26]

Prior to the advent of postfeminism this would have been a restatement of the obvious: Something about a woman's sexual relationship with a man makes her ability to say no to sex a political and conceptual impossibility within patriarchal frameworks. Thus, in 1992 Dale Crawford of South Carolina was aquitted from charges of raping and torturing his wife in the face of what seemed irrefutable evidence produced by the prosecution, namely, a video recording of the rape made by the rapist himself. The jury (although not the arresting police) accepted Crawford's claim that Trish Crawford's cries and screams—at knife point—were of pleasure, not pain.[27] After all, a woman's sexual obligation is written into the marriage contract.[28]

It is only as recently as 1993 that marital rape became a crime in all fifty states.[29] Further, as of this date "thirty-three states still have some exemptions from prosecution for rape, e.g., when the husband does not need to use force because the wife is most vulnerable (temporarily or permanently, physically or mentally legally unable to consent)"![30]

In other words, husbands are exempted from prosecution for rape when a woman's prior consent is impossible. Thus, if a woman is asleep, drugged, or otherwise unable to consent to sex when her husband or boyfriend sexually attacks her, she cannot legally claim that what he did to her was in fact rape. This astonishing exemption from prosecution of marital rape exposes the ideological basis of marital rape and why it has taken so long for it to be recognized as a crime, namely, the assumption that husbands (and also cohabitants or "voluntary social companions" [dates]) own their wives.

In 1994 Kenneth Peacock of Maryland murdered his wife upon discovering her in bed with another man; the judge, Robert Cahill, sentenced Peacock to eighteen months, averring, "I seriously wonder how many men married five, four years would have the strength to walk away without inflicting some corporeal punishment."[31] The phrase "corporeal punishment," implies a relation of authority and subordinate that the judge accepted and legitimized. Though skeptics might scoff at my use of extreme examples of institutionalized male power, in my view the extremes do expose the social framework in which men have an institutionalized right to sexually use and own women.

To turn specifically to the topic of campus antirape activists, with the very concept of date rape they implicitly call men's sex right into question by confounding traditional lines between "seduction" and "rape." In fact, these activists complicate the very notion of consent by threatening to make visible what the liberal model would hide: They make visible the context of social power in which a woman's consent is constrained rather than free, namely, compulsory heterosexuality as the context of rape and resistance to rape. This reconception of rape and the antirape strategies that have followed are the political crux of the postfeminist furor over "rape crisis feminism." To further demystify the convergence of liberalism and antifeminism in this backlash, and to further clarify the radical feminist position, I want to disentangle some of the main claims that postfeminists have made about "victim feminism."

Culture of Victims?

With the charge of "victim feminism," postfeminists describe antirape activism as just one more symptom of a U.S culture that defines Americans as "victims all."[32] Lumping together twelve-step recovery culture, new-age ideologies, and therapies on the one hand, and civil rights struggles (such as for affirmative action) on the other is typical of the nineties polemic against "victim mythology." Roiphe's caricature of antiviolence campus culture as (in what I take to be her one good line) "more oversaturated with self-esteem than cholesterol"[33] shows awareness of the symptom but not the disease: how a recovery model, mass-marketed in trade paperbacks and daytime TV talk shows, has co-opted feminism. In this vein "victimism" has been critiqued by radical feminists.

Feminist theorist Kathleen Barry first defined victimism as an ideology that, by defining a woman's identity in terms of her victimization, reduces a woman to the sum of her damages.[34] Victimism largely results from the "triumph of the therapeutic"[35] in feminist contexts. Many feminists have been led to redefine political realities in almost exclusively psychological terms and hence political change as a matter of individual, personal transformation.[36] This is a model, needless to say, in which the perpetrators are let off scot-free. Writer Louise Armstrong—who has spearheaded feminist opposition to incest—recently applied a radical feminist critique of the therapy model to the incest-survivor movement.[37] In her book *What Happened When Women Said Incest? Rocking the Cradle of Sexual Politics*,[38] she answered the question posed in the title: A recovery culture happened, one that promises endless healing "retreats" for incest survivors. But "[w]hy retreats" she asks—why not "attacks"?[39]

I agree with Armstrong. An internal critique of "victimism" would mean redirecting feminist focus on the perpetrators of violence. But nothing is further from the agenda of postfeminist arguments against "victim feminism." Postfeminists attribute "victim feminism" as readily to feisty feminist guerrilla actions as they do to therapy-group-modeled events. Camille Paglia derides as "panicky 'victims'" the truly gutsy Brown University students who listed the names of alleged rapists on bathroom walls: "The incidence and seriousness of rape do not require this kind of exaggeration."[40] Rather than contest "victim mythology," the real postfeminist agenda seems to be to stop feminists from acting collectively against rape.

To act collectively against rape would mean to lose a grip on something held too dear, namely, that good old faith in the commonness of benign heterosexuality. Indeed, the main "danger" that Roiphe sees in "rape crisis feminism" is "that it creates a dwindling space for men."[41] Furthermore, this liberal "faith" in men demands an individualist fantasy of women as autonomous sexual agents. Every woman is obligated to depend upon herself, not a political movement, to stop rape. As Paglia puts it, "The only solution to date rape is female self-awareness and self-control. A woman's number-one line of defense is herself."[42]

This postfeminist libertarian "solution" to rape is as new as patriarchal morality—in other words, not at all new in its suggestion that women, not men, are responsible for rape.

The Rules of the Fathers—and the Sons

Both postfeminist neoconservatives and liberals say they are "reclaiming female agency" from the "victim feminists": What they really do is make male accountability all but disappear. At one and the same time, postfeminists inflate and reduce women's agency: They inflate female agency with an unreal freedom, yet reductively define female agency as the capacity for negotiating sex in a "newly ambiguous" modern world. Postfeminists cite a shift from old social mores to modern chaos as the cause of date rape, and redefine date rape in terms of ambiguous sexual encounters. From this perspective the radical feminist analysis of rape as an assertion of men's sex right is a flight from ambiguity, an attempt to impose rules on the chaotic flux of sex. Yet radical feminists are also accused of blurring clear boundaries between ambiguous sex and real rape, the latter defined only as coercion through physical force.

Much postfeminist spleen has thus been vent on the Antioch College Code—a policy that prescribes guidelines for determining sexual assault based on a woman's consent (as a clearly stated yes) rather than on proof of men's use of force (and/or on evidence that a woman said no). The Antioch Code illuminates the issue of consent by expanding the definition of sexual assault beyond sheer physical coercion and/or threat of force. I take it that the point is to emphasize and analyze the degree to which women are still feeling pressured by men to have unwanted sex. However, postfeminists, both neocon and liberal, claim that lack of clear distinction between force and unwanted sex "muddies the waters"[43] and ruins things for "real" rape victims.

Roiphe argues that the Antioch College Code revictimizes women, restricting sexual freedom, and cloaking "retrograde assumptions about the way men and women experience sex. The idea that only an explicit yes means yes proposes that women, like children, have trouble communicating what they want."[44] Although Roiphe scoffs at the notion that consent be defined as an "explicit yes," she seems equally incredulous that women cannot just say no to assault. Hence Roiphe claims, for example, that a woman need only resist harassment with a "good slap in the face."[45] This unambiguously puts the onus of consent—or dissent—on the woman. However, as feminist theorist Laura Ring points out, women's "compliance [with sexual harassers] does not emerge from a failure of self-assertion, or 'self-esteem,'" but from the social context of learned femininity, a context that constrains women's ability to resist harassment and rape.[46] Roiphe's model of individual choice abstracts the notion of choice from this social context.

Although postfeminists claim that rules such as the Antioch Code restrict women's and men's (sexual) freedom, the Antioch controversy "force[s] us to acknowledge that the choice is not between regulation and freedom, but between different sets of rules," as educator Eric Fassin suggests.[47] His point becomes exceedingly clear when neoconservatives such as Elizabeth Fox-Genovese join forces with liberal postfeminists in a shared polemic against "victim feminism." Fox-Genovese finds fault with the Antioch Code for shifting the burden in sexual relations from "individual conscience" to "illegitimately imposed" and "external" authority. Fox-Genovese does not conceal her own preference for old-fashioned "internalized norms"—those associated with such apparently legitimate figures of authority as "fathers." Correspondingly, the late-lamented "individual conscience" in Fox-Genovese's narrative is decisively a woman's "burden," a point made abundantly clear in her history of sexual decadence in modern times: Whereas in the old days internalized norms ensured that "nice" girls could only say no, their no didn't hurt boys' feelings. Today, when girls can say yes as well as no, "it is difficult for young men not to take any refusal personally."[48] And this is what accounts for date rape—as if date rape had never happened in the fifties. "Individual conscience" and "internalized norms" mean that a girl should always have to say she's sorry (for refusing or consenting to sex), and men's egos are always in need of protection.

Both liberal and conservative positions "start from a conventional situation, perceived and presented as natural: a heterosexual encounter with the man as the initiator and the woman as gatekeeper."[49] Fox-Genovese, for example, invokes nothing short of biological determinism in her appeal to internalized norms as a way to restrain sexuality. "Sex," she concludes, "still puts women at higher risk than it puts men."[50] Because it is "sex" that is doing things to women, not men, men are naturally granted a new and appealing moral anonymity. In this vein Fox Genovese's term "New Puritanism" for antiviolence feminist activism is transparently disingenuous, as she concedes: "The New Puritanism has . . . emerged not as an attempt to restore some sense of accepted and internalized sexual norms [an attempt she would approve of] but as a determination to wrestle men to the floor."[51] Then why use the term "New Puritanism" for radical feminists at all? Her use of the term allies her with the "bad girls" like Roiphe despite the apparent opposition in how they view the nice girl/bad girl dichotomy. The intellectual muddle has a political logic that is quite straightforward when you consider that the point is much less about sexual expression versus sexual repression or good girls versus bad, than it is about antifeminism versus feminism—when feminism is perceived, rightly, as having something to do with challenging male power as natural and "benign."

The Unbearable Whiteness of Being Normal

The postfeminist good girl/bad girl account of feminism and rape suggests a final twist in my own narrative of postfeminism: Although date rape happens off campus as well as on, and presumably in every community and cultural context, postfeminists persist in skewing the issue as primarily a matter of a middle-class "nice" girl's confusion with the implication that "real" rape is elsewhere. Roiphe and Hoff-Sommers each warm over a familiar tactic when they attack feminism as the self-indulgent pasttime of bourgeois white women. Roiphe goes so far as to suggest that the fear of rape expressed by campus activists is "an idea that springs from privilege. Who besides these well-dressed, well-fed, well-groomed students would expect the right to safety and to march for it?"[52] Hoff-Sommers, for her part, accuses antirape activists of diverting a "disproportionate and ever-growing share of very scarce public resources allocated for rape prevention." Their success in funding antirape services "underscores," she contends, "how disproportionately powerful and self-preoccupied the campus feminists are despite all their vaunted concern for 'women' writ large," in contrast to what she considers the real "defenseless women," off campus.[53]

What are we to make of the sudden emergence of real victims on the scene of this polemic against "victim-feminism"? Postfeminists can see the fight against date rape on campus only as a delusion of privilege because, I suggest, their tenacious faith in normal heterosexuality as benign is bound to an equally tenacious faith in middle-class whiteness as a code for "normal." From this perspective a division between real versus pseudo victims develops: Pseudo-victims are middle-class feminist activists who must be inventing campus date rape because rape (an aberration) can't happen here. Rape doesn't live here in that sanctuary of the middle class—

the college campus. Correspondingly, the nice girl/bad girl division comes into focus as a division between middle-class white women and other women, between "nice" girls who can now say yes, like Roiphe (although "nice" girls like Fox-Genovese will always disapprove) and "bad" girls who could never, in any circumstances, say no—who are missing from both Roiphe's and Fox-Genovese's stories.

The history of the "nice girl" in our culture is buried in assumptions of class and race (as well as of gender)—the angel in the house, the gatekeeper of morality, the chaste, domesticated "lady," are all deeply coded as white and bourgeois. It has been the sex liberal's tendency to subvert the angel by claiming the whore: Hence Madonna is often celebrated by postfeminists as "liberating." But how liberating is Madonna for women who have always been marked and indeed used as "whore" by men in this culture? For example, African American women are still resisting the legacy of rape under slavery, and the corresponding myths stigmatizing the black woman as breeder or whore—as, in other words, the opposite of the white mother/lady. The Angel in the House (Virginia Woolf's phrase) codeveloped with and feeds on its opposite, lower-class/black aberrations. "Black 'whores' make white 'virgins' possible,"[54] as black feminist theorist Patricia Hill Collins states. "In the United States the fear and fascination of female sexuality was projected onto black women; the passionless lady arose in symbiosis with the primitively sexual slave."[55]

"Normality" depends on "aberration." The image of black women and poor women as unruly in sexuality, appallingly fecund, unable to exercise their willpower—in short, the obverse of the "nice girl" as gatekeeper—is vivid in the other backlash against women today in the bipartisan attack on the poor. Much more explicitly than the backlash against campus activists, this backlash filters its version/vision of normal heterosexual relations through a potent dream of whiteness/middle-classness. I believe I can show that both forms of backlash work together (along with many other forces) to help cement "the social contract as heterosexual."[56]

THE "CONTRACT FOR AMERICA" AS A CONTRACT ON FEMINISM: WELFARE REFORM AND AMERICAN MYTH

The Welfare Reform Bill approved by Congress in 1996 is only the latest development in a long history of American policy aimed at social control of poor women of color. The most striking feature of this bipartisan legislation—which slashed funding for welfare, eliminated entitlements, and imposed time restrictions on AFDC recipients—is the extent to which it was driven by myths rather than facts. In fact, some of the myths cited in government reports "have been debunked so often it's amazing they have any bunk left."[57] Yet policy makers flatly ignore the government's own data in reports such as the Center on Social Welfare and Law, which disproves the "common sense" about AFDC: (for example) that it leads to out of wedlock births, fosters "dependency," and supports a general trend away from marriage.[58] How do we explain the grip of beliefs about welfare in this country, a grip so tenacious that policy makers ignore their own data? In a 1998 dissertation on the history of welfare reform, Sandra Meucci offers a revealing perspective on the puzzle.[59]

According to Meucci, race and racism have driven U.S welfare policy since the sixties—in other words, since the period when welfare itself was first gained for people of color after years of exclusively benefiting poor white mothers. In turn, the group disproportionately affected—devastated—by the recent reform is overwhelmingly black and Hispanic. If racism is one key to the death grip that welfare policy has on the American imagination, another is that (Meucci argues) this policy represents an attempt to "reinstall the normative principle of marriage and men as the natural head of the household."[60] Correspondingly, Meucci concludes that welfare policy is a backlash reactive attempt to salvage the social order against two "crises"—namely, feminism and black power movements.

The moral that I derive from Meucci's story is this: Welfare policy is part of a contract on feminism. It attempts to enforce normal heterosexuality, feeding on a myth of "woman" as domestic angel in the house—as white and wedded to man. Whiteness and weddedness blend here in an invisible standard of heteronormality against which all "other" women are measured, indeed punished, as aberrant. Hence a white horror of black women's reproductive sexuality has generated such demons as the "Black matriarch" of the infamous Moynihan report. The Moynihan report, written in 1965, specifically derived poverty among African Americans from family life without fathers and with strong mothers.[61] Documents such as this report reveal the moral agenda—social control of women of color and of black people generally—at the core of supposedly economic policy.

Women on Welfare: Ain't Misbehavin'

The ideological motivation for welfare reform becomes clear when one examines the extent to which the policy is framed and defended in moralist terms. The legislation is part of a broader "assault on feminism" as *Nation* writer Pollitt puts it, in which regulating women's "behavior" becomes the key focus of social policy.[62] In the racialized context of welfare reform this focus on behavior has a punitive thrust. Thus conservative policy analyst Charles Murray—known most recently for coauthoring the racist *Bell Curve*—explicitly defends welfare reform as punishment for promiscuous women: "The act of getting pregnant if you are not prepared to care for a child is not morally neutral, it is a very destructive act . . . [P]art of arranging society so that happens as seldom as possible is to impose terrible penalties on that act."[63] Ruth Conniff comments in *The Progressive*, "The terrible penalties, he explained, include 'severe social stigma' and poverty."[64] In Murray's universe of teenage welfare-mothers, fathers have magically disappeared from the act of pregnancy: Is Murray a secret feminist, then, imagining a world of parthenogenetically conceiving women? Needless to say, this apparent bestowal of powers onto woman-as-agent is anything but.

Murray clings to a key welfare myth, namely that AFDC is a major cause of "teen pregnancy." Writer Mike Males shows us what this marvelous notion actually conceals: "70% of all births among teenage women pregnancies are fathered by adult men over age 20; one in six by men over age 25."[65] Who, then, exactly are the teens in this picture? The category of "teen pregnancy" is further deconstructed by Males: He calls attention to the percentage of these adult-fathered pregnancies that might in fact be the result of sexual abuse, including incest. Statistics on "teen pregnancy," STD and AIDS infection of teens, rape of teens (the cause of fifty thousand teen pregnancies a year), and sexual abuse (in the history of two-thirds of teenage mothers)[66] reveal the invisible structure of social power concealed and presupposed by the right-wing image of the sexual and reproductive licentiousness of the black or Hispanic welfare mother.

The Social Contract as Heterosexual and Women's Poverty

"Behavior" for welfare reformers works similarly to "individual conscience" for postfeminists—it has the magical function of obscuring men's accountability while reinforcing men's dominant position in (hetero)sexual relations. Compulsory heterosexuality has often been the undisguised agenda for welfare reformers such as Jeb Bush: In a 1994 campaign speech he advocated time limits on welfare, declaring that two years was sufficient time for a woman to get herself together and get married. Sometimes the ideology of compulsory heterosexuality is less explicit; it permeates public discourse about women's poverty.

Feminist analysis of women's poverty implies that women's economic status is inextricable from "the obligatory social relationship between 'man and woman'"[67] as insitutionalized in U.S. structures of work and culture. "[M]en are poor as a result of unemployment, while women are poor because of the type of work they do"[68] because "female poverty often exists even when a woman works full time."[69] At a time of economic crisis such as the present, women's "growing share of the shrinking pie," as feminist economist Teresa Amott argues, means the incursion of women workers into the lower and informal sectors of the labor force.[70] This means work that is part-time, temporary, and unstable, often without benefits, characterized by sexual harassment as well as menial tasks: sweatshop, fast food, home-work/piece-work labor. It is this "kind of work"—"women's work"—that pushes women into welfare, where, for one thing, they can get health care for their children.

In sum, the "feminization of poverty"[71] is a consequence of power arrangements assumed as "natural" by the powers-that-be. This assumption is at the core of backlash ideology: Backlashers persist in defining the problem of welfare as women's "dependency" on the state and construe such "dependency" as (at worst) a moral deficiency and (at best) a psychological deficiency on women's part. Women are presumed to be "naturally" burdened with caretaking of children, and of other (real) dependents such as the aged and the sick, as well as of healthy adult men—a burden that is a key contributing factor to women's poverty. This burden is increased by backlash policy that guts social spending and reshifts the work of caretaking ever more firmly onto women's backs. Another presumably natural fact that pushes women into poverty and welfare is male violence: Women's economic dependence on men makes it more difficult to get away from batterer spouses. In turn, their escape from violent husbands or boyfriends is often their entry into (economic) dependency on the state.[72] All these facts of "nature"—women's obligatory role as caretaker, women's vulnerability to male violence in the home, and so on— are conditions of compulsory heterosexuality and therefore of women's poverty.[73] The backlash against "welfare mothers" is part of a larger contract on feminism that aims at maintaining this "state of nature."

Conclusion: Breaking the Social Contract

Radically feminist strategy helps "dispel the illusion that sexuality [and poverty] is a state of nature that individuals must experience outside the social contract."[74] But conservative and neoliberal backlashers want their illusions, and postfeminist backlashers, more perniciously, want their illusions and their feminism—a feminism with illusions intact.[75] Most of all, postfeminists want the illusion of normality against which rape/violence and poverty are aberrant. They must disavow any feminism that claims otherwise and accept only a feminism that poses no threat to men or sign of rage, lest it be tainted by those dirty words, "victim feminism." Feminism is a blot on the American Dream. Feminist protest "makes

women's blood explicit."[76] Feminism stains the fabric of liberal and conservative illusions; it reveals the texture, like an invisible watermark, of
assumed privilege. Members of both backlashes use the charge of "victim mythology" to make real social power disappear. Behind their insistent faith that male and white power, and heterosexuality, are natural and
benign is a lurking fear: Those they call "victim feminists" are a serious
threat to that faith.

8

CRIME WITHOUT PUNISHMENT: PORNOGRAPHY IN A RAPE CULTURE

Krista K. Jacob

> The utopian male concept, which is the premise of male pornography is this—since manhood is established and confirmed over and against the brutalized bodies of women, men need not aggress against each other; in other words, women absorb male aggression so that men are safe from it.
> —Andrea Dworkin, "The Riot Cause"

I vividly remember one of my first experiences with pornography. At the time I was a freshman in college and was fairly naive about the issue of pornography and violence against women. It was the day of a home football game; my roommate Laura, her boyfriend, and I went to a friend's house to watch the game. When we arrived, I was surprised to see a number of my male friends from high school, many of whom I hadn't seen for several years. I noticed that with the exception of Laura and me there were no women at the party. We had been at the party for about an hour when I noticed a group of guys collecting in front of the television. I could hear them shouting and I assumed that the football game had started. Eventually Laura and I decided to join them in the living room. When we got closer, I could hear the words that they had been shouting. "Get her!" "Look at her, she loves it!" I looked at the television and saw a naked woman being held down and kicked by a group of men. One man had his penis in her mouth while two other men hit and kicked her. Her face was terror stricken, and she had marks forming on her body where the men were beating her. She writhed in pain, struggling to get free. I looked around the room, watching the men watching the film. Their facial expressions were a mixture of excitement and anger. "Fist the bitch, come on she can take it!" "Fuck her up the ass!" They laughed and shouted as another man got on top of the woman and started raping her. Laura and I stood there in stunned silence.

I couldn't believe what I was seeing: a group of guys, whom I had known throughout my adolescence, were laughing and cheering while watching a woman being raped and beaten. One guy, who I knew had graduated from a Catholic high school close to my home town, walked over to the closet and retrieved a blow-up doll. A couple of the guys grabbed it and started beating it, imitating the men in the video. One guy pulled his penis out of his pants and stuck it in the doll's mouth, moving the doll's head back and forth. Another guy yelled, "Keep your dick in your pants, there are girls here!" A couple of them looked over at me and Laura and laughed. They saw the outrage in our faces. We looked as humiliated as the woman in the video, which, of course, enhanced their power game. Outraged, Laura grabbed her boyfriend's arm and told him that we needed to leave. He told her to "chill out" and that they were "just joking and having a good time." "Don't you have a sense of humor?" chided the guy standing next to us. Together, Laura and I left the party.

We spent the rest of the day together talking about what we had just witnessed. We felt confused, degraded, and most of all angry. I will never forget the woman in that video: The look on her face and the marks on her body are imprinted in my mind forever.

Because of the profound impact this experience, as well as many others, had on me, I started to volunteer at a rape crisis center as a peer educator and rape survivor advocate. My life is very different now. I have worked professionally as a community educator and rape survivor advocate for seven years, during which I have also been an activist in feminist political groups organizing around women's issues. My work experience as a rape survivor advocate has taught me many things about our culture. The FBI tells us that one in three women will be raped in her lifetime, that one in four girls and one in six boys will be sexually assaulted before the age of eighteen. For many people these statistics are abstract and perhaps unimaginable. For me they are not. The FBI also tells us that a woman is beaten every twelve seconds, and that four to five women are killed each day by their male partners. In my work I see the violent reality of our culture. I hear the stories of these rapes and the beatings, one by one, from the survivors. This violence is not an abstract compilation of statistical information; for millions of women and children it is a part of their everyday lives. Male violence will continue to threaten and devastate millions of lives, until we, as a society, understand and confront the root causes of violence against women and children.

As a feminist, I employ feminist theory, analysis, and activism in my work as a survivor advocate. The term "rape culture" has been used by feminists to give name to a cultural climate that "encourages male sexual aggression and supports violence against women."[1] A feminist analysis of a rape culture requires that we understand violence against women in terms of the social, political, and economic factors that engender a male-dominated patriarchal culture and perpetuate the subordinate status of women. It requires that we refuse biological or genetic "excuses" for male violence that fail to hold perpetrators accountable, but rather engage in a close examination of the multiple components in our culture that contribute to gender-specific violence. Misogynist and sexist attitudes about women are at the crux of a rape culture, and they are perpetuated by many factors in our society, such as the media, family, peers, and institutions. Pornography, one of the most powerful transmitters of misogyny, contributes to a culture in which violence against women is not only encouraged but accepted as the norm.

As antirape activists, we quickly learn that violence against women is a complex and multifaceted issue. Our job is difficult because we are faced with many challenges. Sexism, racism, classism, homophobia, and other forms of discrimination pervade our culture and maintain an institutionalized structure that oppresses specific groups of people, keeping them vulnerable to exploitation. Perpetrators, pornographers, and pimps (or any combination thereof) target oppressed and marginalized members of our society because cultural rejection forces oppressed people to look for any economic alternative in order to survive. For example, many of the women whom I have worked with live in poverty, and as a result they are forced into prostitution/pornography in order to support themselves and/or their children. Many women who are in abusive relationships are prostituted or used in pornography by their boyfriends/pimps. The women do not have control over their money, their bodies, or their lives. Often teenagers will run away from physical and/or sexual abuse happening in their homes only to be lured into the clutches of the street pimps who prey on vulnerable kids. It is a simple and age-old economic equation: The pimps and pornographers are invested in keeping women and children vulnerable; the pimp's/pornographer's economic power is produced by and stolen from the women and children they film and prostitute.

Through my work with survivors, I have learned that there is more than just a "connection" between pornography and violence against women. The two do not exist as isolated phenomena waiting for researchers and social scientists to "prove" that they are linked. Skeptics want to see numbers that correlate relationships. I do not need to see studies to know that pornography and violence against women are inextricably related to one another. The first time that I worked with a little girl who was shown pornography by the perpetrator in order to groom her for sexual abuse, I saw the "connection." And the time that I worked with a little boy whose uncle filmed the ritual throat and anal rapes of this child so that he could continually get off on the child's abuse, even in his absence, I saw the "connection." The countless number of women whose male partners point to pornography as blueprints for the verbal, physical, and sexual abuse they perpetrate "proves" to me that there is a relationship between pornography and violence against women. Detectives and police officers find massive amounts of pornography in the homes of perpetrators. One detective told me he had never searched a perpetrator's house without finding pornographic materials. But still some people remain unconvinced that pornography encourages perpetrators and fosters a cultural climate that is hostile to women and children.

The highly controversial nature of the "debates" within feminist and progressive circles about pornography, have made me feel, at times, like avoiding the issue entirely. However, my work experience as an antirape activist has consistently reinforced for me that pornography is an inescapable part of violence against women and children; therefore, it is imperative that I engage in these debates and share a survivor advocate perspective. This perspective is the impetus behind, and will be the focus of, this essay. My analysis will hinge on a three-part structure. In the first section I will provide a brief overview of the history of responses to pornography. In the following section I will outline antiporn efforts by second- and third-wave feminists, as well as the challenges confronting third-wave antiporn feminists. And, in closing, I will discuss possible solutions for working to end pornography and violence against women and children.

PERSPECTIVES ON PORNOGRAPHY

The history of men's opposition to women's emancipation is more interesting perhaps than the story of that emancipation itself.
—Virginia Woolf, *A Room of One's Own*

These chicks are our natural enemy. . . . It is time we do battle with them. . . . What I want is a devastating piece that takes the militant feminists apart. They are unalterably opposed to the romantic boy-girl society that Playboy promotes.
—Hugh Hefner, quoted in Susan Brandy's "The Article I Wrote on Women That Playboy Wouldn't Publish"

For the purposes of this article, I will provide a brief description of the long and sordid history of pornography. The word "pornography" comes from the Greek root "porne," meaning prostitute or female captive/slave, and "graphos," meaning writing about or description of. Thus, the very root of the word means female sexual slavery. Historically, attacks against pornography have been organized by conservative religious groups interested in censoring or suppressing issues related to sex, such as birth control and sex education; most of their opposition to pornography has been based on the explicit sexual content of pornography. Rooted in narrow and sexist Victorian ideas about women's sexuality, traditional religious movements argue against pornography on the basis that it is "immoral." If we analyze their arguments, we see that their primary purpose is to vilify and repress female sexuality in order to strip women of sexual autonomy and limit women's right to self-determination. Their goals are to legislate morality (as defined by the male-controlled state), give the state power to censor sexually explicit material, and impose their puritan ideology onto others.

Until the second-wave feminist movement, liberals who believed that pornography was an important part of expanding and cultivating human sexuality were the only opposition to this conservative analysis. Historically, and even in contemporary times, liberals and conservatives alike have defined the content of pornography as sex. They do not include in their analysis perspectives of the women who are hurt in the making of pornography, nor do they discuss the collective impact that pornography has on the everyday lives of women. In theory and in practice, both conservative and liberal approaches are male defined, meaning that they operate from an ideological framework that accounts only for the interests of men; their efforts to implement this framework occurs through masculinist relationships, using archaic gendered terms and hierarchical structures. As a result their pornography agendas serve to reinforce male power and privilege, limit feminist freedom of expression, and undermine the liberation of women.

During the second-wave feminist movement, feminists generated an explosion of research on violence against women and unveiled what many women and children were experiencing in their homes, neighborhoods, churches, schools, and so on. They discovered that acts of violence against women and children were not isolated occurrences, but instead were pervasive and endemic to our culture. Their antirape work gave birth to a new analysis of pornography, one that named pornography as a contributing factor to gender-specific violence. In her book *Sexual Politics*[2] (published in 1969), Kate Millett was the first person to demonstrate the importance of an industry that promotes sexual male domination and female subordination to the maintenance of a patriarchal society.[3] Robin Morgan, another important antiporn feminist during the second-wave feminist movement, coined the phrase, "Theory and practice: pornography and rape,"[4] which has been used by antiporn feminists to illuminate the relationship between porn and rape. As a result of the revolutionary work of second-wave feminists, notions of rape and pornography were reconceptualized as fundamental components of women's oppression.

Contrary to conservative religious arguments, antiporn feminists' analyses do not object to the explicit sexual nature of pornographic material, but instead criticize pornography as an expression of misogyny that eroticizes dehumanization and degradation of the female body and unavoidably inflicts harm on women. Contrary to the liberal stance on pornography, antiporn feminists contend that the foundation of pornography is sexual violence, not consensual sexual expression. Antiporn feminists argue that pornography is a direct expression of male domination and female subordination and contributes to a cultural climate that is inherently hostile to women. Thus, by the very existence and definition, and through the images and acts portrayed in it, pornography creates and perpetuates violence against women.

A quick glance at examples of these images and acts is illustrative. In hard-core pornography we are shown images of women being raped, tortured, mutilated, forced to have sex with animals, and even killed for the purpose of stimulating sexual arousal. "Snuff" pornography is a category of pornography that depicts the killing of women through sexual torture. This (of course) is presented by pornographers as sexually arousing. In soft-core pornography women are depicted as dehumanized sex objects existing solely for the purpose of the (primarily male) viewer's sexual enjoyment. When female sexuality is reduced solely to sexual objectification, women are treated as "subhuman" objects undeserving of the respect and equal treatment that one is expected to show other human beings. In both hard- and soft-core pornography, women are stripped of their humanity and sexual autonomy so that the pornographer can profit and the consumer can get off. Consequently, "normal" male sexuality is defined as possessing a proclivity for violence, aggression, and control; and, conversely, "normal" female sexuality is defined as weak, passive, and desiring (male) aggression. This paradigm of male-female sexuality reinforces a dangerous power imbalance that confuses sex with violence.

Many of the adolescent boys in my antirape educational workshops have described learning about female sexuality through pornographic materials. They have stumbled across their father's *Playboy* or a neighbor's *Hustler*, or they have been introduced to these materials by an older friend or brother. Regardless of the medium, these boys' first sexual experiences are with one-dimensional women placed in powerless and vulnerable positions, devoid of thoughts and feelings. Through the pornographic lens, women are reduced to sexuality, and their sexuality is reduced to nudity—an unrealistic nudity that has been "fixed up" by publishers and plastic surgeons. Young men/boys are indoctrinated into notions and images of sex and female sexuality produced by a misogynist industry that manipulates the female body and misrepresents female sexuality. As a result, young men/boys learn unrealistic expectations of women's bodies and develop sexual identities and understandings of sexual intimacy that are based on power, control, and their superiority over women.

In the world of pornography no atrocity is left untouched. Jokes are made about incest, wife battering, the Holocaust, racism, sexism, homophobia, and other forms of oppression. In pornographic cartoons African American men are depicted as having ridiculously large lips and penises. Asian women are shown to be particularly subservient and weak. African American and Latina women are represented as having insatiable and animal-like sex drives. Every form of hatred and abuse is trivialized. For example, Larry Flynt, founder of *Hustler* magazine, carried the cartoon "Chester the Molester," which made jokes about and trivialized pedophilia. Recently Tonya Flynt, the daughter of Larry Flynt, came forward with charges that her father sexually abused her as a child. She reportedly said, "Freedom of speech wasn't used when he [Larry Flynt] was violating me. . . . He just told me this is what little girls do with their fathers."[5] If we listen to the testimonies of women like Tonya Flynt who have been harmed by pornographers, we see that pornographers have a personal investment in keeping us laughing at child rape and other forms of abuse. If we are laughing at sexual abuse, we are less likely to name this abuse as criminal and hold the perpetrators accountable. Pornographers have a direct economic investment in trivializing sexual abuse and discrimination; if they can keep us laughing at such abuses, we will be less likely to work to change a world that keeps certain groups disenfranchised and vulnerable to this exploitation by pimps and pornographers.

In response to arguments that there is no "evidence" that pornography and violence are linked, Catharine MacKinnon, a feminist legal scholar, points to a number of studies demonstrating a connection between the viewing of pornographic material and violence perpetrated against women.[6] These studies show that men exposed to violent pornography are more likely to act aggressively toward women and that viewing pornography can affect men's attitudes about women in detrimental ways. Viewing pornography increases their hostility toward women, their propensity to rape, their tendency to condone rape, and the likelihood that they would rape or force sex on a woman if they knew that they would not get caught. In addition, Judith Lewis Herman, a feminist psychiatrist, has drawn connections between the abusive techniques employed by rapists, pornographers, pimps, and wife batterers:

> The methods that enable one human being to enslave another are remarkably consistent. . . . The same techniques are used to subjugate women, in prostitution, in pornography, and in the home. In organized criminal activities pimps and pornographers sometimes instruct one another in the use of coercive methods. The systematic use of coercive techniques to break women into prostitution is known as "seasoning." Even in domestic situ-

ations, where the batterer is not part of any larger organization and has no formal instruction in these techniques, he seems again and again to reinvent them.[7]

Both Herman's and MacKinnon's conclusions provide scientific support for the argument that pornography is a contributing factor to a rape culture. For those of us who are part of the antisexual violence movement, these "conclusions" are not new information.

THIRD-WAVE FEMINIST RESPONSE

All too often antiporn feminists find themselves alone in the struggle against pornography. The issue is consistently framed as one to be "debated." Rene S., a survivor of pornography and prostitution, believes that pornography is not a matter for debate: "It is ludicrous that we would even think of sitting around and debating these issues instead of going out and doing something to stop it. . . . It is like going up to a woman who is trapped in a brothel and saying to her, 'We can't help you yet because we are still trying to decide if this is a relevant issue or not.'"[8] When understood in these terms, framing pornography as an issue for debate is absurd.

Many feminists who are skeptical of feminist antipornography efforts are well-meaning people who have bought into the propaganda generated by different stakeholders in the pornography industry. Many gays, lesbians, and bisexuals are concerned that their collaboration with antipornography feminists could result in censorship of alternative literature and art. For others, the truth about the harm done to women is simply too overwhelming for them to confront. Listening to the experiences of women and children hurt by pornography is painfully difficult because, as Rene S. states, "we [survivors of porn and prostitution] scare them because we know about a world that they just don't see . . . to hear this is really scary to people."[9] In addition, people who use pornography are not a handful of dirty-minded men; on the contrary, millions of men use pornography on a regular basis. For women and men who have male partners that use porn, confronting the harm caused by pornography can be all the more challenging.

Some feminist and progressive groups are uncomfortable with the idea that the issue of pornography can create unusual, and often problematic, political bedfellows; feminists and fundamentalist religious groups are frequently aligned against pornography, although for dramatically different reasons. This situation is problematic for two reasons: First, it has been used selectively in attempts to discredit antipornography feminists. For example, in some of my political activism I have stood alongside religious groups in demonstrations against the death penalty and welfare cuts; however, this "unusual" alliance has not been used to undermine my politics. Second, critics often forget the alternative: In support of pornography, liberals and civil libertarians regularly join forces with pimps, pornographers, pedophiles, and rapists.

It is nearly impossible to be part of a pro-pornography or pro-prostitution discussion without hearing the same old tired jokes about antiporn feminists. Antiporn feminists are frequently personally attacked and vilified. Myths and outright lies about antiporn feminists are reinforced and perpetuated. They are accused of being procensorship, antisex (both heterosexual and homosexual), antimale, and so on. A more appropriate label for many pro-pornography/pro-sex advocates would be "anti-anti-pornography" advocates, since most of their discourse is centered on attacking feminists and survivors who speak out against the pornography industry. Writings and lectures by pro-pornography writers and activists consist of the usual cheap shots directed against feminists Andrea Dworkin and Catharine MacKinnon, two women who have dedicated their personal and political lives (at great cost) to eradicating violence against women and children. Attacking Dworkin, MacKinnon, and other antiporn feminists has, in fact, become fashionable in current discussions about pornography. Reactionary politics, capricious behavior, and broadside personalized critiques posed by anti-anti-pornography activists require us to challenge their political agenda.

Sadly, survivors of pornography and prostitution are frequently marginalized by the anti-sexual-violence movement. Many survivors of pornography and prostitution share frustrations that pornography and prostitution are frequently dismissed as viable economic choices for women, rather than understood as institutionalized systems of violence against women. One especially telling example of this frustration was the result of a recent controversy surrounding Andrea Dworkin's invitation to speak at an anti-sexual-violence conference sponsored by WCASA (Wisconsin Coalition against Sexual Assault). In short, because of Dworkin's important contributions to the antirape movement, she was invited by a WCASA staff member and a member of the WCASA Board of Directors to be the keynote speaker at their conference to be held in September 1996. Dworkin accepted the invitation and sent back her signed copy of the contract. While waiting to hear back from WCASA, she received a phone call from Louis Fortis, the president of the WCASA Board of Directors. He told her that the board of directors decided that she could not speak at the conference because he did not like her "ideas." He accused her of being procensorship and informed her that because of this, the board had decided that she could not speak at their conference. Chris

Grussendorf, a survivor of pornography and prostitution, authored a letter of protest calling into question the board's duplicitous behavior:

> If free speech is as important as Louis himself claims to believe, then why did Louis prevent Dworkin from speaking? The answer is quite simple: Louis does not like Dworkin, he has the power to cancel her speech, and so he did. Louis has done to Dworkin what he claims she (somehow) does to pornographers and rapists: he censored her in the name of free speech.[10]

Chris's letter was circulated on the Internet and elicited responses of outrage and disbelief from many feminists. Two hundred seventy activists (including Gloria Steinem, Robin Morgan, Catharine MacKinnon, and Nikki Craft) signed on in support of Dworkin. Louis Fortis has since resigned from the board of directors; and to date the WCASA board has not issued a public apology for their egregious treatment of Dworkin. In fact, the WCASA board went so far as to issue a letter implying that Dworkin lied to create controversy. The WCASA staff were not involved in any of these decisions, and since the controversy they have worked diligently to make issues of pornography and prostitution part of their anti-sexual-violence agenda. They have edited an educational journal about pornography and are planning a statewide conference on pornography to educate antirape advocates who work with survivors. Chris Grussendorf says that the goal of her protest was one of "accountability and education." She believes that "activists in the anti-rape movement must maintain a commitment to holding one another accountable in order to preserve the integrity of the movement."[11] Based on the response of the WCASA staff, Chris and her supporters were successful in raising awareness about the truth behind the board's public explanations. Together these activists and professionals will see to it that no survivors are treated as invisible by the antisexual assault movement.

PISSED WOMEN (PROSTITUTION IS SEXUAL SLAVERY TO ERADICATE AND DEGRADE WOMEN)

In February 1997 a small group of feminist activists on the University of Wisconsin-Madison campus, outraged by the popularity of the movie *The People vs. Larry Flynt*, organized a panel discussion entitled "Pop Culture and Pornography: Images of Women in the Media." Panel members included Jolanda Sallmann, from the UW School of Social Work; Chris Grussendorf, a survivor of pornography and prostitution; Joel Diggleman, from the UW Law School; and me, representing the Dane County Rape Crisis Center. Sharlynn Daun, the women's issues director for the University of Wisconsin's United Council, facilitated the discussion. The event drew an audience of approximately 140 people and catalyzed numerous campus and community discussions about the issues of pornography and violence against women. The panel discussion affected people in a profound way: After the conclusion of the panel, numerous small groups of people continued to discuss different ways to raise campus and community awareness about the harms caused by pornography.

Prior to the WCASA controversy and the panel discussion, Chris Grussendorf and Rene S. founded a group called PISSED Women (Prostitution Is Sexual Slavery to Eradicate and Degrade Women) with the goal of raising community awareness about the issues of pornography and prostitution through education and social action. Both Rene and Chris have been used in pornography and prostitution. The group's primary mission is to "educate, agitate, and eradicate the sexual enslavement of women." Due to time and money constraints, the group was slow in getting started. However, as a result of both the "Pop Culture and Pornography" panel discussion and the WCASA controversy, more people (both women and men) showed interest in working with PISSED Women. Several weeks after the panel discussion, Rene, Chris, and new group members spent hundreds of hours organizing a bus tour to expose the realities of prostitution and pornography in the Madison community. The educational tour was called "Madison Exposed" and visited several different Madison establishments that exploit women and children, including the restaurant Hooters, a "massage" parlor, and two local porn shops. The bus tour created a challenging paradigm shift for the male customers of these businesses. Men who patronize these establishments do so in order to look at women as well as to objectify them in other ways; many of them do not believe (or care) that this could be wrong or harmful to women. Ironically, most of the male customers in the tour establishments were painfully uncomfortable by the fact that the tables were being turned: They were being watched by members of the bus tour and would eventually hide or leave the establishments entirely. Objectification looked very different to them when they were the objects.

On April 11, 1997 (several weeks before the bus tour), a woman named Emma Bacon, while working for an escort service, was brutally raped and murdered by her "customer" in a local motel room, which was located across the street from a strip club. Brandon Grady, a twenty-two-year-old Iowa man, had arranged to meet Emma at the motel room, where he eventually murdered her with a sledgehammer. According to investigators, "Grady fatally beat and stabbed the 20-year old woman, mutilated her body and had sexual intercourse with the corpse." At the competency hearing a court-appointed psychologist reported that "Grady enjoyed violent pornography, especially when it involved torture and violence, and he apparently has a collection of pornography." Investigators did find pornographic materials in his home. The psychologist also noted that "Grady describes intense anger and resentment toward society, especially toward females."[12]

In response to this tragic crime, organizers of the bus tour dedicated the day's event to the memory of Emma Bacon. One of the most powerful and emotional stops for me was the Spence Motel, the site of Emma's murder. The bus group stood in front of the motel room while a member of PISSED Women placed a sign reading, "Emma Bacon was murdered here. We miss her," on the motel room door alongside a bouquet of flowers. For many people this powerful experience personalized the theoretical analysis behind a feminist critique of pornography and prostitution and brought the day's events home; tears rolled down people's faces as they stared sadly at the motel room where a young aspiring nurse who loved animals suffered one of the most horrific crimes imaginable. Eventually the motel manager, outraged by our dedication, called the police. Slowly people filed back onto the bus and sat solemnly in their seats. As the bus pulled out of the parking lot, we saw the motel manager rip down the sign and discard the flowers. Outraged, a tour group member yelled out the bus window, "You can take down the sign but we will never forget!"

WHAT CAN WE DO?

We are faced with many obstacles in the fight against pornography. Currently, it is estimated that the pornography industry is an $11-16 billion dollar a year industry. The production and use of pornography have increased dramatically as pornography has become more accessible through mainstream avenues such as the Internet and video rentals. According to *Adult Video News*, a trade publication, hard-core pornography video rentals alone increased from 75 million in 1985 to 665 million in 1996.[13] The pervasiveness of pornography and the economic power of the pornographers are two of the most challenging obstacles confronting antiporn feminists.

Many feminists are working to create honest and empowering representations of female sexuality, but a lack of economic resources and market censorship have been significant barriers to achieving this goal. Additionally, with a sexual tradition defined by men it has been difficult for women to explore their own sexuality, let alone develop a woman-centered erotica. Using stigmatizing words like "slut" and "whore," society shames and humiliates women who dare to take control over their sexuality. Adolescent girls quickly learn that there is a fine line between good girls and bad girls, and that there are severe consequences for "bad girl" behavior. Almost three decades have passed since the "sexual revolution," and adolescent girls/women are still inhibited by the slut-stud double standard that rewards boys/men and shames girls/women for the very same behavior. The "sexual revolution" did very little, if anything at all, for female sexual expression. In the face of such obstacles, female sexual expression and the creation of a woman-centered erotica are difficult, but not impossible, to achieve.

Many antiporn feminists have attempted to create distinctions between pornography and erotica, which is defined as sexual expression that is pleasurable and not violent or degrading to women;[14] however, they have not yet been able to reach consensus on the differences between the two. During the second-wave feminist movement, women developed consciousness-raising groups that served as safe spaces for women to come together, free from the men in their lives, to talk about their experiences as women. The groups were extremely empowering and helped to build solidarity among women. I believe that this consciousness-raising model can serve us well today as we work to create new understandings of erotica and female sexual expression. It is crucial that women come together and, from a grassroots level, generate new understandings of female sexuality through writings, art, discussion groups, and other channels of expression. A Woman's Touch, a women's erotica shop located in Madison, Wisconsin, is a good example of feminists working to redefine and celebrate female sexuality. Their store's focus is on "women and those who love them," and the store carrys an array of books, art, jewelry, lotions, games, toys, and videos. In addition, it offers reading and writing groups, sex toys and massage workshops, ear piercing, art displays, the "Lesbian Introductory Personal Service" (for single lesbians to meet each other), a newsletter, and a Web site. As women, we have been silenced and shamed for too long in the arenas of sex and sexuality; creating and supporting places like A Woman's Touch are important steps in breaking the silence and shame that inhibit creative and empowering female sexual expression.

Issues of free speech and censorship have been central to leftist discourses on pornography. Many people argue that we should counteract the negative effects of the pornographers' bad speech with that of the feminists' good speech. For example, feminist writer Naomi Wolf believes that if we accept the assumption that pornography causes harm to women, the solutions should focus on creating more empowering representations. Instead of "trying to determine which images 'degrade women' and what to do about them, we must take the responsibility of using art, education, information, the power of speech itself to change the aura around scenes of sexual violence."[15] Though it is true that we must exercise our First Amendment right to speak out against the pornographers, as well as create art and literature that does not degrade or hurt women, Wolf's argument excludes the effect of power and wealth differentials in our society. Women, and in particular poor women, do not have access to free speech in the same way as do powerful, wealthy men.

For too long women have been invisible in political discussions about "rights" and "equality" under the law. Patriarchal society defines "reality" in terms of men's activities, and androcentric political discourses ignore the experiences of women. For example, many liberals argue that pornography is an important medium for liberatory sexual expression for women. If pornography is so liberating, why then do we have such a blatant imbalance of women models and men consumers? If pornography is indeed liberating, one would think that men would jump at the chance to have their naked bodies sprawled out in magazine centerfolds; or to be filmed while being tied up, raped, and beaten. But, of course, this is not the case; pornography looks different to the person in front of the lens. Chris Grussendorf challenges us to rethink the notion of "free speech" from the perspective of the women and children used in porn:

> Most of the people I hang out with are survivors of prostitution and pornography and I can tell you that the world is a very different place for us. We see it from our backs with our legs spread wide, we have terror and flashbacks and problems eating and minds split into a thousand pieces. And we are silent. We are silent, we are terrorized, our throats are raw from all the cock rapes; yet, the discourse about our lives is focused on free speech. Not our speech, of course, it is the speech of the pimps and the consumers that is important. As it is now, the pictures of our humiliation, of us being raped and pissed on and tied up are considered to be acts of free speech: Their speech, our bodies. Their speech, our lives. Their speech, our death.[16]

If we want to change the discriminatory reality of our culture, we need to move beyond male-centered and profit-motivated definitions of free speech that mask societal inequities; we must reconstruct our understandings of political concepts such as "freedom" and "expression" so that they are empowering to, and inclusive of, women and children.

I want to express solidarity with feminist activists Catharine MacKinnon, Chris Grussendorf, and Andrea Dworkin, who have been outspoken opponents of the pornography industry. Dworkin and MacKinnon were the first to reformulate pornography as a violation of women's civil rights. Together they coauthored a Minneapolis, Minnesota, ordinance proposal that would have allowed anyone who could prove in a court of law that they had been harmed by pornography to sue the pornographer(s) who profited from the sale of the pornography. The ordinance would not have given the male-controlled state power to censor what it deemed "pornographic"; instead it would have provided a civil, not criminal, recourse for people harmed by pornography to hold their perpetrators financially accountable. Evelina Giobbe, founder of WHIS-

PER (Women Hurt in Systems of Prostitution Engaged in Revolt) responded to the ordinance's rejection:

> Pornography is the ultimate recycling bin of prostitution. You can buy any piece of my young womanhood in the marketplace and yet I cannot have any kind of redress for the pornographic materials that were made of me. The MacKinnon/Dworkin ordinance would have allowed a modicum of relief for women who have been used in porn. It wouldn't have brought an end to an empire.[17]

To date the ordinance has not successfully become a legal reality in any state; however, I believe that MacKinnon and Dworkin are on the right track by creating legislation that could be used to empower women and men who have been harmed by pornographers. The logic of the ordinance follows the model used for anti—sexual-harassment legislation: Under current law, victims of sexual harassment can sue employers who do not put a stop to sexually harassing behavior happening in their workplace. If someone makes a sexist comment, and someone else finds it offensive, we call that discrimination, not "free speech." It is crucial that we understand pornography both as a violation of women's civil rights and as a form of discrimination, not an issue of free speech.

Many civil libertarians charge that the Dworkin/MacKinnon ordinance, as well as the logic in which it was grounded, would give the state power to restrict freedom of speech. In support of this argument they point to the Canadian Supreme Court's adoption of a censorship law (allegedly taken from the Dworkin/MacKinnon ordinance) that resulted in the banning of lesbian and feminist literature. This argument is patently flawed. Canada did not adopt the Dworkin/MacKinnon civil rights law against pornography. The Canadian law did not include the Dworkin/MacKinnon statutory definition of pornography, nor did Canada adopt any of the five civil causes of action that they proposed (coercion, assault, force, trafficking, defamation). In fact, both Dworkin and MacKinnon have spoken out against the Canadian ordinance because it empowers the state rather than the victims. Both Dworkin and MacKinnon believe that giving the state power to censor certain materials would do little to fight the injustices committed by the pornography industry. Again, the liberal argument against the ordinance is an example of an androcentric perspective on pornography because it prioritizes the speech of the male pornographers over the speech of the women and children used in pornography.

CONCLUSION

In general it is important for us as feminists to distinguish ourselves from any ideology or group dominated by male interests in struggles where justice for women is concerned. This includes the civil libertarian approach of "anything goes," as well as the approach of religious fundamentalist groups that seek to police female sexuality. Instead we must educate people about the reality of pornography and prostitution and, at the same time, maintain a commitment to developing solutions that empower survivors and hold their abusers accountable. Because I believe that the fight against the injustices committed by the porn industry must be led by the survivors and fueled by their supporters, I will conclude with the courageous words of survivor and activist Chris Grussendorf:

> I want to leave you with a few ideas on how to fight this mess. In some ways it's quite simple. I say to any perpetrators: Stop using us; stop raping us, stop beating us, stop murdering us in our very homes. You, all of you, must educate yourself and educate others, listen to survivors. Find out what the real issues are, behind the master's smokescreens. Include this information in your political groups; if you work at battered women's shelters, make sure the shelter accepts prostitutes who are trying to escape. If you are with a rape crisis center, make sure the staff is educated on pornography, prostitution, and ritual abuse. Create literature, speak against the pimps publicly as an organization and individuals. If you are a teacher, teach it. If you are a lawyer, represent women who have been hurt. If you are a therapist, accept women who cannot afford your fees, accept women on Medicare and M.A. Fight welfare cuts. Organize antipornography groups, join those already formed. Confront those who make jokes about whores and pornography. Take direct actions against porn stores. Organize around legal ordinances that would make it possible for women to sue their pimps for the harm caused. Fight new porn stores opening up. White people, organize against the racism involved in the zoning and on the pages of the pornography. Help women escape the pimps, hide us, lend us money to move or rent an apartment or get food. Help us get a job outside of the sexual abuse industry. Do not buy pornography. Do not patronize establishments or businesses that sell or promote pornography. Tell them why you are no longer doing business with them. Write letters to the editors, organize boycotts and demonstrations. Support survivors. Respect us. If you have money, give it to organizations that fight sexual violence. Volunteer at rape crisis centers and battered women's shelters. If you have access to media outlets, include this information. But most of all, men and nonprostitute women, work through your collective inability to see the women and girls in prostitution as women who are used and hurt and raped and battered beyond imagination.[18]

PART III
REWRITING THE RULES

9

ASKING FOR CONSENT IS SEXY

Andrew Abrams

In June 1992—the spring term of my junior year—the board at Antioch College passed an amendment to the school's sexual offense policy: a new clause about sexual consent. Basically, the consent clause says that if two people are going to have sex, then whoever initiates the sex needs to ask the other person if it's okay and the other person needs to say yes or no. That way, you'll know that you're not raping or sexually harassing someone; it's not enough to assume that you can tell nonverbally. Ideally, the policy kicks in when you first begin to touch.

Everyone outside the college always wants to know if I follow the policy step by step. They think that it's crazy because they've never tried it.

It makes sense. On TV and in the mass media, all you ever see is people who know each other for five minutes, look in each other's eyes, and then get it on. But the fact is that sex is just better when you talk.

Before the consent policy, I was infatuated with an artist named Leah. She lived downstairs in the dorm and was friends with my roommate. We started hanging out together in the second quarter. I sat down in her room one night and said, "I just want you to know—you probably know this already—but I am attracted to you." She didn't say a word. She wouldn't look at me, wouldn't respond to what I said. Somehow during my second year we became friends. She was very uncomfortable with sex, and so we would lie in bed and I'd ask her: "Is it all right if I kiss you?" "Can I put my hand on your stomach?" The progression was very slow. I asked her permission basically every step of the way. It seems like a lot of work, but it's sexy to ask permission to kiss a woman, and it's exciting to hear her say yes.

People say that Antioch is topsy-turvy: The men are beaten down and the women are on top. But I'm not submissive, I don't feel beaten down, and I've never felt like my life at Antioch was controlled by the agenda of women. The policy isn't asking me to do anything that I don't think I should be doing anyway.

The fall term of my second year was the quarter from hell. A student had died in a van accident, and in a community this small, when one person dies, it's traumatic. The next quarter a woman died of a brain aneurysm during a meeting in front of fifty people, and a friend of mine was killed in a car accident. There were also two student rapes reported on campus. That fall was easily the worst quarter I had as a student at Antioch.

Antioch has a tradition of holding community meetings to discuss campus issues. Around this time a new group, the Womyn of Antioch, showed up at one unannounced. About seventy-five people were there, sitting in a lecture-class auditorium. The Womyn walked in dressed in black, filing down the stairs to the front of the room. They had pieces of tape with the word "RAPED" written on them, and every three minutes they would put one on another woman's back. They explained that every three minutes a woman is raped, and they demanded a policy to deal with sexual offenses on campus. Soon after that they drafted a sexual offense policy and brought it to the administrative council at a hearing packed with student supporters. It became official in 1991. The thing to remember is that the SOP was brought about by students, and that a majority of students still support it.

At the cafeteria, in my friends' rooms, the question I kept on hearing from men was, "What if someone is unfairly accused?" Lots of men see it as a threat even to this day. But why would someone lie about being raped? I can't imagine that anyone would put themselves through all the emotional stress of the hearing process just to attack someone. Basically, you have nothing to worry about as long as you ask.

I think it's important to ask and to be asked in sexual situations, in order to feel comfortable with the person you are with, and to deal with issues about safer sex. Asking a woman if you can kiss her makes it easier to ask whether she has had high-risk partners, to talk about what being safe means to each other. It seems crazy to risk your life just because you're not comfortable talking about condoms. Also, men tend to be more assertive in sexual situations, and I think that the policy balances that out.

I never stayed in one relationship for a long time: That isn't unusual at Antioch. But after a series of sexual experiences—some of them very good ones—I started looking at that as a real problem. About a year ago a woman invited me back to her room. We were fooling around, and at what you might call the height of passion I realized this wasn't what I wanted. I said, "I'm sorry, this isn't comfortable for me." As a man, I'd been brought up to believe that I should be capable, ready, willing all of the time. But the policy made me realize that I had sexual choices—that it was okay sometimes to say, "Time out."

I've been in a relationship with a woman now for close to five months. I met Lorien playing volleyball: She's tall and she's a good athlete. We took Human Sexuality together, but we stayed friends for a year before we started going out. The first time Lorien and I kissed, we talked about the idea of becoming physically intimate for an hour beforehand. Finally she said, "So are we going to kiss or what?" I said, "I think you should kiss me." So she kissed my hand. Then I kissed her hand. She kissed my cheek and I kissed hers. . . .

That doesn't mean that every time we kiss each other we have a ten-minute discussion. You don't always stop when you're falling asleep together to ask, "May I kiss you good night?'" But if we're having sex, we talk about what we want and what feels good. I don't like rough sex and I hate hickeys; I like to be touched softly. But nobody's going to know that automatically. If you don't talk, then all you've got is guesswork. Go home and try it, see what happens. I bet you'll end up thanking me.

10

DEMANDS FROM THE WOMEN OF ANTIOCH

Kristine Herman

The women of Antioch, in response to the recent rapes on campus, demand that the following become Antioch College policy:

1. That a community member who is accused of rape shall immediately (within twenty-four hours of the report of rape) be removed from campus until guilt is assessed; and that if this person is determined to be guilty, that s/he shall be immediately and permanently removed from the Antioch community (a student must be expelled, an employee must be fired);

2. That the Dean of Students and/or the Advocate shall immediately inform the community that a rape has occurred; and that the rape survivor shall determine whether the name of the rapist and/or the name of the survivor shall be publicized;

3. That the rape survivor be informed of her/his rights; and informed of, supported with, her/his rights to prosecute;

4. That a support network be established for rape survivors that includes a new position, a woman Advocate who could act as the rape survivor's representative, and who would ensure that disciplinary measures against the rapist be carried out. This Advocate shall be given the power to enact the above disciplinary measures against said rapist;

5. That a one-credit PE self-defense course shall be offered each quarter;

6. That orientation shall incorporate rape education, rape awareness, and consent workshops for men and women;

7. That a permanent support group for survivors of rape and sexual assault be established in the counseling center.

If these demands are not met by November 13, 1990, we, the women of Antioch, will (1) inform the Antioch community of this lack of support for rape survivors; (2) distribute a (national) press release detailing Antioch College's lack of support for rape survivors and discussing the recent rapes on campus and the lack of effective disciplinary measures taken; and (3) hold a Day of Action wherein radical physical measures will be taken.

–Created 5 November 1990.

THE DEVELOPMENT OF THE ANTIOCH COLLEGE SEXUAL OFFENSE POLICY

This list of demands was formulated by women in the Antioch community after being outraged at administrative handling of two reported rapes on campus. There would be a policy and protocol established specific to sexual offense, even if it meant that some women would sacrifice credits, sleep, sanity, and their degrees.

It took enormous efforts on the part of many women at Antioch to get the Antioch Sexual Offense Policy implemented at last, a policy known nationally as radical, innovative, and, to some, extreme. The policy has been viewed as both paternalistic—for coddling women and treating them as inherent victims—and empowering for both men and women—because of its reliance on verbal consent. But only those of us who were there, saw it come together, understand its history, and lived under it truly know how important and monumental the policy is in the movement to prevent and fight sexual violence.

I entered Antioch College, a small liberal arts college located in Yellow Springs, Ohio, in 1990 at the age of seventeen. Antioch is known for its commitment to social justice and political activism. I began confronting my experience as a rape survivor in the context of the two reported rapes on campus and the early formulations of the Sexual Offense Policy. I nervously attended meetings and participated in the larger protests, but my attitude about the policy was that it was too harsh.

I arrived at college believing that rape was wrong . . . but if a woman was drinking, well, then things became a little ambiguous. After I was raped at the age of thirteen, I internalized the messages that tell us we are responsible and that you can't blame a guy for taking advantage of a situation if, after all, you asked for it. Instead of feeling angry, I felt guilt and embarrassment.

That fall of 1990 there were two reported rapes of students by students. In each incident the woman knew her perpetrator and reported the rape to the dean. At that time there existed only an ambiguous written policy addressing sexual harassment. The dean of students spoke with the perpetrators and made her decision as to what disciplinary measures would be taken if any.

One woman's perpetrator was removed from campus but remained enrolled. The other woman's perpetrator was not removed from campus.

This lax administrative response to these rapes enraged the women at Antioch and led to the list of demands that ended in the student-initiated Sexual Offense Policy. Emergency meetings at the Women's Center drew nightly crowds of over fifty women to discuss and strategize a response to the inadequate administrative response to rape. The meetings were emotional and volatile, as we found divisions among the women's community at Antioch. Some women thought that we should allow input from the men at Antioch; other women felt strongly that we had waited long enough and that support from men was welcomed but their input was not. In the end, men were not involved in the drafting of the original policy.

Over the course of a few crucial days political actions were staged to get the need for a Sexual Offense Policy on the college's official agenda. Over thirty women stood silently along the walls during a meeting of the Advisory Committee to the President: dressed in black, rape whistles hanging symbolically from their necks. This action successfully pressured the committee into putting The List on the committee agenda. Another action, intended to demonstrate the prevalence of rape and enlist the support of other students, took place at one of our weekly campus community meetings. Every six minutes a woman broke out crying as a piece of duct tape was slapped on her back with the word "RAPED" written across it, reflecting that every six minutes a woman is raped in the United States.

A group of fifteen third- and fourth-year women students, many of them friends of the survivors of the two on-campus rapes, wrote the first draft of the Antioch Sexual Offense Policy. Some were so dedicated that they sacrificed graduation because so much time and energy went into developing the policy.

The policy was intended to outline the protocol for addressing incidents of sexual offense on our campus, but it was obvious that to do so required defining what was and was not a sexual offense. The Antioch Sexual Offense Policy outlined six forms of sexual offense: rape (any nonconsensual penetration of the vagina or anus, nonconsensual fellatio or cunnilingus); sexual assault (nonconsensual sexual conduct exclusive of that included in the definition of rape, but including attempted penetrations, attempted fellatio, or attempted cunnilingus); sexual imposition (nonconsensual sexual contact that includes the touching of thighs, genitals, buttocks, the pubic region, or the breast/chest area); insistent/persistent sexual harassment (insistent/persistent emotional, mental, or verbal intimidation or abuse found to be sexually threatening or offensive); nondisclosure of a known positive HIV status or other known sexually transmitted disease. The Sexual Offense Policy requires that all sexual conduct and contact with an Antioch community member must be consensual.

The policy defines consent as "the act of willingly and verbally agreeing to engage in specific sexual act of conduct." It requires consent by all parties in a sexual encounter and states that "obtaining consent is an ongoing process in any sexual interaction. Verbal consent should be given with each new level of physical and/or sexual contact in any given interaction." The media latched on to this controversial element. Camille Paglia found the policy absurd "as if sex occurs on the verbal realm," a belief that is dangerously reminiscent of outdated notions of what sex should be like in an age that sees AIDS as the number-one killer of people between the ages of twenty-three to forty-four years of age, and when one in four college women are victims of rape or attempted rape.

The bulk of the policy is devoted to the procedures available when a sexual offense has occurred. A gradated list of remedies is included in the policy; for instance, an individual found to have committed rape according to the policy's definition is to be expelled immediately, whereas someone found to have been in violation of the policy's definition of sexual imposition may receive suspension or be required to undergo some sort of educational/counseling program.

Equally important in the policy is the element of antirape education, including mandatory sexual consent workshops for all students, and self-defense courses. The Sexual Offense Prevention and Survivors' Advocacy Program features year-round antirape education, residence advisor training, and group and individual counseling services for survivors of rape and sexual abuse.

The Sexual Offense Prevention and Survivors' Advocacy Program was beginning to develop by my second year at college. I came to know other survivors, hear their stories, and I grew angry. I was seeing patterns of violence, not the sporadic, unrelated occurrences of rape by a stranger in the bushes at knife point. My involvement as an advocate for survivors of rape began and grew; I became a residence advisor for a dorm of first-year women and became active in community politics. My opinion about the policy changed drastically, and my job as a residence advisor convinced me that anything short of verbal and willing consent could result in a harmful "sexual experience." In this role I witnessed several first-year students, many of them seventeen years old, assaulted and raped, often under the influence of alcohol. These women came to me, slept in my room because of nightmares or fear of being alone, and asked for support. They needed to be told of their right not to be victimized, regardless of how much they had to drink or whether or not they were flirting, brought someone back to their room, or made the first move to kiss.

In light of these experiences I became convinced that the important work had to begin with prevention—not the standard "teaching women how not to fall prey to sexual victimization," as if the responsibility once again lies with the victim, but addressing the potential perpetrators and circumstances that lend themselves to sexual violence. The emphasis on consent in the policy attempts to do just that, by requiring people to obtain verbal consent for every level of a sexual interaction, and by trying to eliminate the gray areas that exist when people make silent assumptions about what their partner wants, then act without consulting their partner.

Undoubtedly the Antioch Sexual Offense Policy validated all women's and men's rights not to be sexually victimized. By requiring all persons to seek verbal consent, permission, for each new level of a sexual interaction, responsibility is shifted to the initiator of sexual contact. I felt tremendously empowered living on a campus where I was supposed to be asked before being touched, where my voice was required to be heard. Silence does not equal consent. As a survivor struggling to regain a healthy sense of sexuality, it was much easier for me to say no once I was asked than for me to stop nonconsensual advances once someone has already violated my boundaries. For many survivors it is extremely difficult to voice an objection when it is apparent that someone is just moving ahead physically. A freezing phenomenon occurs, wherein we shut down and just wait for it to be over because it has proved either futile to protest a sexual offense in our pasts, or too scary a situation. This is particularly true when there is a noticeable difference in size and physical stature between the survivor and the person we are with. Being asked gives us the space as well as the confidence that our opinion will be respected this time, that this person wants to make sure that we want to move forward physically too.

In June of 1992 the final revision of the Antioch Sexual Offense Policy was passed by the Advisory Committee to the President and approved by the University Board of Directors. The next two entering classes attended mandatory workshops designed to educate students about the policy and its definition of "consent," and to address the importance of, and new students' concerns about, living under the policy. As a result of these workshops and ongoing campus dialogue, the idea of verbal consent was no longer so shocking. The controversy around the Sexual Offense Policy had died down.

In late 1993 a reporter for the *San Francisco Examiner* mentioned the Antioch Sexual Offense Policy in a story about a California campus rape. Immediately following the *Examiner* article, Jane Gross of the *New York Times* did an in-depth article about the Antioch policy, which led to the AP newswire running the story worldwide; and so began the media explosion of 1993. During the 1993-94 academic year, Antioch received visits from, and provided interviews for, hundreds of national and international publications and radio and television programs.

By this point I was working in antirape education in several capacities: I facilitated sexual consent workshops; consulted with the police department regarding their sexual assault protocol; served as an advocate for survivors of sexual offense on campus; and worked as liaison to the Sexual Offense Prevention and Survivors' Advocacy Program for the Student Housing Office. As a result I was asked by the college administration to be a media spokesperson. I participated in panels at nearly a dozen universities and appeared on numerous television and radio programs and talk shows.

The policy, as it received global recognition and attention from figures such as Rush Limbaugh, Katie Roiphe, Camille Paglia, and Doctor Ruth, was criticized on a number of levels, many of which were riddled with misinformation about its contents. Instead of the policy's being viewed as an instrument by which we hoped to curtail the incidence of sexual violence on our campus, we were seen as legislating sex.

MEDIA INTERPRETATION AND RESPONSE FROM OUTSIDE

The media, within their own limited scope and understanding of the policy, defined it in terms of its effects on sexual interactions according to gender roles only. This artificial polarization of men's and women's interests was not based in the reality of the Antioch policy but was an oversimplification of the issue of sexual violence on college campuses. Media coverage framed the Antioch policy in a way that divided men and women into groups with conflicting and competing interests, instead of portraying a policy that created a cohesive community devoted to eliminating the frequency with which sexual violence is perpetrated on college campuses.

A widely ignored aspect of the policy was its intentionally non-gender-specific language. The Antioch Policy recognizes, acknowledges, and validates that men and women can be raped, and that both men and women can be perpetrators of sexual violence. The policy strives to be non-heterosexist and is inclusive of all sexual orientations. To describe the policy as "requiring men to ask women at each level of a sexual interaction" excludes a large portion of our campus and society who are gay, lesbian, and bisexual, and does not acknowledge that sexual violence occurs between people of the same sex.

The policy has also been criticized under the notion that it limits the spontaneity of romantic sexual relations and unrealistically burdens students to talk about sex. Anyone who is currently sexually active must be aware of the dangers of STD/HIV/AIDS infection and the necessity to talk about safer sex. This alone makes the idea of nonverbal sex both outdated and dangerous. Communication is a vital component of sexual interaction. When verbal communication is not a central part of a sexual encounter, false assumptions occur that can result in a sexual assault.

The media have contributed to a backlash against women and the antirape movement by misdirecting the issues. Instead of accurately gathering data on the incidence of rape on college campuses, the media have responded with a different slant to the debates about rape, prevention, and sexual relations. An example of the minimization of the problem of rape can be found in Dr. Ruth Westheimer's comments about the Antioch Sexual Offense Policy on *Eye to Eye with Connie Chung*. Dr. Ruth chose to focus not on rape or sexual assault at all, but instead on the way the policy might affect a man's ability to maintain an erection if he is expected to be verbal during a sexual encounter. This clearly demonstrates the priorities of mainstream media when addressing a movement focused on the prevention of sexual violence.

Part of the fascination about the policy was that it actually redefined rape, and in doing so threatened the ways in which we have all been socialized to conceptualize sex. In the context of the Clarence Thomas hearings and the Lorena Bobbitt story, discussions about sexual abuse, harassment, and rape were occurring nationally. The Antioch Sexual Offense Policy contributed to this debate.

The implications of the necessity for verbal consent are vast in that we, culturally, must look at the mechanisms by which people are socialized and the messages that are sent regarding sexual relations. The *Connie Chung* segment showed a clip from the movie classic *Gone with the Wind*, where Rhett Butler whisks Scarlett O'Hara into his arms as she struggles to get away, beating on him as he carries her up the stairs to their bedroom. The next day she is happy and giddy, implying that she really wanted it or at least enjoyed it. We used to view this—the woman saying no when she really means yes—as a romantic scene; many still do. By Antioch definitions, and considering many of the shifting attitudes about rape, this could now be viewed as a rape scene.

The media's focus on the Antioch Sexual Offense Policy diverted a strong movement of antirape education toward addressing issues of old-fashioned notions about spontaneity, what it means to be romantic, and how the burden of verbal consent will affect men. This is not surprising, given that acceptance of Antioch's definitions of sexual violence, and the expectation of consent, forces us all to reexamine our own sexual histories. Many of us find that we have ambiguous and uncomfortable pasts—

we may have done something that could now be called sexual assault, or we may have experienced a sexual assault but did not call it so at the time.

Challenging "traditional" beliefs about sex has resulted in societal defensiveness and negative reactions to documents such as the Antioch policy, and other instances whereby the status quo is shaken. Another example of this type of response can be seen in the battle against homophobia. Some major corporations are finally beginning to acknowledge domestic partnerships, while some states are responding by passing discriminatory homophobic legislature. The struggles of all women, people of color, and gay, lesbian, and bisexual people overlap in that they threaten to disrupt the dominant paradigm.

Though the general public missed the urgent need for the policy, Antioch College received an incredible response from other universities, with over two hundred requested copies of the policy during the fall of 1993 alone.

POSTGRADUATION IMPACT

In my own life, as a second-year law student with a master's in social work, my work in the antirape movement continues. The Antioch Sexual Offense Policy affected my views on sex and power dynamics in sexual situations. Women and men are not on completely equal ground sexually; many women have internalized messages that tell us we owe sex if a man has spent a lot of money on us, or if we have allowed a situation to go to a certain point. A first-year man in a sexual consent workshop at Antioch once expressed what many men fear about the policy when he said, "But if I have to ask for what I want, I won't get it."

The Antioch Sexual Offense Policy introduced the importance of consent in sexual interactions. It aims to resocialize students to be verbal with each other in sexual situations in order to eliminate different perceptions of the same experience. The efforts of the original drafters of the policy, as well as all of us who participated, and the resulting document are something to be extremely proud of. For many the Antioch Sexual Offense Policy is the embodiment of the principle that the personal is political.

With the issue of sexual violence introduced into the public arena, we must now look at the directions that need to be explored to further decrease the prevalence of rape and sexual assaults on college campuses. Anthropologists such as Peggy Sanday, and feminist theorists such as bell hooks, have begun writing about a "rape culture." Some people consider this to be the third wave of the antirape movement, one that aggressively addresses rape, domestic violence, and sexual harassment in a new light, armed with social science research, statistics, and personal stories. What we have learned from the Antioch Sexual Offense Policy and from the efforts of students on campuses all over the United States is that we are involved in a process of learning from each other strategies, ideas, and tools to combat sexual violence on an interpersonal, campus, societal, national, and international level.

11

THE ANTIRAPE RULES

Jason Schultz

"This will probably offend you," she said, looking down for a moment, "but I need to ask you something." She clenched her hands together in a small ball as she leaned back against the headboard of my bed and took a deep breath. "I need to know why it doesn't bother you." Her eyes reopened and looked to me for answers. My lips pursed and separated.

I thought back to other conversations I'd had like this one. Six years back. You'd think that after half a decade of educating, counseling, and supporting survivors that you've heard everything—every story, every question, every nightmare. But this was a new one. "Well," I said, "it doesn't bother me because I didn't do it. And because letting it bother me would make us both victims of his attack. It doesn't mean I don't hate him. It means I know the difference between hating him and hating you because of what he did to you."

She stared back at me. "You probably don't believe that," I continued. "But it's the truth and it's the same answer I'm going to give you every time you ask. It may not help you feel any better, and that's fine because I'm not saying it to make you feel better. You're going to have to figure out how to believe me. It's my job to understand how you feel and yours to believe that I care."

Ever since I became a rape educator in 1990, I've been acutely aware of the impact of violence against women in my life. On an external level, I now worry much more about my female friends and family. I always try to offer them a ride or walk home. I always wait for them to get inside safely before driving away. I give way to women on the street at night. I make sure other men know I'm watching when they make their moves.

On a more personal level, I've felt the pain of being mistrusted for no good reason, the frustration when past hurts affect present attempts at intimacy, the disbelief when cycles of violence repeat themselves. I've felt the emotional impact of rape in my relationships, my friendships, even my family.

THE CASCADE EFFECT

The first time is always the worst. That cold, hard realization of the effect of rape. The first woman ever to tell me she was raped was a good friend of mine in college. We were both in our first semester at Duke University, giddy with excitement over the future and full of arrogance about our newfound college independence. "No more curfews!" we would shout, fantasizing about all the rules we would break and trouble we would cause.

Eight weeks into the semester, there was a knock at my door. I opened it and in she collapsed, sobbing. She crawled over to my futon and curled up in a shell. "What's wrong?" I asked. "He raped me tonight" was all she could murmur.

In the following months I learned what rape does to friendship. The anger, the sadness, the hurt—it all came flooding out. I tried every method of support I could think of—the strong shoulder to cry on, the overprotective brother, the vindictive vigilante. Nothing changed how she felt. "How can I trust you?" she would blurt out in private. "You could be just like him."

"You could be just like him." Those words echo in my ears every time I talk to men about rape and every time I hear them talk about it. "But I'm not a rapist!" they'll say—all the words that I once said myself. They're right, of course. They're always right. But that's the horror of rape. It doesn't change anything. It doesn't make a difference to a survivor that you're not a rapist. They simply don't care.

I joined the Duke Acquaintance Rape Education Program. I felt stronger, more in control. I learned what caused rape: patriarchy, socialization, cycles of violence. I also felt in control of my own emotions. I knew that when survivors talked to me that it wasn't my fault—I hadn't caused their pain. I was helping them. I was part of the solution, not part of the problem.

But they just kept on coming. A friend . . . a classmate . . . a fellow editor at the student newspaper. Someone I met at a party. Someone I hooked up with after a basketball game. My senior-year girlfriend. Her roommate. The numbers started to build and so did the horrors. Child sexual abuse, STDs, gang rape. I started to keep count. The Number kept growing. All the time I kept thinking and saying to myself, "It's okay. You're helping them. You're making a difference."

And I was. I received countless thank-yous from people I helped and from others as well—faculty in the women's studies department, campus administrators who had their hands tied by the legal department. But no matter how hard I tried to help, no matter how much I listened, The Number kept growing. Sisters, old friends from high school, the cab driver on my way home for Thanksgiving. How? I would wonder. How can we live in a world where every woman I meet has been tortured in this way?

In some ways it was a perverse high. I was the savior. I was the good guy. I heard their stories and believed them. If only more men could be like me, I would think to myself, there wouldn't be all this hurt and madness.

December of my senior year, I lost it. I called up a close friend of mine—someone with whom I had shared much of my adolescent and adult life, someone with whom I could break the rules. "I need to ask you a question," I prefaced. "It's going to sound weird and might possibly embarrass you, but I need to know if you've ever been raped." I went on for a minute explaining what was happening to me, how all the violence in the lives of the people around me was overwhelming my sense of hope.

"Jason," she interrupted. "I have *never* been raped. By anyone. Anytime in my life." My stomach relaxed and the air slowly left my chest in relief. "Thank you," I said. "Thank you so much."

I have no idea how one learns to live with being raped. I can't even imagine what it means to carry that around with you. But I know what it means to live with and care for people who have been raped. I know the frantic phone calls, the frustration of starting over, the joy of witnessing recovery. I know that it's hard to be a man and care for women who've been raped. I know how not to blame myself and not to blame them.

As part of the national antirape movement, I've spent the last eight years talking about sexual violence, mostly on college campuses and mostly to men. Looking back on that now, I realize that we don't need to simply educate men on how not to rape. The reality is that most of us don't rape women. But we do need to educate all men on how to live with, love, care for, and communicate with survivors. We need to share the rules we've learned.

THE ANTIRAPE RULES

When I first heard of *The Rules*, I laughed. *The Rules: Time-Tested Secrets for Capturing the Heart of Mr. Right* was a surprising best-seller self-help book that gave women traditional and prefeminist guidelines for snagging men. Encouraging mind games, *The Rules* include such tidbits as "Let him take the lead," and "Don't call him." What a ridiculous idea, I thought. How could anyone imagine finding the key to a successful relationship in this semblance of pop-cult grocery-store-line pocket trash? I figured the hype about the book was simply the logical outcome of media conspiracy, lack of education, and yet another market built on women's insecurities. Yet as many of us do, I forced myself to read *The Rules*, just to be sure.

I pretty much found what I suspected. Manipulative psychobabble and social conditioning. There were, of course, a few feminist intonations about the "modern girl" and the need to be independent in one's life. But these were couched in the frantic language of the man-crazy woman and the "horror" of being unmarried.

So why was this book selling? I wandered about, asking various female friends. They gave me three reasons: (1) Despite all our good wishes about bicycles and fish, many women *are* frustrated with their attempts to find the right guy; (2) despite the stereotypes, every woman I talked to knew at least one man whom they thought would respond to *The Rules;* and (3) even if you completely disagree with *The Rules*, you still want to read it as a gut check—just to make sure you're still not doing anything wrong.

So while the content of *The Rules* disturbed me, the brilliance of the approach to writing it intrigued me. Then it clicked. Rules . . . that's what men need—not on how to find the right woman (well, maybe, but that's more like a book instead of an essay), but for handling the issue of rape—a topic that makes men about as neurotic as women are made about marriage.

WHERE TO START

That being said, starting to learn about rape is almost always weird for men. There are so many subtle moments and brief insights that we all need to learn. But every journey starts with a single step, or four in this case. Below are several experiences and "rules" that have helped me support survivors of sexual assault in my own life. I offer them up in the hope that we all will start to think about what "rules" truly help us care for, and about, each other.

Rule #1: Believe the Hype

As much of a cliché as it sounds, you probably know someone who has been raped. They may have told you by now or not, but sooner or later they will. When they do, they will most likely disclose information to you in doses. Maybe just the fact that it happened. Maybe the story leading up to it. They may even disguise it as bad sex or a drunken blur. Whatever they do when they tell you, there's one rule to follow: Don't reject them.

Rape centers on control. After someone is assaulted, it often takes great effort to regain control of her or his life. One of the quickest ways to do this is to control who knows about the rape and what they know about it. That is why it is often difficult to get survivors to talk to the police or a doctor or even answer their phone. There are many other reasons why survivors don't tell anyone, such as fear of retaliation, desire to put it behind them and move on, and so on. But the need to control who knows about the rape is often a primary concern. (Hence the need for rape crisis centers to maintain confidentiality.)

When a survivor tells you about her rape, she is beginning to trust again. She is reaching out to you with one of the few parts of her life that she does feel control over. When she does this, she generally wants two things: (1) to have you believe her, and (2) to have you accept her. Often a survivor's worst fear is that telling someone about the rape will trigger another attack or betrayal, this time a verbal or emotional one.

Marilyn Van Derbur Atler, an incest survivor and former Miss America, once talked at Duke about disclosing her survivor status on an airplane. She was sitting next to a businessman, reading a magazine, when he struck up a conversation with her. At one point in the conversation, he mentioned his occupation. He then proceeded to ask her what she did. "I talk about how I survived child sexual abuse," she replied. As you can imagine, the man was struck silent by her comment.

After taking a moment to compose himself, though, he asked a question I suspect most men think about when a survivor discloses to them: "How should one respond to that?" he asked her.

Ms. Van Derbur Atler calmly looked back at him and said, "You say 'I'm very sorry that happened to you.' And you mean it."

Rule #2: Don't Expect Her to Change, or Try to Change Her

The knock on the door had to be Catherine. I opened it and it was. "Surprise!" she yelled, and marched into the room with not one man in tow, but two—one on each arm. "This is Kevin; and this is Dave! Aren't they cute?" she breathed into my face, fresh and full of keg beer. My heart sank.

"Yeah, I suppose they are. Don't you think you're . . . um . . . a little out of it to be hooking up with two guys?" I asked, regretting each word as I spoke.

"Fuck you," she retorted. "I'm a big girl. I'm in control. I'll do whatever I want." She turned around, pushed the two men out the door, and slammed it behind her.

The next afternoon she came to apologize. We both knew she was having a tough time dating again after the rape, especially on campus. She admitted that last night she had been scared of being alone with her dates and said that she came by my room with the hope that I would intervene. I told her that I can't intervene—that part of being supportive is following her lead and letting her run her own life again, not simply transferring control to me.

I asked her why she chose Kevin and Dave. "They don't particularly seem your type," I said, still trying to tread cautiously. Catherine had always gone for more introverted guys as long as I had known her. She started to list a number of excuses: She was turning over a new leaf. They liked her, so why not? She didn't care who she hooked up with anymore.

Finally, she told the truth. "I knew what they wanted," she said. "I knew they wanted sex, so I knew there wouldn't be any surprises. No rape. No force. No betrayal. I knew that if I took the initiative with them that I would be in control and never out of it. I wouldn't have to be afraid that it would happen again." She leaned against the wall, picking off pieces of paint with her fingernails. "I just can't take that risk anymore."

I sat at my desk. I had no idea what to say. "You'll figure it out," I responded.

Watching survivors make dumb decisions and take horrible risks is probably the most frustrating part of being there for them. When Catherine left with the two men, it took every ounce of self-control not to run after her and make sure she wasn't going to be attacked again. But the number-one rule with survivors is to let them forge their own recovery. Catherine also later admitted that she had been testing me in some ways by bringing the men home—to see if I would trust her. I've learned time and time again to be honest with survivors about how I feel—to express disappointment, concern, anger, fear—but ultimately to leave the decisions up to them. Right or wrong, they will need you as a friend the next day more than a savior the night before.

Rule #3: Ask for It

"I've been thinking about kissing you all night," I said.

"Really?" she asked whimsically, testing the waters a bit more.

"And then touching you. All over."

The wind whistled past our ears as we headed back to the hotel. A sudden silence arose between us. "I hope that's okay," I added.

"Sure," she said. "I just . . . well—no one's ever said that to me so far in advance before." She blushed a little. "Usually we're already drunk and naked and at least somewhere near the bed."

I laughed. "Well, I figured it'd be better to make my intentions clear before we got in the elevator. That way you could decide what floor to get off on . . . so to speak." We laughed again, and I felt the tension ease a bit. I opened the outside door for her and we scurried into the lobby.

"So it's really my choice?"

"Yeah," I replied.

She reached out with one hand for the elevator button, then reached with the other for my arm. She smiled as we waited for the doors to open.

Much has been said about supposed politically correct sex: that asking for consent is unsexy, that talking ruins the mood. And for the most part, I agree—if that's all you do. In the midst of confronting violence, it's easy to forget about the fact that being sexy is important to both men and women, to survivors and nonsurvivors alike. Being too clinical, too cautious, or even too earnest often clashes with our fantasies about what turns us on. And no matter how many rape awareness workshops we attend or late-night dorm conversations we have, antiseptic sexual conversations will rarely hit the right spot.

Being sexy means knowing what you really want. If you truly know what you want with the other person, you'll know how to tell them you want it. And you'll also know when they want it too. Spend some time thinking about it. Fantasize about what you think will make you both happy, then take a deep breath and tell her. Style, nuance, attitude, and mystery are all still important elements of seduction. Don't lose them. Just use them in the way they were meant to be used: to elicit true desire and temptation.

Rule #4: Sometimes the Tough Thing Is the Right Thing

I stayed up very late last night, trying to clean the kitchen. It's something I do when I'm nervous—cleaning. It had been a pretty rough day, with the trip to the hospital and all. I wondered what Laura was doing right now. I thought about the hug she had given me right before they took her to her room. "Don't disappear on me," she said, as if I were the one leaving the rest of the world behind. "Remember, I know where you live," she added as the duty nurse searched her suitcase. I nodded, turned, and walked down the hallway, hands in my pockets, eyes on the red carpet beneath my feet.

The counter was a mess. I emptied the wine bottle from the night before and dumped the ashtray. We'd decided that they probably wouldn't allow her to drink or smoke once she was inside, so we took advantage of her last night to binge a little. At one point I caught her staring at me from her seat near the windowsill, bright blue eyes flickering as she exhaled away from my face. "It really means a lot to me," she said softly, turning back toward the light. "I really don't know who else I can trust."

That was exactly twenty-four hours ago. Now she was tucked away inside the psych ward on the other side of town and I was home, loading dishes into the dishwasher. I felt a tremendous sense of relief, mixed with sadness from the separation. I thought about calling the hallway phone number she had left me. I let the thought pass. I took her last cigarette from off the counter and grabbed a match.

Helping survivors recover can hurt. Many of the men I've talked to over the years have told me about "secondary syndrome"—a condition whereby people who are close to a victim of violence begin to experience similar symptoms of post-traumatic stress disorder—almost like emotional osmosis. Lack of sleep, difficulty concentrating, and depression are a few of the common experiences.

But beyond secondary syndrome is an even greater issue for men who support survivors—our own general health and happiness. No matter how giving you are, no matter how gentle you want to be, there are limits to what any one person can offer to another. Anger, depression, and burnout can creep up on us, and before we know it, we're of little use to them or to ourselves.

The bottom line is always to know your limits and make sure you have support for yourself. Find friends to talk to about the situation. Call a help line whenever you feel like it. Take time away from the crisis. Checking Laura into the psychiatric hospital was a difficult decision for both her and me, but we agreed that she needed more help than I could ever give her. Recognizing that limit not only saved her life, but saved our friendship as well. In the end, we realized we wanted both to survive.

PART IV
REVOLUTIONARY CHANGES

12

PEER EDUCATION: STUDENT ACTIVISM OF THE NINETIES

Jodi Gold and Susan Villari

There is a GAP for every generation
Instastyle, instaworn, instantique
History is born in the jeans,
so stop your search
for yourselves
your rallying cry
your Vietnam
Ask the boomers,
and they tell us:
They know from real pain,
activism that meant something
the organic variety
(yet, strangely, with no half life)
Ask any boomer:
Style, Movements, Moments
don't just erupt like they did
in the Wonder Years . . .
                —Mike Fisch, "Don't Call Me Twentysomething"

PEER EDUCATION: THE QUIET REVOLUTION

It was a fairly typical day. Students who volunteered as peer educators were buzzing in and out of the health education office preparing for workshops, responding to the campus media, or seeking advice about a troubled friend. In our usual style, Susan, the director of the office, I, and other members of STAAR, Students Together Against Acquaintance Rape, were frantically preparing for a campus fraternity program scheduled that evening. As we debated what educational exercises to use to facilitate a good group discussion, Susan proudly turned to us and exclaimed "You do amazing social change work!" Never having associated my work in STAAR with social change, I was perplexed by this statement. Hoping to clarify her misperception, I responded, "No, Susan, it's just peer education."

That simple exchange of words in 1992 became a catalyst for many future discussions between Susan and me about nineties-style student activism. As an institutionally funded volunteer service program, how could peer education be viewed as student activism? Yet in our work as educators, we advocated systemic changes—even revolutionary changes—in the way our society views the interconnection between gender, power, sex, and violence. If our primary goal in STAAR was the prevention of rape, could this be accomplished without social change? Believing ourselves to be rational and intelligent beings, we shunned the convenient belief that violence against women is biologically driven by male hormones or just a series of random isolated events. Equally intolerable was viewing acquaintance rape as a matter of miscommunication or regrettable sex. Instead, our collective sensibilities suggested we hold women and men accountable for their behavior without imposing restrictive social and sexual curfews on women. In promoting this viewpoint, we in STAAR believed we could systematically end our community's tolerance of sexual violence. Ultimately, short of locking women away and castrating men, ending sexual violence would mean social change work.

Social change efforts on campuses today are often overlooked or misrepresented by the general public because twenty-somethings have developed their own style of activism, a style that on the surface sharply contradicts the popular image of a student activist. Often working within university systems, concerned students advocate social change through community service projects and peer education programs. Perceived as less confrontational, peer education is rarely associated with student activism. Yet it is the main strategy used today in the campus movement to end sexual violence. Believing that each generation contributes to social and political change in its own unique way, we propose that peer education be viewed as a powerful form of student activism and a vehicle for social change as we move into the next century.

Peer education is defined as "instruction or guidance from equals."[1] It is powerful because people are more likely to hear and personalize a message if it is perceived as coming from someone with a similar age or lifestyle. Though not new, this method is widely used to confront controversial health and social issues defining this generation, such as HIV/AIDS, multiculturalism, and violence.

The 80 million Americans born between 1961 and 1981 have been cynically referred to as "Generation X."[2] Fueled by media images, twenty-somethings are stereotyped as apathetic, apolitical slackers who are more content surfing cable and the Internet than changing the world. But according to Arthur Levine, president of the Teacher's College at Columbia University, the reality is that today's college students are "the most socially active generation since the late 1930s."[3] Conducting an extensive study with Jeanette S. Cureton from 1992 to 1997, he found that two out of three undergraduates were involved in volunteer activities.[4] In our national study of university response to sexual assault, we found that approximately 50 percent of universities provide sexual assault peer education workshops.[5] Despite extensive training, only a handful of these students receive academic or monetary compensation; the overwhelming majority of students simply donate their time. Since 1991 two national student organizations have been founded: SpeakOut: The North American Student Coalition against Campus Sexual Violence, and CCOAR: Coalition of Campuses Organizing against Rape. SpeakOut has sponsored fifteen conferences since 1992, whereas CCOAR has maintained an active national network committed to advocacy and resource development for programs in jeopardy. And yet, in spite of this level of national organizing, many active students are reluctant to view their work as social change.

ACTIVISM IS FOR HIPPIES AND SIXTIES LEFTOVERS

We discovered that many college students define activism based on distorted images of the protests against the Vietnam War, and the civil rights movement. Perceptions of activism have been significantly influenced by vivid media clips of the Berkeley Free Speech Movement, the 1963 March on Washington led by Rev. Martin Luther King, and numerous marches on the Pentagon to protest the war in Vietnam. There is a sense that if you are not Tom Hayden, Martin Luther King, or Gloria Steinem, you are not worthy of such a grand title as "activist." Author and scholar Paul Loeb aptly describes this phenomenon in his book *Generation at the Crossroads: Apathy and Action on the American Campus:*

> That period [the sixties] could be viewed as a model of understanding how ordinary citizens—especially students—worked to end segregation, stop a dubious war, and further democratize this nation. Instead, American culture has focused mainly on its caricatures—ragged crazies spitting on soldiers.[6]

The students we interviewed contribute significant time and energy to the campus movement, yet they still do not feel deserving of the term "activist." Diana Orino, a student from the University of Massachusetts

Everywomen's Center, explained her reluctance: "I don't consider myself 'active' enough to call myself an activist. I fear the responsibility that I would feel if I identified with that term."[7] It seems we are playing the childhood game "Telephone" or "Whisper Down the Lane" when we relay images of activism from one generation to the next. Like the game, the information has become distorted and now appears to be out of reach to an entire generation.

The Random House dictionary defines activism as "the doctrine or practice of vigorous action or involvement as a means of achieving political goals." Working to end sexual violence involves asking tough questions about how women and men relate to each other, how we use power, and how we have sex. Inevitably, this moves sex out of the "bedroom" and into a very public, political domain. In this context activism involves the process of challenging cultural or legal norms that contribute to or sustain sexual violence.

Prior to the nineties anyone who participated in this type of social change work probably would have identified with the terms "feminist" or "activist" or both. Today thousands of students are working to end sexual violence, yet many reject the terms most associated with gender equality and social change—"feminism" and "activism." More often they are comfortable with the term "educator." A peer educator from the University of California at Irvine comments, "I never thought of myself as an activist because it connotes a radical with weird ideas. I do think of myself as educating my peers and fostering change through the rational exchange of ideas." Often students recognize the negative stereotypes of activism on campus and sometimes consciously choose to define themselves as educators in order to appear more accessible to other students and administrators.[8]

COMING OUT OF THE CLOSET WITH FEMINIST ACTIVISM

If the concept of social change and the term "activism" are not controversial enough, throw in the label of "feminism"—which may be the most misunderstood political term in America. Student educators committed to rape prevention have adopted, consciously or not, a radical feminist approach to sexual violence. The word "radical" means "root," and the radical feminist analysis of rape requires eliminating—not simply reforming—the root causes of rape. Radical feminists of the sixties demanded not only stricter rape laws but a complete change in the way that society viewed the causes of rape. Although educator-activists are willing to tackle the hotly debated issues of sex, speech, power, and violence, one-fourth of the campus movement is still reluctant to evoke the feminist label. Ironically, these same students, by virtue of their educational work, are slowly chipping away at the foundations of our rape-supportive culture—a long-held feminist goal.

Although all women and men benefit from the gains made by the feminist movement, a recent Gallup poll found that only 33 percent of women identify as feminists.[9] Barbara Findlen, executive editor of *Ms.* magazine and of the book *Listen Up: Voices from the Next Feminist Generation,* describes the status of young feminists:

> Young feminists are constantly told that we don't exist. It's a refrain heard from older feminists as well as the popular media: Young women don't consider themselves feminists. Actually, a lot of us do. And many more of us have integrated feminist values into our lives, whether or not we choose to use the label "feminist." This is an important barometer of the impact of feminism, since feminism is a movement for social change—not an organization doing a membership drive.[10]

She adds that what is often described as "movement infighting," stems from the fact that not all young feminists are alike. A constant reevaluation of our identity and goals comes from an "honest assessment of our differences as each of us defines her place and role in feminism."[11] Embracing feminism involves making a commitment to political action and learning new tools for social change. Anastasia Higginbotham, a radical young feminist, describes the tools she has obtained through feminism:

> I know new kinds of words now. Words like "revolution," "equality," "dignity," "reproductive freedom." I've mistressed phrases like "Subvert the Patriarchy," "Run with the Wolves," and "Take Back the Night." The one word all phallocrats most fear, I wear like a badge of honor, my pride, my work, my glowing, spiked tiara. That word is "feminist."[12]

Label-phobia is dangerous when it prevents us from taking credit for our generation's significant contributions to social change. We can keep our own unique identity while also embracing the powerful terms from previous social movements. We often hear the defense from educators that if they call themselves feminists, then they will be attacked for their beliefs. "Coming out" as a feminist activist and proudly wearing the label can be a frightening process. A shift of perspective on sexual violence, where the analysis moves away from the idea that rape is a random act and toward an understanding that rape culture creates rape, is inevitably politicizing. Andrea Dworkin in her landmark 1974 book *Women Hating* describes the power of an activist, feminist consciousness:

> The fact is that consciousness, once experienced, cannot be denied. Once women experienced themselves as activists and began to understand the reality and meaning of oppression, they began to articulate a politically conscious feminism.[13]

Finally, embracing feminism unites the anti–sexual violence educator-activist to all men and women advocating equality.

PLAYING GOOD COP/BAD COP

Whether they choose to identify as feminists or activists, many students are working for social change on their college campuses. Although we have developed our own model of community service and collaboration, students in the anti-sexual-violence movement and other student movements recognize the importance of a good old-fashioned protest or rally. Current student activism passes the test—even by the sixties standards of demonstration and protests, with the only major distinction being the presence of laptops and cell phones.[14] Forty percent of all first-year college students participated in some form of politically organized demonstration during 1994—more than double the amount demonstrating during the sixties even at the height of the Vietnam War and civil rights movement.[15] In our study of 466 universities, we found that one-third had organized Take Back the Night marches—student-sponsored marches where women (and sometimes men) walk through their campus and/or community at night to symbolize their inherent right to walk the streets free of male violence and without the need to rely on male protection.[16] In 1993 Women against Rape at Arizona State University took to the streets when charges of acquaintance rape were dropped against a basketball player. Members were arrested when they outlined their bodies on the sidewalks with chalk and wrote slogans such as "Rape is not a sport."[17] On April 9, 1995, the National Organization for Women (NOW) sponsored the National Rally for Women's Lives, protesting violence against women. The rally attracted over two hundred thousand people, mostly students, who protested all forms of violence. This rally also housed the first national showing of the Clothesline Project: a display of six thousand T-shirts made by survivors of violence and hung from clotheslines in front of the Capitol building as a living memorial and monument to the epidemic of gender-based violence. Finally, in 1998, hundreds of students stormed the president's house at Bates College in Lewiston, Maine, angry over reports the college was failing to investigate reports of sexual assaults.[18]

Direct-action tactics combined with less threatening strategies such as education form the model for student activism in the nineties and beyond. Peer education may seem like an innocuous and benign strategy for social change, but in reality it is quite subversive. It secretly colludes with more traditional "in your face" activism by posing as the lesser of two evils. It appears nonthreatening in nature and thus draws in educators from a variety of backgrounds; and it appeals to a campus audience that might otherwise react defensively to what is perceived as the more "radical" approach to social change.

Marian Wright Edelman, past president of the Children's Defense Fund, explained the importance of differing styles of activism for the civil rights movement of the 1960s:

> Malcolm was blunt where King was tactful. . . . He could say the anger, while King could do the softer, encouraging, persuasion, pushing, prodding. . . . There was always a need for multiple voices with multiple strategies pursuing social change.[19]

Erica Gutmann Strohl, cofounder of STAAR, Students Together Against Acquaintance Rape at the University of Pennsylvania, explains the usefulness of the good cop/bad cop approach in the current campus movement to end sexual violence.

> Sometimes the situation is too desperate to work within the system and something needs to be done fast. You need people who will spray paint fraternities or demonstrate outside of judicial conduct hearings. However, one thing that gave STAAR a lot of power was that we could still work within the system. We went to meetings, joined committees, and provided peer education workshops; but, they [high level administrators] understood we could quickly shift. Maybe we would have a sit-in or demonstration or go to the media. It is good to have balance. If you are trying to make real change for real people, most of America is connected to the system. Therefore, you have to change how college campuses act.[20]

SERVICE ACTIVISM: THE INDIVIDUALIST APPROACH TO SOCIAL REVOLUTION

Traditional forms of activism often jump-start many campus anti–sexual violence services and programs, but much of today's social change efforts includes service projects, peer education, and working within the system. In the *Philadelphia Inquirer* Sally Steenland made the following observation on the current state of student activism: "If young people in the sixties spouted grandiose rhetoric about saving the world, young service workers in the nineties are more modest about their goals. Pick an issue, they say; get involved."[21] In *Generation at the Crossroads: Apathy and Action on the American Campus*, Paul Loeb proposed a model of community service for understanding current student activism. He describes how apolitical students become politicized by doing community service work:

> Students have been looking for different ways to voice social concern. They want to act. They want to help. They don't want to deal with complicated issues and factions or the messy contention of politics. Instead, they have

revived approaches to involvement that focus on individual service . . . yet, these same approaches often lead them back toward larger social change.[22]

The work of Nyasha Spears, a Grinnell College graduate, exemplifies this approach to social change. When her classmate, Tammy Zywicki, was abducted and murdered in September 1992 on her way back to their school in Iowa, Nyasha founded the nationally recognized, student-based program FEARLESS. Concerned that Tammy's death was perceived as an isolated event rather than a pattern of gender-based violence, Nyasha used the issue of highway safety as a nonpartisan, "no labels" entree to address violence against women in the farming communities of Grinnell, Iowa. Referring to her work as "service-activism," Nyasha believes the program provides a "service" (helping people to be safer), yet also introduces the idea of gender-based violence to audiences who would not typically hear such messages.[23]

We would like to propose a variation of Loeb's community service model. Campus-based peer education is a form of community service, with the campus as the community. Unlike other forms of community service (such as hunger/homelessness), the issues that peer educators address affect them directly (rape, AIDS, racism, and so on). Students become involved in antirape peer education for a variety of personal reasons. The most common motivation is being or knowing a survivor of sexual assault. Men, who compose one-third of the movement, frequently get involved because a girlfriend discloses being raped. These men focus their anger and accompanying sense of powerlessness into educating other men. Men as well as women are angered by an institutional system that has failed the survivor by not holding the perpetrator responsible. And, of course, some students come from a strong feminist background and choose peer education because they are interested in feminist social change work.

Our research found that concern over public safety and interest in community service were the second most common reasons for getting involved in the campus movement to end sexual violence. Although educators share common motivations, their other student group affiliations, career goals, and politics are quite varied. It is not uncommon to see a fraternity brother facilitating a workshop with a self-identified "radical feminist," or an openly gay man working with the president of the campus Republicans. This diversity reflects young people's preoccupation with not being stereotyped or defined by social causes. Kurt Conklin, advisor to the STAAR program at the University of Pennsylvania, sums up this generationally specific style as an "individualist approach to social revolution."[24]

YOU DON'T GET RADICALIZED FIGHTING OTHER PEOPLE'S BATTLES: PEER EDUCATION AS A FORM OF CONSCIOUSNESS RAISING

Apolitical students who sign up for peer education often graduate with a political consciousness. Leading discussion groups on sex and violence brings students face-to-face with the realities of social and political inequities. In the women's liberation movement, women used consciousness-raising groups to translate personal issues into political action, knowing full well that, in the words of Beverly Jones, "you don't get radicalized fighting other people's battles."[25] Though this was considered a radical action in its time, participants studied the collective reality of women's lives by sharing the truth about their everyday personal experience. These women viewed themselves as the "experts," group discussions becoming their scientific evidence. Issues such as rape moved beyond isolated situations and into a framework that saw sexual violence against women (and children) as a natural result of living in a patriarchal system.

Peer education is the consciousness raising of the nineties. Educators take their personal experiences with violence or their abhorrence of it and translate it into political action. The educators who are survivors or who know survivors get involved because of personal experience. When they connect their experience to that of other survivors and understand patriarchy as the root cause of rape, they begin to develop a political consciousness. Those students who get involved for purely community service or public safety reasons may also become radicalized by peer education. When apolitical students initially become active in antirape education, they are likely to advocate risk reduction and crisis intervention strategies *only*—for example, "Use the buddy system." More often than not educators quickly learn that these are merely Band-Aid strategies and do nothing to eliminate rape. Only by challenging the sociopolitical system that perpetuates sexism, racism, and homophobia can we begin to transform rape culture. By making a commitment to ending rape, peer educators take the first step to gaining a political consciousness.

When college presidents, reporters, and "postfeminists" conveniently disregard rape as regrettable sex, miscommunication, or a drunken mistake, peer educators speak out. Students consider themselves to be the experts on their own experience. Like women in consciousness-raising groups, peer education workshops provide forums for sharing personal experiences and finding solutions. Often women will disclose experiences of being raped, assaulted, or harassed. More often men will ask other men, "Can you separate desire from action?" or women will broach the topic of sexual expression by asking about masturbation or orgasm. Men and women talk to each about the "rules" for hooking up and debate the nonverbal language of sex. Much like CR groups of the women's movement, peer education workshops become opportunities to negotiate uncharted waters.

There are no organized consciousness-raising groups in this third wave of feminism. It is assumed that young women and men will transform the personal into the political because twenty-somethings were able to benefit from some of the advances of feminism. Anti–sexual violence peer education workshops provide consciousness raising on the issues of power, sexuality, and violence. Professors can pose the question, "How does deconstructing gender contribute to the eradication of our rape-prone culture?" but students make this discussion more user friendly by asking, "Is it possible to give nonverbal consent to sex?" or "Are men and women equally responsible for the prevention of rape?" These simple questions provide a springboard for discussions on masculinity, femininity, sexual scripts, and the difference between sex and violence. It would be ambitious to hope that all workshop participants would frame their personal experiences with sexism or male privilege within a political context in just one hour-long workshop. Yet slowly but surely peer educators are helping to build communities intolerant of rape.

ANTRAPE WORK 101: INSTITUTIONALIZED ACTIVISM

While the peer educators are playing good cop/bad cop alongside the more "in your face" activists, there is another equally powerful collaboration at work. Administrators who oversee sexual violence peer education programs have become key allies to students. These staff and faculty members are often activists themselves who got their start in the second wave of the women's movement. The majority of campus-based sexual assault programs are in established student affairs offices with budgets directly funded by the university.[26] Program coordinators are health educators, women's center directors, or deans. These supportive allies often help students negotiate the complicated waters of university bureaucracy. As powerful and trusted mentors, these administrators explain the basic rules of campus politics—that tenured faculty have power and know how to use it, while students have even more power but don't know what to do with it.

Midlevel administrators often find themselves in tricky positions. As paid employees of the institution, they walk a fine line when advocating for institutional change. Teaming up with student activists provides an effective strategy for working "within" and "outside" the system. Non-tenured faculty and staff may be unable to participate in overt political action, but the students they advise still have the freedom to challenge the institution when the need arises.

The institutionalization of antirape work is unprecedented and a major contributing factor to the success of the nineties model of student activism. It should not be viewed as co-optation or a sellout. One goal of women's liberation was to effect institutional change. Today we have older activists writing campus policies and funding peer education programs. In fact, the Ramstead Amendment to the Higher Education Act requires by law that all universities have sexual violence policies. Administrators working with students can work inside and outside of the university to create a campus dialogue on sexual violence. Administrators also provide continuity to the work that student activists initiate but are not able to sustain because they graduate. Of critical importance, the collaboration of administrators and students closes the generation gap and facilitates a connection with previous antirape work.

While campus rape centers are not new, broad-based peer education programs that seek to prevent sexual violence are a recent phenomenon. These programs provide tremendous opportunity and resources for nineties-style activism by significantly increasing the number and effectiveness of young people engaged in the movement for sexual equality and gender equity.

Oversimplified media proclamations that feminism is dead, or that this generation is apolitical, coupled with the harangues of antifeminist critics, make it challenging to be a feminist activist. Here are our suggestions on how to participate in the social and sexual revolution to liberate women and men and ultimately end sexual violence.

- Appreciate your roots. Know your herstory. The anti-sexual-violence movement is built on the foundation of radical feminism and the antirape movement of the seventies. By connecting ourselves to previous powerful movements, we do not lose our identity, but we actually increase our power.
- Collaborate. Seek out administrative allies and activist professors. Programs cannot sustain themselves without significant administrative support.
- Call yourself whatever you want. Whether you prefer peer education or guerrilla tactics, recognize that loud and soft protest are needed to achieve the common goal of ending sexual violence. Play good cop/bad cop.
- Politicize your work. If we view sexual violence as inevitable, then the best we can do is respond to rape. If we believe that we can pre-

vent and eliminate rape, then we must address the power inequalities that maintain our rape-prone society. A political consciousness is integral to true rape prevention work.

- Advocate for a new system of power that promotes gender equality and protects human dignity.

13

KICKING INTO CONSCIOUSNESS THROUGH SELF-DEFENSE TRAINING: GETTING PHYSICAL IN BOTH THEORY AND PRACTICE

Martha McCaughey

I was once a frightened feminist. I used to think I was resisting violence through all the sexual assault prevention education I did. But the lectures I gave and the articles I wrote did nothing to quell the increasing fear I experienced—or, I suspect, the increasing fear I instilled in my female students. I would lecture on rape and battery at the university, only to feel intimidated by the hostile men who would inevitably approach me afterward. I showed the standard pornographic images of women being dominated and mutilated by men and hoped that my audience would detest them as much as I did, only to hear the occasional male student oohing and aahing at the graphic displays. I rallied to Take Back the Night, listening to one testimony of victimization after another, and went home depressed. There I would check all my closets because I'd read interviews with convicted rapists who said they'd hidden in women's closets before attacking them.[1]

A friend, to whom I confessed that all of this was crippling me psychologically, suggested I take a self-defense class. It was here that I met an incredible group of women who offer more than the kind of education and cultural critique I'd been presenting. Women here seemed unconcerned about questions of political purity, about nonviolence, about using "the master's tools," or about being masculinist. Women here practiced how to knock out and maim attackers; some were even learning how to kill an attacker, sometimes with a weapon, sometimes with their bare hands. The power and pleasure and physicality of this training drastically altered my understanding of feminist resistance, assault prevention, and consciousness raising.

After spending some 140 hours as a participant-observer in a wide variety of self-defense classes, I began to question why I and my colleagues in sexual assault prevention ignored self-defense. It's not that we would protest the woman who did fight off an attacker, but that we didn't ever emphasize such a possibility. Self-defense didn't seem like a necessary part of our strategies to stop sexual assault. To some it hasn't even seemed like a viable strategy. For instance, a member of my university's Take Back the Night organizing committee said, "If men aren't going to stop violence, there's *nothing* a woman can do to stop it."

My own activist circle isn't unique. Despite the fact that self-defense training was an important part of 1970s feminism—much as learning to fix your own car and embracing financial independence—self-defense rarely appears in books providing the history of the women's movement, or in the current anthologies of the anti-gender-violence movement. In the three recent groundbreaking anthologies about violence against women—*Transforming a Rape Culture*; *Violence against Women: The Bloody Footprints*; and *Gender Violence: Interdisciplinary Perspectives*[2]—we find only one article about women's self-defense.[3]

To make matters worse, the latest tool for organizing and disseminating political information, the Internet, usually repeats the problem. Surfing the Net recently, I found that the vast majority of college women's centers that have Web pages provide lots of on-line information about how to avoid attack and where to go if it happens. Very few provide any information about how to defend yourself or where to go to learn how to defend yourself. Indeed, the list of links you can follow echoes eerily the pattern of thinking I found in much feminist activism around this issue: What is gender violence? CLICK HERE for a definition. Men assault women a lot, CLICK HERE for statistics. Women are therefore vulnerable, CLICK HERE for a statement about why this is unjust. How to engage in prevention, CLICK HERE—and here we see avoidance advice such as, "Don't walk alone at night," "Don't drink too much," "Don't accept a drink someone else poured because it could contain Rohypnol, the 'date rape drug,'" and "Communicate clearly on dates—say no when you don't want to do something with a man." After this, however, there are no links to what to do if these avoidance strategies fail.

There's a missing link between all the avoidance measures a woman is supposed to employ until a man tries to assault her (despite women's avoidance measures, men still attack them) and the aftermath of his attack. If the avoidance measures fail, CLICK HERE—and there's no mention of twisting the testicles, breaking a kneecap, or gouging out eyes. Instead, we read instructions about not taking a shower, going to the hospital, and so on. It's as though women's fighting back and stopping an assailant isn't even possible.

Another Web site provides tips for student activists who want to fight violence against women. Campus Action, a coalition of student activists on ten campuses in New York's capital district, provides on-line "action tips" to concerned women's groups who want to take action against sexual harassment and assault (*http://www.crisny.org/~campact/actideas.html#Sexual Assault*). Their action guide includes about every activist strategy—joining the campus action task force, holding speak-outs, displaying the Clothesline Project, setting up a student-run sexual harassment log, joining a Take Back the Night rally, pressing for sessions on sexual assault at student orientation—except the recommendation to establish self-defense training programs on campus. While college women are encouraged to act to resist men's violence through educational campaigns and stylized speak-outs, women are not encouraged to thwart, or treated as if they could thwart, an attack that might come their way. Self-defense is not part of the action a woman can take; indeed, in this regard women are considered already immobilized.

My colleagues, fellow activists, and I had emphasized that violence against women was men's responsibility (and I still believe that it is), but in so doing we'd done nothing more than try to mobilize men around guilt or empathy for the "weaker sex." We ourselves had swallowed whole the rape myth that men cannot be stopped. Some scholars have even studied the "effectiveness" of campus Rape Prevention Education Programs by measuring how effectively those programs instilled a sense of vulnerability in women (because other research shows that people who feel vulnerable tend to restrict their "risk-taking" behaviors).[4] Such an approach never challenges the rape myth that men are strong and impenetrable and women are weak and vulnerable.

I suggest that talk of women's fear, victimization, and vulnerability only solidifies men's sense of power over women and women's sense of disempowerment. Of course, the activists in the anti-sexual-assault movement do not dichotomize feeling empowered and talking about victimization. For many, talking about victimization is empowering in the context of the "safe space" of feminist organizing. Agency and empowerment, however, cannot come solely through discussion of victimization in safe spaces; to the extent that they do, some activists find threatening any attempts to focus on a different kind of empowerment, namely, a celebratory empowerment that emphasizes concrete resistance.

Feminist activists, then, have as much to learn from self-defense as self-defense has to gain from feminist activism and analysis.[5] It is not that no feminist on a college campus today is involved with self-defense, but that the most visible, well-read, and well-funded projects usually do not include self-defense. This essay is about why that may be the case, and why that should change.

Self-defense presents an important challenge both to rape culture and to many of the organizing efforts set up to transform rape culture. Rape culture is a culture that accepts gender-motivated attacks as normal, natural, and even sexy—a culture whose models of masculinity, femininity, and sexuality sustain and rationalize men's violence against women. Violence against women depends upon the myth of male strength and female weakness, and so rape culture depends upon the impossibility and inappropriateness of women's aggression. The cultural norms that regulate who gets to use violence legitimately have kept women positioned as the weaker sex and have fueled the frequency and ease with which men assault women. Cultural ideals of manhood and womanhood include a political, aesthetic, and legal acceptance of men's aggression, and a deep skepticism, fear, and prohibition of women's. The set of cultural assumptions that positions aggression as a primary marker of sex difference fuels the frequency and ease with which men attack women, and the cultural understanding that men's violence is an inevitable, if unfortunate, biological fact.

Rape culture requires that we see women's aggression as ugly and unfeminine. A beautiful woman is a "real knockout" but she isn't really supposed to able to knock a man out. In fact, feminine beauty connotes precisely the opposite of strength and power. Strength, power, aggression, and bravery are coded socially as male. After all, we don't commend acts of heroism with "You've got ovaries!" In fact, women's ovaries and other body parts have been invoked historically to rationalize our inferiority and exclusion from prized and financially rewarding social spheres.

All women in this country are held accountable to the norms of feminine manners, though many women's life situations or choices make it impossible to live up to them. Lesbians, for instance, have been dubbed "aggressive" simply because they desire women.[6] African American women have been stereotyped as domineering, overpowering, and castrating, despite the fact that they are just as likely as any other women to be victimized by male violence (and, historically, even more likely, since a racist system of slavery positioned them as the property of white men).[7] And feminists, in their efforts for women's freedom, have been labeled "ball busting" and "male bashing"—as though stopping wife beaters and rapists is comparatively more offensive than the perpetrators' actual female bashing and woman hating.

The everyday practices in a rape culture show boys and girls their respective places in the world. As one self-defense instructor put it, "It's every child's birthright to body sovereignty. [But] in boys, we overemphasize it; in girls, we 'no,' beat, incest, and rape it out of them." Male domination requires specific kinds of bodies. Rape culture is an embodied ethos. What counts as feminine comes down to physical vulnerability and subservience to men, and that's why self-defense training challenges femininity. Feminist philosopher of the body Iris Marion Young argues that often girls do not develop a relationship with their bodies as agents, as instruments of action.[8] Hence, many of us learn to "throw like a girl," that is, to withhold our strength, to approach a physical task in a timid manner.

That girls and women tend not to make full use of the body's potential[9] would explain why so many of us don't use our full strength when we first kick a punching bag or a padded instructor in self-defense class. Some women even apologize to the padded attacker after striking him. Moreover, the rules of polite, empathetic, feminine communication make setting limits verbally awkward and embarrassing. This explains why so many of us on the first day of self-defense class have to practice over and over before we can yell "FUCK OFF!" without smiling.

I have asked self-defense instructors, who have witnessed more students than I have, to tell me the biggest hurdle their students must overcome when learning to defend themselves. Their answers all reflect the way prescriptive femininity is an obstacle to competent verbal and physical aggression. They tell me that their students need to overcome being nice, overcome a fear of hurting people, overcome a fear of guns, overcome a physical hesitancy, and overcome a disbelief in their own physical power.

To help women discard their feminine hesitancy and imagine new possibilities for action, self-defense instructors share success stories, model strength, critique our sexist culture, and provide an encouraging atmosphere. The best self-defense courses I have seen provide female-only or female-student-only environments that help women learn about the physical power they possess. And they help women practice using that power.

The coaching, then, is only the beginning: Women have to enact the aggressive posture in mock-attack scenarios. For those unfamiliar with self-defense mock fights, here are the field notes recounting one of my mock fights in a padded-attacker course:

> "Hey, Martha, I know you from the university. I was in your sociology class," says the man casually.
>
> "I see," I respond. "Well, I'm in a hurry to get somewhere now."
>
> "Just wait a minute. I've always wanted to tell you how attracted to you I was. Maybe we could get together."
>
> "I don't think so. No." At this point I raise my hands casually to a protective position so that I can protect my face or strike his if necessary. My legs are shoulder-width apart and pivoting so that I'm always facing him. I quickly look around to see if anyone else is in the area.
>
> He touches my arm, urging, "I thought you liked me."
>
> "Don't come any closer," I say firmly. This is the intense part. If he persists, I have to make a decision to fight. And if I make this decision, I have to be prepared to continue fighting to the knockout.
>
> He steps closer, trying to put an arm around me. I deliver a heel-palm

strike up his nose, and, just as his head tips back, I knee him in the groin. He doubles over momentarily, and I drop to the ground on my side, ready to kick him in the head.

He lunges for me. "Damn you, bitch! You broke my nose."

"KICK! KICK! KICK!" Several blows to his head knock him out. I get up, look around me, assess the assailant, see that he is indeed knocked out, run to safety, and shout "9-1-1"—the official end of the fight.

Of course, in real life the verbal self-defense alone might well be enough to scare off an assailant. But this kind of course trains women for the worst, and so students often fight through to the knockout blow.

Self-defense provides a knowledge at the bodily level distinct from that at the intellectual level. Self-defense, then, requires not only a theoretical understanding of body or voice. Women must inscribe it into their bodily schema. Self-defense training provides a stirring sensorial atmosphere that engages the body.

Practicing assertiveness under real-life conditions of fear and attack—under high-stress, high-adrenaline conditions—most realistically captures the emotional and physical conditions under which women would have to defend themselves. The sensorial quality of the activity presents the stakes of self-defense—you can feel them as the adrenaline rushes through your body, hear them in women's stern words, and taste them when it's your turn to eat the mat. Fighting a mock attacker makes you tangibly, organically invested in the scene.

One firearms instructor I talked with trains women to shoot under stressful conditions, so they get used to the feeling; and they discover that they can shoot quite well under those conditions. She has a "garbage mouth" come in and shout obscenities and threats to her students who, at her command, must shoot at their targets. This gives gun students the sense of trauma that they might have while shooting, incorporating their fighting techniques into that sensibility one has when one is afraid. Another, lower-intensity technique is the "spaz drill," which involves the shooter clutching her gun, aiming at the target with as hard a grip as possible until her hands shake, then shooting while shaking.

Despite the unpleasantness of attack simulations, there is a certain pleasure in the combat. We train not only to ensure physical survival; we train for dignity, to survive socially as people with a certain sense of entitlement. In this way the increased sense of value a woman has for herself is etched onto her body through the physicality of the practice of self-defense training.

The physicality of the practice, the emotional character of the venture, and the sensorial nature of the atmosphere solidify in women a new body. One self-defense student explains, "Whereas therapy may take weeks, to talk about it, this just brings it up immediately. . . . I go into these really intellectual things, whereas the body just needs to go 'Whoa, like, what are you doing? It's not okay.'"

An instructor told me that the physicality of self-defense training is what makes the difference over all sorts of traditional forms of consciousness raising. She said, "I spent years in rallies, feminist therapy, et cetera, and when I get a woman in her body for forty hours and she has a kinesthetic experience of her power, that's a major difference." A padded-attacker-course student explained:

> I'm a lot more sensitive to my boundaries—this began during the training, and I preface this with saying prior to the training I had studied boundaries, and disorders of boundaries, through therapy, psychology school, AA, Adult Children of Alcoholics, etc., and I had done a little bit of "boundary work"; but in Model Mugging I did the real work—I became hyperaware of my boundaries.[10]

Self-defense students learn a new set of reflexes that encompass attitude, technique, body, will, and spirit. That's why some self-defense teachers call the new proud, assertive, and willful demeanors they see blossoming in their students "the fighting spirit." The change is quite literally metamorphic. A karate student said that many aspects of her life have changed as a result of her training, including her dreams at night:

> My dreams over time have changed from being always stopped and hiding and people trying to kill me and rape me to where right in the dream I would say, "I know karate." And I would either stop them from doing it right there or wake up just as I was about to and then other times I'd be fighting back. And I know that what was happening was a real shift like in my understanding of who I am in the world and what I can do.[11]

The embodied ethos of rape culture is radically contested and restructured as women are forced to adopt and make habit new gestures and voices. Women's "victim bodies" metamorphosize into "fighting bodies".[12] The attacker and his victim do not exist in some primal predator-prey relationship; those are precisely the terms of the event that self-defense rejects. When a woman resists an attack, she confounds the script of helpless female victim and unstoppable male attacker. This is the political, and feminist, importance of self-defense.

Self-defense taught me how gender ideology operates not just at the level of ideas, of social interaction and relationships, but at the level of the body as well. When women perform a decidedly unfeminine script, they challenge gender reality. Gender ideology is expressed at the level of the body—it's a soma-reality. Self-defense makes a new soma-reality possible.

Why, then, has self-defense training remained a marginal, overlooked, and sometimes even scorned part of the anti-gender-violence movement on college campuses? It is not as though feminist activism has ignored the body. Whether it's reproductive rights, beauty culture, pornography, eating disorders, alternative sexualities, rape, or woman abuse, a large portion of feminist activism and theorizing concerns the body and its control, representation, violation, or discipline. But, ironically, under this framework we can't as easily imagine the female body as an agent for social change. The body in feminist discourse has been construed as the object of patriarchal violence, and violence has been construed as something that is always oppressive, diminishing, inappropriate, and masculinist. The self-defense movement challenges us to rethink these central assumptions about the body and violence.

Women's pleasurable engagement with violence in the context of their past and/or potential victimization by men's violence presents somewhat of a quandary for feminists. But as long as we continue to construe violence as something patriarchal and bad, whose binary opposite must be good, virtuous, feminist nonviolence, and deny the complexities of deciding which is which, we will see men as the only ones capable of violence and agency. The corollary of this is that the female body will continue to be seen as a nonagent—an object of patriarchal violence.

Feminists have construed violence as patriarchal and have used the concept of violence to imply an oppressive, bad intent. Thus self-defense is, at worst, dismissed altogether as "masculinist" or is, at best, embraced carefully as not really violent, since it stops the violence of someone with bad intent. But I insist that we admit that self-defense trains women for violence in certain circumstances, should they arise. We need not hide our ability and willingness to use violence to protect ourselves, any more than we should hide our desire for intimacy without intimidation, or our insistence upon sex with consent. The knowledge of one's ability and willingness to use violence lies behind the all-important shift in self-perception and attitude that self-defense training accomplishes. We must show women how to interrupt the embodied ethos of rape culture, train to thwart attacks, and disrupt rape culture by embracing the very threat of violence that men have used to keep women in line. This does not mean teaching women to become bullies or perpetrators of violent crime. It means that we uphold women's legal right to self-defensive violence.

Embracing women's capacity for violence is not a political compromise, a position of relinquished social ideals. Embracing women's right to self-defensive violence is embracing women's status as equal citizens who have boundaries and lives worth defending. Feminists need not claim women's rights by positioning women as morally or otherwise superior to men. By analogy, our feminist foresisters didn't deserve the right to vote because they'd bring special values to the voting booth. They deserved the right to vote as equal citizens. We deserve the right to defend ourselves for the same reason. And when women advocate nonviolence without themselves being capable of violence, it makes less of an impact than if they had a real choice.

By challenging the passivity and vulnerability of the female body and by challenging sexist notions of legitimate violence, self-defense presents us with a new set of possibilities—not just for individual women but for the women's movement as a whole. Feminist resistance to violence against women has made incredible progress. Since the 1970s we have broken the silence about what used to be private, individual, even secret experiences of child abuse, rape, sexual harassment, and spouse abuse. Feminist scholars and activists have rightfully positioned these problems as social problems, and have developed crisis centers and shelters, hotlines and legal services for victims, Take Back the Night rallies, women's centers on college campuses, research and educational campaigns, SafeWalk programs, nighttime ride services, emergency phones, and streetlights. But women's self-defense culture taught me that our resistance can be much more tangible, and that we can get a lot more preventative than streetlights.

Some might dismiss self-defense as more individualistic and less collective than the aforementioned programs—as though self-defense affects only the individual woman and her sense of personal empowerment. But I insist that we need self-defense and a "physical feminist" vision incorporated into the organizational efforts of the anti-sexual-assault movement. Self-defense does not privatize women's problem with violence: "Physical feminism" is not some simple, individualized, fight-by-fight feminism; physical feminism offers a new theoretical understanding of sexed embodiment important for dismantling rape culture. Self-defense and the critique it offers of the embodied ethos of rape culture demand collective action, new policies, and legislative change.

For example, we need to get some of the millions of dollars that Clinton's crime bill provided to deal with the problem of violence against women, in the form of the Violence against Women Grants Office. Currently, the grants given by this office don't even mention self-defense training as something it funds, and I was told by a representative from the grants office over the phone, "We don't fund prevention." Most of the funds go to training police officers, servicing victims, and prosecuting offenders—making women's postabuse lives more tolerable and perpetrators' postabuse lives more punishing. We need to show the importance of self-defense to groups like this who, like myself a few years ago, haven't seen self-defense as a necessary part of an anti-gender-violence movement.

Take Back the Night rallies should offer stories of women's self-defense victories or include a self-defense demonstration. Students should be starting clubs for self-defense so they can get whatever money their university provides to student clubs for funding programs and other events to increase student awareness of self-defense. Activist strategies might include a vision of self-defense—for instance, instead of painted signs announcing, "A Woman Was Raped Here," why not signs warning, "A Woman Kicked a Rapist's Ass Here"? Why not scare men, for a change, instead of women? If research has shown that an increased sense of vulnerability to danger leads to self-imposed behavioral restrictions to reduce risks, then perhaps men need to feel more vulnerable so that they'll restrict their abusive behavior.

College-student orientation programs are more likely now to include a sexual assault awareness session. Let's push for those programs to include a self-defense training session. College women's centers can make self-defense more available—but they need financial support from the likes of university administrators and the Violence against Women Grants Office. Of course, many women can't afford to pay for self-defense training, which can cost up to five hundred dollars for a comprehensive course. This is all the more reason why self-defense must be incorporated into the already-existing organizations of the women's movement. Many women can't afford to leave their batterers, but thanks to women's shelters they have help doing so. Many rape victims can't afford the fees for therapy, but thanks to rape crisis centers and women's centers, they can speak with trained counselors and with other survivors. These organizations need to help bring self-defense to more women in that same way.

Self-defense challenges some of the core assumptions of rape culture—the assumption that women's bodies don't have boundaries, that men's bodies are strong and impenetrable, that women are naturally vulnerable to men, and that women need to restrict their behavior in order to avoid attack. Self-defense need not be seen as a second step, to be taken after women gain an initial awareness or fear of the problem of violence against women. In fact, if fear increases as a first step, the second step may never be taken because fear in feminist discourse is so powerfully associated with immobility.[13] Self-defense does not deny women's fear of attack but attaches that fear to active resistance rather than to immobility.

In transforming women's bodies, the physical activity of self-defense can transform women's minds, offering a new political consciousness. Self-defense training is a feminist consciousness-raising session in the classic sense—and by enlisting the body, it expands our notion of what consciousness is. Consciousness involves not just a mind, detached from a body. We have protested male domination as it has exploited, controlled, violated, and misrepresented the female body. It's time now to enlist the female body as an agent for social transformation. Male domination is already an embodied politics. It's time for feminism to get physical, too.

14

BECAUSE VIOLENCE IS A WEAPON OF OPPRESSION, ANTIRAPE MUST MEAN ANTIOPPRESION

Janelle L. White

A PERSONAL *AND* POLITICAL EXPERIENCE

"Who's zoomin who?"

—Aretha Franklin

In November 1995 I attended the Seventeenth Annual National Coalition against Sexual Assault (NCASA) Conference and Women of Color Institute. Having directly worked in the antirape movement for only two years, at the University of Michigan's rape crisis center, I was thoroughly excited about participating in this particular conference, which was my first NCASA conference. As a doctoral student, I have had the opportunity to attend all too many conferences. But this one was different, special to me. First, many of the writings and much of the work of white women and women of color working on the "front lines" of the antirape movement led me to expect progressive theory *and* practice at this conference. By "progressive" I mean ideology shaped by the recognition that forms of oppression—based on race, gender, class, sexual orientation, ability, and religion—are interconnected. But it does not stop with just this recognition. Instead, truly progressive ideology stimulates action—individual and collective—that attempts to address oppression in all of its manifestations simultaneously. Such a conference opportunity also brought with it the expectation that, for a change, I would not be forced to explain any aspect of myself—a Black feminist activist-scholar involved in confronting, resisting, and challenging violence against women. In addition, I was excited by the prospect of finding new sister-allies in the antirape struggle. And, finally, I looked forward to the opportunity to thank women in the movement for the work they do—educating about sexual violence, advocating for survivors, and taking direct action to change the social structure that allows violence against women to thrive. I knew that a woman who would likely acknowledge only that she was "doing her part" had empowered me to save my life and had empowered many other women. I wanted to say thank you to her and to let her know that the work she had done and continues to do has affected me to such an extent that I want to do—must do—my part too. I wanted and have begun to register my thanks in action.

So it was with great hopes and expectations I attended this conference in 1995. I was devastated by what I found there. A group of white women refused to participate in the White Women against Racism Caucus. They cited being excluded from the Women of Color Institute as their reason. At the conference "Speak Out," which was provided to give participants the opportunity to talk about their conference experiences, various white women "spoke out" to demand that I and other women of color devote our energy to educating them about racism. A city councilman, who was to serve as our parliamentarian during the annual business meeting, refused to serve in this capacity after an NCASA executive board member publicly identified herself as a lesbian. There was little collective outrage registered by (straight) conference participants at this man's blatant act of homophobia. Finally, I saw Kata Issari—my advocate, ally, and friend—step down from her position as president of NCASA after serving only half of her term. Of course, all the various incidents that I witnessed during the conference—of which these cited are only a few—alerted me to the problems that Kata and other progressive women of color must face working in this coalition and in the antiviolence movement in general.

And, unfortunately, I must note that the 1996 Eighteenth Annual NCASA conference held in San Francisco was not much different from the 1995 conference. I'll give one example. A white woman refused to leave a group that was designated as women of color only. The group asked the woman to leave; yet she refused. Later, in discussing this occurrence, a conference participant made a significant revelation about the incident. She said, "How is what happened here different from when men won't listen to women, imposing themselves against women's will?" And at the 1997 NCASA Conference held in Cleveland several women walked out of a session that was to focus on ally building between white women and women of color. These women walked out to do their own antiracism education because the conference session did not acknowledge white skin privilege. Nor did it delve into white women's historical privilege in the antirape movement, privilege that has manifested itself in white women holding positions of power and ultimately charting the direction of the movement.

These incidents bring to my memory various essays and articles written by progressive women in the antiviolence movement. In "Women and

Male Violence," Susan Schecter writes provocatively on the issues of men in the movement and male responsibility for violence against women:

> In the battered woman's movement, most shelters that include males use them in limited staff roles or as a minority of board members; women retain primary leadership and control. . . . Feminists who see themselves as organizers and activists do not believe that it is the responsibility of the women's movement to divert its resources, in an ongoing way to men. Nor do they want to see agencies proliferate whose only task is to help violent men. . . . Traditional social service agencies will initiate more [male] treatment programs and the movement will have to stay organized and vigilant to ensure that psychological explanations [of male violence], devoid of an analysis of power, do not replace political ones.[1]

Donna Landerman clearly articulates why it is of utmost importance that the antirape movement be antiracist:

> From both an ideological and practical point of view, it is essential for the anti-rape movement to investigate racism and incorporate an anti-racist perspective, because racism in major ways both causes and defines rape. If we are to successfully aid women who have been raped, prevent rape, and eventually eliminate rape, it is necessary to understand and attack rape in all its forms and at all its roots. Racism and cultural and class oppression are some of those roots of rape, and lead rape to take different forms in the lives of women of various races, cultures, and classes.[2]

Finally, Suzanne Pharr connects homophobia and heterosexism to sexual and domestic violence perpetrated against women:

> How many of us have heard battered women's stories about their abusers calling them lesbians or calling the battered women's shelter a lesbian place? The abuser is not so much labeling her a lesbian as he is warning her that she is choosing to be outside society's protection (of male institutions), and she therefore should choose to be with him, with what is "right." He recognizes the power in woman-bonding and fears loss of her servitude and loyalty: the potential loss of his control. The concern is not affectional/sexual identity; the concern is disloyalty. The labeling is a threat. . . . Our concern with homophobia, then, is not just that it damages lesbians, but that it damages all women. We recognize homophobia as a means of controlling women, and we recognize the connection between control and violence.[3]

I was experiencing intense cognitive dissonance, unable to reconcile these words of progressive women that I had read and reveled in and what I was seeing and experiencing at these conferences. I must recognize that I talk about these experiences not to make anyone feel bad or guilty, but because they provide us an opportunity for education and social change.

All agents of the antiviolence movement encounter an external backlash daily, but some of us also experience an internal backlash. By backlash I mean a reactionary response to social change. This response stems from an unwillingness to redistribute institutional power and resources or concede individual power and privilege. And by no means is this backlash symptomatic only of NCASA. For example, the 1995 National Student Conference on Campus Sexual Violence not only failed to offer any workshop sessions on rape and racism, but also gave rise to a major disagreement between those students who wanted to discuss the link between racism and sexual assault and those students who saw rape as a distinctly separate issue from racism.

We have to address this internal backlash head-on in order to progress. This means that we cannot write enough about how racism, classism, and heterosexism reinforce sexism. This means that we cannot educate enough about how violence is rooted in oppression. Therefore, I take this unique opportunity to elucidate the connections between forms of oppression; to speak out about the alienation and exploitation of women of color and the marginalization of issues important to us in the antirape movement; and to emphasize the need for the antirape movement to confront its own racism, homophobia, and class bias. I also hope to offer some strategies on how we might begin to do this.

ELUCIDATING THE CONNECTIONS

Audre Lorde wrote, "There is no hierarchy of oppression." What did the feminist poet-activist mean by this? Ultimately she is saying she will not choose between her identities. Any movement that fails to recognize her multiple identities or asks her to recognize only her Blackness or her gender or lesbian identity is a movement in which she refuses to participate. Such a movement holds the seeds of its own failure and destruction.

If we look deeply, we will see that violence—in the form of sexual assault, battering, lynching, genocide, and other hate crimes—is endemic to all forms of oppression. Thus, violence is one area of intersection between all forms of oppression. And, in fact, acts of bias violence often involve more than one form of oppression. For example, lynching—most obviously an expression of racism—often included bizarre sexual mutilation of the victim. It seems clear that the white male perpetrators of such violence were expressing not only their racist ideology of white supremacy but also their sexist fantasy of masculinity.

By the same token, rape—most obviously an expression of sexism—also often involves other forms of oppression. When women, regardless of their sexual orientation, are threatened with rape when they show affection toward other women, we see homophobia acting in concert with sexism. This all too common occurrence is a manifestation of these two forms of oppression interacting with and bolstering one another. Suzanne Pharr, who cochaired the National Coalition against Domestic Violence and the Lesbian Task Force of that coalition, calls homophobia a weapon of sexism. So, clearly, members of the sexual assault prevention movement must challenge homophobia as well as sexism if we hope to be effective.

The intersection of oppressions also affects how acts of bias violence are perceived. Feminist legal scholar Kimberlé Crenshaw notes that rape is "racialized."[4] In the United States rape has been historically racialized in the image of the white female victim and the Black male rapist. This does two things. First, women of color are absolutely invisible in this equation. We are socially constructed as "unrapeable." Second, white men are protected by this mythology. They are let "off the hook"; they do not perpetrate rape. But we know that 90 percent of sexual assaults occur between individuals of the same race and socioeconomic class.[5] We also know that in 84 percent of all rapes the survivor knows her rapist.[6] Such a racialized image of rape obscures these facts and the everyday attacks that white women experience at the hands of white men. So this racist mythology not only harms women and men of color, but also white women. Here, racism and sexism cohabit the same space.

All this goes to show that constructing sexism as the paramount evil is not only inaccurate, but absolutely self-defeating. This is in part because we cannot neatly separate sexism from homophobia or from racism. Over time forms of oppression have become intertwined. Movements that fail to take this into account cannot fully succeed and may cause more harm. I think Kimberlé Crenshaw, writing about the antirape movement, says it best: "This movement inadvertently participates in exclusionary politics because some of us fail to comprehend the anti-violence movement as an anti-oppression movement."[7]

WOMEN OF COLOR AND THE ANTIRAPE MOVEMENT

African American feminist and activist Barbara Smith wrote in *This Bridge Called My Back* that "A bridge gets walked over." Latina feminist-activist Cherríe Moraga responded with, "Yes, over and over again."[8]

There are a number of ways in which women of color are marginalized, alienated, and exploited within the sexual assault prevention movement. When I write of women of color, one often only thinks about race. But women of color also have sexual orientations and class backgrounds. This means there are a number of conversations about privilege and power that are going on and must go on among women of color. I say this to acknowledge that we women of color also have work to do in addressing homophobia, class privilege, and our own internalized sexism and racism.

Yet too often I have heard about and experienced abuses of power and privilege by white women working in the antirape movement. I want to mention some of my experiences and the experiences and sentiments of a few of my sister-allies. This will serve three purposes. First, it will present some painful incidents that exemplify the kinds of interactions that occur frequently at rape crisis centers but may have not yet been labeled as problematic. Second, these accounts will serve as a testament of the work we still need to do. And third, writing of these incidents will break the silence that has surrounded them for too long. If there is one thing I have learned in the antirape movement, it is that I do not have to remain silent about my oppression or the oppression I see around me. Audre Lorde wrote, "Your silence will not protect you." And silence has not protected me, although it has protected those who have victimized me and other women. Ultimately, the work of Pearl Cleage and the collected essays and works of Audre Lorde gave me strength to stop protecting the perpetrators of violence and oppression and helped me find my voice.

The first experience I call "Teach Me What I Need to Know. Now!"

Previously I mentioned white women at the annual NCASA conference wanting women of color to educate them about racism. My sister-ally Jamie Lee Evans, who coordinates the teen education program at San Francisco Women against Rape, shared with me one way she and other progressive women deal with this problematic maneuver. When a white woman asks a woman of color to "school" her on a race issue, or an economically privileged woman asks a working class or poor woman to educate her on a class issue, the woman being asked to do the educating says "Fifty." This means the education costs fifty dollars, to be exact.

Too often marginalized groups are burdened with the onus of educating the privileged. In providing this service upon demand, we are nothing other than exploited labor, because we are seldom remunerated for playing the role of educator. I have no problem helping in the education of more privileged women in the movement, especially if I know that these women have empowered themselves to seek self-education about their privilege and power and educate other women like themselves on these issues, but I will not be *the* education, nor should I be expected to serve in that capacity.

Too often I and other women of color have been faced with white women wanting us to provide the primary education on racial inequality. When we adamantly refuse, the response is, "I want to learn, but you refuse to teach me." This is a strategic maneuver, because it takes responsibility off a particular white woman and lays it squarely on my shoulders and the shoulders of other women of color in the movement. Racism becomes my fault and the fault of other women of color who refuse to be exploited in such a manner. Sounds painfully familiar, doesn't it?

Like what we in the antirape movement call "blaming the victim"? Here again we see tactics that serve to reinforce oppression overlapping. Tactics used to keep sexism alive are the same tactics used to keep racism alive. My sister-ally Amy Mong Wok, former director of public education at the Austin Rape Crisis Center, noted that it is a sad phenomenon that women in the antirape movement work tirelessly to empower survivors of sexual assault, yet some of these same women declare themselves unable to empower themselves enough to take on their own education. I think this realization is profound.

The next experience I call "Our Practice Doesn't Match Our Rhetoric."

Recognizing the interconnection of oppression got one of my sister-allies in a difficult position at the campus rape crisis agency where she volunteered. A homeless woman who had been sexually assaulted on campus property specifically asked for service through my friend's rape crisis center. My friend was beeped and asked to do an outreach to this survivor at the local hospital. The policy of this woman's agency is to provide counseling and outreach to college faculty, staff, students, *and* to any person assaulted on the college campus. So my friend answered the call. The next day she was chastised for going on this call. My sister-ally strongly feels that the survivor's homelessness played a part in her reprimand. A quote from Beth Richie's book *Compelled to Crime: The Gender Entrapment of Battered Black Women* addresses this disheartening situation. Beth writes, "this grass-roots feminist movement has had limited success in creating the social changes necessary to end violence against women, partly because it has failed to address the needs of those whose lives are most marginalized."[9]

The agency involved in this incident purports to embrace the philosophy that violence against women is rooted not only in sexism, but also in racism, class exploitation, and heterosexism. The sad part is that my sister-ally stopped volunteering at this center after five years of service, citing this experience, a lack of appreciation for her long-standing commitment, and other organizational changes and obstacles as primary reasons. A tremendous asset was lost because she brought to the agency not only her perspective as a woman of color, but also her experiences as a "non-traditional" student, having started work on her undergraduate degree while in her forties. She was the only volunteer in this age group; of course, older women who are survivors of sexual assault often prefer to talk to women of their age, just as women of color survivors may prefer counseling from another woman of color. Nonetheless, my sister-ally's commitment and tenacity kept her connected to antiviolence work. She moved on to facilitate a support group for battered Black women at a domestic violence shelter in the Midwest.

I call this third experience "Trust Me, I Am a Survivor."

Even more disturbing and equally difficult to talk about is that some survivors of sexual violence use their survivor status as a shield to hide behind when confronted with their own racism, heterosexism, class bias, anti-Semitism, and/or ableism. Psychologically this makes sense. Survivors often feel an intense victimization, and it is difficult to recognize that at times they can and do victimize others. Yet hiding behind one's survivor status so as not to have to deal with one's personal power and privilege is self-defeating, and defeating to the antirape movement.

We must challenge survivors when they act oppressively. It does not help our healing to be allowed to act in oppressive ways; in fact, it may only contribute to our further victimization. I know that at San Francisco Women against Rape we train our rape crisis counselors to interrupt oppressive dynamics that may arise when doing crisis intervention work with survivors, their friends, and families. It is not easy or comfortable to do, but it is necessary if we really want to challenge the root of violence, which is oppression.

I call this next experience "Women of Color as Tokens" or "The Old 'We Can't Find Any Women of Color' Line."

It has become popular to try to integrate the staff and volunteer programs of predominately white rape crisis centers with people of color. I too have been a proponent of this. But I am beginning to question and reconsider this strategy. This does not mean that I am advocating segregation. But rape crisis centers must seriously ask themselves if they are really ready to accommodate people of color. In other words, how much are they willing to change and give up to become safe places for people of color? For example, NCASA plans an annual Women of Color Institute to provide a space solely for women of color to engage with one another on issues important to women of color. The structured inequality that women of color face in society and within the antirape movement is why this institute is warranted and was started. Unfortunately, some women, as mentioned previously, see the institute not as an opportunity in the struggle against rape, but as a threat.

It is not enough only to learn how to recruit volunteers and staff of color, you must consider how they are made to feel when working in the organization. Are their critiques of the organization silenced or met with skepticism and/or defensiveness? Are only particular types of people of color recruited (such as those who are more compliant)? Do women of color or other marginalized people become tokens, a photo opportunity used to illustrate a supposed commitment to communities of color? Will people of color be expected to do all the "race work" in the agency (such as recruiting staff and volunteers of color, constructing educational programs for "minority" communities, doing all/most outreaches to communities of color)? Such "sham diversity" is worse than no diversity at all.

The flip of this coin is the "We can't find any women of color to work or volunteer here" line. Granted, in some areas there are very small populations of people of color, making it difficult to recruit. But too many organizations hide behind rather than confront this difficulty. Many agencies seem not to recognize the basic economic fact that women of color may not be able to afford to volunteer their time, or that women of color may not have as much access to graduate education. There are some solutions. It may be possible to offer less economically affluent women stipends to attend volunteer trainings. Also, recognize the trend toward professionalization that is occurring nationally in the antirape movement *and* resist it. Do we want to build an exclusive movement of women with graduate degrees? And if we do, what does that mean? Of course, I say this as someone who is working on a graduate degree, and who wants to be certain that my educational privilege is not used to impede another woman's participation in the movement.

The last experience I call "Insidious Co-optation."

In 1985 student protests at the University of Michigan ultimately led to the formation and university funding of the Sexual Assault Prevention and Awareness Center (SAPAC). In the early years SAPAC was largely student run and activist oriented, with a relatively nonhierarchical distribution of power. The students who formed SAPAC believed that education was as important as direct services to survivors. Without education—not only about rape, but also about sexism and other forms of oppression, there would be no chance of changing the attitudes that contribute to sexual assault. These students also attempted to maintain an involvement with the off-campus community, working hard to connect campus and community, because rape and sexual violence know no boundaries. And, finally, many students of color, gay men, and lesbians served as volunteers and paid staff.

All of this has greatly and slowly changed. Students have much less of a say in the workings and decisions of SAPAC. The distribution of power is now entirely hierarchical—with no apologies. In 1995 there were fewer students of color and no counselors of color. And out of a group of twenty-one peer educators, there was only one "out" lesbian and no gay men. The focus has changed from an equal emphasis on service provision and education to a primary emphasis on services for survivors. There is a distinct division between campus and community. And though the mission statement still includes an analysis of violence against women as rooted in oppression, it is difficult to see this theory in practice in the everyday workings of the center. I know so much about the changes at

SAPAC because I worked there as the co-coordinator of the Peer Education Program.

I do not believe that this is a phenomenon experienced only at SAPAC. This is part of a national trend in the antirape movement. Nancy Matthews (1994) writes that "as the state becomes involved in the anti-rape movement, it recasts the feminist definition of rape as a political issue into the problem of an individual victim." University administrations can double for the state, and—at public schools—are the state. Thus, campus rape crisis centers are in precarious positions where they can be easily co-opted. Here I must also add that rape crisis centers that accept federal funds are also put in precarious situations. University administrations have an interest, in the words of Nancy Matthews, in "managing rape" in order to minimize liability and make the school more attractive to parents of prospective students. Arguably, other social institutions are interested in "managing rape" too. They have no interest in pursuing a progressive feminist political agenda, particularly with the current backlash against political correctness.

Those of us with a genuine interest in preventing rape must resist this thrust to "manage" rape. Unfortunately, at SAPAC resistant individuals have tended to be purged while more cooperative individuals have been hired. I believe this to be a common pattern at campus rape crisis centers that have chosen to or been forced to affiliate themselves with the administrations of their college or university. Of course, this means we must be ever vigilant and strategic in finding spaces within the antirape movement for resistance.

In January of 1996, when I first wrote about the mainstreaming and co-optation of the antirape movement in preparation for a talk I gave in Norfolk, Virginia, I wrote about it with great fear and trepidation. So often at SAPAC my critiques of the organization and antirape movement had been dismissed or evoked defensiveness or anger. This had led to oral and written reprimands by my supervisors, which strongly reminded me of the common tactic of warning survivors of domestic abuse to "keep it in the family." I knew that I would be taking a great risk in speaking about this at the Virginia conference, but I refused to be immobilized because of a fear of institutional repercussions. One of the first steps in recovery— and change—is acknowledging that there is a problem. This was to be my opportunity for public acknowledgment.

As it turns out, my fear and trepidation were well grounded. About one week before I was to deliver my keynote at the student conference in Norfolk, I was fired from my position at SAPAC. Although that termination was an incredibly traumatic experience, it also offered some important opportunities for resistance and change. One example of this resistance is the work of the Ann Arbor Coalition for Community Unity. After my termination this coalition, which formed in 1994 in the wake of a poorly handled serial rapist investigation, and which is committed to addressing sexism and racism simultaneously, issued a statement to feminist agencies in the Ann Arbor area. This statement stressed the importance of addressing abuses of power within women's agencies. Here is an excerpt from the letter, which was written by the women of the coalition:

> Audre Lorde told us that when we, as women, fall back on the same tactics that the patriarchy uses to control us, tactics of sexism, racism, silencing, and dismissal, we become self-defeating as a movement. Instead of working to end the conditions that create and perpetuate violence against women, we enable them. Every time we silence other women's criticism of our work, or punish dissent, we commit an act of violence. Violence, after all, is the abusive or unjust exercise of power. And when we perpetuate this kind of emotional and spiritual violence against women within our movement, we condition women to accept the physical and sexual violence we are fighting daily.

Although my termination was troubling, what was more troubling was the treatment of committed SAPAC volunteers who were critical of my dismissal and critical of the operations of SAPAC. These volunteers took the difficult and principled position of engaging in a work stoppage. Although none of these volunteers wanted to stop doing educational workshops on the issues of rape, dating violence, and sexual harassment, they felt they had no other choice. They attempted to get the structural problems addressed internally, but to no avail. Sadly, the resisting volunteers were purged from the organization solely because of their dissent. I mourn their dismissal as a loss to the antirape movement. What is most compelling about this is that these volunteers are the ones who have remained most loyal to the mission statement and philosophy of SAPAC, a philosophy that recognizes that violence is rooted in all forms of oppression and urges individuals to address all forms of inequality.

I wanted to address my termination because I know what happened to me is not an isolated incident. Too many women have been pushed out of the antirape movement for challenging oppressive dynamics in the movement, be it through termination, layoff, reassignment, or burnout stemming from numerous obstacles and lack of support. And perhaps it is easier to talk about my experience because I was surrounded with overwhelming community support and I was not ultimately pushed out of the movement. But the victimization I faced at the hands of this movement was painful. Therefore, I want to recognize the contributions of those women who face obstacles in the antirape movement and because of those obstacles are no longer working in the movement. Your contributions and commitment to confronting oppression are stellar, have reshaped this movement, and will not be forgotten.

ACTIONS TO CHALLENGE OPPRESSION

The Dalai Lama wrote, "It's not enough to have compassion. You must act."

The following is a list of some actions that those of us working in the anti-sexual-assault movement can begin to take to challenge oppression on all fronts.

1. *Build coalitions.* Strengthen your relationships with antiracist, lesbian and gay, antipoverty, domestic violence, youth, and disability rights activists and organizations. If you do not have relationships already, extend invitations to talk together about each other's concerns and goals. Do not wait until a crisis arises. Show solidarity by attending each other's events or writing letters to your local paper regarding your stance on other issues of oppression in your community. Working in isolation, duplicating efforts, or "protecting your turf" are luxuries none of us can afford.

2. Prioritize the planning and implementing of antioppression trainings in your agency. Make a commitment and a plan to host workshops regarding racism, homophobia, classism, ageism, anti-Semitism, and ableism. Workshop agendas should include opportunities for participants' identification of personally held oppressive attitudes, as well as opportunities to develop analysis of how racism, classism, and other forms of oppression impact sexual assault and assault survivors. End workshops by planning how to implement knowledge gained during training in the daily work of your agency. If no one in your agency is qualified to facilitate antioppression workshops, ask for help from outside.

3. Rewrite your mission statement to include an analysis of violence as rooted in oppression. Make your mission statement public. Constantly review whether your programs reflect your mission statement. Ask the question, What are we doing to end the conditions that make violence against all women permissible? Figure out what you are not doing, then do it.

4. Incorporate people of color and other marginalized groups into your agency. Do this only if you plan to sincerely accommodate them as full partners in the movement with legitimate concerns about racism, class bias, homophobia, and so on. The expectation that the concerns of marginalized people be raised in "nice" ways is offensive. Don't expect this. Our concerns are valid and should be addressed no matter how they are articulated. Your willingness to take the preceding action-steps that I presented is a good indication of whether or not you are ready to incorporate people of color and other marginalized groups into your agency. At San Francisco Women against Rape white women participate in monthly mandatory antiracism discussion groups, and we have established task

forces for women of color. This shows a recognition of the responsibility white women have to address their own race privilege, and it acknowledges the need for women of color in a movement historically dominated by white women.

5. Create or strengthen the education component of your agency's work. Prevention of violence happens through education. Empower women by providing a space to talk about their experiences and to discuss strategies for fighting sexism and sexual assault. Encourage men to take responsibility for violence against women through education challenging stereotypes and beliefs about men's and women's roles, the nature of sexism, and their relationship to other issues of oppression. Host general community awareness-raising events to talk about the myths and realities of sexual violence.

6. Make sure all educational outreach recognizes the interconnection of oppression. This means volunteers doing education must be aware of the connections. So make sure that a generous portion of volunteer training delves into how racism, homophobia, and class exploitation cause violence against women, shape how that violence is experienced, and influence whether and how the survivor is able to fight back.

7. Work toward less organizational hierarchy. In the antirape movement such hierarchy often means less control by staff and survivors utilizing services. Collectives are ideal, but if it is not a structural option, build in collective practices. Hierarchies allow for abuses of power. Hierarchies manifest themselves in patriarchy, white supremacy, and capitalism. Audre Lorde writes that the master's tools will not dismantle the master's house.

8. Use direct action (for example, dramatic protest, civil disobedience). Don't shy away from this. If we are dissuaded from taking direct action, it's time to worry. You might need consider if there is solely an interest in "managing rape" and not enough interest in actively changing the institutional structures that allow rape to happen. Read the work of Pearl Cleage, Cherríe Moraga, Gloria Anzuldúa, Beth Richie, Gloria Yamato, Barbara Smith, and Audre Lorde, just to name a few. But do not stop there. Keep reading, thinking, and acting!

There are a number of women I must thank who have educated me, supported me, and sustained me as I work in the antirape movement. First and foremost, I thank Pattrice Jones for her love and unwavering belief in me as an activist and writer. Linda Willis, Carmen Crosby, Teri Rosales, Aishah Simmons, Tamara Xavier, and Ain Boone, your commitment to social justice and social change inspires me and keeps me in the fight. I also acknowledge Beth Richie, Edith Lewis, and Patricia Hill Collins for showing me that I can be both an activist *and* scholar. Thank you for struggling with me on that issue. I also must recognize Mary Beijian for her help in developing the list of Actions to Challenge Oppression. Mary, you are a true ally. Finally, I thank Jamie Lee Evans. You take tremendous risks for social change and to end violence against women. I am with you my sister-friend to the end!

15

MEN-ONLY SPACES AS EFFECTIVE SITES FOR EDUCATION AND TRANSFORMATION IN THE BATTLE TO END SEXUAL ASSAULT

Stephen Montagna

When the axe came into the forest,
the trees said "The handle is one of us . . . "

I believe we all suffer from divisionary and polarizing thinking, are all out
of balance in different degrees at different times particularly because of win-
lose ethics, from which in the long run everyone suffers. Developing a non-
enemy ethic in my life means refusing to hate and refusing to win at a cost
to others. I am trying to look for the human face behind the enemy image
and in this find a possible transformation of relationship.

—K. Louise Schmidt,
Transforming Abuse: Nonviolent Resistance and Recovery

Six years ago I moved to Madison, Wisconsin, from the East Coast to pursue my master of fine arts degree, and to get away from the East Coast.
In a certain sense, I was also trying to get away from Nancy.

Nancy and I had dated, quite briefly, at the end of my senior year of
undergrad. Our charming, promising, and nonsexual (though physical)
relationship was punctuated with the discovery that she had been cheating on me with another man. Under any circumstances this would be
upsetting; my frustration was enhanced by the fact that we had specifically held back from becoming intimate sexually because her previous
partner had focused so much of that relationship on intercourse. This
former partner, our argument would reveal, was in fact the man she had
been sleeping with behind my back. In the wake of that catastrophic scene
in my kitchen, with tears rolling down cheeks and the threat of dishes
being thrown, I fell back on the support and comfort of friends. The conclusion arrived upon by my little clan of coed compatriots was unani-
mous. I had been too nice to her in the relationship: "She's a bitch . . . you
shouldn't take that stuff from a woman . . . be more aggressive . . . go out
and get it."

Getting "it" was, after all, a man's central occupation.

These phrases ran around inside my head, ricocheting like a mantra, and amplifying until the original sentiment, their desire for me not to be hurt, became the seed of the twisted promise to myself to obtain sexual satisfaction—even if it meant hurting someone else. Fate lent a hand, with an offer to teach and get my graduate degree halfway across the country. It was perfect: Moving far away would help me forget the hurt Nancy had caused me. Furthermore, in the Midwest I would meet thousands of available women and "get what I wanted" from them.

The summer passed. I moved. I started grad school on a campus nearly ten times larger than the one I had spent my undergrad years on; the amount of potentially available females was staggering. Despite this, I was terrified of actually asking someone out, and completely confused about the language my friends had passed along to me. It was language that inferred a kind of aggression that wasn't really inside me. It felt foreign. One day in the student union, I happened upon a brochure for the organization Men Stopping Rape. The pamphlet spoke not only about avoiding bad behavior with women in your life, but also of reaching out and connecting with other men. I decided to attend a meeting and check them out; I thought, if nothing else, it will impress the girls.

The environment of the MSR meeting was so welcoming and transformational, that I not only returned for subsequent meetings but went on to partake in the workshop presenter training, and eventually moved into presenting workshops both on the UW campus and in the Dane County community. My life, as they say, has never been the same.

"Just what do men talk about?" I don't want to explain that yet; I like to leave a little mystery, create a little cliff-hanger: What exactly happened in those mysterious MSR meetings? My withholding this information is a little tongue-in-cheek gibe, an in-joke if you will, with many of the women I've come into contact with in my six years with Men Stopping Rape who want to know what exactly it is we do.

This question has become quite controversial, in fact. Recently, a debate arose on the electronic forum CCOAR (Coalition of Campus Organizations Addressing Rape) over what men's participation in the antirape education movement should be (if any!?). Further compounding this controversy is the fact that we at MSR specifically advocate "men only" spaces for most of our workshops; men, in a room alone, talking about rape.

For a number of reasons, many women feel threatened when they hear about men working in the area of sexual assault prevention education. On one level, they feel cheated because after working so hard to raise awareness for women's rights and issues, here come the men trying to shine the spotlight back on themselves. Also, since sexual assault crosses borders of gender, orientation, and physical space, it is easy to fear anyone who mounts a soapbox: Just what do they stand for? What is their definition of assault? Where do they stand politically? What is their prescribed cure?

The most potent threat posed by men doing work with men, is that we are, statistically speaking, the "perpetrating class." The predominant number of assaults, regardless of the gender of the victim, are perpetrated by males. There is a long history of assaults taking place in, or being informed by activities in, traditionally male-only environments (Peggy Reeves Sanday has already so eloquently and bravely researched fraternity traditions—if you haven't read her work you are missing something[1]). As one person explained to a fellow MSR presenter, "Men collude"; in other words, when men are alone together, sexism rules.

Now, I want to be perfectly clear that I am not (repeat: not, not, not) saying that the agenda of the feminist movement is to attack men. From my perspective what most feminists out there are trying to do is deconstruct the system of patriarchy—the institutionalized implementation of a bias against anything perceived to be weak (that is, anything female or effeminate, or any display of dependence). The difficult thing is that most men have a hard time understanding feminism. While most feminists are addressing bad behavior, men hear it as an attack on their biology. They cannot separate a feminist critique of "the system of patriarchy" from a criticism of themselves as men.

One of the reasons this is true is that, in my experience, men's issues have been absent from rape prevention programs. On college campuses, in particular, sexual assault prevention education is done "quick and painlessly" during freshman orientation, never to be revisited, unless the student willingly takes a women's studies course. Higher education's rallying cry for preventing assault is that old standard: "No means no." The recipe is simple: Teach women how to say no and how to defend themselves (against what?—why, against men of course . . .), throw in a little lesson to the men on how to respect women. Add a warning about alcohol. Mix.

The message is still about women, though. Men are not taught how to respect each other, how to be safe around other men, or that men have boundaries too. Absent from sexual assault prevention education is the realization that perpetrator behavior is a result of misinformation handed down from generation to generation through the popular culture (movies, magazines, music), and further, that this misinformation can be unlearned.

On the CCOAR list one person posted an inquiry as to what others were doing across the country to educate men. Several people responded, including myself, describing the programming we do in MSR. The ensuing dialogue was skeptical. An educator from the University of Washington commented that at her school, "no matter what group was being presented to, there would *always* be a female presenter present." Her assumption seemed to be that men in a room together, alone, would simply talk about sex, while sexism would go unchallenged. Furthermore, she proclaimed that men's resistance to rape prevention training in coed settings with female presenters was a result of their inability to accept women as authority figures.

Another list member submitted a number of questions, including "What kinds of things are men more comfortable talking about if women aren't present that need to be talked about in rape education?" and "Do you see a danger in supporting male-only rape education groups, given that this may be extended to arguments to exclude women from other arenas of male bonding (such as fraternities, which research data demonstrates are such frequent sites for sexual abuse)? How do you negotiate the contradiction effectively?"

It is true that male-only environments have been at the root of many sexist acts and beliefs, and it is specifically for that reason that male-only environments must be used in unlearning those habitual behaviors. Popular science so far hasn't found sexism to be buried in the Y chromosome. It comes from behavior and attitudes passed on across generations and cultures. Why have such attitudes permeated male-only spaces? Simple: We are terrified of each other.

Men's exchanges are fraught with the underlying threat of violence, and informed by homophobia (for our purposes, homophobia is not just the fear of homosexuals—it is the institutional belief that men cannot be intimate with each other—emotionally or otherwise). In a culture where we are shamed for showing feelings, men learn to express any type of feeling as rage. If we feel threatened, we do everything we can to pose a larger threat. In such an arena women become both targets of criticism and objects we use; the stories we tell each other about what we do with women on dates (or claim to have done) become tools used to maintain status among our circle of men.

At Men Stopping Rape, we feel our job is to reconstruct the male-only space as one where sexism can be identified and challenged. More important, we seek to create a space where men can build trust and safety with each other in a way that would no longer require women or their bodies to be used as a means of maintaining status. For men to see and hear another man talking about sex, sexuality, and sexual assault is radical; no one has ever talked to them about this stuff before in a clear, informative way.

Regarding the comment that men resist female presenters because they cannot accept women as authority figures, while it is certainly true that men have such a problem, resistance is not absent in a male-only workshop. Truth be told, their resistance is not so much against the woman as it is against the feminine. For instance, when I go in to present a workshop, I am not an authority figure in their eyes at first; I am an "other." Their homophobia is in place, so I'm automatically gay to them (debased to the "level of the feminine") because, after all, aren't all sensitive men gay? They perceive that I have come simply to chastise them and slap their wrists.

There are several benefits to having a male facilitator and a male-only environment. In a coed workshop with a female presenter, the men would be less likely actually to say some of the things on their minds. They are too busy trying to avoid being called on, and too busy posturing for the benefit of the other females present. When women are absent, their agenda is to assert themselves; they do not censor themselves. Second, I myself was raised as a man, and can address on that fundamental level the ways in which our culture teaches aggression and coercion.

Men need to hear about sexual assault in a context that does not automatically place them in the role of perpetrator simply based on gender. While the concept of "No Means No" is important for men to hear, and while they do need to learn about respecting women as human beings—as individuals—they further need to hear that they themselves have a right to set boundaries. In other words, men cannot possibly be taught how to respect women when they have no concept of what it means to have the right to control their own physical boundaries. All their lives men are taught that their masculine identities are dependent upon their ability to put their bodies at risk. They are expected to excel in athletics; they are expected to develop muscular, strong physiques; they are taught that anything emotional makes them weak. If we really want to reach men on the issue of sexual assault, a starting point must be to relearn masculinity; if we really want women to be safe around men, we must teach men to be caring, communicative, and supportive with each other.

"No Means No" is further compounded by the fact that men are told that our masculinity, our sexuality, and our identity as men are directly connected to our ability to get a woman to say yes. Men's ability to grapple with the concepts of no and yes is impaired by the culturally taught bias against communication. For decades these men have been bombarded with images in print and in the movies of men who simply "make their move," "don't ask, take," and, the definitive slogan, "just do it." Where does communication fit into such a paradigm? In workshops I lead men in an exploration of these stereotypes. "How many of you have seen a movie in which two people have sex?" I ask. All of their hands go up. "How many of you have seen films in which they actually talked while they were having sex?" Almost every hand goes down.

Men have had no models to show how communication can improve sex—not just make it more safe, but also more enjoyable. When I facilitate a workshop, one of my goals is to take "No Means No" to the next level—or, perhaps more accurately, flip it around. As a man, I am responsible for only two things: *my* feelings and *my* needs. It is my responsibility to myself to let the person I'm with know what I'm feeling, what I would like to do; how that person reacts is not my responsibility. By working against the grain of society, which historically has viewed asking as "unromantic" because it "ruins the mood," I present communication as part of a package of my taking responsibility for myself. By asking I am not ruining the mood, I am in fact creating the mood; I am letting my partner know my sexual desires. I am presuming no privilege to it, nor any power over her/him to get what I want.

All this is done in an effort to get men to reject the myth that our avoidance of communication goes beyond fear of being uncool; men don't ask because they are afraid of rejection. ("Rejection!" I call out to the workshop participants. "The number one cause of death among men!") My initial question to the workshop participants is "How do you know she wants a kiss?" which yields the typical stereotypes of our pop culture: "She looks at you in a certain way," "She moves closer to you," or some intricate combination in which she looks at you, then away, then down, then back at you. The irony is that many men take this as "yes" and never bother to ask what their partner may actually feel like doing. "If all this body language is in place, and you're telling me that you know she wants a kiss," I ask them, "then you have your answer. Where is the risk in asking?"

There is nothing buried deep in the male soul that impels us to force someone to pleasure us. It is the pressure from without, from our male peers, from our cultural teaching, that pushes us constantly to score (to find a way, as the old frat phrase goes, to "work out a yes"). To live in a world ruled by the principles of patriarchy means a constant repression of feelings, a commitment to being violent, to putting your body at risk, to expressing affection either by slapping your male friends' backsides, or, with women, scoring. Men have been denied that middle ground: affection, compassion, sensuality, compatibility, cooperation.

In coed workshops it is very effective to have a male-female presenter team; it is very important to model a positive, cooperative male-female dynamic, and it has been very effective in such workshops I've done in the past. However, I feel the work is incomplete if both genders don't get some time in the workshop in a same-sex-only setting. Female presenters are often unable to deal with the topic from a man's perspective. This is not meant to sound like a criticism; the fact is, it is not their job to deal with our oppression and pain—they have their own to work on, and that is plenty.

However, as a community invested in ending sexual assault—not just avoiding it but ending it—we must involve and engage men. We negotiate the contradiction of men-only spaces as sites for sexism, assault, and collusion by giving them a directly contradictory experience: a men-only space that challenges them to be accountable for their actions, while at the same time provides a forum for expressing their feelings of oppression. Much of the debate around the issue of men-only spaces has been caused by lack of understanding between men and women of each other's processes. So I am trying to paint an accurate picture of what occurs in one of our workshops so that we can move beyond generalizations (and the fear caused by our assumptions) and into more focused critique.

Thus, we arrive back at my little cliff-hanger. It was in such a men-only meeting, my third MSR meeting, in fact, in which a conversation took place that changed my life. In a discussion being led by Michael, one of MSR's founders, we came upon the topic of consent. In response to a question Michael was tossing around the circle of six men, I said, "Yes, of course you ask the woman your are with—up to a point." Michael encouraged me to go further with my comment: What was that "point"? I launched into a detailed explanation of "fail-safe"—the point at which a man is so committed to orgasm that, like our B-52 bombers (notice the military allusions in our sexual discourse), he cannot be called back to base. In other words, I reiterated, "I reach that certain point at which I cannot stop."

Michael leaned back in his chair and nodded with a skeptical squint in his eyes. After a moment he offered: "Let's play a little game . . . it's just an exercise, just to think about. You've gone on a date with a woman. You've talked and asked questions, you've gone back to your place, and you've both consented to having sex. Along the way you're asking and checking in and everything is fine; you start having intercourse, you're inside her, and everything feels great. The woman suddenly says, 'Stephen, wait . . . I'm not feeling well, I don't know, maybe something I ate . . . . Could we just hold up for a second?' Does she have the right?"

With that last question he leaned forward in his chair with a penetrating, inviting expression on his face; the inference was that it was a question to be answered not out loud, but in my own heart. My brain raced; the only possible answer to that question kept bumping into the brick wall of my social programming—"No . . . no, she can't . . . how can she . . . ," or even better, "How dare she?" The feeling was one of being cheated, having my power taken away; and yet my conscience could not accept any other answer but yes. To answer any other way is to put that woman in a category one step removed from human being.

None of the other men in the circle reacted with anger toward me; instead they sat silently nodding. The profound quality of that moment sticks with me to this day. To move beyond the superficial "We shouldn't rape, I know it's bad" to recognizing that what perpetuates a culture of rape is the inability of society to grant a woman the most fundamental of human rights: sovereignty over her own person. Further, then to make the connection that such a right was exactly what I wanted for myself—sovereignty over my own body, my own life.

Ultimately, the most effective sexual assault prevention education programming must allow for coed workshops copresented by male and female facilitators to be augmented by separate single-sex discussions. Too often men's sexism is reaffirmed because they imagine feminism as a great big ax coming at them to remove their sexuality, to empower women at the expense of men. As a man reaching out into my community of men, I am spreading the message that the true intent of feminism is equality. For men that means being accountable for our actions; it also means empowering ourselves to reconstruct masculinity in a way that allows us to be caring, communicative, and supportive, not only with intimate partners, but with each other as well. A true ending to the rape culture in which we now live will come only when we can educate men about how much more rewarding consensual relationships can be, not only for the women in our lives, but for ourselves.

PART V
INSTITUTIONAL CHANGE

16

RAPE AND THE MEDIA: PUTTING A FACE ON RAPE

Elizabethe Holland

Arguably the greatest debate in journalism on the subject of rape in recent years has been whether to publish or broadcast the names of victims.

The most-mentioned reasons against naming victims: The stigma that envelopes rape might prevent victims from coming forward if there is a chance they will be named, particularly if they have the further risk of having their reputations and judgment impugned during court proceedings; making known a victim's identity could put that person at further risk, especially if an attacker hasn't been arrested.

The most-mentioned reasons for naming them: If the accused is named, such should be the case with the accuser; to hold back a victim's name keeps rape's stigma alive instead of making it clear that rape is nothing for which a victim should blame him- or herself or feel shame.

Most media outlets have taken the stance that victims' identities should be shielded, and, except for the occasional slew of columns and articles on the topic after a well-known figure is linked to a sexual assault, there the issue sits—when perhaps another facet needs to be considered.

While the debate has been over whether to give a victim's name, I wonder if the media's energy might be better spent giving victims a face.

That the stories of two rape victims, Susan and Tim, came to print was almost accidental. Susan and I happened to meet in a restaurant while I was a crime reporter in the Florida Panhandle; Tim had read my articles and wanted me to know I wasn't telling the whole story—not at all intending, at least initially, to share his. Over time they agreed to talk and let their stories be printed.

That we came together this way indicated to me how difficult it is for reporters to describe the impact of rape. Victims' names often are stricken from records, and when they're not, rape victims, more often than not, don't dare discuss their experiences with a reporter. What if their names got out, if their attackers found them, and who trusts the press this day and age anyway? they ask.

A reporter is left to string together sterilized, cold facts on a police blotter. The victims seldom are given faces and lives on the page or in a newscast; the crime seldom is described as the horror it is and the horror it can perpetuate.

When Susan realized I was a reporter, she riddled me with questions about the sentencing of a rapist that week. She wanted to know if it had been mentioned in the paper, and how long she could expect this man, a first-time offender, to be behind bars. Her interest and intensity gave her away as his victim.

She, a thirty-two-year-old divorced mother of three, said she would tell me her story but that she wouldn't feel comfortable if her name was used in the newspaper.

Susan endured hours of detailing the crime, from describing her attackers' thick leather gloves, to the sound of her children running around in the dark, to the feel of a gun at her temple. She told me of her fear that he would kill her children and of the lingering effects the attack had on a son who felt responsible for not stopping the intruder from raping his mother. She told me of the drawn-out court case, of hearing strangers right in front of her tell the judge what a fine man this rapist was: and of the strength it took to take the stand to tell them how wrong they were.

The first time Tim called me, he was nervous, curt, even a little angry. He wanted to know why I never wrote about men who had been raped, only women. I told him that I wrote what the police and their records told me and that I seldom, if ever, came across cases of male rape. He hung up on me.

Tim called a week later, and again a week after that, each time pushing his point but not telling me what I already had surmised. It was the fourth or fifth call that Tim told me his name and acknowledged that he had been raped.

We met, and Tim painfully regurgitated his story. Thirteen years prior, he had decided to save money by hitchhiking to a wedding in Detroit rather than flying there. In Nashville a man in a Volkswagen picked him up, but when Tim wanted off at an exit, the car kept moving. The man, a serial rapist who preyed on male hitchhikers, put a knife to Tim's throat, stopped the car, and raped him.

Tim wanted desperately to leave the nightmare in Tennessee and rebuild his life, but an investigator there encouraged him to testify. All of the other victims had backed out, and Tim was the only one who could stop this man, and he did.

Neither Susan nor Tim wanted to relive what had happened to them by seeing their experiences dissected in a newspaper. They talked because they wanted others to know what another person's terrible decision had done to their lives. They wanted people to know that victims don't ask for this and that rape lasts much longer than the time in which it takes place.

They gave rape victims faces and lives—without giving their names—and they exhibited how far-reaching rape's effects can be.

But they are exceptions.

In such a crime-ridden society, rape has become nearly commonplace and is often treated as such.

A woman walking home from work is yanked into an alley and raped. A major newspaper, already crammed with news from all sectors, relays the crime in two or three paragraphs, listing few, bare facts. We learn it was a woman, where it happened, the approximate time, perhaps whether she was otherwise injured, if there was an arrest. If something extraordinary or somehow unusual occurs—the victim is kidnapped, is a child, or the rape is believed to have been committed by a serial rapist—the incident will receive more space in the paper and on the television news.

Otherwise, the article describing an incident that will forever change this woman is quick, to the point. The victim is faceless, and only the readers who care to ponder the crime consider what she must have gone through and what is yet to occur.

If anything, that rape has become common enough to elicit only two or three paragraphs in a newspaper should be a signal to the media how critical it is to report more and more in-depth about rape.

The media, however, are in a tough situation when it comes to rape. The public rails at the media for publishing so much crime and painting the world negative, so journalists wonder how to treat it. Victims—the small percentage who do report the crime—so often prefer not to receive media attention, so two or three paragraphs' worth may be the maximum amount of information available.

For those media outlets that want to educate the public about rape, it's not as simple as deciding to tell more victims' stories and track their survivals. Tracking information on sexual assaults can be trying. Police information can be vague and deficient, and even legal definitions of sexual assault state to state can muddy the reporting process.

Reporting about rape on college campuses can be especially difficult. Although a federal law, the Crime Awareness and Campus Security Act, was passed in 1990 to raise public awareness about campus crime, the law suffers from loopholes and lack of enforcement. The law requires that all post-secondary schools that receive federal funding disseminate annual reports to current and prospective students and employees. The reports must include campus safety policies and crime statistics—including sex offenses.

Further, institutions are supposed to alert students and employees "in a timely manner" to crimes that may threaten the community. A victim's bill of rights provision added in 1992 says schools also must promote awareness about acquaintance rape and other sex offenses, as well as form policies for reporting such crimes.

The intent of the law is admirable, but the picture it creates for safety-conscious parents, students, and employees is, more often than not, incomplete. Some campus authorities don't bother to include sexual assaults in their statistics if a victim decides against filing a report. And acquaintance rape produces deeper problems. Authorities realize considerable instances of acquaintance rape go unreported, thus the number of rapes committed is vastly undertabulated.

Critics say the number of sexual assaults committed nowhere approaches what statistics show. And if the numbers aren't there, it looks as if rape is not a significant problem. And when it doesn't appear to be a major concern, it gets less attention from students, employees—and the media.

Were victims more forthcoming in reporting rape, there would still remain the issue of how they are portrayed. Although rape awareness has stemmed instant judgments of victims to some degree, victims are still judged. People, some media included, want to know what a victim was wearing, why she was out that time of night, why she took that drink, why she didn't know better.

Susan's attack took place in her home. The rapist had plotted the attack and broken in through her garage. He left no room for people to blame Susan, an innocent woman at home, asleep in bed.

Tim's story was one of an unsuspecting person sought out by a perpetrator with a plan that had been carried out before.

Although there are times when victims' stories prove problematic and require raised eyebrows, there seem to be far more instances of victims being questioned or judged on material irrelevant to their cases. The media are not always responsible for pursuing such tidbits, but are often guilty of using or overplaying them.

Some of the more well-known examples are the cases involving William Kennedy Smith, Mike Tyson, and, most recently, allegations against professional football players Michael Irvin and Erik Williams.

After charges were pressed against William Kennedy Smith—who later was acquitted—a string of details about Patricia Bowman, the woman who alleged Kennedy had raped her, hit the papers. Among them: that she had performed poorly in school, had a child out of wedlock, had a load of speeding tickets, and had somewhat of a wild streak.

Desiree Washington, the woman Mike Tyson was convicted of raping, incited quick judgments because she was in Tyson's hotel room when raped. The boxer's defense was that she must have known—he being a womanizer and she being in his room—that he wanted sex.

In the case involving Michael Irvin and Erik Williams, Nina Shahravan accused the two of being instrumental in a gang rape in which she was the victim. That story was found to be a hoax, and Shahravan eventually pleaded guilty to perjury.

Despite Shahravan's awful lie, she should not have been classified as she was in news reports. Over and over again she was referred to as a "former topless dancer," as if anyone who had ever held such a job couldn't possibly be victimized. Shortly after her story was revealed to be a sham, a sports broadcaster for a major network commented on the air that such a lie should have been expected from the woman—she having been a stripper, and all.

In two seconds of airtime, the broadcaster took a cruel swipe at any woman who has held such, or similar, employment. His words essentially pronounced all women with like backgrounds untrustworthy and incapable of telling the truth about rape simply because of their employment.

With judgments like these receiving so much attention by the media, it is easy to understand why more victims don't trust journalists or the legal system. By reporting a rape, they risk having their lives placed under a microscope and picked apart, piece by piece. Sometimes, in the interest of justice, it is warranted that they have their lives picked apart. But even then, not all of the pieces need to be displayed.

Something Susan said spoke volumes. After talking with investigators and enduring a medical exam, a sheriff's deputy called her a lady. He didn't judge her because she was a divorcee or because she wore silk pajamas the night she was raped. He respected that she had been victimized and thought no less of her because of that.

"That really set the pace for me," she said. "I didn't do anything wrong."

A newspaper editor can't decide to give the topic of rape the treatment it deserves and then expect perfect coverage overnight. Even the best, most fervent intentions and scads of space in newspapers wouldn't be enough to allow for proper coverage right away. There would exist the problems of reaching victims and encouraging them to tell their stories, and finding ways to get timely, detailed accounts from law-enforcement officials, among other issues.

But the decision to do a better job in itself would be a start. Reporters could try to make better contact with victims to better represent their stories. They could talk to social scientists, criminologists, and other experts to figure out why rape occurs. They could talk to activists and educators to report what is being done to teach people about rape, and what is being done to prevent it. They could learn to treat rape not as a trend story, but as the ongoing issue it is.

They could step back and examine how rape and its victims have been portrayed in the media and set standards for how they should be addressed. Editors could determine which reporters on their staffs are most able to tell these stories properly and establish the trust of victims and other sources.

Journalists could go beyond the debate of whether to name victims and focus more on giving victims something that will far better address the impact of rape than printing one's identity. They could give them faces.

17

TRAINING CAMP: LESSONS IN MASCULINITY

Nate Daun Barnett, with Michael DiSabato

In high school few things mattered. At least that was my impression as I struggled to communicate with my peers. We avoided discussing class work because we were afraid to demonstrate how little we understood. We did not discuss politics because it was so removed from the world we knew. And we discussed culture only in the popular sense of the word, which of course was limited to movies and music. Instead, we focused our attention on the two things that interested us most: sports and women. The former we knew well, and the latter we tried desperately to know.

We struggled to understand our female classmates, but seldom did we include them in our discussions. Talking with them seemed logical, but as shy, awkward, pimple-faced pubescent boys, we found it nearly impossible. Instead, we relied on the next best thing: other guys. One conversation, in particular, taught me an important lesson that I will never forget. The conversation took place with my closest high school friend and ten or twelve guys from the football team. We finished practice and, like many times before, gathered to discuss Dave's love life. Of course, love is not what we were after; we were really only concerned with whether or not he'd had sex. Dave was not the only victim of this harassment; he was simply the only one with a girlfriend at the time. Each conversation was the same; we questioned him about Sheila and he blushed. Then he told us to shut up and the harassment intensified. Some guys were more relentless than others, but Dave never said a word. We could have constructed a shrine with his picture, and the conversation would have been the same.

But this time it was different. Dave mentioned to a few guys after one of these sessions that he and Sheila were going to have sex, and the word spread like fire. I was particularly curious because we were best friends and he'd never mentioned it to me. So that Monday night, after weeks of

interrogation from our teammates, Dave said, "Yes, we did it; we had sex."
With this exclamation came a huge roar of celebration from the paparazzi.
Everyone slapped high fives, shook their lockers, and barked like dogs
to show their approval. But as the excitement faded, our group disbanded.
There was nothing more to discuss. The goal was achieved. Our vicari-
ous sexual experience had reached climax, and we all rolled over.

Afterward Dave and I waited for our ride home from practice, and I
asked him if it was true. After a moment of hesitation he asked if I could
keep a secret. Sheila did not have sex with Dave, but he was afraid to
admit it to the guys. The pressure Dave felt in the locker room forced him
to make a difficult decision. He could be honest about the relationship and
face the humiliation of failure in the eyes of his peers, or lie about having
sex and gain the approval of the team while jeopardizing the relationship.
Not an easy decision to make at fifteen years of age. Of course, Sheila
found out and he was both humiliated and alone.

In the years since that incident, I realize that Dave could have made
another decision. He chose to lie about having sex, but he could have
chosen to force sex on Sheila. To Dave, our approval meant a great deal.
It meant so much that he was willing to risk his relationship to impress
all of us. What would have happened if Dave had felt the need to prove
it to himself? The result might have been very different.

In this chapter we will explore the dynamics of the locker room culture that influences young male athletes to make these difficult decisions.
Additionally, we will examine the way masculinity has been defined
through athletic competition and discuss the sense of entitlement athletes
develop and the role coaches play in teaching and perpetuating sexist
attitudes and assaultive behaviors. Finally, we will explore the phenomenon of gang rape and discuss possible intervention strategies for educators. To illustrate, we will discuss the experiences of Michael DiSabato, a
former All-American wrestler at a major Big Ten university in the Midwest. His account of growing up an athlete, from Little League baseball
to Division I wrestling, is indicative of the aspirations of many young men
and boys. His insights will assist us in formulating a game plan for com-
bating the maladaptive attitudes young athletes learn through sport. It
should be recognized throughout that the key to our success is to reach
men like Michael who have the power to influence the sexist attitudes of
those athletes who rape.

The purpose of this chapter is not to indict the athletic community for
the violent nature of our society. We could argue that sports are a product of an already violent, competitive culture. Instead, we hope to illuminate the significant influence athletics have on the development of young
boys in the United States, and some of the ways competitive sports have
inadvertently contributed to the sexism prevalent in our society. Only

when we are aware of the danger can we effectively restructure the experience to define masculinity inclusive of a feminist perspective.

DEFINING MASCULINITY

During the 1990s masculinity has been a central focus of public discourse, and its definition has been called into question. The military has been forced to recognize women in their military academies, highly respected political figures have been called on their deviant sexual behavior, and athletes have been increasingly implicated in various charges of sexual misconduct. These institutions, which were once exclusively male, are no longer the safe havens for maladaptive masculine behavior and sexist tradition they once were. These men are scrambling to understand the new rules of gender relationships and are anxious to protect the institutions they were once so proud of.

To understand these changing roles, we must first examine how society defines the masculine and feminine. Michael Kimmel identifies fear of other men as a cornerstone of masculinity. "[Men] fear humiliation, losing their competitive ranking among men, being dominated by other men."[1] This deep-seated fear of other men is rooted in our fear of inferiority. Adler believed that this fear motivates us to overcome our weaknesses by striving for superiority.[2] But since we have learned that to be feminine is to be weak, we must necessarily deny any identification with femininity and measure our superiority relative to other men.

O'Sullivan describes the traditional masculine man as independent, successful sexually (in terms of numbers of partners), physically tough, and financially secure.[3] To fulfill these expectations, we either exhibit our superiority or we degrade those we are most threatened by. Quite often this denigration involves relegating the other to the status of woman. Terrence Crowley explains, "as I aggrandize myself, I demean my opposite. As I deify the masculine, I necessarily vilify women. The degradation not only makes attack permissible, it makes it a moral imperative."[4] By defining masculinity and femininity in opposition to one another, we set the stage for gender inequity.

The feminist perspective challenges this notion by asking men to acknowledge the privilege society grants them and to embrace an egalitarian alternative. This is not an easy task because in a competitive, male-defined, sports-dominated society such as the United States, in order to accept egalitarianism, men are expected to relinquish the power they possess. Jason Schultz maintains that as men, we cannot give up that power.[5] He likens men's critical examination and work against male privilege to holding our hand over a burning candle: We can hold our hand over the flame as long as we wish, but if it becomes too hot, we can always pull our hand away. Similarly, as men we can fight sexism and challenge patriarchy, but when it becomes too risky and too personal, we can always pull our hand away. Women, on the other hand, can never pull their hands away from sexism. The uncomfortable and often damaging flame of misogyny continues to harm them. That advantage will always be ours so long as inequality exists. So instead of enduring the pain, our goal should be to extinguish the flame. To do so, we must examine the means by which this inequality is reinforced.

THE INFLUENCE OF ATHLETICS

There are many characteristics of our society that support and encourage sexist tradition. Perhaps the most influential in the lives of young boys is athletic competition. I grew up with sports from the time I was born. My father, and his father, were die-hard football fans, and the Buffalo Bills were their team. Each Sunday, from September to December, they planted themselves before the television set to consume almost three hours of hard-hitting action; they leapt from their chairs and screamed in jubilation whenever the Bills scored, and became frustrated, pensive, and argumentative if a call went against them. The early nineties brought to the Nickel City a collective vitality and energy that could be extinguished only by four consecutive Superbowl loses. Buffalo sports fans, including the men in my family, experienced what social psychologists call Basking in Reflected Glory.[6] Our collective esteem was defined, in part, by the success of our hometown heroes. We learned to identify with athletics and the men who compete. We saw in athletes what we dreamed about for ourselves. If our team lost, we felt the disappointment. Conversely, if our team won, our egos were inflated, we reveled in the shared success, local holidays were declared, and we welcomed our heroes with ticker-tape parades.

If sports competition could have so significant an impact on those filling the stands, what effect does it have on the men who participate? Michael's experience as a young boy growing up in Columbus, Ohio, serves as an illustration:

> Sports have always been a part of my life. My childhood memories are dominated by thoughts of my brothers and I playing football, baseball, and basketball in the backyard of our home in Columbus, Ohio. Our heroes were Archie Griffen and the Ohio State Buckeyes, Pete Rose and the Big Red Machine, Reggie Jackson and the New York Yankees, and John Havlicek and the Boston Celtics. Our discussions at dinner became arguments over who was the greatest center fielder in baseball or who was the

best running back in football. I still remember a summer evening in 1976 when my mother called us down from bed to watch a youthful Ray Leonard win the Olympic Gold Medal in boxing at the Montreal Olympic Games. I felt very close to my parents that evening. I must have been eight years old at the time, yet this memory remains embedded in my heart.

Michael learned at an early age that athletes were to be admired and emulated. They were great people who could do anything. They were infallible. They were the men we could look up to and someday hope to be like. They were also the men our fathers adored. Michael describes feeling close to his parents that evening of the summer Olympics not because Ray Leonard was especially important, but rather because it gave him an opportunity to bond with his parents. By age eight Michael had learned to associate intimacy with athletic competition; he also learned that to receive adoration and affection from his family, particularly his father, he would need to excel at sports.

Growing up in an athletic environment teaches men to be masculine by emphasizing how not to be feminine. The following are examples of this tendency. While playing catch in the backyard, Dad asserted himself in a very serious, coachlike manner. "Stop throwing like a girl," he yelled. In Little League, at tryouts for the all-star team, the coach jeered a feeble attempt to hit the ball: "You swing like a pansy." During training camp for high school football, the coaches threatened, "Many of you girls will not make it to the end of the week." For those who persevered, the weekly insult was "You hit like a pussy," or in reference to pain, "Take it like a man." Each of these coaches exploited a fear of being inferior, and they equated inferiority with femininity. If our coaches and fathers thought exhibiting feminine qualities showed signs of weakness and helplessness, then to make us feel stronger, we must deny any identification with the feminine. Coaches have modeled the use of this tactic, and the locker room has served as a classroom to reinforce its value.

THE LOCKER ROOM CULTURE

The locker room is a breeding ground for male aggression and the denigration of women. It is seen as a bastion for male privilege and a place where boys learn to become men.[7] To the outside observer the locker room appears to be a safe place for men to be themselves without fear of ridicule. In truth, it is a fragile environment based on tenuous, superficial relationships. Two conflicting forces underlie the facade of the locker room culture: competition and fear.

Curry identifies competition as the foundation of the locker room.[8] Athletes are competing with other teams in their conference or division, they are competing with one another for status and position on the team, and they are looking to enhance their position with their peers through egregious use of alcohol and the sexual exploitation of women. They are constantly vying for acceptance and are acutely aware that one bad game or one small injury could change their status in the locker room permanently. No matter what level an athlete is at, or what status he has attained on the team, each is aware that others wait anxiously to replace him. At no point is a male athlete completely secure in this environment.

The locker room culture extends well beyond the confines of steamy showers and musty cubicles. It refers more to the way male athletes relate to one another off the field. The locker room is merely symbolic of the privilege these men often receive as athletes. Michael shares an experience from a recruiting trip as a high school senior that illustrates the pervasive nature of the locker room culture:

> For the most part, the party was a typical college party. We drank beer as fast as we could to avoid harassment from our potential teammates. Although at the time I was not much of a beer drinker, I managed to drink enough to avoid attracting attention from the "beer police" yet not enough to become excessively drunk. Most of the night was spent drinking and listening to music. Something happened at this party, however, which was not typical of most of the parties I attended prior to this point in my life. Midway through the evening and after most of us had several beers in our system, one of the veteran athletes informed my friend and I that the real fun was about to begin. One of his teammates strolled up to a female guest and proceeded to pick her up in the air via a reverse body lock and bit her buttocks while his teammates counted to eight. Our host informed us that this game was called the "rodeo," and that although some of the women in attendance got upset, all of them enjoyed it for the most part.
>
> This game went on most of the night with only one of the victims becoming extremely upset. The problem was that this person happened to be the one I chose for the "rodeo." She threw her beer on me and slapped me as I turned my back. She ran off in embarrassment as most of the members of the team came to congratulate me for conquering such a feisty opponent; one of those who congratulated me was the head coach. Immediately following this incident, the embarrassment I felt was quickly replaced with the typical male bonding, which I have since come to view with disdain. Not one of my potential teammates or the coaching staff informed me that what I had done was out of line; to the contrary, I was officially on my way to full acceptance into the male sports culture, where the objectification of women is commonplace and aggression toward women is nurtured.

The recruiting trip experience may be the most telling aspect of the locker room culture. Athletes and coaches are eager to impress the new recruit, and they will do everything in their power to make a favorable impression. In order to show their best side, they give the young athlete a glimpse of the coveted benefits of membership. These new recruits are courted by the active members of the team and tempted to join by the freedom of membership and camaraderie of brotherhood. This enticement is used to convince the new recruit to attend the school. Once training camp begins, the tables turn. Now the recruit must prove himself worthy of membership. Only then will he earn the benefits that were dangled like carrots during the recruiting trip. This process is similar to the rush process for Greek letter social fraternities.[9]

The locker room culture can be illustrated in many ways but is probably best understood through the conversations that take place between teammates. Curry has observed that, in the locker room, conversations fell into two categories: "(a) the dynamics of competition, status attainment, and bonding among male athletes, and (b) the dynamics of defending one's masculinity through homophobic talk and talk about women as objects."[10] Don Sabo adds that few conversations in the locker room regard serious intimate partners or relationships with female peers.[11] This sort of discussion would open an athlete to the ridicule of their teammates. Most often their conversations are attempts to relate through common or shared experience. Some men tell tall tales of legendary success on the field or the wrestling mat. Others tell similar stories of sexual prowess in the bedroom. One conversation Michael was privy to as a wrestler illustrates this:

Athlete 1: (After a long practice, while sitting in the sauna) Man, I was unstoppable today. I must have had fifty takedowns or so without giving up one. I don't think anyone touched my leg.

Athlete 2: What kind of shit have you been smoking! I beat the shit out of you during our match. You live in a fantasyland; what color is the sky in your little world?

Athlete 1: You could never take me down. Shit, all you do is stall and block everything I try.

Athlete 2: Yeah, you are the expert on everything—except women of course. Maybe that is why you can't get laid if your life depended on it. Hell, I am starting to think you are an f——n' fag.

Athlete 1: F— you! (Leaves the sauna)

This conversation illustrates Curry's observations very clearly. The first exchange is an attempt by athlete 1 to attain status by emphasizing his dominance on the mat; he conveys the message to athlete 2 that he is the best. The latter, not to be outdone, reminds his teammate that he was not nearly that successful in their match. This statement is made to reaffirm athlete 2's status and protect his esteem. He then follows with a comment that is indicative of Curry's second category of locker room talk. By referring to athlete 1's sexual inadequacy, he has changed the competition

from the mat to the bedroom and even asserted that athlete 1 is homosexual, defending his own masculinity while simultaneously attacking
that of his peer's. In doing so, he relegates athlete 1 to an inferior status
and has claimed superiority.

The Principle of Pain

One way men counter this sort of abuse in the locker room is to approve their status through the endurance of pain. In many locker rooms,
particularly those belonging to aggressive contact sports teams like football, hockey, wrestling, and basketball, you will find the aphorism, "No
Pain, No Gain," displayed prominently near the coach's office or over the
weight room entrance. It emphasizes that to win you must be willing to
endure pain. At the end of the game, the most celebrated players are often those who played through injury to support the winning (or losing)
effort. Rarely are athletes commended for choosing not to play through
an injury. In fact, the typical response is one of derision: "He couldn't take
it" or "Where was he when we needed him?" The latter insinuates that
the athlete failed his team, that he was weak. Perhaps he was not a de-
pendable contributor after all.

Timothy Beneke observes the celebration of tattoos, sculpted physiques,
and scars as indicative of athletes' willingness to endure pain to prove
masculinity.[12] Never have we been more aware of this pain principle than
in the early months of 1998 when three wrestlers died as they worked
feverishly to shed enough weight to qualify for a lower class of competition.[13] They subjected themselves to immeasurable pain, like countless
wrestlers before them, in the hopes that they would qualify to wrestle a
smaller, weaker opponent. This does not guarantee a victory, but if the
athlete loses, his teammates will know that he made every sacrifice in his
attempt to win. In some ways this serves to protect the esteem of the athlete because he may attribute the loss to the weakness that resulted from
the pain he endured. In either case, the athlete has won in the eyes of his
teammates.

The Entitlement of Male Athletes

Just as athletes learn that the endurance of pain will translate to success on the field and status in the eyes of fans, coaches, and peers, they
are also taught that success will afford them countless privileges off the
field. This sense of entitlement is ingrained from childhood and recon-
firmed at each new level of competition. Mariah Burton Nelson observes

that by the time athletes reach college, they have already reaped numerous benefits ranging from scholarships, trophies, and fan mail to leniency in the classroom.[14] Merrill Melnick refers to this as the support of an athletic justice system.[15]

Take, for example, the case of Tom Watson, former football player at Syracuse University.[16] In 1986 Watson was convicted of sexual misconduct in a court of law, yet the school maintained he had not violated university policy. Despite the conviction he was allowed to remain in school, maintain his scholarship, and stay on the team; his only punishment through the university came in the form of a five-game suspension levied by the university's chancellor. More recent was the conviction of former high school wrestling star, Alex Kelly.[17] After the first attempt at conviction was declared a mistrial, Kelly fled to Europe, where he was supported financially by his parents. After ten years a fugitive, Alex returned to the United States and was tried and convicted of the 1986 rape of a former girlfriend. These cases illustrate that even if the courts hold them accountable, athletes will find leniency with their families, peers, coaches, and institutions—the athletic justice system.

The Spur Posse, of Lakewood High School in California, was probably the most horrific illustration of this sense of entitlement.[18] These young men, mostly athletes, developed a competition of sexual conquest. For each woman they had sex with, they scored a point. Goals were set according to the jersey numbers of their favorite athletes; Michael Jordan, for example, would be the code name for twenty-three sexual conquests. But what was more disturbing than the Spur Posse scandal itself was the response of the athletes' fathers. Instead of expressing remorse for the women who felt victimized, many of the fathers lauded the virility of their young and potent prodigies. These boys learned, once again, that their actions, at worst, might be merely against the law if they were caught—a lesson learned many times through athletic competition. The courts might hold them accountable, but if they receive support and adulation from their fathers and coaches, the risk may seem worth it.

Michael DiSabato describes a similar phenomenon at the collegiate level:

> Athletes develop deviant competitions which allow them to bond in a masculine manner. Several athletes within my peer group (which included athletes who competed in wrestling, football, track, soccer, hockey, tennis, gymnastics, and basketball) developed a "game" similar to that which was made famous by the Spur Posse. The "game" not only consisted of tracking the number of women the athlete had sex with but also included the number of times they had sex during the "session."
>
> Members of a very successful athletic program at a major Midwestern university developed the most disturbing version of this "game." The team

included several national champions, all-Americans, World/Olympic med-alists, and assistant coaches. They awarded points to those who were able to penetrate various orifices during one sexual encounter; in other words, these athletes would award two points to an athlete who successfully pen-etrated a woman's vagina, one point for an athlete who received oral sex, three points to an athlete who had anal sex, and five points for something outrageous, like a nose or ear. The goal of the "game" is to ejaculate into the orifice. If the athlete ejaculates, he scores (with scoring closely resem-bling the scoring system of the athlete's competitive sport), whether or not the sex was consensual. Many, if not most, of these encounters involved some form of sexual assault.

This extreme example of the game illustrates how clearly integrated athletic competition and sexual conquest become for male athletes. The game has placed ejaculation at a premium, with little regard for the woman at all. The woman merely serves as a playing field on which men compete for sexual supremacy with one another. If this were not harmful enough, consider the consequences of group sexual assault, remarkably similar to head-to-head competition. Former football players at Glen Ridge High School in New Jersey shocked a nation when they turned this into a spectator sport.

Gang Rape: The Epitome of Sexist Male Bonding

A situation remarkably similar to the Spur Posse debacle, the Glen Ridge High School incident, left the country shocked and angry. A group of thirteen high school athletes persuaded a young retarded girl to return with them to the basement of the cocaptain of the football team.[19] She agreed when the members promised her a date. Upon returning, four of the men raped and sodomized her with a broom handle and a miniature baseball bat in front of an audience of their peers. The four men did not deny what took place, but they did claim it was consensual. In March 1993 three of the young boys were convicted of first-degree aggravated sexual assault, and the fourth was convicted of third-degree conspiracy.[20]

The Glen Ridge boys represent something we wish we could discount as an aberration—an unexplainable, random act of hatred perpetrated by monsters. Our response here reminds me of our collective response to the 1996 case of Susan Smith and the drowning of her two young children,[21] and to the rash of teen shootings during the early months of 1998. We wish desperately to believe that these atrocities could not happen in our own backyards. Gavin DeBecker warns us that this collective denial prevents us from reading the warning signals of violence.[22] Take, for example, the fifteen-year-old boy in Springfield, Oregon, who sprayed countless bul-lets into a crowd of his peers, killing three and injuring at least twenty-three others.[23] He had been arrested the day before and released to his parents for the unlawful possession of a weapon on school premises. Shortly after the incident, his parents were found shot to death in their home, which was secured by countless homemade bombs crafted by the young teen. Should we have predicted this senseless outburst of violence?

Similarly, group sexual assault or gang rape may not be the anomaly we desperately hope it is. Peggy Reeves Sanday notes "the widespread tendency on the part of college administrators to ignore or cover up reports or specific instances. In protecting the male students involved, the school is also protecting its image."[24] Administrators protect these men by dissociating asocial behavior from the perpetrator and attributing it to something else. Our response to the Springfield, Oregon, incident was similar. While searching for answers, we blamed society, we second-guessed the parents, and we debated the issue of gun control, but we refused to believe that a fifteen-year-old boy from a good home in rural America was capable of such barbarity. Similarly, we refuse to believe that our childhood heroes and athletic role models could also be sexual predators.

It is important to realize that gang rape is not about sexual gratification; it is a confirmation of one's heterosexuality and an opportunity for men to be sexually intimate with one another through the use of an objectified female form. A group of men masturbating to a pornographic movie, often referred to as a circle jerk, is an illustration of the same misogynistic behavior. We long for ways to be close with one another, but we are taught that intimacy is expressed through sex and that sex with other men is deviant. Our homophobia forces us to choose between sharing our feelings and being labeled as feminine, or denying our emotional desire to be close while maintaining our status as masculine men. Our limited concept of intimacy prevents healthy expressions between men and forces either isolation or deviant rituals of masculine affirmation. Gang rape is far too frequently the result.

EDUCATING MALE ATHLETES

The key to reaching male athletes is to believe that each and every one of them is essential to eradicating sexual violence. We must see athletes as partners in the fight to end violence against women. We must also remember that violence and aggression are the product of twenty or more years of socialization and cannot be unlearned through a single workshop. The process of educating these men must be comprehensive. Tom Jackson indicates that the most critical first step in working with male athletes is to gather support from the coaching staff.[25]

The Role of Coaches

If locker rooms are a classroom for sexism, then coaches are the professors. Players observe coaches and emulate their behavior. Athletes simultaneously admire and fear them. If the head coach says a program is mandatory, no player will dare question his authority. To do so would be to jeopardize his status on the team. Look, for example, at the message Michael received during the "rodeo." His initial reaction was one of guilt and regret, but the moment the head coach congratulated him, his behavior was validated and his fear was washed away. If the coach had reprimanded the players for their harassing behavior, the sexist tradition of the rodeo would not have continued. What message do you think Indiana University head basketball coach Bobby Knight sent when he said in response to a question from Connie Chung, "If rape is inevitable, relax and enjoy it"?[26]

Rick Pitino, on the other hand, sent a very positive message. Under his guidance the University of Kentucky was the only Division I basketball program to have a woman assistant coach.[27] Her presence forced the elimination of sexist jokes in the locker room, and it helped members of the team develop respect for women as athletes and as people.

The coaches are essential in gaining access to athletes and supporting antirape messages, but who should deliver that message? Jackson suggests utilizing male athletes as educators in the locker room.[28] Athletic teams are cohesive groups of individuals that share many common experiences. They are reluctant to accept a message delivered by an outsider, particularly if the message is delivered in an accusatory fashion. Michael confirms, "former athletes who have established credibility within the fraternity of sport, are more likely to receive support from the coaching staff, and are likely to present material to male student-athletes in a manner which recognizes their unique experiences." A fellow athlete will appreciate the intensity of training, the long hours, the pressures of competition, and the personal sacrifices. Jackson Katz has been extremely successful with the Mentors in Violence Prevention (MVP) program, quite simply because he understands the experience of college athletics. As a former football quarterback, he is acutely aware of the resistance educators face when addressing male athletes. He personalizes the issue for men and gives them ways to become part of the solution rather than the problem.

As Curry points out, many of these men avoid participating in the sexist tradition of the locker room altogether.[29] Unfortunately, most turn their backs on the sexist and often assaultive behaviors of their peers. Katz likens this complicity to the "bystander effect," a phenomenon commonly observed in studies of people's reluctance to help others in distress.[30] This emphasis challenges men to reach beyond the personal by refusing to tolerate the violence perpetrated by their teammates. It challenges the notion that all men are potential rapists, and it allows men to identify with the majority who do not rape.

Tom Jackson employs a slightly different approach, which explores the athlete's approximate development of moral judgment.[31] In his work with Division I athletes Jackson has found that a disproportionate number of athletes are at premoral levels of development. At this stage behavior modification is best achieved by illustrating the consequences of one's actions. The loss of money or the threat of jail time are two of the most salient consequences to athletes. The caution, "If you rape a woman, you run the risk of being drafted in a later round," may be convincing enough to prevent these players from committing acts of sexual violence.

Kilmartin asserts that any approach designed to reach men must include a discussion of our socialization as men.[32] This aspect is so critical, and yet it is often overlooked. We discuss the definitions of sexual assault, the frequency with which it occurs, the impact it has on survivors, and the fact that men are the perpetrators, but seldom do we examine the ways we learn to be aggressive or the fear we have of one another. We do not talk about the pressure we feel to perform or the stigma surrounding failure. And we do not discuss the lessons we learn on the playing field that tell us aggression will lead to success. If we took more time to examine these issues as they pertain to our masculine identities, we would be empowered to own the problem, assess our behaviors, and make changes where they are necessary.

Finally, we must emphasize male accountability in our presentations. As Alan Berkowitz suggests, if we continue to focus on women, we reinforce the attitudes that allow men to deny responsibility for the problem.[33] The simplest way to minimize the focus on women is to work with men in single gender groups. The presence of women in a presentation reinforces their belief that this is a woman's issue. By removing women from the equation, at least during the initial stages, it becomes an issue men cannot deny. They may resist the message, but it will be theirs. This is especially effective when discussing with men the way we define masculinity.

CONCLUSION

There is no clear solution to the problems we face, but one thing is clear: Change must happen at a societal level. The social construction of masculinity must be restructured to be more inclusive of a feminist perspective. Male athletes must learn to see women as equals in competition, in the classroom, and in relationships. Men have been taught to objectify women, and athletic competition has reinforced that. Equal opportunities for women, like the WNBA and the introduction of women's softball as an Olympic sport, are steps in the right direction, but we must simultaneously redefine the male athletic experience to value personal accomplishment and deemphasize competition. And we must stop equating inferiority with femininity in male athletics. Only when these changes occur will we see true equality for women and men and, ultimately, the eradication of violence from our relationships.

18

SEXUAL VIOLENCE: THE LEGAL FRONT

Brett Sokolow

Issues surrounding sexual violence transpire on many different levels having multiple layers and varying facets. This essay offers a legal perspective on sexual violence, which is itself a many-layered context. Sexual violence will take on great and small shades of meaning for the prosecutor, the victim's rights lawyer, the defense lawyer representing accused perpetrators, the lobbyist working to change state and federal sexual assault laws, the college legal counsel, the sexual assault policy consultant, the legal theorist, and the legal reformer. What these practitioners share is a common vantage point from which to view a decade of significant changes on the legal front of the anti-sexual-violence movement.

Since the late 1980s we have witnessed legal changes in policy, philosophy, statutes, attitudes, rules of evidence, and legal services for victims. As the 1990s draw to a close, Congress is seriously entertaining debate on a Victim's Rights Amendment to the U.S. Constitution (we might better term it a Survivor's Rights Amendment), and a three-hundred-page draft of the 1998 Violence against Women Act (VAWA II) is being circulated among stakeholders to gain input before it is introduced before Congress later this spring. These new legislative enactments may soon add to the legal arsenal of tools—an arsenal that has grown tremendously in size within this last decade. But rather than looking forward, this chapter affords us an opportunity to look back to see what really has been accomplished, and to see what extent these juris-systemic changes have impacted the reality of sexual violence in America.

SYSTEMIC CHANGE

New Definitions

The most significant change to the reality of sexual violence has been a reformulation of the definitions we use to proscribe sexually violative behaviors in our society. More accurately, this decade has brought us a retreat from the legislative baggage that has been tacked onto statutory definitions of rape and sexual assault over many decades, in deference to a reemergence and modernization of the common law definitions of these crimes. Before states enacted voluminous criminal codes, our law was taken from a basic set of rules that were borrowed from England and known as the common law. At common law, most crimes could not be consented to, though most intentional torts and a select few crimes were exceptions to the rule. For example, when two boxers brutalize each other on Pay-per-View, the common law would have considered those boxers to have committed criminal battery as well as the tort of battery upon each other. Yet the boxers' consent to the prize fight effectively abrogates any illegality that might otherwise have existed. Like battery, common law rape—the carnal knowledge of a woman by a man not her husband—was a crime unless it was effectively consented to.

Over time, as these common law rules became codified by states, they collected moral, religious, and evidentiary baggage that transformed this consent construct into a definition requiring the use of force, a showing of resistance, or other physical harm in addition to that caused by the act of forced intercourse. Force was often defined very narrowly, as physical force. Under these codes only women could be raped, and rape was limited to vaginal penetration exclusively. Degrees upon degrees of sexual misconduct, sexual battery, sexual assault, forcible intercourse, and involuntary intercourse became part of the legal lexicon.

To a great extent we are still today saddled with statutory definitions of multivariate complexity, but states are beginning to reclaim the consent concept of the common law. At least for some degrees of sexual assault, a majority of states now have adopted consent-based definitions. Force may be an aggravating factor, or may serve as additional proof, but it is increasingly being abandoned as the sine qua non of rape. Where codes previously provided that sex against one's will constituted rape, modern revision now holds that rape is sexual intercourse without one's consent.

This shift represents a subtle yet all-important change. The onus of giving consent is taken away from the object of the sexual initiator, instead requiring that the initiator gain that consent from the object of the sexual attention before any permissible sexual activity may take place. This reemergence of consent-based doctrine recognizes and ratifies a simple principle of the common law—our personal sovereignty. We have the right not to be acted upon unless we wish to be acted upon and communicate that wish to the actor. Our silence is not our permission. You may not take my wallet simply because I have not said you cannot have it. Moreover, this restoration of the common law principles of consent aids in the uniform application of the laws. A murder victim never was required to resist an attacker in order to prove it was murder. A mugging victim need not resist a thief in order for the theft to occur. So this reformulation restores a sense of symmetry to sex crime codes where anomaly has heretofore reigned.

Expanding the Scope of Rape Laws

This definitional change has other important aspects as well. Adding to this sense of legal symmetry, state laws are recognizing that men and women are no different with respect to rape, and that definitions ought to apply to both sexes uniformly, as both potential victims and potential perpetrators. Similarly, we have seen a shift away from defining rape by reference to vaginal penetration only, adopting broader orifice-based statutes. In many states where force-based definitions are still in use, judges and juries are not waiting for the legislatures to act. They are moving the case law progressively forward, hoping that the statutes will soon catch up. In other areas of the country, the statutes have led public opinion, and the legal system is teething on the new formulations, not quite yet ready to let go of the old.

One final area of definitional change is that some states are creating, while some are abolishing, the categorization of rape by the relationship of the victim and perpetrator. No clear national trend is emerging. Some states that have used "rape" and "sexual assault" terminology are now using terms like "stranger rape," "acquaintance rape," and "date rape" to make legal distinctions based on the relationship of those involved. Some states consider "stranger rape" to be more severe than rape situations where the parties are known to each other. They create harsher recommended sentences for "real" stranger rapes, and lesser punishments for "other" rapes. Some states even go so far as to classify some date rapes as misdemeanors, which is a discouraging antivictim practice.

Still other states have had such categorizations previously and are returning to a uniformity of terminology where all rape is rape. These states have recognized that victims of known assailants do not suffer less because they were not attacked by strangers, and often experience the added trauma of a violation of trust that is not experienced by those whose victimization is at the hands of unknown assailants.

Defining Rape on Campus

Leading the advance guard, as always, are our colleges. Not bound by state statutory definitions, colleges have led the way in adopting consent-based definitions in their conduct codes, even when the states in which they are sited steadfastly adhere to outmoded constructs. Colleges are also leading the way in defining more precisely what "effective consent" means. Although most states have chosen an incapacitation standard (for example, one who is physically incapacitated by use of alcohol, other drugs, or otherwise is not capable of giving effective consent), many colleges have adopted intoxication or impairment-based standards, which are more restrictive, because they prevent the giving of informed consent at lesser levels of alcohol and drug consumption.

Victim's Rights on Campus

Definitional changes mark only some of the progress colleges are making. Many colleges will now issue campus-based restraining orders against students to prevent harassment or stalking. Some colleges are experimenting with allowing students involved in sexual assault campus trials to bring attorneys as advisors, and many others offer victims the empowering option of presenting their own case against the accused.

Backward Steps for Colleges

Not all is improvement on the college front, however. Mediation has become an important tool for resolving campus sexual misconduct cases, but the enormous popularity of mediation may be going too far. Whereas most sexual misconduct may be amenable to such informal resolution where it is desired by the victim and provides an educational opportunity for the accused, colleges are also offering mediation for incidents of rape. All too often the result is a slap on the wrist for a felony, and victims who later regret not pushing for a more formal resolution. The real danger of mediating rapes comes from the few colleges that use the mediation process to keep the incidents quiet, sweeping campus rapes under the carpet and leaving rapists at large on campus to rape again.

Also disturbing is the trend of some colleges to refuse to deal adjudicatively with sexual assault on campus. Many college administrators simply feel that colleges are ill equipped to handle such serious crimes, and that the criminal courts offer the proper venue. Although they may be right in an ideal world, it is both possible and necessary for colleges to hear sexual assault cases, and it may well be required by law. With the average criminal case load reaching a backlog of eighteen months in most areas of the country, it is simply untenable for colleges to refuse to hear cases, thereby leaving potentially dangerous rapists free to victimize again.

Colleges have a duty to protect their students from foreseeable crimes, and waiting for a criminal trial is not an adequate response. Further, though training may be costly in terms of personnel and expense, many colleges are dealing quite successfully with campus sexual violence, proving that with enough commitment, it is entirely possible to address such incidents in a campus forum. It is also arguable that courts could read the two campus-directed laws discussed in the following sections to require that colleges create policies, procedures, and protocols for dealing with incidents of campus sexual violence, and that colleges that refuse to hear these cases are in violation of federal law.

Marital Rape Laws

Still another facet of rape law that continues to be transformed is in the area of marital rape. From common law property concepts, where the wife was the property of her husband and was therefore his to do with as he desired, a thirty-year movement has chipped away at such notions to the point where every state now proscribes marital rape at some level. Some states make marital rape a crime but assign a lesser punishment than for "real rape." Other states condone rape within marriage unless the couple is legally separated or a restraining order has been violated. Refusal to provide sex to a spouse is still grounds for a fault divorce in some states. The few concessions that states have made to activists in this area have been gained only after exceptional struggles and often would never have happened without strong support from female state legislators.

A More User-Friendly Approach in State Courts

This decade has seen changes in more than just the definitions of sex crimes. States are changing their legal procedures to reflect greater victim sensitivity in a venue that has often been as likely as not to revictimize those it purportedly seeks to vindicate.

Victim advocates are now part of many prosecutorial offices, whereas little concern was given to such positions in the past. They guide victims in important decisions and provide information to victims and their families on an often confusing and complicated process.

Many states now afford rights to test accused rapists for HIV and allow the victim to reveal those test results to other sexual partners they have had since the rape. State penal codes also are likely to provide for increased penalties when HIV is knowingly transmitted to a victim during a sex crime, including possible murder charges.

Greater numbers of courts are acknowledging the sensitivity of rape and child abuse trials by allowing victims to give testimony from separate rooms, or by closed-circuit so that they do not have to face intimidation by the in-court presence of the attacker. So called "tender years" testimony is exempt from many common evidentiary restrictions.

Sequestration rules that have been used by defendants to exclude from the courtroom those who might be key supporters of the victim are increasingly coming under attack. So, too, the laws of evidence are gaining modern sensitivities and victim's rights savvy. Rape shield laws recognize in most jurisdictions that the victim's past sexual history is not a subject relevant to the victim's conduct with the accused. Some courts have even gone so far as to recognize that even past conduct with the accused may not bear any direct relation to whether or not consent was given for the incident in question.

NEW LAWS

The Violence against Women Act

The fight against rape as a form of domestic violence has been more successful on the federal level than on the state level. In 1994 Congress enacted the Violence against Women Act (VAWA), and a federal Violence against Women Office was established to administer the provisions of this law. While grassroots antiviolence activists tend to question the importance and effect of VAWA so far, it is viewed by victim's rights attorneys as a quantum leap, the results of which will be felt strongly in the years to come as courts develop a body of case law on VAWA-based decisions.

VAWA is a broad congressional enactment, attempting to address violence against women on many different levels. For example, VAWA's many separate provisions include:

- education and evidentiary training on sexual assault, domestic violence, and stalking for state court judges and personnel;
- grants to prevent crime on public transportation and to study the problem and research solutions;
- grants for the establishment of training programs for parole and probation officers and others who work with released sex offenders;

- research, development, and proposal of model legislation and rules of evidence for the protection of confidential communications between sexual assault and domestic violence survivors and their counselors;
- compilation and dissemination of information on community treatment programs to all convicted federal sex offenders before they are released from confinement;
- a study of and postal regulations on procedures to secure the confidentiality of the addresses of domestic violence shelters and abused persons;
- creation of a national research agenda to increase the understanding and control of violence against women;
- provisions allowing a federal court to order mandatory HIV testing of those charged with sex crimes, even in the absence of a state right to test an alleged perpetrator in a state prosecution;
- provisions appropriating funds for and requiring the completion of a national baseline study on campus sexual assault;
- provisions appropriating funds for and requiring the completion of a report on battered women's syndrome;
- provisions requiring an audit of federal domestic violence record-keeping practices, and a requirement to include domestic violence and intimidation crimes in the National Incident-Based Reporting System, and to provide Congress with an annual report thereon evaluating the effectiveness of state antistalking efforts and legislation;
- provisions announcing the sense of the Senate regarding the need for a violence against women initiative to address the issue of statutory rape;
- grants to states to create and improve local, state, and federal stalking and domestic violence tracking databases, with recommendations on improvements for intrastate communication and data sharing between civil and criminal courts;
- funding and a requirement for research and reporting on how states may collect centralized databases on the incidence of sexual and domestic violence;
- funding and a requirement for a study to produce a national projection of the incidence of domestic violence-related injuries, health costs, and recommended health care strategies for reducing the incidence and cost of such injuries;
- rural domestic violence and child abuse enforcement assistance grants;
- studies of the extent and understanding of the nature of gender bias

in the federal courts and the establishment of a clearinghouse to disseminate the results of the study;

- federal criminalization of interstate domestic violence and creation of a civil rights action for damages resulting from gender-motivated crimes of violence.

The constitutionality of the provisions of this final paragraph have been the most widely debated and hotly contested of all the VAWA provisions within the legal community, and quite a few test cases have already been filed. Thus far only one court has held these provisions to be unconstitutional, and that decision was overturned on appeal. Six other courts have upheld the law, including two federal appellate circuits. Should these provisions ultimately withstand constitutional scrutiny, they will provide survivors a potent VAWA-based means of prosecuting those who commit interstate violence, and of collecting damages from those who act violently upon them on the basis of their gender.

Title IX

VAWA is not the only federal legal tool that has been drafted for the prevention and aid of victims of sexual violence. Two landmark pieces of congressional legislation could have profound impact on the issues of college safety and college sexual assault victim's rights. In the early 1970s Congress enacted Title IX to recognize and federally proscribe sexual harassment at colleges as a form of gender-based discrimination. Mirroring Title VII's employment-based discrimination scheme, Title IX prohibits quid pro quo and hostile environment sexual harassment by granting a civil cause of action for damages and injunctive relief to victims. Yet it has taken nearly thirty years for Title IX to be applied in the context of sexual violence. Thus its discussion here is quite timely.

Since its enactment Title IX's scope has been a subject of much question and debate. Should a cause of action lie against only the perpetrators, or also against the college if it somehow contributes to the creation of a hostile environment? Should sexual assault be considered a form of sexual harassment under Title IX? Should the scope of Title IX extend beyond college employees to reach all members of the college community? Federal courts are finally supplying us with the answers to these tough questions. The courts are slowly but surely opening up and expanding the reach and scope of Title IX's provisions. It cannot yet be said with certainty that the answer to the above questions is uniformly yes, but the trend that is emerging so indicates.

A federal appeals court has gone so far as to hold that rape is the ultimate form of sexual harassment, and that colleges that knowingly fail to adequately address incidents of student-on-student campus rape may be liable for creating a hostile environment. This evolution of Title IX represents an exciting, though still nascent, means of bringing campus rape out of the shadows and into the courts.

The Student Right-To-Know and Campus Security Act

A second federal law, also still in the incipient stages of its application, may soon provide campus victims of sexual violence with yet another tool for vindicating their rights in civil suits. Even in its present form the 1990 Student Right-to-Know and Campus Security Act (as amended by the Campus Sexual Assault Victims' Bill of Rights in 1992) is the only federal law that clearly and specifically addresses the requirements that colleges must meet with regard to campus sexual assault and assault victims' rights, if colleges want to continue to receive federal Title IV Higher Education Act assistance (millions of dollars). Presently, the following are the main provisions of the Campus Security Act (CSA) which directly affect sexual assault:

- a requirement that colleges collect, publish, and distribute in an annual campus security report to students a comprehensive set of campus crime statistics for the previous year, including reported forcible and nonforcible sex offenses;
- a requirement that every college must state in its annual security report its policy on sexual assault and its disciplinary hearing procedures for sex offenses;
- a requirement that colleges must include in the annual campus security report a description of educational programs provided by the college to promote awareness of rape, acquaintance rape, and other sex offenses;
- an affirmative statement of student rights, including:
  - the right of both the accuser and the accused in a campus sexual assault hearing to have the same opportunity to have others present in support or advisory capacities;
  - an amendment to the Family Education Rights and Privacy Act of 1974 (FERPA) to provide the right of the victim to know the outcome of a campus hearing in which sexual assault is alleged;
  - the right of students to be informed of their options to notify proper law enforcement authorities, including on-campus and local police, and the option to be assisted by campus authorities in

notifying such law enforcement authorities, if the student so chooses;

• the right of survivors to be notified of available counseling, mental health, or student services for victims of sexual assault, both on campus and in the community;

• the right to notification of and options for, and available assistance in, changing academic and living situations after an alleged assault incident, if so requested by the victim and if such changes are reasonably available;

• a requirement that colleges make timely notification to the campus community of situations that pose a potential threat to student safety, when reports of such events or situations are received by any campus security authority;

• a requirement that the annual campus security report contain procedures students should follow if a sex offense occurs, including who should be contacted, the importance of preserving physical evidence as may be necessary to the proof of criminal sexual assault, and to whom the alleged offense should be reported.

However good the CSA may look on paper, its actual value as a tool for survivors remains in question. Colleges have mostly treated the CSA as a paper tiger, because enforcement has been almost nonexistent. A 1997 study found a substantial compliance rate of about 46 percent, and it was only in 1997 that the Department of Education (DOE) finally created an apparatus for reporting violations. The first reports of violations began to come in, and DOE has investigated five of the eight reports it has received. DOE has never sanctioned a college for noncompliance, and its evaluation reports invariably deal with reporting violations rather than college violations of the affirmative victim's rights included in the CSA. Private suits by students to enforce the provisions of the CSA are impossible under the current framework, because the law specifically provides that DOE enforcement is the only method available.

Campus Security Laws on the Horizon

Yet all of that may soon change. H.R. 715, the Accuracy in Campus Crime Reporting Act (ACCRA), was introduced before Congress in February of 1997. It awaits action in the House Postsecondary Education Subcommittee, and has collected sixty-six cosponsors. Reflecting congressional frustration with the pace of DOE enforcement of the CSA, ACCRA would amend the CSA to allow a private right of action—students could sue colleges for violations of the CSA. ACCRA would also implement a mandatory Title IV funding penalty for all colleges that the DOE finds to be in noncompliance.

These are not the only provisions of ACCRA that have colleges finally sitting up and taking notice of the CSA. ACCRA would also open campus police logs and disciplinary hearings to the public, allowing for widespread dissemination of campus crime information. Aiming to prevent colleges from covering up crime in confidential campus courts, the campus safety group Security-On-Campus, Inc., authored the ACCRA legislation. Many in Congress have recognized the misguided reasoning behind such provisions, noting that publicizing campus trials will have a chilling effect on reporting. Victims will be less likely to report violent crime such as rape if they fear that private details of traumatic incidents will be revealed on the front page of the campus newspaper. With fewer victims reporting, we will be given a false sense of the true extent of campus crime, rather than a clearer picture.

The status of ACCRA remains in limbo. The drafters of VAWA II have included the most beneficial provisions of ACCRA into their omnibus bill, while eliminating the provisions that would violate student privacy rights. But Congress may want action sooner and is set to include select provisions from ACCRA into its Higher Education Reauthorization bill in the spring of 1998, thereby mooting some of the campus sexual assault provisions in VAWA II. Many of the cosponsors of ACCRA are on the House Postsecondary Education Subcommittee, so it will be interesting to see how many of the ACCRA draft bill's provisions are eventually incorporated as amendments to the CSA and FERPA.

A Look in the Toolbox

A decade of new or newly changed laws and modernized legal practices have acted to alter the legal reality of sexual violence at many different levels within our jurisprudential system, though it is clear that many of these laws, though no longer in their formative stages, are nevertheless having a painfully long effectiveness gestation. Those who work with these laws must meet this snail's pace with the frustration of activists, but the patience of lawyers.

Thus, while the impact and results remain unsure at present, what is clear is the cohesive impact on victims' rights law. Sexual assault, long considered solely a state criminal issue, has been modernized and federalized in both civil and criminal contexts. Victims of sexual violence now have access to the jurisdiction of the federal courts and federal civil rights and discrimination claims, where only unavailing state claims existed before. What changes these laws have wrought on our long-term legal fabric will become known only as increasing numbers of survivors, civil rights lawyers, and judges work more and more to finely hone and sharpen these new legal tools.

AFTERWORD

Top Ten Ways the Campus Movement Against Sexual Violence Is Misunderstood

John Stoltenberg

I went to college during the fabled 1960s, to a church-affiliated school perched on a hilltop. The campus was as isolated by midwestern religious piety as it was circumscribed by flat cornfields and pastures. The tallest building in town was a Malt-O-Meal factory, and several miles away was a plant that churned soybeans into Cool Whip. Having grown up on an intellectual diet of porridge and artificial dessert topping, I had developed a taste for chewier stuff, so during my undergraduate years I sought meaning for my life through existential philosophy and avant-garde theater. I lapsed from the Lutheran faith I was raised in. I wrote trenchant satire reviews and plays. I cultivated the pose of the dissident artiste. I hung out with Baez- and Dylan-besotted folkies. And I was suspended for drinking on campus (during a bacchanalian cast party after a ribald production of *Lysistrata,* the ancient Greek antiwar sex comedy). But on contemporary matters of sex and justice I was naive beyond belief. The words "sexual politics" would have meant nothing to me, and the phrases "sexual harassment" and "acquaintance rape" were still two decades from being coined.

No college student today gets to be as clueless as I was back then. Survivors of sexual assault and battery have spoken, beginning in the late sixties with the first public speak-outs against rape. Marches and rallies against violence against women have been staged. Laws of evidence and civil redress have changed. Federal legislation has put institutions of higher learning on notice that they must fully disclose on-campus sex crimes and underwrite sexual-assault prevention programs. Academic communities have become well versed in the sex talk of illegality—a strained jargon in which words like "unwanted," "nonconsensual," and "forcibly" are slung like sandbags against the floodwaters of eroticized inequality. College students no longer matriculate in an insular subsociety where—in the name of "passion," "fun," or "boys being boys"—everyday violations of human worth and dignity exact a price paid only by the victim, in silence and in private. Occasionally, these days, the perp pays too.

Today's college students are more astute about the prevalence of sexual importuning among their peers than any generation in history. Although earnest efforts begun by post-sixties women's liberationists managed to give most varieties of sexual violence a name, the ensuing feminist movement could not make the violence end, and students today are the legatees of both that success and that failure. Students have *had* to learn what they now know about sexual violence, and many have learned the hard way.

At this unique juncture in sexual-political history there has grown up a remarkable new student movement that is both misperceived and misunderstood. It is a movement that dares to envision a world without sexual violence. It is a movement of awesome vitality. It is a movement peopled with sturdy survivors and steadfast friends of survivors, young women and young men planning, leading, organizing together—a fact that would surely have been incomprehensible to my undergraduate male classmates. In those days, as an oft-repeated wisecrack had it, women went to college only to get their M.R.S.

I recall that sexist joke with a rueful cringe at the extent to which the naïveté of my generation continues. For anyone who spent their college years during the eighties or earlier, information about the burgeoning campus movement against sexual violence has been scanty at best. Alumni associations do not make a big point of keeping potential donors apprised of the latest student-initiated antirape campaign. Other media, to the extent that they provide any coverage at all, tend to be skewed and dumbed down, portraying academia as being awash in either "date-rape hysteria" (once a cover story in *New York* magazine) or "do-me feminism" (a cover story in *Esquire*). By contrast, the antiwar movement of the late sixties was covered at length and in depth. Students huddled around TV sets to learn about not only the latest bombing raids but also new flashpoints of protest combusting on campus. To paraphrase a well-worn antiwar chant: The whole world was watching. When young people's antiwar convictions combined with the fresh fervor of "sexual liberation," the mix was potent and provocative: "Girls say yes to boys who say no" went the catchphrase (translation: Girls prefer to have sex with draft resisters). Today's middle-age, mostly male, media decision makers seem stuck in time, missing those good old days of their youth. They don't much get what's going on now.

The new student movement against sexual violence is more pervasive than any media have yet reported. It has spread to just about every campus in the country in some form or another, but it has gone largely unremarked by those journalists, social critics, and pundits whose broad brush strokes paint most citizens' picture of the political landscape. I have wondered to myself why this is so, and I have come up with several explanations—ten, to be exact. This new campus movement is so historically unprecedented that it simply does not fit neatly into former frames of reference. It is like anything truly new: not very visible at first, because if one has no recognizable frame of reference, one can easily see nothing there.

I

Although the campus movement against sexual violence is a bona fide new political movement on the U.S. scene, it is almost entirely nonpartisan. This makes it invisible in a media climate obsessed with left and right. On the weather screen of "real" politics, only liberal or conservative pressure zones appear, predicting whether the day will be fair or foul, depending upon one's party predilection. But the campus movement against sexual violence subverts such dichotomous political thinking. Its weathervane tracks a very different prevailing wind.

The young people in this movement come from all over the political compass. I recall sitting in a diner one night after an exhilarating day spent observing one of the movement's annual national conferences. As I was introduced to the young activists around the table, one identified himself as a member of the campus Young Republicans. His affiliation produced nary a squirm, no consternation. The challenge of preventing and ending sexual violence among their peers, they all seemed to understand, transcended party politics—a point many national feminist leaders have failed to grasp. A 1995 NOW rally in Washington, D.C., for instance, ostensibly organized as a protest against violence against women (the cause for which thousands of earnest students had been recruited), turned inexplicably partisan, ostentatiously anti-Republican, like a big bait and switch. At one point a NOW vice president took the microphone, pointed behind her to the Capitol, and railed at the top of her lungs against the Republicans there, denouncing them for the epidemic of violence against women. As I watched the event on C-SPAN, I wished for someone to come to the mic and give the crowd a reality check: "The major federal piece of anti-rape and antibattery legislation, the 1994 Violence against Women Act, had bipartisan support from beginning to end! We must continue to hold *both* parties accountable!"

The young women and men who are taking seriously the meaning of sexual violence throughout American life will not be easily duped into partisan demagoguery. Their vision and their activism reach to an underlying societal problem that neither political party can claim to know how to solve. Not only middle-class, white, urban, heterosexual, able-bodied, and professional Democrats get raped, battered, incested. The potential constituency for the vital new young people's movement against sexual violence draws upon no "special interest" category thus far identified by pollsters. As such, this movement promises to revolutionize the meaning of politics itself.

2

I come from a generation that was defined by a war, the Vietnam War. My parents come from a generation that was also defined by a war, World War II. For both my agemates and my parents' agemates, a foreign war figured in their lives as a coming of age. Who fought in the war, what happened to those who went, what happened to those who stayed home—all shaped us and the world we knew. The impact of those military engagements was to follow both my agemates and my parents' agemates long into their lives as they began families and careers and lives of community service. Something about each of those wars set both those generations apart from any generation before.

Today's student generation has been set apart by a very different sort of war. In response, some have started a new sort of antiwar movement. It is a movement to make this a world in which violence is not sexy. It is roomful-by-roomful presentations to teach fellow students that inequality is not sexy. It is one-by-one conversations between friends and lovers to get clear that sexism is not sexy. It is intimate talks about respect and consent that today are a core part of peer sex education and sexual-assault-prevention outreach on campus after campus.

Back in the anti–Vietnam War movement of the sixties, many young women of conscience organized politically in behalf of young men whose bodies were then at risk, because those young men were subject to the draft and deployable as cannon fodder. I remember, I was one of them; and I was lucky, I escaped. Women of conscience stood by men of conscience and united in a movement that changed the hearts and minds of this nation and helped bring that immoral military operation to an end. In those days, every major news-gathering medium wanted to listen in, overhear, and report what young people against that war were thinking and doing, because everyone somehow understood that, like it or not, what the antiwar movement was accomplishing was having a vast ripple effect on this country's consciousness.

Today, a potentially even more powerful social-change movement has begun. Today young men of conscience have begun to understand their vital role and responsibility in the movement against sexual violence, and this time it is they who are organizing in behalf of the women whose bodies are most at risk. These young men are talking to one another and to other young men. They are standing up and speaking out. They are creating campus groups and actions. They are taking on their fair share of the work, for they understand that they cannot in conscience sit on the sidelines while women confront sexual violence alone. Nothing like this has happened before in human history.

When student antiwar activists of the sixties brought new ideals and values into their subsequent work, family, and civic lives, the cultural and political impact of their movement was felt throughout the larger society for decades. No one could have guessed back then that this fledgling youth counterculture, vibrantly antimilitarist, would not only help halt a war but one day inform this nation's governance at the highest level. Today, too, it is easy not to reckon the profound cultural and political sea change portended by the values and ideals of the campus movement against sexual violence. But who knows? Perhaps someday men's war against women will finally be over—and perhaps this country will elect a president who in her student days was in the movement that helped end it.

3

Soon after 1960 a major new generational upheaval began to occur in the United States: Young people started rebelling against their parents, flagrantly, en masse. So-called baby boomers, especially those who continued their education after high school, recoiled from the stultifying fifties values represented by their mothers and fathers. A spirit of antiauthoritarianism wafted over American campuses like smoke from a popular intoxicant, and it went straight to students' heads, inspiring a rash of rousing slogans: "Stop the war!" "Fuck the establishment!" "Smash the state!" "Off the pigs!" "Up against the wall, m———f——!" and (the clincher) "Don't trust anyone over thirty!" When the enterprising popular-culture industry caught on and cashed in—this was capitalist America, after all— the raw, insurgent sound of rock and roll fueled this postpubescent fury to a frenzy, and political protest became a fashion statement. For many young people—groping for a meaningful identity post-Hiroshima, post-Holocaust, post–legal segregation—it was as if life was not worth living if they had not rejected, in some significant measure, the values they associated with their parents' and grandparents' generation.

Rebellion against authority is every generation's badge of honor, of course, and today is no exception. Tattoos and body piercing would hardly have become de rigueur if required by Mom and Dad. But as the face of contemporary authority has changed, so has young people's antiauthoritarianism. Institutions of higher learning are no longer viewed as "the enemy"; they are a necessarily respected means to employability. Activist students no longer hold their schools accountable for large-scale societal change ("Evict recruiters from companies that manufacture napalm!" "Sell off investments in South African apartheid!"). Instead, students are vocally demanding that they receive the quality of educational experience their pricey tuitions paid for. As the nation begins the twenty-first century, its students appear to be less like a social-change insurgency and more like a consumer-rights lobby.

But appearances can be deceiving. Case in point: the campus movement against sexual violence. Although it first emerged in the eighties along with students' heightened expectations for institutional delivery of educational services, the difference, inspired by feminism, is that now those demands include higher standards of security and safety from sexual assault. That's a tall order for befuddled career administrators, for whom building an endowment fund is more doable than making a campus rape-free. Enter the host of student peer educators, student-health-office staffers, women's-center directors, and other low- or no-paid people eager to change their colleagues' hearts and minds. These ardent, loosely networked educators and activists not only storm and occupy buildings; they make appointments with deans and regents. They not only hold sit-ins; they requisition budgets. They not only wave placards and bellow; they crusade by persuading. They set up, for example, antirape programming for first-year students, athletes, and fraternities and get administrators and coaches to make these programs mandatory. They work *with* institutional authority, not *against* it. Especially after a horrific incident of sexual assault galvanizes campus fury, recalcitrant administrators tend to come around and cooperate: It makes them look good. Increasingly under strict scrutiny for the sexual welfare of students, administrators generally recognize the cost-benefit ratio in funding sexual-assault-prevention education: It's peanuts to them compared with paying out elephantine attorney's fees and settlements in rape and sexual-harassment lawsuits. To an extent unimaginable in the sixties, academic administrations have become the patrons of a student-led social-change movement.

What is remarkable is that within this historically unprecedented economic matrix, the campus movement against sexual violence is slowly but surely invigorating a brand-new antiauthoritarian consensus. The authority against which these young people are rebelling is not "out there" some-where, a nameless, faceless, evil abstraction ("the military-industrial com-plex!"); nor is it simply a sublimated grudge match against Mom and Dad (as was common in the sixties and early seventies). The authority today's young people have come up against face-to-face—and sometimes far more intimately than that—is the authoritarian presumption of ownership and access in sex, the desire to conquer and dominate and control, the sadism of contempt—all the sexual authority structures, behaviors, and mind-sets that inhabit their peers (and sometimes themselves), damage their friends (and sometimes themselves), annihilate trust (and sometimes their most longed-for relationships). Today's college students struggle against this sexual-authority complex passionately and creatively. Although this gendered and gendering authority was often identified during the past three decades of second-wave feminism (as "patriarchy" by the polite, "phallic imperialism" by the blunt), it has never before been so palpable, and never so recognizable as such, to so many agemates, all of whom live together in a relatively closed community. But experience this sexual au-thority they definitely do, and from a variety of standpoints, from above and below, from top and bottom. They experience this sexual authority's visceral connection to vectors of wealth, age, race, sexual orientation, and other degrees of separation. And they are inventing language to commu-nicate that experience concretely, in order to interrupt and disempower that sexual authority not only in between their budding bodies but in the body politic at large. The generational shift signified by this campus move-ment is not yet reckoned as a revolt against tyranny. Little wonder, for it is completely new on this earth.

4

The history of sexual ethics can be summarized simply. It boils down to a calendrical catalog of proscribed and prescribed sexual partners and practices: when and to whom you can't/must perform whatever sex act it is that you can't/must do. Until the advent of pharmacological birth control, a few of these strictures made sense. Now that there's AIDS, pro-visos have had to be added. But in the outburst of experimentation and exploration between the Epoch of the Pill and the Era of the Plague, most of those tired old sexual ethics were cast off with heady abandon. To this day there is deep confusion about which strictures are shame-inducing, religion-based claptrap and which principles might actually matter in the way people connect through sex. There are still fervent antimoralists who keep pushing the envelope, transgressing any dead-letter rule they can still turn up, as if the priapic trajectory aroused in the sixties could extend to eternity, or at least into middle age. But as many young people are discovering, especially within the communications hubbub of college campuses, an ethicsless sex life can be emotionally hazardous if not deadly. One can really get screwed.

What has been lacking is a secular sexual ethics that speaks to the question of *how:* As a sexual encounter begins, and then as it proceeds, and even when it is over, what interpersonal values and considerations matter? How does a person act ethically during sex with one's freely chosen sexual partner? What conduct and communications are appropriate and inappropriate when? How can respect and caring affirm one another's sexual selfhood? How can sexual responsiveness and responsibility not be torn asunder? The old rules and regulations do not specify. They don't even provide a clue.

Feminists tried over the years to invent such an egalitarian sexual ethics, but they did not have conspicuous success. They got as far, for instance, as "no means no"—which was a vast improvement over the view of women as men's chattel property that for centuries had been encoded in western patriarchal religions and male-supremacist laws. But feminists did not really get to "yes—now how?" Their attention was distracted. As in any war—where mobile field hospitals are not ideal settings for mapping out subtle diplomacy—feminists had their hands full doing triage on multitudes of survivors of worst-case scenarios. Meanwhile, a trendy counterculture began to infect the body politic, nearly ravaging mainstream culture. Widely known by the euphemism S/M, it was actually a counterrevolutionary sexual ethics that codified how to have hierarchical sex pulsate with "power" and "danger." This was an ethics intended not only to embody authoritarianism but to get off on it. This was an ethics designed to supplant any impulse for coequal communing, any passion for justice, any sensory experience of mutually owning one's own eroticism fully awake to one another's sexually embodied selfhood. So it has come to pass that the modern-day campus movement against sexual violence, rather by default, has had to take up the challenge and try again—as if starting from square one—to invent an egalitarian sexual ethics of *how.* They may be just the right age at the right time to succeed. Out of their everyday emotional and sexual experiences, and out of their hopes for a future in which there is true sexual freedom—sex free of coercion and violence, sex free of hurt and self-hate—these students are creating a new ethical consensus about what actually makes good sex good. One key is mutual respect for bodily integrity. Another is informed consent, followed closely by the corollary that consent to do something is not carte blanche to do something else. Perhaps the most widely known instance of this emergent consensus was a comprehensive, nine-page policy developed in 1991–92 by students at Antioch. It spelled out the meaning of consent in sexual contact and conduct; it defined and prohibited a list of offenses that included rape, sexual assault, "sexual imposition," and nondisclosure of a known HIV-positive status; and it detailed fair hearings procedures and remedies in case of violation. This pathbreaking, gender-neutral sexual-ethics initiative was mocked on *Saturday Night Live* and widely reviled by media commentators who had neither read it nor talked—as I had the good fortune to do, at a national student movement conference—to students who drafted it. The Antioch policy was more revolutionary for its time than was the "Port Huron Statement," the impassioned manifesto that launched Students for a Democratic Society (SDS) in 1962. "In its heyday," writes Dave Dellinger in his 1975 book, *More Power Than We Know: The People's Movement toward Democracy*, SDS was "the brightest and the best of the New Left and antiwar organizations—the largest, most dynamic, most imaginative and innovative." Its manifesto was widely regarded as "anti-American" by people who could not conceive of a more equitable country. Similarly the Antioch students' policy was widely criticized as being "antisex." As Andrea Dworkin writes in the 1997 preface to her book *Intercourse*, "Equality in the realm of sex is an antisexual idea if sex requires domination in order to register as a sensation." The campus movement to end sexual violence is predicated on the notion that equality *belongs* in sex. Where else, after all, can equality be sensed and celebrated so intimately and ecstatically?

At a subsequent national student movement conference I attended, several young men had put together a workshop they titled "Eroticizing Consent." Inspired, they told me, by media for gay men intended to eroticize condom use, they wanted to talk about what can be erotic in two people's honesty and honoring when yes indeed means yes. No religious teachings go there; nor do public school sex-education programs. The explorers of this uncharted landscape of sexual ethics are sexually active undergraduates in the campus movement against sexual violence, and they have only just begun this journey. They are still finding their way by trial and error, comparing notes, and leaving helpful pointers along their trails.

5

During the early years of the women's movement there was a "metooism" among some men, and it produced various men's auxiliaries. *Men too* wanted to do consciousness raising. *Men too* wanted to manage their sex-role dysphoria. *Men too* wanted to sob. So beginning in the early seventies they formed men's groups to do so. Truth to tell, few women then in the feminist movement would have wanted it any other way; they quite liked being relieved of the burden of sustaining men's egos. Out of that separation of convenience grew the so-called antisexist men's movement, which by the mid-eighties got dubbed "profeminism."

The teensy but tenacious profeminist men's movement was subsequently eclipsed by several rapidly growing and rabidly antifeminist men's movements—men's rightists, mythopoets, weekend warriors, religious fundamentalists, racial nationalists. Attendance at the profeminist movement's annual national "men and masculinity" conferences fell off, and profeminism stopped attracting younger men even as more and more were casting their lot with their feminist women friends. One concrete accomplishment of the profeminist men's movement was a new academic field called men's studies, and quite a few young men enrolled. A growing number of male undergrads were also majoring or minoring in women's studies. Yet neither of these constituencies ever really rallied under the banner of profeminism. The main reason was that profeminism had originated in a time when women and men organized to work on sexual-political issues separately. The generation joining in the campus movement against sexual violence in the early nineties never knew that time and never had need to. Even when male students form a campus men's group today—to talk about issues of sex and gender, or to prepare and present sexual-assault-prevention programs for other men—they are never really separately constituted the way older profeminist men's organizing was, for every day they socialize and organize with young women friends (and sometimes lovers) who also energize the local movement against sexual violence. In this lively community of proactive peers, they pick up a rich range of mixed-gender communication styles and skills that were unknown to their profeminist forebears—ways of respectful talking and intensive listening that go a long way toward dispelling the stressed male-female distrust that older feminists have known so well.

This rapprochement may seem completely unremarkable to college-age people today. But second-wave women's liberationists, those who coalesced in consciousness-raising groups in the sixties and seventies, could not possibly have imagined the easy collegiality, respect for differences, and shared responsibility that typify young women and men in today's campus movement against sexual violence. I remember, after a speaking engagement in Winnipeg in 1995, being invited into a meeting of a political group of women and men in their teens and early twenties, some students and some not, several part of the local anarchist/punk scene. They were discussing an upcoming action, a plan to distribute informational leaflets about date rape to local bars. At one point an issue arose on which there was disagreement in the group. I forget now what it was, but as they talked it through, I could not help noting that no one raised their voice or interrupted. No one lobbed verbiage barbed with sarcasm. No one sighed the snort that signals exasperation or derision. Just simply, as each person spoke (briefly, no one for much longer than anyone else), the whole circle listened intently. There was no "chair," no one called on successive speakers; but by some code or inflection I never discerned, they all seemed to intuit when one had finished and whose turn it was to speak next.

I thought this episode a fluke until I realized I'd had a very similar experience at a national student movement conference the year before. The setting was a classroom at Duke packed with about a hundred conference participants representing campuses around the United States. Two groups, Men against Rape and Sexism, from Iowa State University, and Men Advocating Change, from the University of California, Davis, were co-presenting a workshop about outreach to men. A leader of one group mentioned in passing that they gave rape-prevention presentations only to all-male groups. A woman raised her hand and asked him why. I sensed that her question arose from some possible disagreement or reservation, though there was no testy edge in her voice. The male presenter replied, describing the group's experience (they'd found there was greater receptivity to the message when men presented to men), and he answered the woman's straightforward question without defensiveness or pique. As divergent opinions were articulated, there was never any eruption in the room of pro/con fervor or rancor; everyone simply listened closely. I could not help flashing on an image of the same room suddenly filled with feminist women and profeminist men my age. I imagined what might occur if a man there made a case for sex exclusivity and a woman challenged him about it. Teeth might clench. Throats might tense. There might be superficial civility, but inside everyone a well-tuned sensor would go on instant alert, for they would now be on the road through a man-woman minefield.

Something of the sort occasionally also happens in the campus movement against sexual violence. Before annual Take Back the Night marches, for instance, young men sometimes bristle at being asked by women to show support from a distance. But the wonder is that gender tension does not flare up routinely. When a male student leader was designated to chair a meeting or a planning committee at several conferences I observed, the relaxed dynamics in communications—female/female, male/male, and female/male—were in stark contrast to political meetings I could recall from the seventies when sexist male bonding and contentious male-female exchanges were the norm.

It occurred to me that the student activists of this generation were communicating about sex equality in a way that older folks—media types, certainly, but even many staunch veteran feminists—might not recognize or understand. Expecting to hear dissension across the gender divide, that's what they would hear, and not the new nuances. To be sure, the gender divide is something that younger activists are well aware that they've inherited (even as they tend not to believe it's inherent). Yet as they continue through their outreach against sexual violence to communicate and cooperate and colead across it, they are not only learning and inventing new ways to walk. They are discovering new ways to talk altogether.

6

The students in the campus movement against sexual violence are a new sort of "children's crusade." It is unlike the one that Sting sings of in his 1985 ballad by that name (about young, virgin soldiers betrayed on bloody battlefields in World War I). It is also not a replay of what media called the children's crusade in 1968 (the young people who buoyed Eugene McCarthy's maverick campaign for the Democratic presidential nomination on an anti–Vietnam War platform. "Clean for Gene," they were, all spiffed up and hopeful). Today's children's crusade is generationally unique, for it consists of sons and daughters of mothers whose lives were changed by feminism.

The story of this crusade is still unfolding, but it could not have begun to be told were it not for the women's movement. Divorce, for instance—often "blamed" on feminism—has played a larger role in this generation's upbringing than in any in American history. Countless students now on campus have witnessed, and deeply endorsed, their mother's decision to get out of a marriage in which she was treated badly. Countless students and their siblings are the proud beneficiaries of their mother's breadwinning and economic resilience. Such single moms have become role models of self-respect to both daughters and sons. Meanwhile the women's movement has ratcheted up this generation's expectations of what a pair bond should look like from the get-go: egalitarian and respectful, an economic collaboration, mutual mentoring, zero tolerance for violence and abuse. Changes that feminism has wrought in the workplace, where many students' mothers have had fulfilling careers, have made the college guy on the prowl for a compliant, stay-at-home wife a lone wolf indeed.

Much has been said about the salutary effects of the women's movement on daughters; much less has been said about its impact on sons, and it is in the campus movement against sexual violence that the most significant new stories are being told. Here it is not uncommon to hear sons freely and frequently acknowledge the women who have been primary agents of positive change in their lives—their mothers, sisters, classmates, girlfriends. Role modeling by older men is more complicated and conflicted, because a son's relationship to his father (who is increasingly also his mother's ex) can as well pitch him into fury against sex equality as prepare him for affectionate alliance with strong feminist women. Although the women's movement has opened unprecedented opportunities for daughters' self-definition, it has not done as much for sons, whose options for self-definition remain under crushing pressure to prove manhood. In particular, feminism has not diminished the extent to which sons' attitudes must conform to those of other men for whose power or approval they must constantly vie. Today, however, the mixed-sex campus movement against sexual violence has begun to create social supports for young men to make choices that significantly diverge from the requisite pack mentality. Young men's autobiographical honesty about the high-stakes dramas inside various male-male worlds will be a major contribution to the movement against sexual violence as a whole, for we cannot comprehend what happens between men and women without knowing more about what is happening between men: how manhood is contested and validated, and what males feel compelled to do to comply with such tests. As silence around coercive male-male dynamics is broken, there will be more egalitarian options for the self-definition of all sons—including those whose conscience already rebels at playing the manhood-as-dominance game, the ones most likely to gravitate to the campus movement against sexual violence.

While visiting Duke in 1994, I listened in on a conversation among members of Men Acting for Change, a campus group that met regularly to talk personally and present programs about gender, sexuality, sexual violence, and homophobia to fraternities and other campus groups. Unprompted, each young man shared a story of his ambivalence about other men. One young man belonged to a fraternity and knew personally not only some twenty female survivors of rape but also about a quarter of their male assailants. Another had never before felt safe enough in men's company to speak of having been sexually molested as a youth by a male relative. Yet another served as a volunteer in a counseling program where he met regularly with men sent there because they had abused their wives, and he had to manage his strong feelings about what they had done. Such matters would likely go unspoken were it not for the context of activism against sexual violence—a sort of sanctuary from gender conformity—in which their friendships formed. Against the prevailing male-male force field that pressures young men to betray not only the women in their lives but also their own best selves—and against the Faustian deal they can cut to claim gender-class privilege through antifeminist backlash—these young men had glimpsed the possibility for a personal selfhood that was far better than that, and not alone.

7

Activism against campus sexual violence bobbed up in the wake of not only the second-wave women's movement but also the gay-and-lesbian movement. Back when these two movements had their radical origins, in the late sixties and early seventies, they were much more aligned philosophically than they are at present. Radical feminist women (including lesbian feminists) did not want a piece of the patriarchal pie; they wanted a whole new menu. Radical activist faggots and fairies did not want a place at the table—at least not while straight men's power sat at the head. The two affinity groups in their first bursts of revolutionary zest were rather like two overlapping circles in a Venn diagram. Today both movements are more diverse and mainstream. Though each has its own internally divisive controversies (about who is a real feminist, for instance, and about whether bisexuals and transsexuals belong), the feminist movement as a whole and the umbrella movement now named gay/lesbian/bi/tran (GLBT) have become like separate spheres, adjacent only rarely in coalitions. Many queer undergrads, swept up in competing claims for their extracurricular attention, sense a disconnect between campus GLBT and antirape activism. They may suppose this is because peer-education programs against sexual violence address primarily heterosexual assault—or because GLBT groups tend to throw better parties. But what young queers may not realize is how this tension they sense derives from a time before they were born—a history of conflict that haunts relationships between the two movements to this day.

In the years after radical feminists protested the Miss America Pageant in Atlantic City in 1968, and patrons at a gay bar called Stonewall fought back during a police raid in 1969, I was in my mid-twenties and living in New York City. I recall my amazement at finding out that where these two movements intersected there was a network of very feminist queers (or "flaming faggots," as the editors of *Double F* magazine called themselves). They had figured out from radical feminists that the stigma of being queer originates in male supremacy, which derogates females and all that is "feminine"; therefore it made perfect sense to these folks to make common cause with women in fighting to "smash patriarchy." Before long, I witnessed this feminist-faggot insight be totally eclipsed by gay men who were choosing a very different and completely reactionary strategy. Seeking enfranchisement in the culture as "really virile men," they had no incentive to change or challenge their own attitudes toward women. After all, if the reason gay men were disdained was that they were deemed akin to females, the best way to propitiate their straight-male tormentors was by demonstrating their distance from women. The gambit worked. It brokered male bonds. A political fissure between gay men and feminist women became a chasm. And in the blink of an eye there appeared count-less gay-male chambers of commerce—cruise bars, bathhouses, bookstores with back rooms, and dungeons with harnesses for fistfucking and tubs for piss-and-shit shows. On the streets of Greenwich Village, I saw gay men wearing neo-Nazi uniforms and white men in black leather leading black men on chain leashes. An idealized hypermasculine physique—with bulging upper torso, impossibly slim waist, mammoth genitals—was in-troduced into gay male pornography through drawings by an artist named Tom of Finland. As a child growing up during World War II, he was awed by, and enamored of, the masculinity of the Aryan-wannabe soldiers who occupied his country, and he turned his SS recollections into illustrated exaggerated fantasies that became homoerotic icons for gay men—even as, contradictorily, the gay movement was adopting as its emblem the Holocaust's pink triangle. In the years before Stonewall, clan-destine coteries of urban male homosexuals would longingly admire pho-tos of young men in posing straps in "physical culture" magazines, swoon over "rough trade" (straight-acting, somewhat menacing young men whom they would fellate, often for a fee), and dress up their distaste for women as "camp." After Stonewall, as author Daniel Harris has astutely observed, anal intercourse, which in the forties and fifties had been rare, suddenly became a common and expected practice among young, urban gay men, who now sought to *become* the icons of masculinity that had been the object of previously closeted homosexual desires. The feminist-faggot critique of heterosexist male supremacy—including its misogyny, race hate, and sexual sadism—got shoved aside as urban gay men en masse began to remake their bodies, rework their wardrobes, and brand gay male liberation as the avant-garde of S/M sex.

I still remember the pall that settled over the roomful of gay men when, during a 1974 Gay Academic Union conference, I finished giving a scath-ing critique of the sexist politics of the male-dominated gay-liberation movement. "Unless we change, we cannot claim to be comrades with women," I concluded. "Until we change, the oppressor is us." That speech cost me many friendships and made me persona non grata on the gay political scene. It was subsequently published and reprinted (as "Toward Gender Justice," the first coinage of the phrase "gender justice" that I know of), and it was widely read, including in the early eighties by one of the first student-initiated antisexist men's organizations (Men's Discus-sion Group, formed by mostly straight-identified young men at Brown). Meanwhile gay men by the thousands, having eroticized male dominance and embodied in themselves the idealized hypermasculinity for which they longed, were discoing deliriously under a mirrored ball about to shatter, and their self-absorbed, femiphobic movement could not be counted an ally by anyone remotely concerned with sexual abuse.

As all this was going on in the gay circle, something quite the reverse was happening in the women's-movement circle. Certain leaders of the National Organization for Women, cofounder Betty Friedan famously among them, tried to drum out lesbians—which left lesbian feminists, already not welcome by gay men, homeless. Meanwhile, as radical feminism was being purged from the male-dominated gay movement, it was gradually moving from the margin to the center in the women's movement. In those early days, sexual violence was a fringe issue in the women's movement. Not only wasn't there much talk about it; there was hardly any activism. For years, as I recall, Friedan would regularly issue warnings to the women's movement not to jeopardize its mainstream credibility by embracing "militants" who were agitating around issues of violence against women. She kept calling it a "diversion." The marginality of violence against women in those days may be difficult to imagine for young people who have only known the women's movement with an agenda against sexual violence at its core. In words declared by the 1995 Beijing World Conference on Women: "The human rights of women include their right to have control over and decide freely and responsibly on matters relating to their sexuality, including sexual and reproductive health, free of coercion, discrimination, and violence." Nobody in the women's movement of the early seventies could possibly have predicted such a global consensus.

AIDS altered the homophile movement drastically. Gay men were dying, lesbian women were not, compassion became the order of the day, and gay men learned new respect for their lesbian sisters. Suddenly there was gender parity in the leadership of gay-and-lesbian organizations (an issue over which many self-respecting dykes in the seventies had abandoned their brethren in droves). And suddenly movement leaders began to look critically at patterns of drug abuse, compulsive promiscuity, rampant amoebas and other sexually transmitted diseases among gay men—not least because many of the men most heavily involved in that urban subculture, their immune systems already shot and their rectums ripped from fisting, were unwittingly the first to succumb.

Today's GLBT pride festivals, protests, and raves on campuses across the country bear scarcely any resemblance to the self-hating and self-destructive gay underground of decades gone by. The fact that that past has been displaced by a campus culture in which diversity is not only tolerated but openly celebrated—and sexual orientation is no biggie—is a miracle of generational healing. At that fleeting age just past adolescence when all things seem possible, when sexuality is in flux and identity a work in progress, students on campuses today—and those soon to arrive from high school—are inciting some of the best of GLBT activism.

At this juncture in time, therefore, I believe that a historic potential exists, particularly within the campus movement against sexual violence, for those two separate circles—the feminist and the queer—to converge again. Over the past several years, antiviolence projects have sprung up in GLBT communities in several major U.S. cities for the specific purpose of preventing, and serving the survivors of, violence between and against queers. Domestic violence is no longer viewed as a solely heterosexual problem. Male-on-male rape, including gay on gay, is at last being taken seriously. Male survivors of molestation, including those who grew up queer, have borrowed page after page from feminist-inspired politics and healing work with female survivors of incest and childhood sexual abuse. On some campuses, self-defense programs are available specifically addressed to the needs of GLBT youth. Slowly but surely, the feminist movement's pathbreaking work on sexual violence has begun to inform the GLBT community's worldview. The GLBT movement is still not overfond of radical feminist theoretical analysis, yet among college students doing practical work against sexual abuse and assault and those doing practical work against homophobia, there are profound new cross-referencings. The topic of homophobia, for instance, is a standard component of antirape education for heterosexual men—almost no such program is without it—not only because men's panicky urge to prove themselves not homosexual is what drives many a rape but because homophobia contributes to a campus rape culture: It makes men fearful of challenging other men's antiwoman attitudes. Campus antirape educators emphasize homophobia for another reason: It paralyzes men's feelings, making them less able to say no when they fear it would be unmanly to decline an offer of heterosexual sex or unstudly to express their desire for a more egalitarian sexual relationship, whatever their partner's gender. The social orbits of students in peer sex education and GLBT groups increasingly overlap, just as do the gender emergencies from which each seeks respite, and out of this historically unprecedented convergence could come a new political synthesis, I predict, one in which there need be no fear of being feminist and no fear of being queer, for both signify brave and honorable dissidence to the same stultifying system. Some may not see the point. Some feminist elders, bitterly remembering gay men's betrayal in the early seventies, may be wary or even alarmed. Some older gay politicos and loyalist lesbians may send warnings to their troops not to fraternize with the enemy. But they will have misunderstood, because the time has come for the work that needs doing to come full circle.

8

In the sixties, when I was an undergraduate, college administrations were expected to act in loco parentis (in place of a parent). Now and then the children acted up and had to be punished. I was on the campus of Columbia University the night in 1969 when its president sent in the police to reclaim several buildings that had been occupied by unruly brats. At a signal, hundreds of police on foot and scores of police on horseback, all wielding nightsticks, rampaged and stampeded across the quad, nearly trampling me and clobbering many others who had come out in support. Gee, Dad, that was some spanking. Today's conservative right would have enthusiastically approved.

Political conservatives who extol "family values" would also not see the sense in which the campus movement against sexual violence is a new family-values movement. Nowadays the familial configuration of campus life has altered considerably. One of the most dramatic changes has been the impact on student life, for over a decade now, of coed dorms, where young women and young men meet one another coming and going more like brother and sister than like alien species. The same sibling spirit prevails in all sorts of campus affinity groups, including those that are part of the movement against sexual violence. The family values being learned on campuses today now also include familiarity with family violence— battery, marital rape, incest. Because these topics are talked about frankly—especially among students hooked into the movement against sexual violence—students are better prepared to form families with a vow that violence shall never occur in theirs. Lucky the child who is entrusted to the care of such parenting.

Sibling revelry has had an impact on the way students date and have sex. In the easygoing familiarity that comes of dailiness in shared housing, there is far more opportunity now for acquaintanceships to grow into friendships that evolve into sexual relationships and then back into friendships. The free-form family that plays together on and off campus (and stays together for a time) has made possible a generationally new cultural consensus about sex. In large part this change is due to the new antiauthoritarianism I described earlier (the growing awareness among students who are alert to the roots and reality of sexual violence that sex asserting authority is passé and sex expressive of mutuality and equality is now greatly to be desired). Older political types tend not to recognize this new antiauthoritarianism as such. But whereas the sexual liberation movement launched in the sixties resisted authority *through* sex ("Make love not war"), contemporary young people's antirape radicalism renounces authority *in* sex. During sex between a man and a woman, for instance, this means that he is not the presumptive overlord nor she the presumptive chattel property. This also means that whether male or female or in between, neither partner need dominate the other in order for either to feel sexual.

Exactly how eroticized equality happens between two people is not self-evident. Sex-ed curriculums do not explain it, nor does pornography (which today is the main medium of sex education for young men). Nevertheless, in what is one of the most significant social experiments in history, the new antiauthoritarian brothers and sisters are (to borrow a refrain from Aretha Franklin and the Eurythmics) "doing it for themselves." For many of them, the influence of radical feminism can be felt in their passion for gender justice. For many of them, too, the influence of the radical GLBT movement can be felt in their resistance to categorization. Sex is becoming less the necessary site for ascertainment and assertion of sexual identity in a hierarchy, and more a fluid or elastic space for experiencing now one sexual expression then another on a level playing field.

Whether this social experiment ever comes to light and transforms the nation's consciousness about eroticism and equality will depend, in large measure, on the students in the campus movement against sexual violence. It is they who are living it. It is they who understand why it matters. It is they who are best situated to speak of it with one another. And it is they who could clue in the country.

9

The sexual revolution that began in the sixties had both a bright side and a dark side. The bright side was represented in The Summer of Love (1967), Stonewall (1969), *Roe v. Wade* (1973). The dark side was a cynical sex commerce that peddled licentiousness as liberation and alienation as an inalienable right. Like any good capitalist enterprise, the sex industry produced something for *some* people by expropriating it from *other* people. A massive disinformation campaign gave the impression that so-called sex workers were happy as clams. Meanwhile women and runaway, sexually abused youth slipped into poverty and homelessness at an unprecedented rate, becoming a vast labor pool from which sex profiteers could pick and choose. On the backs of people they prostituted (including technologically), the sexual revolution created a new owning class, a nouveau riche of pimps and pornographers who had—like organized-crime figures (which many of them were)—cadres of lawyers running interference for them in courts. Not a few of the new sex barons had roots in the political left, such as the man who first marketed a movie called *Snuff*. It showed a man disemboweling a woman and holding up her uterus while he orgasmed, and in 1976 it was advertised throughout the New York City subway system with posters showing a woman's body sliced to pieces by a scissors and the tagline "Made in South America . . . where life is CHEAP." Outside a mainstream movie house where it played in Times Square, I joined with hundreds of women and men in nightly protests. The distributor and promoter, a former lefty, made a killing.

Contributions from sex-industry profits flowed liberally into almost all the causes now associated with "sexual freedom"—abortion rights and gay-and-lesbian groups, sex-research and sex-education institutes—as well as into the campaign chests of politicians who could be trusted not to tamper with the trade. It takes a certain courage to criticize exploitation committed by one's benefactor. Through the seventies and early eighties, pornographers bought a lot of people off.

But the political influence of the sex industry was greatest as a propaganda machine against radical feminism. "These chicks are our natural enemy. . . . It is time we do battle with them," wrote *Playboy* founder Hugh Hefner in an in-house memo that inadvertently got leaked. "What I want is a devastating piece that takes the militant feminists apart. They are unalterably opposed to the romantic boy-girl society that *Playboy* promotes." From the seventies on, *Playboy, Penthouse,* and *Hustler* regularly ran articles that distorted and derided feminist initiatives against acquaintance rape, sexual harassment, wife beating, child abuse, and pornography. Many of the media misrepresentations that persistently undercut efforts against sexual violence can be traced back to these articles, which were read not only by millions of ordinary men but by media decision makers and opinion shapers in the context of photographs that facilitated masturbation. The notions that date rape is but morning-after regret, that women batter as much as men, that sexual harassment laws clamp down on sex, that women concoct tales of having been sexually abused as kids, that antipornography feminists are in bed with the right—all of these red herrings first flopped on board in so-called men's sophisticate magazines. Now they're swallowed hook, line, and sinker.

Political liberals who extol "sexual liberation" would probably not recognize the sense in which the campus movement against sexual violence is a new sexual-liberation movement. In 1993 I watched, along with millions of Americans, a remarkable group of young men and women on *20/ 20,* an ABC News program. The young men spoke graphically about the negative effects that pornography, including *Playboy,* had had on their sex lives and their relationships with women. The young women spoke about the negative effects of pornography on their body self-image and their partners' expectations. The broadcast was perhaps the most frank coverage of pornography's interpersonal effects ever to appear on network television. The young men and women, who were all from Duke, included members of Men Acting for Change. *Playboy,* responding later to the broadcast, referred to them as "the pointy-headed, wet-behind-the-scrotum boys at Duke."

As fish that have never swum in clear water see a polluted pond as home, so do young people now experience the world befouled by porn. Countless values that are now normative in youth culture first crossed over into the mainstream from sex-industry propaganda—the expectation that men are hot sex machines or else not real men, an ideal body type that most women could approximate only with breast implants (because the requisite calorie deprivation does not leave enough adipose tissue there), the anatomical standard for gay "hunks" and "twinks" that author Michelangelo Signorile has aptly termed "body fascism." The notions that women who are raped "provoked it" or were "asking for it" or "deserved it" would never have felt so viscerally true to so many men if not for the scenario, recycled endlessly in straight porn, in which a woman resists but is ravished anyway, then fawns over her rapist. The bulk of the women in run-of-the-mill pornography (not the token stars) come from, and return to, lives of quiet desperation; they are quickly replaced by younger women—the inanimate lens of the camera having provided a brief respite from johns' innumerable penetrations. Along the shelves in a typical gay male video shop one can find such a mausoleumful of porn stars, now dead of drugs and AIDS, that masturbating to their sex scenes is virtual necrophilia.

Meanwhile a few young people within the campus movement against sexual violence have begun to speak from what they know, including their own bodies and one another's, and they are beginning to speak of what the pornography industry has imbued in them and suffused their sexual feelings with—the values, the expectations, the standards and practices that were dumped upstream in time long before they were spawned. They are beginning to understand that the waters are deeply troubled. They are beginning to understand that the values promoted in pornography do not help one experience eroticized equality. Perhaps those values may prevent it.

The sexual revolution that began in the sixties was about liberation *through* porn. It may now come to light, thanks to some young people's quest for a genuinely egalitarian sexual ethics, that the new antiauthoritarian sexual revolution will be about liberation *from* porn. If so, I would expect that anyone still loyal to the dark side of the sexual revolution begun in the sixties will not understand the campus movement against sexual violence at all. They may just have to stay in the dark.

10

At some point or another, anyone who wants too sincerely to end sexual violence runs up against a new nihilism, a pessimism peculiar to our times: the belief that sexual violence cannot possibly ever actually *end*. This dim view is based in the entrenched conviction—bolstered by academic bluster and media blather alike—that men are one way, women another, and if sometimes age-old rites of dominance and submission get out of hand, well, that's too bad, but that's just the way we are. Rape is in our nature; our species has not yet evolved it out of our system, and we cannot. Men are one way. Women are another. *Vive la différence.* Never the twain.

This may prove the point on which the campus movement against sexual violence is most misunderstood, the point at which it draws the most blank, uncomprehending stares, the point at which it is deemed most dangerous to the status quo, for the students in this movement are genuinely hopeful. They are profoundly optimistic. They are radically idealistic. They believe that sexual violence *can* end. They believe that women and men of conscience *can* work together to bring that future into being, perhaps not in their lifetimes but *someday.*

They make me proud to share their hope.

&)

NOTES

INTRODUCTION

1. Sarah Ferguson, "Sex on Campus: How Making Love Became the Vietnam of the Nineties," *Village Voice,* April 1991, 9.

2. *The American Woman 1996–97, Woman and Work* (New York: W. W. Norton, 1996), 269.

3. Peggy Sanday, *A Women Scorned: Acquaintance Rape on Trial* (New York: Doubleday, 1996), 191–92.

4. Kate Millett, *Sexual Politics* (New York: Simon and Shuster, 1990), 23.

5. Harry Kalven Jr. and Hans Zeisel, *The American Jury* (Boston: Little, Brown, 1966), 254. See also Peggy Sanday, *A Women Scorned* for complete history of acquaintance rape, 184–207.

6. Menachem Amir, *Patterns in Forcible Rape* (Chicago: University of Chicago Press, 1971), 245.

7. Redstockings of the Women's Liberation Movement, *Feminist Revolution* (New York: Random House, 1975), 141.

8. Susan Brownmiller, *Against Our Will: Men, Women and Rape* (New York: Ballantine Books, 1975), 257.

9. Diana Russell, *The Politics of Rape,* 2d ed. (New York: Stein and Day, 1984), 13.

10. Russell, *Politics of Rape,* 59.

11. Sharon Sayles, "Ten Years: 1972–1982: Working against Sexual Assault," Archives of the National Coalition against Sexual Assault, Pittsburgh, Pa., 2.

12. Interview with Ruth Koenick, coordinator of Rutgers University Sexual Assault Services, June 1994.

13. Interview with Ellie DiLapi, director of University of Pennsylvania's Women's Center, June 1994.

14. Interview with Jennifer Beeman, director of University of California, Davis, Rape Education and Prevention Program, July 1994.

15. Beth Ribet, "Fighting Campus Sexual Violence: Notes about the Coalition of Campus Organizations Addressing Rape," unpublished paper, Irvine, Calif.

16. Karen Barrett, "Date Rape: A Campus Epidemic," *Ms.*, September 1982, 51.

17. Mary P. Koss, Christine A. Gidycz, and Nadine Wisniewski, "The Scope of Rape: Incidence and Prevalence of Sexual Aggression and Victimization in a National Sample of Higher Education Students," *Journal of Consulting and Clinical Psychology* 55 (1987): 162–70.

18. Robin Warshaw, *I Never Called It Rape: The Ms. Report on Recognizing, Fighting, and Surviving Date and Acquaintance Rape* (New York: Harper and Row, 1988), 11.

19. Jodi Gold, Jessie Minier, and Susan Villari, "Creating Campuses Intolerant of Rape: Peer Education and the Institutional Response to Sexual Violence" presented at the 6th International Conference on Sexual Assault and Harassment on Campus, Long Beach, California, November 1996.

20. Gold, Minier, and Villari, "Creating Campuses Intolerant of Rape."

21. Interview with Willa Young, director of Women Student Services and Rape Education and Prevention Programs at Ohio State University, July 1994.

22. Interview with Julie Steiner, director of the University of Michigan Sexual Assault Awareness and Prevention Center (SAPAC), July 1994.

23. Interview with Jamie Tiedemann, director of University of Minnesota's Sexual Assault Services, August 1994.

24. *Time*, June 3, 1991, 55.

25. Interview with Myra Hindus, Princeton University, June 1994.

26. Warshaw, *I Never Called It Rape*, 24.

27. Warshaw, *I Never Called It Rape*, 44.

28. Julie K. Ehrhart and Bernice R. Sandler, *Campus Gang Rape: Party Games?* Project on the Status and Education of Women (Washington, D.C.: Association of American Colleges, 1985).

29. Peggy Reeves Sanday, *Fraternity Gang Rape: Sex, Brotherhood, and Privilege on Campus* (New York: New York University Press, 1990).

30. Carol Bohmer and Andrea Parrot, *Sexual Assault on Campus* (New York: Lexington Books, 1993), 22.

31. The North American Student Conferences on Campus Sexual Violence began at the University of Pennsylvania, Philadelphia, in 1992. Jodi and I coordinated this first conference and, at the time, we had no idea that this conference would continue into its eighth year. Since 1993 one to three conferences have been held each year, with 1998 seeing its first Canadian conference. SpeakOut: The North American Student Coalition on Campus Sexual Violence was founded in 1994 to help oversee and coordinate these North American student conferences.

32. Py Bateman, "Keynote Address," First Annual National Student Conference on Campus Sexual Assault, University of Pennsylvania, Philadelphia, March 1992.

33. Arthur Levine, "A New Generation of Student Protesters Arises," *Chronicle of Higher Education*, February 26, 1999, A52.

34. Paul Rogat Loeb, *Generation at the Crossroads: Apathy and Action on the American Campus* (New Brunswick, N.J.: Rutgers University Press, 1994), 61.

35. Gold, Minier, and Villari, "Creating Campuses Intolerant of Rape."

36. *Ms.*, July/August 1995, 95.

37. Interview with Ruth Koenick, June 1994.

38. From the CCOAR listserv, June 1996.

39. Michael Kimmel, "Clarence William, Iron Mike, Tailhook, Senator Packwood, Spur Posse, Magic . . . and US," in *Transforming a Rape Culture*, eds. Emile Buchwald, Pamela Fletcher, and Martha Roth (Minneapolis, Minn.: Milkweed Editions, 1993), 121.

40. Judy Mann, "Sexists on the Net," *Washington Post*, November 15, 1995, E17.

CHAPTER I

1. In *Sexualizing the Social*, ed. Atkins and Merchant (New York: St. Martin's Press, 1996), 77–101.

2. New York: Lexington Books, 1993.

CHAPTER 3

Versions of this chapter have appeared in other publications. "Same-Sex Rape of Male College Students" reprinted with permission of the Helen Dwight Reid Educational Foundation, published by Heldref Publications, 1319 Eighteenth Street, N.W., Washington, D.C. 20036-1802, copyright 1997. Preface for *Male on Male Rape: The Hidden Toll of Stigma and Shame*, Plenum Publishing Corp.

1. B. D. Forman, "Reported Male Rape," *Victimology: An International Journal* 7 (1982): 235–36; P. A. Frazier, "A Comparative Study of Male and Female Rape Victims Seen at a Hospital–Based Rape Crisis Program," *Journal of Interpersonal Violence* 8 (1993): 65–76; A. P. Kaufman, "Male Rape Victims: Noninstitutionalized Assault," *American Journal of Psychiatry* 137 (1980): 221–23.

2. "Bureau of Justice Statistics' National Crime Victimization Survey, 1994." *Bureau of Justice Statistics Bulletin.* April 1996.

3. A. N. Groth and A. W. Burgess, "Male Rape: Offenders and Victims," *American Journal of Psychiatry* 137 (1980): 806–10; G. Mezey and M. King, "The Effects of Sexual Assault on Men: A Survey of 22 Victims," *Psychol Medicine* 19 (1989): 205–9.

4. Groth and Burgess, "Male Rape," 806–10; R. Hillman, "Adult Male Victims of Sexual Assault: An Underdiagnosed Condition," *International Journal of STDS and AIDS* 2(1991): 22–24; R. McMullen, *Male Rape: Breaking the Silence on the Last Taboo* (London: Gay Men's Press, 1990); P. L. Huckle, "Male Rape Victims Referred to a Forensic Psychiatric Service," *Medicine, Science, and the Law* 35 (1995): 187–19.

5. Groth and Burgess, "Male Rape"; Mezey and King, "Effects of Sexual Assault"; Hillman, "Adult Male Victims"; McMullen, *Male Rape*; Huckle, "Male Rape Victims."

6. Groth and Burgess, "Male Rape"; McMullen, *Male Rape*; and R. E. Funk, *Stopping Rape* (Philadelphia: New Society, 1993).

7. Groth and Burgess, "Male Rape," 809.

8. D. F. Duncan, "Prevalence of Sexual Assault Victimization among Heterosexual and Gay/Lesbian University Students," *Psychological Reports* 166 (1990):

65–66; D. Island and P. Letellier, *Men Who Beat the Men Who Love Them: Battered Gay Men and Domestic Violence* (New York: Harrington Park Press, 1991); C. K. Waterman, L. Dawson, and M. J. Bologna, "Sexual Coercion in Gay Male and Lesbian Relationships: Predictors and Implications for Support Services," *Journal of Sex Research* 26 (1989): 118–24.

9. Frazier, "Comparative Study"; Mezey and King, "Effects of Sexual Assault."

10. McMullen, *Male Rape*; Huckle, "Male Rape Victims"; Funk, *Stopping Rape.*

CHAPTER 4

1. U.S. Department of Justice, *Violence against Women: A National Crime Victimization Survey Report* (Washington, D.C.: 1994).

2. "African American Women in Defense of Ourselves," *New York Times*, November 17, 1991, 47.

3. Elsa Barkley Brown, "Imaging Lynching: African American Women, Communities of Struggle, and Collective Memory," in *African American Women Speak Out on Anita Hill-Clarence Thomas*, ed. Geneva Smitherman (Detroit: Wayne State University Press, 1995), 100–124.

4. Toni Morrison, "A Knowing So Deep," *Essence*, May 1985, 230.

CHAPTER 5

1. Mary P. Koss, Christine A. Gidycz, and N. Wisniewski, "The Scope of Rape: Incidence and Prevalence of Sexual Aggression and Victimization in a National Sample of Higher Education Students," *Journal of Consulting and Clinical Psychology* 55(1987): 162–70.

2. Catharine MacKinnon, *Feminism Unmodified* (Cambridge, Mass.: Harvard University Press, 1987).

3. Dianne Herman, "Rape Culture," in *Women: A Feminist Perspective*, 4th ed., ed. Jo Freeman (Mountain View, Calif.: Mayfield, 1989).

4. Esther Ngan-Ling Chow, "The Feminist Movement: Where Are All the Asian American Women?" in *Making Waves: An Anthology of Writings by and about Asian American Women*, ed. Asian Women United of California (Boston: Beacon Press, 1989).

5. Esther Ngan-Ling Chow, *Acculturation of Asian American Professional Women* (Research Monograph) (Washington, D.C.: National Institute of Mental Health, Department of Health and Human Services, 1982).

6. Peggy Sanday, "The Sociocultural Context of Rape: A Cross-Cultural Study," *Journal of Social Issues* 37(1981): 5–27.

7. Chow, 1989.

8. Renee E. Tajima, "Lotus Blossoms Don't Bleed: Images of Asian Women," in *Making Waves: An Anthology of Writings by and about Asian American Women*, ed. Asian Women United of California (Boston: Beacon Press, 1989).

9. Anne Mi Ok Bruining, "Speak Out: Working with Asian Women," in *Reclaiming Our Lives: A Training Manual for Those Working with Victims/Survivors of Sexual*

Assault, ed. Elba Crespo and Candace Waldron (Boston: Massachusetts Department of Public Health, Women's Health Unit, 1987).

10. Andrea Dworkin, *Pornography: Men Possessing Women* (New York: E. P. Dutton, 1979), 53.

11. Robin Warshaw, *I Never Called It Rape* (New York: Harper and Row, 1988). Dworkin, *Pornography,* 17.

12. Ann W. Burgess and Lynda L. Holmstrom, *Rape: Crisis and Recovery* (Bowie, Md.: Robert J. Brady, 1979).

CHAPTER 6

Dedicated to the women, children, and men who have been, and continue to be, harmed by pornography and prostitution.

1. See Sianne Ngai, "The Writing on the Wall," *Brown Daily Herald,* October 31, 1990.

2. Brown University Department of Police and Security Services Incident Report #89-05939 [hereinafter Police Report]:

> 06 Sept. 89: Contacted Mr. Oliver at 134 hrs. this date. He states that it was definitely Mr. Lori that wrote the message on the complainant's door. He states that he witnessed him do it. He states that it was just a joke and that the subject doesn't even know the complainant. . . .
>
> 15 Sept. 89: This officer also received a call from the complainant this date inquiring about the status on the investigation. It was explained to the complainant [that the case was still] "open pending deans [sic] decision" [but the investigation was over] at which point she requested to be given the address of the subject so that she could address him personally. This officer explained to the complainant that this was not department policy to give out such information at which point the complainant became very upset.

3. Letter from David Inman, dean of students, Brown University, to Joseph Oliver, student, Brown University, September 25, 1989 (on file with author) (hereinafter Letter to Joe Oliver). The letter reads, in relevant part:

> The [incident] clearly constituted sexual harassment, a Major Offense at Brown. . . . You reported that a number of males were intoxicated in the vicinity of Ms. Brown's room. In a follow up report you admitted to participating in the incident but thought it a joke. . . . I have to accept your word on this. . . . You did admit that you had been drinking and that the whole matter was alcohol related. For that alone, I issue this Warning.

The letter concluded, "Ms. Brown has been sympathetic in your regard because she is also your Resident Counselor. Perhaps you can return this in kind by a letter of apology to Ms. Brown for the drinking that evening which contributed to the whole sordid atmosphere."

4. See, e.g., *Beauharnais v. Illinois,* 343 U.S. 250 (1952) (principle of group libel). Beauharnais held that group defamation—including publications that expose the

citizens of any race, color, creed, or religion to contempt—could be made criminal without violating the First Amendment. See also *New York Times Co. v. Sullivan*, 376 U.S. 254 (1964). Sullivan tilted First Amendment law in the direction of the conclusion that individual libel is actionable but group libel is not, making injury to the reputation of *individuals* legally real and consigning injury to the reputation of *groups* to legal limbo.

5. See Catharine A. MacKinnon, *Only Words* (Cambridge, Mass.: Harvard University Press, 1993). "Suddenly, harassment became an issue of speech. Practices of bigotry and inequality were transformed into discussions and debates. Threats became statements of political ideology. What had been judicially understood as acts of discrimination became a dialogue about ideas" (52).

6. Jerry Adler, "Taking Offense: Is This the New Enlightenment on Campus or the New McCarthyism?" *Newsweek*, Dec. 24, 1990. The article explains:

Philosophically, PC represents the subordination of the right to free speech to the guarantee of equal protection under the law. The absolutist position on the First Amendment is that it lets you slur anyone you choose. The PC position is that a hostile environment for minorities abridges their right to an equal education (52).

With the debate thus framed, the *Newsweek* article goes on to denounce all efforts challenging "the intellectual tradition of Western Europe" (48), "attempting to redistribute power from the privileged class (white males) to the oppressed masses" (53), and promoting diversity and "multiculturalism" (54).

7. George F. Will, "New Guise for Assault on Free Speech," *Houston Chronicle*, October 30, 1993.

8. *American Booksellers v. Hudnut*, 771 F.2d 323 (7th Cir. 1985, *aff'd*, 475 U.S. 1001 (1986).

9. Mary T. Schmich, "Accusers Use Graffiti in Campus Rape Debate," *Chicago Tribune*, December 9, 1990, 20.

Previously, the term "Magic Marker terrorist" was applied by the university to KKK members who scrawled racist and homophobic graffiti in a dormitory during April 1989. It is no coincidence that, shortly after being described with the same label used by the University to describe Ku Kluxers, the women defending the antirape graffiti were labeled a "lynch mob." See Karen Ziner, "Breaking down the Wall of Silence," *Providence Journal*, November 26, 1990. Reichley described the KKK incident at Brown and analogized it to the "Rape List": "Somebody put graffiti on the wall which was racist and certainly anti-gay. . . . [This time,] the scribblings on the wall are anti-male and they are no more tolerable. . . . Period."

10. Robert Mathiesen, "Of Restroom Graffiti: Beware Of Witch-Hunting," *Brown Daily Herald*, November 5, 1990.

11. See Carol F. Karlsen, *The Devil in Shape of a Woman* (New York: Norton, 1987).

12. Mathiesen, "Of Restroom Graffiti": "Just as there is no crime so heinous that some person might not commit it, so is there no false accusation so harmful that some person might not make it."

13. I thank Sarah Benson for this insight.

14. *Whitney v. California*, 274 U.S. 357, 376 (1927) (Brandeis, J., concurring).

15. Sheila Blumstein, "Blumstein Knocks Graffiti," *Brown Daily Herald*, November 13, 1990. In citing instances of "anonymous communications," Dean Blumstein offered two: the "Rape List" and a swastika embedded in a painting on the stairwell wall of campus building; see also Eliza Engelberg, "Blumstein Should Make System Work," *Brown Daily Herald*, November 15, 1990: "Rather than addressing what in the system has caused what she terms 'vigilantism' (i.e. action which occurs outside the system), [Blumstein] has chosen to attack the women who wrote the list, equating them with Nazis (both have recently written graffiti at Brown) and Joe McCarthy (both have made accusations)."

16. See Blumstein, "Blumstein Knocks Graffiti." Compare with L. L. Sommers, "Vigilantism Defined," *Brown Daily Herald*, November 30, 1990:

> Vigilantism is punishment of persons extralegally and it is against the law.
>
> If women had meant to publicly accuse without explanation, wouldn't they have written on dorm walls, public sidewalks, etc., where the accused could really have felt attacked? What they did was more akin to telling their friends about their bad experiences with certain men. Now that it is public, no one asks for an explanation. The Administration threatens that if explanation is forthcoming[,] those responsible may be expelled from the University. This confirms what these anonymous women have suggested: the University is not interested in helping them with their problems, it is interested in silencing them.
>
> Should we be outraged at these women or should we be afraid that they are among those who have spoken out about the insensitive and frightening comments by those in authority who have been told of such instances? How many of those on the rape list have been reported to deans, R.A.s, etc.? Does anyone care to ask?

17. See Meredith Moss, "Flier Calls Doyle Cen. Fascist," *Brown Daily Herald*, December 6, 1990.

18. Moss, "Flier Calls." See also Will, "New Guise" (expressing concern that "white heterosexual males" are targets of political correctness).

19. Schmich, "Accusers Use Graffiti," 20 (emphasis added).

20. Henry Louis Gates Jr., "Let Them Talk," *New Republic*, September 20 and 27, 1993.

21. Blumstein, "Blumstein Knocks Graffiti" (emphasis added). See generally MacKinnon, *Only Words*, 78. MacKinnon sheds light on how the law of libel works to the favor of dominant groups, and targets the powerless for liability:

> [Expressions] that criticize the sexual distribution of power in particular are often, in my experience, supported by reference to the law of libel. Libel law, just one subdivision of the law of speech which lacks sensitivity to the substance of social inequality, has become a tool for justifying refusals to publish attacks on those with power, even as it targets the powerless for liability.
>
> The [current] law of libel has had the effect of licensing the dominant to say virtually anything about subordinated groups with impunity while supporting the media's power to refuse access to speech to the powerless, as it can always cite fear of a libel suit by an offended powerful individual.

This situation is exacerbated by the fact that it is subordinated groups who are damaged by group defamation and mostly the privileged who can make credible threats to sue even for true statements that make them look bad." (80–81)

22. See generally MacKinnon, *Only Words*, 81. The men at Brown had no trouble framing their injury in the legal terms of defamation. MacKinnon offers an insight as to why: "Reputational harm to those who are allowed to be individuals—mostly white men—is legal harm. Those who are defined by, and most often falsely maligned through, their membership in groups—namely almost everyone else—have no legal claim."

23. Alexander Downes, "I Am Not a Rapist," *Brown Daily Herald*, November 2, 1990 (emphasis added).

24. Adam Gillitt, "Surprised and Angered," *Brown Daily Herald*, November 13, 1990 (emphasis added).

25. Ann Russo, "An Unhealthy Climate for Women," *Women's Review of Books*, February 1992, 26.

26. As a result of the "Rape List" controversy, Inman was demoted to director of student activities. See Michael Rothman, "The Deanery Shuffle: Office of Student Life Overhauled after Sexual Assault Controversy," *College Hill Independent*, August 30, 1991.

27. Letter from Dean Inman (on file with author). The letter reads, in pertinent part:

> You may or may not be aware that your name has been included in a list of names that has been appearing in various female toilet stalls on campus. The list suggests that those listed have engaged in sexual assault or harassment. Some of those listed have filed complaints. You may wish to do the same. I have notified Police and Security to respond immediately if we receive information of further inscriptions, to file an official report and stay until it is removed by Plant Operations. At this time we have no knowledge of the perpetrators or their motives. If you would like to speak to me about this or meet with others so listed, please contact me.

28. Brook Conner '91, Andreas Schmitz '91, John Boscardin '91, Noah Green '91.5, Eliot Fisk '92, Joe Oliver '93, David Gardi '93, Andre Haynes '93, Eric Marderstein '94, and Maurice Fitzmaurice '94 were all men on the "Rape List" against whom female students had previously tried to press charges through the university disciplinary system for sexual harassment or assault.

Brook Conner was sent home a week early for spring break in connection with sexual assault allegations. The woman pressing charges was denied a hearing. The woman who tried to press charges against Andreas Schmitz was told that the disciplinary review board would not take a sexual assault case, and that if she tried to press charges against Schmitz for rape, the university might press countercharges against her for drinking. John Boscardin was ordered to write a letter of apology to the woman who tried to press charges against him for date rape. Eliot Fisk was ordered to write a letter of apology to the woman who tried to press charges against him for stalking and sexual harassment. Joe Oliver and David Gardi both received letters of warning and were ordered to write letters of apology to me when I tried to press charges against them for sexual harassment. Jesselyn Brown, "Sexual Violence at Brown University" (Honors thesis, Brown University, April 1992).

When the disciplinary system was revamped after the "Rape List" controversy and some women decided to reinitiate disciplinary proceedings, Green was put on a semester of full probation, Marderstein was sanctioned and put on probation for the remainder of his undergraduate years, Fitzmaurice was suspended for a year, and Haynes was expelled. The University Disciplinary Council Public Record of Major Disciplinary Hearings (record on file with author).

29. See Karen Houppert, "Wildflowers among the Ivy," *Ms.*, September/October 1991, 54. Part of the dialogue on the bathroom walls appeared in the article: "There is antiwoman graffiti all over this fucking university. If we wrote the Rape List on top of all the graffiti maligning women, maybe it would finally be erased too!"

30. Vartan Gregorian, "One Is Too Many: Sexual Assault Is a National Tragedy and Disgrace," *Brown Daily Herald*, November 30, 1990.

31. Brown University Department of Police and Security Services Incident Report #90-_____ (on file with author).

32. See Meredith Moss, "Graffiti Maligns Activist: Response to Bathroom Graffiti against Jesselyn Brown '92 Reveals Complaint Process Is Still Not Operating Smoothly," *Brown Daily Herald*, December 11, 1990.

33. An account of this incident follows:

> I later called President Gregorian. He said that despite the front page *Herald* article, he was not aware that I had been hurt in the graffiti. I asked him if I was entitled to the same letter received by male students under similar circumstances and he assured me "absolutely" I was. He told me to make sure and check my mailbox when I returned to Brown after Christmas vacation.
>
> I asked what to do if there was nothing from Inman in my mailbox (though I figured something would definitely be there because Gregorian now had a week to order Inman to get the letter in the mail before my arrival). Gregorian told me to go to the Office of Student Life and tell Inman I wanted the letter. I explained that morally I refused to do this because 1) Inman is already aware of the situation, 2) it is not my duty as a student to be continually having to tell Dean Inman how to do his job, and 3) I find it demeaning that I would be expected to have to beg the Office of Student Life for a letter when I am the one who has been twice victimized during this recent incident.
>
> Gregorian explained that he was a "hands-off manager," and that he doesn't go chasing deans telling them how to perform their jobs. He just kept telling me over and over to check my mailbox when I returned. I asked one more time what to do if there was nothing from Inman in my mailbox. He replied, "Give 'em hell!" (letter on file with author).

34. Sarah Crichton, "Sexual Correctness: Has It Gone Too Far?" *Newsweek*, October 25, 1993, 52.

35. Katie Roiphe, *The Morning After: Sex, Fear, and Feminism on Campus* (1993), 19.

36. Roiphe, *The Morning After*, 6: "The image that emerges from feminist preoccupations with rape and sexual harassment is that of women as *victims*, offended by a professor's dirty joke, verbally pressured into sex by peers. This image of a delicate woman bears a striking resemblance to that fifties ideal my mother and the other women of her generation fought so hard to get away from" (emphasis added); see also Crichton, "Sexual Correctness," 52: "The obsession with correct codes of behavior seems to portray women not as thriving on their hard-won independence but as *victims* who can't take care of themselves" (emphasis added). See Ronald Dworkin, "Women and Pornography," New York Review, October 21, 1993 at 38 n.9: "MacKinnon's frequent use of 'you' and 'your,' embracing all female readers, invites every woman to see herself as a *victim* of the appalling sexual crimes and the abuses she describes, and reinforces an implicit suggestion that women are, in pertinent ways, all alike: all passive, innocent, and subjugated" (emphasis added); Richard Posner, "Only Words" (Book Review), *New Republic*, October 18, 1993, 36: "MacKinnon's conception of American women as eternal *victims*, cowed, fearful, intimidated and silenced . . . may once have been true, though I greatly doubt it" (emphasis added).

Compare with Catharine A. MacKinnon, *Feminism Unmodified*: *Discourses of Life and Law* (Cambridge, Mass.: Harvard University Press, 1987). MacKinnon's response to this criticism is that she is just telling it like it is:

[T]he parade of horrors demonstrating the systematic victimization of women often produces the criticism that for me to say women are victimized reinforces the stereotype that women "are" victims, which in turn contributes to their victimization. If this stereotype is a stereotype, it has already been accomplished, and I come after. To those who think "it isn't good for women to think of themselves as victims," and thus seek to deny the reality of their victimization, how can it be good for women to deny what is happening to them?" (220)

37. Camille Paglia, "It's a Jungle Out There, So Get Used to It!" *Utne Reader*, January/February 1993, 61.

38. Betty Friedan, *The Second Stage* (New York: Summit Books, 1981), 362; see also Crichton, "Sexual Correctness," 56. Crichton quotes Betty Friedan: "I'm sick of women wallowing in the *victim* state . . . We have empowered ourselves. We are able to blow the whistle on rape. I am not as concerned with that as I am with violence in our whole society" (emphasis added).

39. Naomi Wolf, *Fire with Fire: The New Female Power and How It Will Change the Twenty-first Century* (New York: Random House, 1993), 135, 161–62.

40. For a salient article contesting the claim that "women are making themselves victims," see Susan Faludi, "I'm Not a Feminist, But I Play One on TV," *Ms.*, March/April 1995, 30. In response to the charge that feminists are paranoid whiners who like to imagine women as helpless victims, Faludi writes:

[W]omen have resisted efforts to discourage them from pursuing their rights and independence; far from embracing victimhood, they have fought challenges to their freedoms tooth and nail. I would go one step farther here and argue that women's unladylike, un-victim-minded response to a backlash is, in fact, the enduring legacy of feminism. If feminism stands for anything, it is the belief that women can and must stand up and speak out. Feminism identifies victimization not so we can wallow in it, but so we can wallop it. (36)

41. Peter Hellman, "Crying Rape: The Politics of Date Rape on Campus," *New York*, March 8, 1993, 36 (emphasis added).

42. Professor Alan Dershowitz, "The Administration of Freedom of Speech," guest lecturer for Yale Law School, April 21, 1994.

43. Police Report. But see MacKinnon, *Only Words*, 48 ("Many courts have rejected defenses that the abuse being litigated was only a joke").

44. Letter to Joe Oliver. ("Although I can not hold you responsible for the actions . . . I believe that an apology from you to Ms. Brown, a sister Brown student, would be most appropriate.")

45. Catharine MacKinnon once asked how many elaborate ways can be found to say "Shut up!" Catharine MacKinnon, "Feminist Theory Workshop" and "Free Speech and Social Structure," guest lecturer for Yale Law School, April 22, 1994. Being told to "drop it" was one not-so-elaborate way. What later happened with the ritual erasure of the "Rape List" was.

46. Interview with Catharine MacKinnon, Professor, University of Michigan Law School, in New Haven, Conn., April 22, 1994. As examples of the kinds of speech that make those in power uncomfortable, she suggests: "Feminists trying to get published and the publishers won't do it; the way Andrea Dworkin's work is reviewed and distorted; the way prostitutes are never listened to."

CHAPTER 7

I want to thank Deborah Rifkin, Heather Claussen, Irene Reti, and especially D. A. Clarke for invaluable comments on the substance and style of this essay as I was drafting it.

1. Christine Hoff-Sommers, *Who Stole Feminism? How Women Have Betrayed Women* (New York: Touchstone, 1994), 19.

2. Rosi Braidotti and Judith Butler, "A Feminism by Any Other Name," *Differences: A Journal of Feminist Cultural Studies* 6, no. 2–3 (1994): 27–60, 54.

3. Suzanna Danuta Walters, "'Postfeminism' and Popular Culture," *New Politics* 3, no. 2(1991): 103–12, 110.

4. Walters, "Postfeminism and Popular Culture."

5. Carole Pateman, *The Sexual Contract* (Stanford, Calif.: Stanford University Press, 1988), 20.

6. Hoff-Sommers, *Who Stole Feminism*, 16.

7. Quoted in L. A. Kauffman, "Feminism for the Few," *S. F. Weekly*, November 24, 1993, 11.

8. Renée Denfield, *The New Victorians: A Young Woman's Challenge to the Old Feminist Order* (New York: Warner, 1995).

9. Laura Ring, "And If Morning Never Comes? Roiphe, Resistance, and the Subject of Women," *Radical America* 25, no. 2 (1994): 57–64, 59.

10. Stephen Steinberg, "The Politics of Memory," *New Politics* 3, no. 2 (1991): 64–70.

11. This is Katie Roiphe's term. *The Morning After: Sex, Fear, and Feminism on Campus* (Boston: Little, Brown, 1993).

12. Elizabeth Fox-Genovese, "Beyond Individualism: The New Puritanism, Feminism, and Women," *Salmagundi*, no. 101–2 (1994): 79–94.

13. *New York Times* review quoted in Patrice McDermott, "On Cultural Authority: Women's Studies, Feminist Politics, and the Popular Press," *Signs: Journal of Women in Culture and Society* 20, no. 31 (1995): 668–84, 669. McDermott points out that "In addition to the favorable reviews in two newspapers, Roiphe was the cover story of the *New York Times Magazine* and the lead story in the *Washington Post*'s 'Style' section, was interviewed for the fashion magazine *Mirabella*, and was featured in four other women's glossies."

14. Roiphe, *Morning After*, 6.

15. The term "sexual liberal" was first used, to my recollection, in the context of a 1987 conference held at NYU School of Law, "The Sex Liberals and the Attack on Feminism," organized by antipornography radical feminists. In this context the term "liberal" is a specific critique of the self-characterization "sex radical" by the pro-pornography camp, although it more precisely designates a libertarian position. I keep the term "liberal" in the spirit of what I see as a necessary radical feminist critique of liberal individualism. See the anthology that grew out of the conference, *The Sexual Liberals and the Attack on Feminism*, ed. Janice G. Raymond and Dorchen Leidholt (Tarrytown, NY: Pergamon Press, 1990).

16. Roiphe, *Morning After*, 26.

17. Tad Friend, "Yes. (Feminist Women Who Like Sex)," *Esquire*, February 1994, 48–56, 55.

18. Quoted in Laura Flanders, "The 'Stolen Feminism' Hoax," *EXTRA!* September/October 1994, 7.

19. Wendy Kaminer, "What Is This Thing Called Rape?" *New York Times Book Review*, September 19, 1993, 42.

20. This is Roiphe's characterization of Andrea Dworkin's ideas. *Morning After*, 46.

21. Denfield, *The New Victorians*, 119–20.

22. With the term "institutionalized heterosexuality" I am not criticizing women's desire for men. I am criticizing a system that establishes heterosexuality as the norm for "healthy" sexual relationships and stigmatizes those who fall outside the norm as "perverse," and I am asking how this "normative" heterosexuality helps institutionalize and eroticize the existing power hierarchy between men and women. "Homophobia is a weapon of sexism," as Suzanne Pharr among others maintain, because it tars any woman who crosses the line of her gender role. Thus homophobia reveals the extent to which heterosexuality remains a bulwark of sexism. It may very well be the case that many individual heterosexual relationships are benign. What I am concerned with is the question of why an acknowledgment of benign heterosexual relationships becomes a "faith"—a faith that leads liberals and postfeminists to deny the feminist insight that there is a connection between rape and institutionalized heterosexuality. In my opinion the faith and the fear it represents (that heterosexuality is not so benign) confirms the degree to which heterosexuality remains compulsory rather than freely chosen. See Suzanne Pharr, *Homophobia: A Weapon of Sexism* (Inverness, Calif.: Chardon Press, 1988) and Radicalesbians, "The Woman-Identified Woman," in *Radical Feminism*, ed. Anne Koedt, Ellen Levine, and Anita Rapone (New York:

Quadrangle, 1973), 240–45.

23. Diana Scully and Joseph Marolla, "Riding the Bull at Gilley's: Convicted Rapists Describe the Rewards of Rape," in *Feminist Frontiers III*, ed. Laurel Richardson and Verta Taylor (New York: McGraw Hill, 1993), 402–13, 403.

24. Adrienne Rich, "Compulsory Heterosexuality and Lesbian Existence," in *Powers of Desire: The Politics of Sexuality*, ed. Ann Snitow, Christine Stansell, and Sharon Thompson (New York: Monthly Review Press, 1983), 177–205.

25. More than 75 percent of rape victims know their attackers according to *Rape in America: A Report to the Nation*, prepared by the National Victim Center and Crime Victim's Research and Treatment Center (Arlington, Va.: National Center for Victims of Crime, 1992).

26. Catharine A. MacKinnon, "Rape: On Coercion and Consent," in *Toward a Feminist Theory of the State* (Cambridge, Mass.: Harvard University Press, 1989), 171–83.

27. National Clearinghouse on Marital and Date Rape, Berkeley California. See their Web site: *http://members.aol.com/ncmdr/index.html*. The video that Dale Crawford made of his assault on his wife might have had the opposite effect on the jury of that intended by the prosecution. As feminist theorist Karen Davis has pointed out, if pornography works to predispose people to view rape as sex, it especially does so when what we're viewing is a video of that rape. Personal communication, 1992.

28. See Pateman, *Sexual Contract* for a historical overview and radical analysis of this political fact.

29. "State Law Chart," National Clearinghouse on Marital and Date Rape.

30. "State Law Chart," National Clearinghouse on Marital and Date Rape.

31. Anna Quindlen, "Old Math: Women's Worth Is Less," *San Jose Mercury News*, October 26, 1994.

32. David Rieff, "Victims All?" *Harpers*, October 1991, 49–57.

33. Roiphe, *Morning After*, 37.

34. Kathleen Barry, *Female Sexual Slavery* (Englewood Cliffs, N.J.: Prentice-Hall), 35.

35. Philip Rieff, *The Triumph of the Therapeutic: Uses of Faith after Freud* (New York: Harper and Row, 1966).

36. Important radical feminist critiques of therapy and/or victimism can be found in Mary Daly, *Gyn/Ecology: The Metha-Ethics of Radical Feminism* (Boston: Beacon, 1978) and Janice G. Raymond, *A Passion for Friends: Toward a Philosophy of Female Affection* (Boston: Beacon, 1986). Also see Bonnie Mann, "Validation or Liberation: A Critical Look at Therapy and the Women's Movement," *Trivia* 10 (1987): 41–56.

37. My point is not to underrate the urgency of the healing process for individuals in therapy or recovery but to address the extent to which this model of individual recovery has been seen as an adequate substitute for collective, political action.

38. Louise Armstrong, *What Happened When Women Said Incest? Rocking the Cradle of Sexual Politics* (New York: Addison-Wesley, 1994).

39. Louise Armstrong, "Surviving the Incest Industry," *Trouble and Strife* no. 21: 29. In "What Happened When Women Said Incest," Armstrong explains that she no longer uses the term "incest industry," as it is a phrase that has been co-opted by the backlash.

40. Camille Paglia, "Rape and the Modern Sex War," in *Debating Sexual Correctness: Pornography, Sexual Harassment, Date Rape, and the Politics of Sexual Equality*, ed. Adele Stan (New York: Delta, 1995), 21.

41. Quoted in Friend, "Yes. (Feminist Women who Like Sex)," 49.

42. Paglia, "Rape and the Modern Sex War," 25.

43. This is one of Hoff-Sommers's favorite phrases in *Who Stole Feminism?*

44. Roiphe, *Morning After*, 62.

45. Quoted in Ring, "And If Morning Never Comes?" 62.

46. Ring, "And If Morning Never Comes?" 61.

47. Fassin, "Playing by the Antioch Rules," in *Debating Sexual Correctness*, ed. Adele Stan (New York: Delta, 1995), 99.

48. Fox-Genovese, "Beyond Individualism," 90.

49. Fassin, "Playing by the Antioch Rules," 99.

50. Fox-Genovese, "Beyond Individualism," 89.

51. Fox-Genovese, "Beyond Individualism," 91–92.

52. Roiphe, *Morning After*, 45.

53. Hoff-Sommers, *Who Stole Feminism?* 221.

54. Patricia Hill Collins, *Black Feminist Thought: Knowledge, Consciousness, and the Politics of Empowerment* (Routledge: New York, 1990), 176.

55. Jacqueline Dowd Hall quoted in Hill Collins, *Black Feminist Thought*, 170.

56. Monique Wittig, "The Straight Mind," in *The Straight Mind* (Boston: Beacon, 1992).

57. Katha Pollitt, "Just the Facts," *Nation,* June 24, 1996, 9.

58. Pollitt, "Just the Facts."

59. Sandra Meucci, "The Race to End Welfare: Reproduction Politics and U.S. Policy" (Ph.D. diss., Board of Sociology, University of California, Santa Cruz, March 1998).

60. Meucci, "Race to End Welfare," 7.

61. Daniel Patrick Moynihan, *The Negro Family: The Case for National Action*, for the Office of Policy Planning and Research (Washington, D.C.: Government Printing Office, 1965).

62. Katha Pollitt, "Fetal Rights: A New Assault on Feminism," *Nation,* March 26, 1990, 409–16, 410–11.

63. Quoted in Ruth Conniff, "Big Bad Welfare," *The Progressive,* August 1994, 18.

64. Conniff, "Big Bad Welfare."

65. Mike Males, "Infantile Arguments," *These Times*, August 9, 1993, 19.

66. Studies cited by Males, "Infantile Arguments," 19–20.

67. Wittig, "Straight Mind," 27.

68. Elizabeth Higginbotham, "We Were Never on a Pedestal," in *Race, Class, and Gender: An Anthology*, ed. Margaret L. Andersen and Patricia Hill Collins (Belmont, Calif.: Wadsworth, 1993), 183.

69. Karin Stallard, Barbara Ehrenreich, and Holly Sklar, *Poverty in the American Dream: Women and Children First* (Boston: South End Press, 1983), 9.

70. Teresa Amott, *Caught in the Crisis: Women and the U.S. Economy Today* (New York: Monthly Review Press, 1993).

71. Diana Pearce, "The Feminization of Poverty: Women, Work, and Welfare," *Urban and Social Change Review*, February 1978.

72. As Sandra Meucci found in her study of women on AFDC, "Regardless of class background . . . sexual abuse of the daughter and battering of the mother were common themes in the lives of 50% of the women." "The Moral Context of Welfare Mothers: A Study of U.S. Welfare Reform in the 1980s," *Critical Social Policy* 34 (January 1992): 52–74, 62–63.

73. Other key conditions of women's poverty are, of course, the hierarchical structure of a labor market that has historically excluded women (and people of color) and/or relegated women and people of color to the lowest-paid, menial types of work. See Amott, *Caught at the Crisis.*

74. This is Eric Fassin's comment about the Antioch Code, "Playing by the Antioch Rules," 100.

75. I am inverting the title of Fox-Genovese's book, *Feminism without Illusions: A Critique of Individualism* (Chapel Hill, N.C.: University of North Carolina Press, 1991).

76. I am citing a principle and aesthetic of resistance imagined by Andrea Dworkin: "I will take the blood of women implicit in the weaponry and I will make it explicit; and from this I enunciate another political principle, which is, The blood of women is implicit, make it explicit." Andrea Dworkin, *Mercy* (London: Secker and Warburg, 1990), 328.

CHAPTER 8

Special thanks to Chris Grussendorf, Rene S., Jolanda Sallmann, and Christopher Zenk.

1. Emille Buchwald, Pamela Fletcher, Martha Roth, eds., *Transforming a Rape Culture* (Minneapolis: Milkweed Editions, 1993), preamble.

2. Kate Millett, *Sexual Politics* (New York: Ballantine Books, 1969).

3. Laura Lederer, ed., *Take Back the Night: Women on Pornography* (New York: William Morrow, 1982), 190–92.

4. Lederer, *Take Back the Night*, 134–40.

5. Gloria Steinem, "What's Wrong with This Picture?" *Ms.*, March/April 1997, p. 76.

6. Catharine MacKinnon, "Francis Biddle's Sister: Pornography, Civil Rights, and Speech," in *Feminism Unmodified* (Cambridge: Harvard University Press, 1987), 187–89.

7. Judith Lewis Herman, *Trauma and Recovery* (New York: Basic Books, 1992), 76.

8. Rene S., personal communication, May 20, 1997.

9. Excerpted from "WCASA Censors Andrea Dworkin," letter by Chris Grussendorf, taken from the Andrea Dworkin home page *(www.igc.apc.org/ womensnet/dworkin/index.html).*

10. Chris Grussendorf, personal communication, June 21, 1997.

11. Grussendorf, personal communication, June 21, 1997.

12. Elizabeth Brixey Courts, "Defendant Ruled Fit to Stand Trial in Motel Murder," *Wisconsin State Journal*, May 24, 1997.

13. "The Business of Pornography," *U.S. News and World Report*, February 10, 1997, 42.

14. Gloria Steinem, "Erotica vs. Pornography," in *Transforming a Rape Culture,* ed. Emilie Buchwald, Pamela Flectcher, and Martha Roth (Minneapolis: Milkweed, 1993), 33–45.

15. Naomi Wolf, *Fire with Fire: The New Female Power and How It Will Change the Twenty-first Century* (London: Fawcett, 1994), 103.

16. Chris Grussendorf, "Pornography Is Not Fantasy," *Feminist Voices,* April 14-June 12, 1997.

17. "Pornography: Stop It? Use It? Ban It?" *Ms.,* January-February 1994), 43–44.

18. Chris Grussendorf, "Fight Back," University of Redlands, Redlands, Calif., November 1996.

CHAPTER 12

1. Jeffrey M. Gould and Annie R. Lomax, "The Evolution of Peer Education: Where Do We Go from Here?" *Journal of American College Health Association* 41, no.6 (1993): 235.

2. Author Doug Coupland coined the term "Generation X" in his book by the same name. See *Generation X* (New York: St. Martin's Press, 1991).

3. Arthur Levine, "A New Generation of Student Protesters Arises," *Chronicle of Higher Education,* February 26, 1999, A52.

4. Levine, "A New Generation."

5. Jodi Gold, Jessie Minier, and Susan Villari, "Creating Campuses Intolerant of Rape."

6. Paul Rogat Loeb, *Generations at the Crossroads: Apathy and Action on the American Campus* (New Brunswick, N.J.: Rutgers University Press, 1994), 4.

7. Interview with Diana Orino, Duke University, January 29, 1994.

8. In fairness to the many students whose work we are attempting to capture, we have chosen the term "educator-activist" to describe those who participate in this campus movement.

9. Gallup poll survey (release date 12/92) sponsored by *Newsweek.* Telephone survey including interviews with 750 adult women.

10. Barbara Findlen, ed., *Listen Up: Voices from the Next Feminist Generation* (Seattle: Seal Press, 1995), xiv.

11. Findlen, *Listen Up,* xiii.

12. Anastasia Higginbotham, "Chicks Goin' at It," in *Listen Up: Voices from the Next Feminist Generation* (Seattle: Seal Press, 1995), 3–12.

13. Andrea Dworkin, *Women Hating* (New York: Penguin, 1974), 18–19.

14. Levine, "New Generation," A52.

15. *The American Freshman: National Norms for Fall, 1967–1969* (Los Angeles: UCLA Higher Education Research Institute, 1969). This survey was begun in 1966 by the American Council on Education and since 1973 has been coordinated by the Higher Education Research Institute.

16. Gold, Minier, and Villari, "Creating Campuses Intolerant of Rape."

17. "Sexual Assault," *About Women on Campus* 2, no.2 (1993),1.

18. "Sexual Assault," *About Women on Campus* 7, no.4 (1998),8.

19. Malcolm X display at the National Civil Rights Museum, Memphis, Tenn. Original source unknown.

20. Interview with Erica Guttman Strohl, June 15, 1994.

21. Sally Steenland, "Two Twentysomethings Who Are Getting Involved: Young Volunteers in the Nineties Have More Modest Goals Than Those in the Sixties," *Philadelphia Inquirer,* December 7, 1993.

22. Loeb, *Generations at the Crossroads,* 231.

23. Nyasha Spears, "No Time to Wait for a Revolution: Nineties Style Activism through Service," unpublished paper, 1994.

24. Interview with Kurt Conklin, Philadelphia, Pa., December 11, 1997.

25. Beverly Jones, "Toward a Female Liberation Movement," in *Feminist Revolution* (New York: Random House, 1975), 145.

26. Gold, Minier, and Villari, "Stop the Violence."

CHAPTER 13

I have benefited enormously from conversations with all of the following people and groups who invited me to speak about the ideas presented, in revised form, here: Elizabeth Corbett and Roni Morganstern of Fightback! of Central New York; Lorne Coleman of Escape Women's Self-Defense and Empowerment in Atlanta, Georgia; Emory University's Women's Center; Northwestern University's Women's Center; and Hillel Cultural Life of Evanston, Illinois. Thanks also go to Ingrid Banks (Black Studies, Virginia Tech) and Jocelyn Hollander (Sociology, University of Oregon) for comments on a draft of this chapter.

1. See Diana Scully, *Understanding Sexual Violence: A Study of Convicted Rapists* (Boston: Unwin Hyman, 1990), for an analysis of convicted rapists' accounts of their actions.

2. Emilie Buchwald, Pamela R. Fletcher, and Martha Roth, eds., *Transforming a Rape Culture* (Minneapolis: Milkweed Editions, 1993); Pauline Bart and Eileen Geil Moran, eds., *Acquaintance Rape: The Hidden Crime* (New York: John Wiley and Sons, 1991); and Laura T. O'Toole and Jessica R. Schiffman, eds., *Gender Violence: Interdisciplinary Perspectives* (New York: New York University Press, 1997).

3. D. A. Clarke, "A Woman with a Sword: Some Thoughts on Women, Feminism, and Violence," in Buchwald, Fletcher, and Roth, *Transforming a Rape Culture.*

4. Michael D. Gray, Diane Lesser, Edna Quinn, and Chris Rounds, "The Effectiveness of Personalizing Acquaintance Rape Prevention: Programs on Perception of Vulnerability and on Reducing Risk-Taking Behavior," *Journal of College Student Development* 31 (1990): 217–20.

5. For a fuller discussion of this idea, see my book *Real Knockouts: The Physical Feminism of Women's Self-Defense* (New York: New York University Press, 1997).

6. George Chauncey Jr., "From Sexual Inversion to Homosexuality: Medicine and the Changing Conception of Female Deviance," *Salmagundi* 58–59 (1982–83): 119; Lynda Hart, *Fatal Women: Lesbian Sexuality and the Mark of Aggression* (Princeton, N.J.: Princeton University Press, 1994), 9.

7. Linda L. Ammons, "Mules, Madonnas, Babies, Bathwater, Racial Imagery, and Stereotypes: The African American Woman and the Battered Woman Syndrome," *Wisconsin Law Review* 5 (1995): 1003–80. Angela Davis, *Women, Race,*

and Class (New York: Vintage Books, 1983). U.S. Department of Justice, "Violence Against Women: Estimates from the Redesigned Survey" (National Crime Victimization Survey) by Ronet Bachman and Linda E. Satzman, NCJ-154348, (Washington, D.C.: Office of Justice Programs, Bureau of Justice Statistics, 1995).

8. Iris Marion Young, "Throwing Like a Girl and Other Essays," in *Feminist Philosophy and Social Theory* (Bloomington, Ind.: Indiana University Press, 1990).

9. Young, "Throwing Like a Girl," 145.

10. Quoted in John Gaddis, "Women's Empowerment through Model Mugging: Breaking the Cycle of Social Violence," Ph.D. diss., University of California, Santa Barbara, 1990, 166–67.

11. Quoted in Johanna Turaj, "Finding the Kiai: Training at a Women's Karate School and Its Relationship to Self-Esteem," manuscript, Smith College School of Social Work, 1993, 61.

12. Sharon Marcus, "Fighting Bodies, Fighting Words: A Theory and Politics of Rape Prevention," in *Feminists Theorize the Political*, ed. Judith Butler and Joan W. Scott (New York: Routledge, 1992).

13. Nayda Burton, "Resistance to Prevention: Reconsidering Feminist Antiviolence Rhetoric," in *Violence Against Women: Philosophical Perspectives*, ed. Stanley G. French, Wendy Teays, and Laura M. Purdy (Ithaca, N.Y.: Cornell University Press, 1998), 188.

CHAPTER 14

This chapter was originally presented at the Fifth National Student Conference on Campus Sexual Violence (1996) and at the Minnesota Coalition Against Sexual Assault Annual Conference (1997).

1. Susan Schecter, *Women and Male Violence: The Visions and Struggles of the Battered Women's Movement* (Boston: South End Press, 1982), 259.

2. Donna Landerman, "Breaking the Racism Barrier: White Anti-Racism Work," in *Revealing the Web of Life: Feminism and Nonviolence,* ed. Pam McAllister (Philadelphia: New Society, 1982), 320.

3. Suzanne Pharr, *Homophobia: A Weapon of Sexism* (Little Rock, Ark.: Chardon Press, 1998), 14–15.

4. Kimberle Crenshaw, "The Marginalization of Sexual Violence against Black Women," *National Coalition against Sexual Assault Journal* 2, no. 1 (1994): 1–6, 15.

5. U.S. Department of Justice, *Violence against Women* (Rockville, Md.: Bureau of Justice Statistics, 1994).

6. Robin Warshaw, *I Never Called It Rape: The* Ms. *Report on Recognizing, Fighting, and Surviving Date and Acquaintance Rape* (New York: Harper Perennial, 1994), 11.

7. Crenshaw, "The Marginalization," 15.

8. Cherrie Moraga and Gloria Anzaldua, eds., *This Bridge Called My Back: Writings by Radical Women of Color* (New York: Kitchen Table Women of Color Press, 1983), xv.

9. Beth Richie, *Compelled to Crime: The Gender Entrapment of Battered Black Women* (New York: Routledge, 1996).

CHAPTER 15

1. Peggy Reeves Sanday, *Fraternity Gang Rape: Sex, Brotherhood, and Privilege on Campus* (New York: New York University Press, 1990).

CHAPTER 17

1. Michael Kimmel, "Clarence, William, Iron Mike, Tailhook, Senator Packwood, Spur Posse, Magic . . . and Us," in *Transforming a Rape Culture*, ed. Emilie Buchwald, Pamela Fletcher, and Martha Roth (Minneapolis: Milkweed Editions, 1993), 127.

2. James Prochaska and J. Norcross, *Systems of Psychotherapy: A Transtheoretical Analysis*, 3d ed. (Pacific Grove, Calif.: Brooks/Cole, 1994).

3. Chris O'Sullivan, "Fraternities and the Rape Culture," in *Transforming a Rape Culture*, ed. Emilie Buchwald, Pamela Fletcher, and Martha Roth (Minneapolis: Milkweed Editions, 1993), 23–30.

4. Terrence Crowley, "The Lie of Entitlement," in *Transforming a Rape Culture*, ed. Emilie Buchwald, Pamela Fletcher, and Martha Roth, (Minneapolis: Milkweed Editions, 1993), 348.

5. Jason Schultz, personal communication, March 21, 1996.

6. Timothy Beneke, *Proving Manhood: Reflections on Men and Sexism* (Berkeley: University of California Press, 1997).

7. Mariah Burton Nelson, *The Stronger Women Get, the More Men Love Football* (New York: Avon Books, 1995), 76.

8. Timothy J. Curry, "Fraternal Bonding in the Locker Room," *Sociology of Sport Journal* 8 (1991): 119–35.

9. Peggy Reeves Sanday, *Fraternity Gang Rape: Sex, Brotherhood, and Privilege on Campus* (New York: New York University Press, 1990), 135–55.

10. Curry, "Fraternal Bonding," 123.

11. Don Sabo, *Power at Play*, ed. Don Sabo and Michael Messner (Boston: Beacon Press, 1992).

12. Timothy Beneke, *Proving Manhood: Reflections on Men and Sexism* (Berkeley: University of California Press, 1997).

13. Associated Press, "NCAA Changes Rules in the Wake of Wrestling Deaths," *Boston Globe*, January 14, 1998.

14. Nelson, *Stronger Women Get*, 146.

15. Merrill Melnick, "Male Athletes and Sexual Assault," *Journal of Physical Education and Research Development* (May-June 1992): 32–35.

16. Constance Johnson, "When Sex Is the Issue," *U.S. World and News Report*, October 7, 1991, 34–35.

17. Denise Lavoie, "Fugitive Student Convicted of '86 Rape of Neighbor," *Philadelphia Inquirer*, June 13, 1997.

18. Kimmel, "Clarence, William," 127.

19. Jaymz Haynes, "Gender Issues Speaker Talks Wednesday of Horrific Assaults," *Wabash College Bachelor*, March 19, 1998.

20. Nelson, *Stronger Women Get*, 132.

21. Rick Bragg, "A Killer's Only Confidant: The Man Who Caught Susan Smith," *Spartanburg Herald-Journal*, August 4, 1995.

22. Gavin DeBecker, *The Gift of Fear and Other Survival Signals That Protect Us from Violence* (New York: Dell, 1997).

23. William Claiborne, "Youth Jailed in Oregon School Rampage," *Washington Post*, May 22, 1998.

24. Sanday, *Fraternity Gang Rape*, 14.

25. Thomas Jackson, "Rape Prevention Program for Athletes: Special Characteristics of NCAA Division I Athletic Programs," in *Rape 101: Sexual Assault Prevention for College Athletes*, ed. Andrea Parrot, Nina Cummings, and Todd Marchell (Holmes Beach, Fla.: Learning Publications, 1994), 38–43.

26. Melnick, "Male Athletes and Sexual Assault."

27. Nelson, *Stronger Women Get*, 147.

28. Jackson, "Rape Prevention Program."

29. Curry, "Fraternal Bonding."

30. Jackson Katz, "Reconstructing Masculinity in the Locker Room: The Mentors in Violence Prevention Program," *Harvard Educational Review* 65, no. 2 (1995): 163–74.

31. Jackson, "Rape Prevention Program."

32. Christopher Kilmartin, "Integrating the Gender Context," *Connections—WCASA Quarterly Educational Journal* 12, no. 1 (1998): 8–10.

33. Alan Berkowitz, "A Model Acquaintance Rape Prevention Program for Men," *New Directions for Student Services* 65 (San Francisco: Jossey-Bass, 1994), 35–42.

APPENDIX I

RESOURCES

Campus Outreach Services, Inc.

304 Overlook Lane
Gulph Mills, PA 19428-2634
(610) 941-5997
http://www.campusoutreachservices.com

Provides sexual assault education, policy, and risk management services for high schools, colleges, and military academies.

Coalition against Trafficking in Women

http://www.uri.edu/artsci/wms/hughes/catw

Feminist nongovernmental human rights organization committed to fighting all forms of sexual exploitation of women and children. Works with national and international policy makers, women and human rights advocates, and the United Nations.

Men Stopping Rape

306 North Brooks Street
Madison, WI 53715
(608) 257-4444

Offers variety of educational materials including posters, brochures, and videos.

National Association for Women in Education

Suite 210
1325 Eighteenth Street, N.W.
Washington, D.C. 20036-6511
(202) 659-9330
http://www.nawe.org

The Women's Issues Project of the National Association for Women in Education publishes an excellent quarterly newsletter called *About Women on Campus,* which highlights specific campus cases and available resources related to sexual assault and harassment.

National Coalition against Sexual Assault (NCASA)

125 N. Enola Drive
Enola, PA 17025
(717) 728-9764
http://www.ncasa.org

A feminist organization that provides leadership to the movement to end sexual violence through advocacy, education, and public policy. Also sponsors national conferences.

National Organization of Victim Assistance (NOVA)

1727 Park Road, N.W.
Washington, D.C. 20010
(800) 879-6682
(202) 232-6682
http://www.try-nova.org

Founded in 1975, NOVA is a small nonprofit organization dedicated to improving services for victims and survivors of violent crimes and disasters, offering a twenty-four-hour hotline, conferences, legislative advocacy, and a national clearinghouse.

The New York City Gay and Lesbian Anti-Violence Project

647 Hudson Street
New York, NY 10014
24-hour hotline: (212) 807-6761
Office: (212) 807-6761

Founded in 1980, this is New York City's primary resource for lesbian and gay survivors of sexual assault. This organization publishes an excellent brochure on male rape.

Rape, Abuse and Incest National Network (RAINN)

252 Tenth Street, N.E.
Washington, D.C. 20002
(202) 544-1034
(800) 656-HOPE (national referral to local service)
http://www.rainn.org

National organization founded by musician Tori Amos.

The Safe Schools Coalition, Inc.

P.O. Box 1338, Dept. S112
Holmes Beach, FL 34218-1338
(800) 537-4903
http://www.ed.mtu.edu/safe

Consortium organizer of the *International Conference on Sexual Assault and Harassment on Campus* held annually.

Santa Monica Rape Treatment Center

1250 Sixteenth Street
Santa Monica, CA 90404
(800) END-RAPE
http://www.endrape.org

In addition to offering twenty-four-hour medical and legal advocacy services, distributes rape prevention posters, brochures, and videos appropriate for use on college campuses.

Security on Campus, Inc.

601 South Henderson Road
Suite 205
King of Prussia, PA 19406
Hotline: (888) 251-7959
(610) 768-9330
http://www.campussafety.org

Founded by Howard and Connie Cleary after their daughter was sexually assaulted and murdered by another student at Lehigh University in 1986. Excellent resource for legislative issues related to campus crime and the reporting of sexual assault.

SpeakOut: The North American Student Coalition against Sexual Violence

http://members.aol.com/nascasv

Organization of U.S. and Canadian campus activists and educators committed to ending sexual violence. Since 1992 SpeakOut has sponsored fifteen North American student conferences. Also serves as clearinghouse for campus programs, resources, and speakers.

Violence against Women Office (Department of Justice)

National Domestic Violence Hotline (800) 799-SAFE
http://www.usdoj.gov/vawo

This is the first federal-government-funded hotline established as part of the 1994 Violence against Women Act.

APPENDIX 2

ADDITIONAL CONTRIBUTORS

We conducted 266 student interviews and 50 phone interviews with sexual assault program directors; surveyed 605 universities and colleges; and traveled to over a dozen conferences and universities conducting research for this book. We met passionate activists and educators and were inspired every step of the way. We would like to recognize the following students whose work we learned from but were unable to include in this publication. Their commitment to this project and the movement is greatly appreciated.

- Willy Airaldi. Ohio State University. *They Say Every Man is a Potential Rapist.*
- Rachel Bennett. Evergreen State University. *Antirape Activism at Evergreen.*
- Chloe Bergman. University of Pennsylvania. *The Naked Truth about Freedom, Responsibility, Sexual Health and Pornography.*
- Amy Best. Ithaca College. *Empowering Ourselves, Educating Others: (Re)presenting Assault Accounts in the University.*
- Anne DePrince. Duke University. *Breaking the Silence on Campus: Adult Survivors of Child Sexual Abuse on Campus.*
- April Elliot. Virginia Commonwealth University. *The Virtual Reality of Rape: Violence in Cyberspace.*
- Morgan Friedman. University of Pennsylvania. *Student Activism of the Nineties: The Convenience of the Internet.*
- Rus Ervin Funk. *Rape and Racism: Overlapping Tools of Oppression.*
- Sara Hall. Addison, N.Y. *Sexual Harassment at My High School.*
- Cathy Harris. Brown University and New York University School of Law. *Peer Education at Brown.*
- Loolwa Khazzoom. *defining . . . the violence, the power.*

- Kirsten Lee and Nate P. Gilbertson. Valpraiso University. *Moving from Institutional Rape to Sexual Equality: A Shift from Power Over to Power With.*
- LeAnn Levering. Duke University. *Resist and Survive: The Need for Self-Defense Training in the Antirape Movement.*
- Carrie Lezotte. East Lansing, Michigan. *The Ups and Downs, Why I Do What I Do, My Life as a Filmmaker/Feminist/Activist/Woman on the One of Us Project.*
- Lisa Raucci. University of Illinois.
- Michele Rendeiro. *Rhode Island Task Force on Sexual Assault.*
- Elizabeth Ribet and Laura McKieran. *Female on Female Violence: Forms, Implications, and Consideration for Feminist Youth.*
- Naomi Mara Alena Mahogany Sachs. Brown University. *The Antirape Movement in the United States 1970–1992: An Analysis of Interactions of Race, Gender, Class, and Sexual Assault.*
- Nyasha Spears. Grinnell College. *The Invisible Revolution: Nineties-Style Activism through Service.*
- Tristan Svare. University of Pennsylvania and California Western School of Law. *A Brief History of the Crime of Rape, and the Origins of the Rape Reform Movement.*
- Heather Teeter. *Nightswimming.*
- Becky Temple. University of Virginia. *Rape in High School.*
- Adam Thorburn. *What Every College Student Needs to Know about Pornography.*
- Doug Wubben. Iowa State University. *Best Liberated Guy on the Block: Why Men Do Rape Education and How.*

APPENDIX 3

SPEAKOUT: THE NORTH AMERICAN STUDENT COALITION AGAINST SEXUAL VIOLENCE

Vision: *To build a community intolerant of sexual violence.*

Mission: *SpeakOut: The North American Student Coalition against Sexual Violence recognizes, unites, and enhances the efforts of campus activists throughout the country working to end sexual violence. We strive to promote public discourse on sexual violence while changing social and political institutions.*

Goals:

- To create and foster a communication network between campus programs and campus activists, both dealing with sexual violence, nationwide.
- To work collaboratively with other antiviolence efforts.
- To create a national consciousness of the campus anti-sexual-violence movement.
- To address cultural, racial, economic, and religious factors affecting sexual violence.
- To affect campus, local, state, and national policies regarding survivor's rights.
- To affect campus, local, state, and national policies regarding the adjudication proceedings and perpetrator sanctions and treatment.
- To challenge cultural norms and social constructs contributing to a sexually violent culture.
- To provide a forum for the exchange, evaluation, and development of exemplary models for education and prevention.
- To recognize and build credibility of peer-to-peer education and to promote its implementation.
- To foster leadership development and organizing skills of campus activists.

Objectives:

- To insure the continuity of the North American Student Conferences on Campus Sexual Violence.
- To create an electronic communication network.
- To establish and maintain a national database.
- To work with other organizations and task forces relating to sexual violence issues.
- To document the work of activists in the movement.
- To publish a newsletter to be distributed to all members.
- To promote the student anti-sexual-violence movement and the credibility of peer-to-peer education by presenting at professional conferences.
- To consult with national organizations and media in efforts to promote the accomplishment of the national anti-sexual-violence movement.

APPENDIX 4

CREATING CAMPUSES INTOLERANT OF RAPE: PEER EDUCATION AND THE INSTITUTIONAL RESPONSE TO RAPE

Jodi Gold, Jessie Minier, and Susan Villari

ABSTRACT

This study addresses student activism, peer education, and administrative responses to sexual assault on college campuses. After reviewing the empirical literature on acquaintance rape in America, the authors report their results by way of national profiles of campus programs. They identify a positive association of the campus sexual assault policy with comprehensive staff-provided services. They also find student involvement in the development of this policy correlated with broad-based peer education programs. The authors hypothesize that greater student involvement and more student-administrator collaboration lead to comprehensive peer education programs, increased rape reporting, and potentially more extensive efforts to prevent sexual violence.

> This groundbreaking study provides the first national picture of American higher education's response to sexual violence. Specifically, this study supports the critical roles of student activists and peer-educators in our efforts to prevent and respond to violence against women.
> —Dr. Bernice R. Sandler, Senior Scholar in Residence
> National Association for Women in Education

INTRODUCTION

In 1985 the United States Department of Health and Human Services declared violence, including sexual assault, a primary public health issue in this country. Contemporaneously, Koss (1988) found that over 25 percent of college-aged women were either victims or intended victims of rape, and 84 percent of these women knew their assailants. In another study

273

published in 1988, Aizenman and Kelley concluded that women were most vulnerable to rape during their last year of high school and first year of college. Furthermore, Amir (1971) concluded that most rapists were between fifteen and twenty-four years of age. From these data one can only conclude that our young men are assaulting our young women at alarming rates. Consequently, many researchers have sought the risk factors associated with sexual assault. In the review of studies that follows, we differentiate *psychocultural* factors, those myths and patterns of behavior on which an individual relies to make sense of how to act toward others, from *environmental-situational* factors, aspects of college life and youth that potentiate psychocultural risk factors. This classification is of conceptual interest, to aid understanding of the processes that lead to sexual assault, and is predicated on a cultural analysis of rape. With the ultimate purpose of minimizing psychocultural risk factors and reducing the incidence of sexual assault, we assessed the prevalence and impact of peer education and student activism on college campuses.

REVIEW OF THE LITERATURE

A number of studies have identified psychocultural factors correlated with sexual assault. In Williams and Holmes (1981) peer pressure to perform sexually in order to confirm one's sexuality was highly related to sex-role socialization in which men are expected to dominate and exert force in social situations. With regard to rape myths, Check and Malamuth (1983) found that rape myths, such as "No means yes" and "If a woman leads a man on, she owes him sex," were widely accepted in American society. In addition, such beliefs were more widely subscribed to by males (Burt 1980). These myths reflect presumptions of male social and sexual entitlement (Crowley 1993). Consequently, rapists, potential rapists, and greater society warrant acquaintance rape as just another way sex happens and hold the woman accountable for the man's behavior. Concerning personality characteristics, Mosher and Anderson (1986) determined that a hypermasculine personality correlated positively with behaviors such as treating women abusively, threatening women verbally, and forcing women to have sex. Finally, citing her cross-cultural studies of rape, Sanday (1996) concluded that America is a rape-prone society. Furthermore, she stated, "rape is part of a cultural configuration that includes interpersonal violence, male dominance, and sexual separation . . . an expression of a social ideology of male dominance." It is important to recognize that potential rapists typically bring these factors with them to the college setting.

Among the environmental-situational risk factors identified, the most significant one associated with the campus has been misuse of alcohol and other drugs (Abbey 1991, Koss and Dinero 1989). One potential explanation is that alcohol misuse increases the risk of misperceiving sexual intent (Abbey 1991). Besides substance misuse, Muehlenhard and Linton (1987) implicated gender differences of control over dating situations, such as a male initiating the date, paying the expenses, and driving the couple. Such circumstances, while reflecting real power differentials between genders in society, supported the male's sense of entitlement, already noted with the psychocultural risk factors (Lundberg-Love and Geffner 1989). In recent years researchers have also identified situations with cohesive all-male groups as significant situational factors that increase the risk of rape. Martin and Hammer (1989) have posited that such all-male groups lead their members to doubt their heterosexuality and seek reaffirmation of it through single-perpetrator and gang rape. Sanday (1990) has theorized that this type of gang rape results from a cohesive group's desire for homosexual affection in a homophobic culture. To resolve this conflict, the men use the woman as an object that confirms their heterosexuality and as a vehicle through which they are able to have sex with each other. In addition to these situational factors, Parrot (1991) recognized the newfound freedom and inexperience of college students as general risk factors unique to the college environment.

Although many studies have sought to identify risk factors specific to the potential victim, such factors are not ethically useful for purposes of response and prevention. In their national study of college students, Koss et al. (1987) determined that neither personality characteristics nor rape-supportive beliefs were significantly associated with higher incidence of victimization. Koss et al. (1987) did find a higher incidence of rape among women who participated in college social activities, but it is important to realize that restricting women's behavior is not the solution to rape. Considering college social activities as a risk factor implies that women are responsible for men's behavior and that restricting women's social freedom is a desirable method for rape prevention. This focus on the potential victim's behavior distracts from the perpetrator's attitudinal and behavioral patterns that support and maintain our rape-prone culture. We are not, however, minimizing the importance of developing counterrape strategies, such as self-defense and assertiveness training (Bart and O'Brien 1985, Koss and Harvey 1991, McCoughey 1997).

PURPOSES OF THIS STUDY

Our study focused on the relationships among an explicit campus sexual assault policy, student involvement in the implementation of that policy, and the presence or absence of various staff-provided and peer-led programs addressing sexual assault on campus. Theoretically, staff-provided and peer-led programs attempt to modify behavior by providing cognitive (informational) and affective (emotional) interventions. Empirically, Sloane and Zimmer (1993) found that peer education was the most effective method of changing the values and beliefs of other college students. Yet we surmised that peer education did not exist in a vacuum. In particular, administrative and staff responses to sexual assault on campus may have an impact on the comprehensiveness of peer-led programs on a college campus.

This paper presents the findings of a national survey of college campuses. With a focus on distributional differences between student-led and staff-provided programs, this study also seeks to determine the relationship, if any, between student activism related to the campus sexual assault policy and the prevalence of programs. Two sets of profiles, based on the presence or absence of a campus sexual assault policy and the presence or absence of student involvement with the implementation of that policy, were generated. After discussing the significant relationships, we identified limitations of this and similar studies and the need for future studies specifically addressing the impact of student involvement with efforts to prevent sexual assault on college campuses.

METHODOLOGY

A six-page survey instrument was distributed to 1,100 student-affairs officers in the winter of 1995. With many questions focusing on student-led programs, the need for reliable data was seen. The instrument was sent to members of the National Association of Student Personnel Administrators, persons who would have knowledge of the campus and interest in completing the instrument with care. Consequently, the results are not generalizable to all schools in the United States. The findings are likely to be an overstatement of the programs and policies across the country due to the likely sample bias in using a list of colleges and universities actively interested in their students' affairs and behaviors. Of the 1,100 survey instruments mailed in early 1995, we received 605 responses by May 1995, yielding a 55 percent response rate.

The questions in the instrument may be classified into four categories: campus characteristics (e.g., enrollment size, campus setting, degrees awarded); whether, when, and why the campus developed and implemented a policy specific to sexual assault; what programs and services were provided by staff; and what programs and services were provided by students. To minimize error in responses to quantitative questions, the instrument provided response intervals. For example, for the question,

What year was the policy developed? four responses were listed: (1) Before 1985, (2) 1985–89, (3) 1990–93, (4) 1994–95. Finally, for tests of significance, the authors used the chi-square or Z distributions where appropriate.

AGGREGATE RESULTS

The survey results show that 84 percent of the respondents had a policy specific to sexual assault as of 1995. Of those campuses with a policy, 72 percent implemented their policy within the previous five years, whereas 28 percent had a policy in place before 1990. When asked to select the two primary factors in the implementation of that policy, 47 percent of the respondents reported the recommendation of staff or faculty, 37 percent reported a university task force, and 35 percent reported a legislative mandate. Only 10 percent indicated student activism or a high-profile case. On the other hand, when asked if students had been involved in the implementation of the extant policy, 62 percent reported student involvement. Of the campus characteristics, none provided significant additional information.

Table 1 shows the percentages of campuses, regardless of policy, with twelve common staff-provided services, eleven common student-provided services, and fifteen common issues addressed by student groups. Of staff-provided services, counseling/support services were nearly ubiquitous, found in 93 percent of the institutions. Least common were training programs for faculty (20 percent) and campus-based rape crisis centers (10 percent). Of student-provided services, awareness campaigns were most prevalent, on 51 percent of campuses, compared to the least common peer hotline services (9 percent). A separate finding of interest, 13 percent of all campuses had a student group or program with a primary focus on men's issues (i.e., sexual assault, masculinity, sexuality). Finally, the most common issue addressed by student groups was the role of alcohol and drugs in sexual assault, at 62 percent of institutions. In contrast, at approximately 10 percent of institutions, students addressed childhood sexual assault, racism and rape, and the pornography debate.

PROFILE RESULTS

The services provided and issues addressed were divided into two groups, creating a profile of those campuses with a policy and those campuses without. Of eleven staff-provided services, eight were more prevalent on campuses with policies than on campuses without. In contrast, only three

Table 1 Services Provided and Issues Addressed as % of Respondents

Existing Services Provided by Staff:

Counseling/Support Services	93%
Educational Workshops About Sexual Assault	81%
Safety Escort Service	73%
Orientation Program About Sexual Assault	68%
Specific Educational Brochure On Sexual Assault	62%
24-Hour Crisis Intervention Services	55%
Training for Staff	47%
Legal/Judicial Advocacy	38%
Rape Victim Escort or Advocates Program	30%
Training for Faculty	20%
Campus-Based Rape Crisis Center	10%

Existing Services Provided by Students:

Awareness Campaigns	51%
Student-Led Sexual Assault Educational Workshops	46%
Safety Escort System	45%
Peer Counseling	39%
Self-Defense Courses or Programs	30%
Take Back the Night March	30%
Support Group for Survivors	17%
Escorts for Rape Survivors	16%
Sexual Assault Survivor Speak-Outs	15%
Peer Hotline	9%
Campuses with a Men's Issues Group	13%

Issues Addressed by Any Student Group:

Role of Alcohol/Drugs in Sexual Assault	63%
Aspects of Healthy Sexuality	48%
Peer Sexual Harassment	43%
Gender Role Socialization	38%
Definition of Consent	37%
Physical Self-Defense	35%
Relationship and Domestic Violence	34%
Sexism	34%
Verbal Confrontation Skills	30%
Faculty-Student Sexual Harassment	28%
Sex and Violence in the Media	23%
Homophobia and Rape	18%
Male Rape	13%
Childhood Sexual Assault	11%
Racism and Rape	11%
Pornography Debate	9%

of ten student-provided services and four of sixteen issues addressed by student groups differed significantly between groups. These results are presented in table 2. Of the staff-provided services, only counseling/support services, educational workshops about sexual assault, and campus-based rape crisis centers lacked significant association with the presence or absence of a policy.

Of the schools with a policy, two groups were created based on whether or not students were involved in the development or implementation of the campus sexual assault policy. The results were two more profiles, provided in table 3. As evident, all but one of the issues related to sexual assault were addressed by more student groups on those campuses with student involvement in policy development or implementation. The only issue addressed that exhibited no significant effect was the "pornography debate." With regard to student-provided services, the profile contrast was also extensive. Of ten student-provided services, seven were more prevalent on campuses with student involvement in the development of the sexual assault policy. Only "peer counseling," "self-defense courses," and "peer hotline" were distributed without significant profile differences.

DISCUSSION

As the first nationwide survey of its kind, this study yielded a summary quantitative description of what colleges are doing with regard to sexual assault. Most college administrations implemented a policy regarding sexual assault during the 1990s and primarily in response to internal recommendations or a legislative mandate. Fewer schools implemented a policy before 1990 or primarily in response to student activism or a high-profile case. We did find a significant positive relationship between student activism and early policy adoptions as well as between legislative mandates and later policy adoptions, those after 1990 ($p < 0.05$). Although various states enacted measures requiring policies on, and responses to, sexual assault, the legislative mandate most likely to have affected policy adoptions was the 1992 Ramstad Act (PL 102-325). This amendment to the Higher Education Act of 1965 required colleges to establish explicit policies regarding sexual assault (Bohmer and Parrot 1993). As evident, three years after the Ramstad Act became law, 16 percent of the educational institutions surveyed lacked a policy specific to sexual assault, in violation of federal requirements. Given the student-supportive bias of the population sampled, as mentioned earlier, this figure is likely to be an underestimate. This finding reflects a lack of effective information gathering or enforcement at the national level.

Table 2 Schools with Policy v. Schools without Policy

Services Provided by Staff:

	. . . at 496 Schools with Policy		. . . at 91 Schools without Policy	
	Mean	(95% Conf. Interv.)	Mean	(95% Conf. Interv.)
Counseling/Support Services	95%	(0.93, 0.97)	87%	(0.80, 0.94)
Workshops on Sexual Assault	84%	(0.81, 0.87)	71%	(0.62, 0.81)
Safety Escort Service	76%	(0.72, 0.80)	60%	(0.50, 0.71)*
Orientation on Sexual Assault	71%	(0.67, 0.75)	49%	(0.39, 0.60)*
Brochure on Sexual Assault	66%	(0.62, 0.70)	49%	(0.36, 0.57)*
24-Hr Crisis Intervention	59%	(0.54, 0.63)	35%	(0.25, 0.45)*
Training for Staff	50%	(0.46, 0.55)	31%	(0.21, 0.40)*
Legal/Judicial Advocacy	40%	(0.36, 0.44)	22%	(0.13, 0.31)*
Rape Victim Escort Program	33%	(0.29, 0.37)	13%	(0.06, 0.20)*
Training for Faculty	23%	(0.19, 0.26)	5%	(0.01, 0.10)*
Campus Rape Crisis Center	10%	(0.07, 0.13)	10%	(0.04, 0.16)
Total Staff Provided Services	6.1	(5.9, 6.3)	4.3	(3.8, 4.8)*

Existing Services Provided by Students:

	... at 496 Schools with Policy		... at 91 Schools without Policy	
	Mean	(95% Conf. Interv.)	Mean	(95% Conf. Interv.)
Awareness Campaigns	55%	(0.50, 0.59)	33%	(0.23, 0.43)*
Student-Led Workshop	48%	(0.43, 0.52)	36%	(0.26, 0.46)
Safety Escort System	46%	(0.42, 0.50)	40%	(0.29, 0.50)
Peer Counseling	40%	(0.36, 0.44)	32%	(0.22, 0.42)
Self-Defense Courses	31%	(0.27, 0.35)	26%	(0.17, 0.36)
Take Back the Night March	33%	(0.29, 0.37)	15%	(0.08, 0.23)*
Support Grp for Survivors	18%	(0.14, 0.21)	12%	(0.05, 0.19)*
Escorts for Rape Survivors	17%	(0.14, 0.20)	9%	(0.03, 0.15)
Survivor Speak-Outs	16%	(0.12, 0.19)	12%	(0.05, 0.19)
Peer Hotline	10%	(0.07, 0.13)	7%	(0.01, 0.12)
Total Student Provided Services	3.1	(2.9, 3.2)	2.2	(1.7, 2.7)*

(continued)

Table 2 *Continued*

Issues Addressed by Existing Student Groups:

	... at 496 Schools with Policy Mean	(95% Conf. Interv.)	... at 91 Schools without Policy Mean	(95% Conf. Interv.)
Alcohol/Drugs in Sex	65%	(0.61, 0.69)	49%	(0.39, 0.60)*
Aspects of Healthy Sexuality	51%	(0.46, 0.55)	36%	(0.26, 0.46)
Peer Sexual Harassment	45%	(0.40, 0.49)	32%	(0.22, 0.42)
Gender Role Socialization	41%	(0.36, 0.45)	24%	(0.15, 0.33)*
Definition of Consent	40%	(0.36, 0.44)	22%	(0.13, 0.31)*
Physical Self-Defense	35%	(0.31, 0.39)	35%	(0.25, 0.45)
Relation'p/Domestic Violence	35%	(0.30, 0.39)	30%	(0.20, 0.39)
Sexism	35%	(0.31, 0.39)	30%	(0.20, 0.39)
Verbal Confrontation Skills	32%	(0.28, 0.36)	22%	(0.13, 0.31)
Faculty-Student Sex Harassment	29%	(0.25, 0.33)	20%	(0.11, 0.28)
Sex and Violence in the Media	24%	(0.20, 0.28)	14%	(0.07, 0.22)
Homophobia and Rape	19%	(0.16, 0.23)	11%	(0.04, 0.18)
Male Rape	14%	(0.11, 0.17)	5%	(0.01, 0.10)*
Childhood Sexual Assault	11%	(0.09, 0.14)	8%	(0.02, 0.13)
Racism and Rape	11%	(0.09, 0.14)	9%	(0.03, 0.15)
Pornography Debate	10%	(0.07, 0.13)	8%	(0.02, 0.13)
Total Issues Addressed	4.5	(4.2, 4.9)	3.2	(2.4, 4.0)*

*Difference significant at the 95 percent confidence level.

Table 3 Schools with Student Involvement in Policy v. Schools without Student Involvement in Policy (excluding schools without a policy)

Services Provided by Staff:	. . . at 309 Schools with Students Involved		. . . at 157 Schools without Involvement	
	Mean	(95% Conf. Interv.)	**Mean**	(95% Conf. Interv.)
Counseling/Support Services	96%	(0.94, 0.98)	96%	(0.92, 0.99)
Workshops on Sexual Assault	88%	(0.85, 0.92)	77%	(0.70, 0.84)*
Safety Escort Service	80%	(0.75, 0.84)	71%	(0.64, 0.78)
Orientation on Sexual Assault	81%	(0.77, 0.85)	57%	(0.49, 0.65)*
Brochure on Sexual Assault	70%	(0.65, 0.75)	58%	(0.50, 0.66)
24-Hr Crisis Intervention	64%	(0.59, 0.69)	51%	(0.43, 0.59)
Training for Staff	51%	(0.46, 0.57)	47%	(0.39, 0.54)
Legal/Judicial Advocacy	45%	(0.39, 0.50)	31%	(0.23, 0.38)*
Rape Victim Escort Program	41%	(0.36, 0.47)	19%	(0.13, 0.25)*
Training for Faculty	27%	(0.22, 0.32)	12%	(0.07, 0.17)*
Campus Rape Crisis Center	14%	(0.10, 0.17)	3%	(0.00, 0.06)*
Total Staff Provided Services	6.6	(6.3, 6.8)	5.2	(4.9, 5.5)*

(continued)

Table 3 *Continued*

Existing Services Provided by Students:

	. . . at 309 Schools with Students Involved		. . . at 157 Schools without Involvement	
	Mean	(95% Conf. Interv.)	Mean	(95% Conf. Interv.)
Awareness Campaigns	66%	(0.60, 0.71)	38%	(0.30, 0.45)*
Student-Led Workshop	59%	(0.53, 0.64)	28%	(0.21, 0.35)*
Safety Escort System	53%	(0.47, 0.58)	36%	(0.29, 0.44)*
Peer Counseling	45%	(0.39, 0.51)	33%	(0.26, 0.41)
Self-Defense Courses	33%	(0.28, 0.39)	24%	(0.17, 0.31)
Take Back the Night March	39%	(0.34, 0.45)	22%	(0.16, 0.29)*
Support Grp for Survivors	22%	(0.18, 0.27)	10%	(0.05, 0.14)*
Escorts for Rape Survivors	21%	(0.17, 0.26)	9%	(0.04, 0.13)*
Survivor Speak-Outs	20%	(0.15, 0.24)	8%	(0.03, 0.12)*
Peer Hotline	11%	(0.07, 0.15)	8%	(0.04, 0.13)
Total Student Provided Services	3.7	(3.4, 3.9)	2.2	(1.8, 2.5)*

Issues Addressed by Existing Student Groups:

	...at 309 Schools with Students Involved		...at 157 Schools without Involvement	
	Mean	(95% Conf. Interv.)	Mean	(95% Conf. Interv.)
Alcohol/Drugs in Sex	75%	(0.70, 0.80)	51%	(0.43, 0.59)*
Aspects of Healthy Sexuality	58%	(0.52, 0.63)	42%	(0.34, 0.50)*
Peer Sexual Harassment	37%	(0.31, 0.42)	23%	(0.16, 0.30)*
Gender Role Socialization	49%	(0.44, 0.55)	27%	(0.20, 0.34)*
Definition of Consent	49%	(0.44, 0.55)	26%	(0.19, 0.33)*
Physical Self-Defense	43%	(0.37, 0.48)	21%	(0.15, 0.27)*
Relation'p/Domestic Violence	40%	(0.35, 0.46)	27%	(0.20, 0.34)*
Sexism	43%	(0.37, 0.49)	22%	(0.16, 0.29)*
Verbal Confrontation Skills	37%	(0.31, 0.42)	23%	(0.16, 0.30)*
Faculty-Student Sex. Harassment	37%	(0.32, 0.43)	16%	(0.10, 0.22)*
Sex and Violence in the Media	31%	(0.26, 0.36)	13%	(0.07, 0.18)*
Homophobia and Rape	25%	(0.20, 0.30)	9%	(0.04, 0.13)*
Male Rape	18%	(0.14, 0.22)	6%	(0.03, 0.10)*
Childhood Sexual Assault	14%	(0.10, 0.18)	6%	(0.02, 0.09)*
Racism and Rape	17%	(0.12, 0.21)	2%	(0.00, 0.04)*
Pornography Debate	11%	(0.08, 0.15)	8%	(0.03, 0.12)
Total Issues Addressed	5.5	(5.0, 5.9)	3.0	(2.5, 3.5)*

*Difference significant at the 95 percent confidence level.

With regard to programs and issues, the data painted a picture of diversity across the institutions surveyed. Certain programs and services were more prevalent than others. Of the services provided by staff, those at a majority of the responding campuses (more than 50 percent) tended to be services already provided by the institutions in other contexts. Colleges, in general, have orientation programs and information brochures; they also tend to provide counseling/psychological services or safety escort services. The high prevalence of educational workshops about sexual assault (81 percent) could be explained by the colleges' familiarity with the workshop format. Colleges address many other issues, such as campus safety and alcohol abuse, through educational workshops. Just below the 50 percent threshold was training for staff. We hypothesize that this service was fairly common because of the broader need to train student personnel officers, resident advisors, and similar employees. On the other hand, legal/judicial advocacy services and rape victim advocacy services were rather uncommon, at 38 and 30 percent of institutions, respectively. These low frequencies were not very surprising, given the tension between satisfying legal/constitutional requirements and fulfilling the educational mission of the institution. The assumption of multiple institutional roles may be a source of potential conflict (Bohmer and Parrot 1993). At the bottom of the list were faculty training and a campus-based rape crisis center, the former being a challenge to academic prerogative, and the latter requiring substantial resources and sometimes overlapping with a community rape crisis center.

With regard to student-provided services, perhaps the most significant finding was their lower overall frequencies in comparison to those provided by staff. This disparity, we hypothesize, reflects the generalized and flexible nature of the most common staff-provided student support services, noted previously. In contrast, student-provided services tend to involve more commitment than simply modifying an existing service. One finding of interest was the similarity of the least common programs. Support groups for survivors (17 percent), escorts for rape survivors (16 percent), sexual assault survivor speak-outs (15 percent), and peer hotlines (9 percent), all tend to be driven by survivors of sexual assault. Because rape victims have continued to experience psychological and social stigma (Koss 1988), this finding on the college campus is not surprising. Clearly, it is still difficult for rape survivors to come forward, let alone organize programs for the treatment and prevention of sexual assault.

The issues addressed by student groups also exhibited a variation in frequency. The "role of alcohol and drugs in sexual assault" was the most common issue addressed, probably because it is both the most significant cofactor identified and the least complex and threatening issue for students to raise (Abbey 1991). In contrast, the issues of "homophobia and rape," "racism and rape," and "pornography debate" are very complex, requiring the linkage of rape to power inequities within society (Sanday 1996, Kimmel 1993, Russell 1993). In addition, "male rape" and "childhood sexual assault" continue to be perceived as uncommon, regardless of their empirical incidence rates (Struckman-Johnson and Struckman-Johnson 1992, DePrince and Quirk 1995).

In addition to the aggregate results already presented, this study identified relationships among the existence of a policy, the involvement of students in the development of that policy, and the presence of various programs and services to address sexual assault on college campuses. As previously noted, schools without a policy were logically excluded from the profiles derived from the involvement of students in an existing policy. The importance of having a policy was evidenced by the finding that eight out of eleven staff-provided services were more prevalent at campuses with a policy specific to sexual assault (shown in table 2). More analysis was required on the minimal effect a policy had on student-provided services (three out of ten) or on issues addressed by student groups (four out of sixteen). The second set of profiles based on student involvement (table 3) provides useful data. The campus profiles based on student involvement with the policy showed a positive relationship between student involvement with the campus policy and the presence of student-provided services and student groups addressing issues related to sexual assault.

We hypothesize that having an institutional sexual assault policy affects services provided by staff more than it affects student-led services. Obviously, the presence of a policy affects everyone on campus, not only the staff. With regard to the provision of programs, however, those employed by the institution appear to have responded to the mere presence of a policy on campus. We believe this may be a reflection of staff roles as service providers, as opposed to the typical roles of American students as consumers on college campuses. With student involvement in the development and implementation of that policy, however, students appear to have become invested in the campus response to sexual assault. If effective preventive programs rely on students to engage both the cognitive (informational) and affective (attitudinal) perceptions of the community, then student involvement boosts the efficacy and comprehensiveness of sexual assault prevention programs. In other words, with students involved in the development of the policy, campuses have more prevention programs with which to modify a campus culture conducive to rape. Although this survey sought information regarding the initial implementation of the campus sexual assault policy, we suspect an engagement of students in the continual assessment and reevaluation of campus policy may yield similar benefits. This is one possibility for future research.

The effects of a campus sexual assault policy and student involvement in the development of that policy as outlined in this study suggests the importance of an emergent, collaborative relationship between students and administrators. A concomitant hypothesis is that student effectiveness in peer-led interventions on college campuses is related to how the institution supports or empowers student activism. We note here our understanding of student activism and student involvement as synonymous. Our definition does not match with those of our respondents who reported student activism in only 10 percent of policy adoptions but student involvement in 62 percent of policy adoptions. Perhaps campus administrators misunderstand student activism in the 1990s by associating it with the confrontational style more attributable to the 1960s. We suggest that student activism in the 1990s and the 2000s now has a different face, emphasizing peer education, community service, and collaboration with campus faculty and staff. As the data show, those campuses with student involvement tended to have not only a more comprehensive staff-provided program but also a broader peer-led program. The implications of this collaborative relationship are many.

As Sanday (1996) has documented, however, college administrators have typically not been at the forefront of acquaintance rape prevention. Since 1992 the Ramstad Amendment requires administrators to address rape on their campuses. The most effective way for college administrators to comply with this federal requirement, as our study supports, is through collaboration between students and staff. Staff may be responsible for implementing policies and supporting students, but the students will be most effective in changing the cultural norms that contribute to sexual violence.

LIMITATIONS AND FUTURE RESEARCH

This study provides no incidence data or correlations between student involvement and reported rapes. This limitation reflects the lack of a national database of reported rapes by campus. Although the Student Right-to-Know and Campus Security Act of 1990 requires campuses to make public reported rapes, these statistics are not yet collected and made public by any federal agency. In addition, the act uses Federal Bureau of Investigation definitions of rape, lacking a categorical division between acquaintance rape and stranger rape. Two future studies could fill this void by correlating peer education with increased rape reporting and, in the longer term, with decreased rape incidence. The significant underreporting of acquaintance rape on college campuses limits any conclusions based on reported rape data alone. As a result, we reiterate Koss and Harvey's 1991 recommendations for use of rape incidence data, both officially reported and questionnaire gathered. In addition, this study does not delve into the qualitative intricacies of student-administrator collaborations across college campuses. The large-scale, statistical nature of this study precludes any in-depth analysis of student-administrator collaborations. We recommend future study of this relationship.

CONCLUSION

This paper addresses theoretical aspects of acquaintance rape prevention on college campuses and presents the first profile of campus responses to sexual assault across America. We conclude that student involvement in policy development is positively associated with more student-provided programs to prevent sexual assault on campus. The importance of student involvement becomes evident with the high prevalence of acquaintance rape on campuses and with the efficacy of student leadership in affecting attitudes and beliefs. This study suggests the emergent role of the student-administrator collaboration. We recommend future study into this evolving relationship as well as into the effects of student involvement with acquaintance rape prevention on both rape-supportive culture and incidence of rape, reported and unreported. Our findings imply that in order to build a campus community intolerant of rape, staff and faculty need to include students in all phases of the institutional response to rape.

WORKS CITED

Abbey, A. (1991). "Acquaintance Rape and Alcohol Consumption on College Campuses: How Are They Linked?" *Journal of American College Health* 39: 165–69.

Aizenman, M., and Kelley, G. (1988). "Incidence of Violence and Acquaintance Rape in Dating Relationships among College Males and Females." *Journal of College Student Development* 29: 305–11.

Amir, M. (1971). *Patterns in Forcible Rape*. Chicago: University of Chicago Press.

Bart, P., and O'Brien, P. (1985). *Stopping Rape: Successful Survival Strategies*. Elmsford, New York: Pergamon.

Bohmer, C., and Parrot, A. (1993). *Sexual Assault on Campus: The Problem and the Solution*. New York: Lexington Books.

Burt, M. R. (1980). "Cultural Myths and Supports for Rape." *Journal of Applied Social Psychology* 38: 217–30.

Check, J. V. P., and Malamuth, M. N. (1983). "Sex Role Stereotyping and Reactions to Depictions of Stranger vs. Acquaintance Rape." *Journal of Personality and Social Psychology* 45: 344–56.

Crowley, T. (1993). "The Lie of Entitlement." In *Transforming a Rape Culture*, ed. E. Buchwald et al. Minneapolis: Milkweed Press.

DePrince, A., and Quirk, S. (1995). "Towards an Institutionalization of Denial?" *Journal of Psychohistory* 23: 141–44.

Kimmel, M. (1993). "Clarence, William, Iron Mike, Tailhook, Senator Packwood, Spur Posse, Magic . . . and Us." In *Transforming a Rape Culture*, ed. E. Buchwald et al. Minneapolis: Milkweed Press.

Koss, M. P. (1988). "Hidden Rape: Sexual Aggression and Victimization in a National Sample of Students in Higher Education." In *Rape and Sexual Assault*, ed. A. W. Burgess. New York: Garland Press.

Koss, M. P., and Dinero, T. E. (1989). "Predictors of Male Aggression among a National Sample of Male College Students." *Human Sexual Aggression: Current Perspectives. Annals of the New York Academy of Science* 528: 133–46.

Koss, M. P., Gidycz, C. A., Wisniewski, N. (1987). "The Scope of Rape: Incidence and Prevalence of Sexual Aggression and Victimization in a National Sample of Higher Education Students." *Journal of Consulting and Clinical Psychology* 55: 162–70.

Koss, M. P., and Harvey, M. R. (1991). *The Rape Victim: Clinical and Community Interventions*, 2d ed. Newbury Park, Calif.: Sage.

Lundberg-Love, P., and Geffner, R. (1989). "Date Rape: Prevalence, Risk Factors, and a Proposed Model." In *Violence in Dating Relationships: Emerging Social Issues*, ed. M. A. Pirog-Good et al. New York: Praeger.

Martin, P. Y., and Hammer, R. A. (1989). "Fraternities and Rape on Campus." *Gender and Society* 3: 457–73.

McCoughey, M. (1997). *Real Knock-Outs: The Physical Feminism of Women's Self-Defense*. New York: New York University.

Mosher, D. L., and Anderson, R. D. (1986). "Macho Personality, Sexual Aggression, and Reactions to Guided Imagery of Realistic Rape." *Journal of Research in Personality* 20: 77–94.

Muehlenhard, C. L., and Linton, M. A. (1987). "Date Rape and Sexual Aggression in Dating Situations: Incidence and Risk Factors." *Journal of Counseling Psychology* 34: 186–96.

Parrot, A. (1991). *Acquaintance Rape and Sexual Assault: A Prevention Manual*, 5th ed. Holmes Beach, Fla.: Learning Publications.

Russell, D. (1993). *Against Pornography: The Evidence of Harm*. Berkeley, Calif.: Russell Publications.

Sanday, P. R. (1996). *A Woman Scorned: Acquaintance Rape on Trial*. New York: Doubleday.

———. (1990). *Fraternity Gang Rape: Sex, Brotherhood, and Privilege on Campus*. New York: New York University Press.

Sloane, B., and Zimmer, C. (1993). "The Power of Peer Health Education." *Journal of American College Health* 41: 241–45.

Struckman-Johnson, C., and Struckman-Johnson, D. (1992). "Acceptance of Male Rape Myths among College Men and Women." *Sex Roles* 27: 85–100.

United States Department of Health and Human Services. (1985). *Healthy People 2000: National Health Promotion and Disease Prevention Objectives.* Washington, D.C.: United States Printing Office.

Williams, J. E., and Holmes, K. A. (1981). *The Second Sexual Assault: Rape and Public Attitudes.* Westport, Conn.: Greenwood Press.

APPENDIX 5

THE ANTIOCH COLLEGE SEXUAL OFFENSE POLICY

Approved by the Board of Trustees in June 1992

All sexual contact and conduct on the Antioch College campus and/or occurring with an Antioch community member must be consensual.

When a sexual offense, as defined herein, is committed by a community member, such action will not be tolerated.

Antioch College provides and maintains educational programs for all community members, some aspects of which are required. The educational aspects of this policy are intended to prevent sexual offenses and ultimately to heighten community awareness.

In support of this policy and community safety, a support network exists that consists of the Sexual Offense Prevention and Survivor's Advocacy Program and Counseling Services. The Advocate (or other designated administrator) shall be responsible for the initiation and coordination of measures required by this policy.

The implementation of this policy also utilizes established Antioch governance structures and adheres to contractual obligations.

CONSENT

1. For the purpose of this policy, "consent" shall be defined as follows: the act of willingly and verbally agreeing to engage in specific sexual contact or conduct.
2. If sexual contact and/or conduct is not mutually and simultaneously initiated, then the person who initiates sexual contact/conduct is

Excerpted from the actual policy distributed by Antioch College in June of 1992.

responsible for getting verbal consent of the other individual(s) involved.

3. Obtaining consent is an ongoing process in any sexual interaction. Verbal consent should be obtained with each new level of physical and/or sexual contact/conduct in any given interaction, regardless of who initiates it. Asking "Do you want to have sex with me?" is not enough. The request for consent must be specific to each act.

4. The person with whom sexual contact/conduct is initiated is responsible to express verbally and/or physically her/his willingness or lack of willingness when reasonably possible.

5. If someone has initially consented but then stops consenting during sexual interaction, she/he should communicate withdrawal verbally and/or through physical resistance. The other individual(s) must stop immediately.

6. To knowingly take advantage of someone who is under the influence of alcohol, drugs, and/or prescribed medication is not acceptable behavior at Antioch College.

7. If someone verbally agrees to engage in specific contact or conduct, but is not of her/his free will due to any circumstances stated in (a) through (d) below, then the person initiating shall be considered in violation of this policy if:

a) the person submitting is under the influence of alcohol or other substances supplied to her/him by the person initiating;

b) the person submitting is incapacitated by alcohol, drugs, and/or prescribed medication;

c) the person submitting is asleep or unconscious;

d) the person initiating has forced, threatened, coerced, or intimidated the other individual(s) into engaging in sexual contact and/or sexual conduct.

APPENDIX 6

SENATE JUDICIARY TESTIMONY PROVIDED BY ACTIVIST ON VIOLENCE AGAINST WOMEN ACT

This is a transcript of the testimony of Erica Strohl, a University of Pennsylvania student and founder of Students Together against Acquaintance Rape (STAAR), appearing before the Senate Judiciary Committee hearings on Senator Biden's proposed Violence against Women Act (S.2754). The act was passed into law in 1990.

TESTIMONY ON ACQUAINTANCE RAPE

Good morning. My name is Erica Strohl; I am from Minneapolis, Minnesota, and I will be a senior at the University of Pennsylvania in Philadelphia this fall. I'd like to thank Senator Biden's office for inviting me to be here today. I come as a cofounder of Students Together against Acquaintance Rape (STAAR), which is an organization dedicated to educating students on the issue of acquaintance rape at the University of Pennsylvania.

Amid the college greens, the football stadiums, the great brick libraries, and the social scenes of college campuses across America is the very serious and pervasive problem of acquaintance rape. From the ivy-covered halls of the elite eastern schools, across the great sweeping campuses of the midwestern state systems to the magnolia-lined walks of the southern universities, acquaintance rape is destroying the lives of women students. This crime does not begin or end on college campuses; it is painfully frequent in high schools, both public and private, and among working women in offices, farms, and factories.

At the University of Pennsylvania, an Ivy League school of eight thousand undergraduates, acquaintance rape occurs perhaps once each weekend, possibly more. While to most, this number will seem frightening, if not unimaginably high, I believe it holds true for most institutions of higher learning. Unlike many schools, Penn is fortunate to have an excellent women's center, which offers advocacy and counseling to students who are survivors of sexual assault. This job in itself is overwhelming, and leaves little time for education or prevention.

Although STAAR is mainly an educational group, educators often act as advocates to individuals by taking calls at home or going through the reporting process with students. The need is so great that STAAR educators are sometimes approached on campus or in classes by people they do not know and are asked for help. Mainly, however, STAAR educators present workshops in coed teams in dormitories, fraternities, and sororities. STAAR is supported by the coalition of student groups including the feminist and Greek organizations. Our day-to-day operations are run through Penn's student health services with professional advising from the director of health education. During its first year STAAR presented fifty-five workshops reaching over one thousand students. Peer education works because students trust other students. STAAR educators are not professionals or administrators, but we do know about college life.

The reality of acquaintance rape hit home for me midway through my first year at Penn, when a friend of mine was raped in a fraternity. She fit the stereotype—she was eighteen, at college, trying to fit in, and she had drunk more than she could handle that night. As her friends, we too fit the stereotype—we asked her why she went upstairs. We didn't believe that these guys whom we knew could actually be rapists. We didn't tell her it wasn't her fault or that there was help available. In fact, we didn't say much at all.

Susan was one of the forty-five survivors of rape I have come into contact with at Penn.

During that same year, I also learned about the practice of "beaching," or "ledging" as it is called at some schools. Basically, in a beaching incident a woman is brought into a room where other fraternity brothers or men are waiting on an outside ledge or balcony unbeknownst to her. During sex, either consensual or coercive, the other brothers walk into the room, frightening and embarrassing the woman. Needless to say this is horribly demeaning, but not an unusual event at colleges around the country. Days or months after, the "beached" woman is often harassed and laughed at by the men that participated in the event. To the woman this experience may be extremely psychologically damaging, while the participants get off scot-free with what they consider a funny joke or a pledge prank. Beaching is a part of a continuum of sexually assaultive behavior that can lead to gang rape or acquaintance rape.

When people try to speak out about rape, there is a great deal of resistance. Many educators receive harassing phone calls. One STAAR educator who publicly disclosed she was a survivor received calls warning her that the rape could happen again. Universities are reluctant to respond firmly and quickly to the problem for fear that their reputations will be tarnished. Invariably, people respond to the problem by saying, "not our school—not our boys—they come from good families." They want to believe that rape is committed by men of color who jump out of alleys with lead pipes.

The problem of acquaintance rape is further compounded on college campuses because alcohol abuse is prevalent and peer pressure for men to be sexually active is so strong that they do not hear the word "no" clearly.

Unfortunately, STAAR is one of the few acquaintance rape educational groups in the country, though we are currently working with other campuses to set up programs. For change to occur, universities must first acknowledge that the problem exists and convey to the student body that the crime will not be condoned or covered up. When a rape occurs, survivors must have access to counseling and the choice of pressing charges. These services must work equally well when the perpetrator is the star quarterback, or the best economics professor, or the son of a trustee.

The role of education is to let people know what acquaintance rape is and that it is a crime. It lets survivors know that what happened was illegal as well as awful. When the information is available, I believe that there will be fewer rapes because some women will be able to see the situation coming and get out. Education also raises men's awareness and makes it more likely that they will recognize and stop inappropriate action within their peer groups, as well as not participate in the action themselves. All universities should have rape prevention education, as it is likely the most common crime committed on campus.

Once a rape occurs, it is often difficult to strike a balance between protecting the accused until proven guilty, and protecting the victim from further violence. For instance, victims of acquaintance rape must often face their assailant in the classroom or at the dormitory, thereby further disrupting their lives and making it difficult to study, much less succeed in the classroom. When universities refuse to deal with the problem, they are in effect denying women access to equal educational opportunities.

No matter how much education is done, we cannot compete with eighteen years of socialization. Education about respect and equality must begin in elementary school. The climate of violence against women is overwhelming and growing worse all the time. Statistics for all types of violence against women are rising, and people still refuse to acknowledge that it might happen to their daughter, mother, sister, or themselves. There must be a concentrated effort to send a message that this violence is not acceptable and that perpetrators will be punished and survivors supported. Once the environment is safer, more women will report crimes of sexual violence. Most universities have little or no resources to deal with this wide-scale crisis. Incoming students are warned about pickpockets, muggings, racism, and alcoholism—they deserve to know about rape as well.

Thank you.

APPENDIX 7

THE STUDENT RIGHT-TO-KNOW ACT AND THE CAMPUS SECURITY ACT OF 1990

Title II of Public Law 101-542, The Student Right-to-Know Act and the Campus Security Act of 1990, also known as the "Clery Bill" in memory of Jeannie Clery, enacted by Congress and signed into law on November 8, 1990, amended section 485 of the Higher Education Act of 1965 by adding campus crime statistics and security reporting provisions for colleges and universities.

20 U.S.C. Section 1092

(f) Disclosure of campus security policy and campus crime statistics— (1) Each eligible institution participating in any program under this title shall on August 1, 1991, begin to collect the following information with respect to campus crime statistics and campus security policies of that institution, and beginning September 1, 1992, and each year thereafter, prepare, publish, and distribute, through appropriate publications or mailings, to all current students and employees, and to any applicant for the enrollment or employment upon request, an annual security report containing at least the following information with respect to campus security policies and campus crime statistics of that institution:

(A) A statement of current campus policies regarding procedures and facilities for students and others to report criminal actions or other emergencies occurring on campus and policies concerning the institution's response to such reports.

(B) A statement of current policies concerning security and access to campus facilities, including campus residences, and security considerations used in the maintenance of campus facilities.

(C) A statement of current policies concerning campus law enforcement, including—

(i) the enforcement authority of security personnel, including their working relationship with the state and local police agencies; and

(ii) policies which encourage accurate and prompt reporting of all crimes to the campus police and the appropriate police agencies.

(D) A description of the type and frequency of the programs designed to inform students and employees about campus security procedures and practices and to encourage students and employees to be responsible for their own security and the security of others.

(E) A description of the programs designed to inform students and employees about the prevention of crimes.

(F) Statistics concerning the occurrence on campus, during the most recent calendar year, and during the 2 preceding calendar years for which the data are available, of the following criminal offenses reported to campus security authorities or local police agencies—

(i) murder;

(ii) sex offenses, forcible and nonforcible;

(iii) robbery;

(iv) aggravated assault;

(v) burglary; and

(vi) motor vehicle theft.

(G) A statement of policy concerning the monitoring and recording through local police agencies of criminal activity at off-campus student organizations which are recognized by the institution and that are engaged in by students attending the institution, including those student organizations with off-campus housing facilities.

(H) Statistics concerning the number of arrests for the following crimes occurring on campus:

(i) liquor law violations;

(ii) drug abuse violations; and

(iii) weapons possession.

(I) A statement of policy regarding the possession, use, and sale of alcoholic beverages and enforcement of state underage drinking laws and a statement of policy regarding possession, use, and sale of any illegal drugs and enforcement of Federal and state drug laws and a description of any drug or alcohol abuse education programs as required under section 1145g of this title.

APPENDIX 8

CAMPUS SEXUAL ASSAULT VICTIM'S BILL OF RIGHTS (1992)

The security provisions of the Student Right-To-Know Act and the Campus Security Act of 1990 were amended in 1992 by the Campus Sexual Assault Victim's Bill of Rights to require that schools develop policies to deal with sexual assault on campus and provide certain assurances to victims.

20 U.S.C. 1092

(7)(A) Each institution of higher education participating in any program under this subchapter and part C of subchapter I of Chapter 34 of title 42 shall develop and distribute as part of the report described in paragraph (1) a statement of policy regarding—

    (i) such institution's campus sexual assault programs, which shall be aimed at prevention of sex offenses; and

    (ii) the procedures followed once an offense has occurred.

(B) The policy described in subparagraph (A) shall address the following areas:

    (i) Education programs to promote the awareness of rape, acquaintance rape, and other sex offenses.

    (ii) Possible sanctions to be imposed following the final determination of an on-campus disciplinary procedure regarding rape, acquaintance rape, or other sex offenses, forcible or nonforcible.

    (iii) Procedures students should follow if a sex offense occurs, including who should be contacted, the importance of preserving evidence as may be necessary to the proof of a criminal assault, and to whom the alleged offense should be reported.

    (iv) Procedures for on-campus disciplinary action in cases of alleged sexual assault, which shall include a clear statement that—

(I) the accuser and the accused are entitled to the same opportunities to have others present during a campus disciplinary proceeding; and

(II) both the accuser and the accused shall be informed of the outcome of any disciplinary proceeding brought alleging a sexual assault.

(v) Informing students of their options to notify the proper law enforcement authorities, including on-campus and local police, and the option to be assisted by campus authorities in notifying such authorities, if the student so chooses.

(vi) Notification of students of existing counseling, mental health, or student services for victims of sexual assault, both on campus and in the community.

(vii) Notification of students' options for, and available assistance in, changing academic and living situations after an alleged sexual assault incident, if so requested by the victim and if such changes are reasonably available.

(C) Nothing in this paragraph shall be construed to confer a right of action upon any person to enforce the provisions of this paragraph.

In summary:

The security policies released pursuant to the Campus Security Act shall specifically address sex offense prevention and include the following provisions in cases of alleged sexual assault:

- Accuser and accused must have same opportunity to have others present.
- Both parties shall be informed of the outcome of any disciplinary proceeding.
- Survivors shall be informed of their options to notify law enforcement.
- Survivors shall be notified of counseling services.
- Survivors shall be notified of options for changing academic and living situations.

SELECTED BIBLIOGRAPHY

Allen, Paula Gunn. "Violence and the American Indian Woman." *Working Together* (April 1985): 1–5.

Amir, Menachem. *Patterns in Forcible Rape.* Chicago: University of Chicago Press, 1971.

Ammons, Linda L. "Mules, Madonnas, Babies, Bathwater, Racial Imagery, and Stereotypes: The African American Woman and the Battered Woman Syndrome." *Wisconsin Law Review* 5 (1995): 1003–1080.

Asian Women United of California, eds. *Making Waves: An Anthology of Writings By and About Asian American Women.* Boston: Beacon Press, 1989.

Bambera, Toni Cade. *The Black Woman: An Anthology.* New York: Penquin, 1970.

———. *Deep Sightings and Rescue Missions.* New York: Pantheon, 1996.

Barrett, Karen. "Date Rape: A Campus Epidemic?" *Ms.* 11, no. 3 (1982): 49.

Bart, Pauline, and Eileen Geil Moran, eds. *Violence against Women: The Bloody Footprints.* Thousand Oaks, Calif.: Sage, 1993.

Bechhofer, Laurie, and Andrea Parrot, eds. *Acquaintance Rape: The Hidden Crime.* New York: John Wiley and Sons, 1991.

Bohmer, Carol, and Andrea Parrot. *Sexual Assault on Campus.* New York: Lexington Books, 1993.

Brownmiller, Susan. *Against Our Will: Men, Women, and Rape.* New York: Simon and Schuster, 1975.

Buchwald, Emilie, Pamela R. Fletcher, and Martha Roth, eds. *Transforming a Rape Culture.* Minneapolis: Milkweed Editions, 1993.

Burchess, Ann W., and Lynda L. Holmstrom. *Rape Crisis and Recovery.* Bowie, Md.: Robert J. Brady, 1979.

Burton, Nayda. "Resistance to Prevention: Reconsidering Feminist Antiviolence Rhetoric." In *Violence Against Women: Philosophical Perspectives,* ed. Stanley G. French, Wandy Teays, and Laura M. Purdy. Ithaca, N.Y.: Cornell University Press, 1998.

Chandler, Zala. "Voices beyond the Veil: An Interview with Toni Cade Bambera and Sonia Sanchez." In *Wild Women in the Whirlwind: Afra-American Culture and the Contemporary Literary Renaissance*, ed. Joanne M. Braxton and Nicola Mclaughlin. New Brunswick, N.J.:Rutgers University Press, 1990.

Chauncey, George Jr. "From Sexual Inversion to Homosexuality: Medicine and the Changing Conception of Female Deviance." *Salmagundi* 58–59 (1982–83): 114–46.

Chow, Esther Ngan-Ling. *Acculturation of Asian American Professional Women* (Research Monograph). Washington, D.C.: National Institute of Mental Health, Department of Health and Human Services, 1982.

Cleage, Pearl. *Mad at Miles: A Blackwoman's Guide to Truth.* Southfield, Mich.: Cleage, 1990.

Cleaver, Richard, and Patricia Myers, eds. *A Certain Terror: Heterosexism, Militarism, Violence, and Change.* Chicago: Great Lakes Region Friends Service Committee, 1993.

Crenshaw, Kimberle. "The Marginalization of Sexual Violence against Black Women." *National Coalition against Sexual Assault Journal* 2, no.1 (1994): 1–6, 15.

Crespo, Elba, and Candace Waldron, eds. *Reclaiming Our Lives: A Training Manual for Those Working with Victims/Survivors of Sexual Assault in Massachusetts.* Boston: Massachusetts Department of Public Health, Women's Health Unit, 1987.

Dash, Julie. *Daughters of the Dust: The Making of an African American Women's Film.* W. W. Norton, 1992.

Davis, Angela. *Women, Race, and Class.* New York: Vintage Books, 1983.

———. *Women, Culture, and Politics.* New York: Random House, 1989.

Delacoste, Frederique, and Felice Newman, ed. *Fight Back! Female Resistance to Male Violence.* Minneapolis: Cleis Press, 1981.

Dworkin, Andrea. *Our Blood: Prophecies and Discources on Sexual Politics.* New York: Harper and Row, 1976.

———. *Pornography: Men Possessing Women.* New York: E. P. Dutton, 1979.

———. *Intercourse.* New York: Free Press, 1987.

———. *Life and Death: Unapologetic Writings on the Continuing War against Women.* New York: Free Press, 1997.

Ehrhart, Julie K., and Bernice Sandler. *Campus Gang Rape: Party Games?* Project on the Status and Education of Women. Washington, D.C.: Association of American Colleges, 1985.

Estrich, Susan. *Real Rape.* Cambridge: Harvard University Press, 1987.

Evans, Sara M. *Personal Politics: The Roots of Women's Liberation in the Civil Rights Movement and the New Left.* New York: Vintage Books, 1980.

Fairstein, Linda A. *Sexual Violence: Our War against Rape.* New York: William Morrow, 1993.

Faludi, Susan. *Backlash: The Undeclared War against Women.* New York: Crown, 1991.

Freeman, Jo. *The Politics of Women's Liberation: A Case Study of an Emerging Social Movement and Its Relation to the Policy Process.* New York: David McKay, 1975.

———, ed. *Women: A Feminist Perspective.* 4th ed. Mountain View, Calif.: Mayfield, 1989.

Gaddis, John. "Women's Empowerment through Model Mugging: Breaking the Cycle of Social Violence." Ph.D. diss., University of California, Santa Barbara, 1990.

Giddings, Paula. *When and Where I Enter: The Impact of Black Women on Race and Sex in America*. New York: Bantom Books, 1984.

Gray, Michael D., Diane Lesser, Edna Quinn, and Chris Rounds. "The Effectiveness of Personalizing Acquaintance Rape Prevention: Programs on Perception of Vunerability and on Reducing Risk-Taking Behavior." *Journal of College Student Development* 31 (1990): 217–20.

Griffin, Susan. "Rape: The All-American Crime." *Ramparts* 10, no. 3(1971): 26–35.

———. *Pornography and Silence: Culture's Revenge against Nature*. New York: Harper and Row, 1981.

———. *Rape: The Politics of Consciousness*. San Francisco: Harper and Row, 1986.

Guy-Sheftall, Beverly, ed. *Words of Fire: An Anthology of African-American Feminist Thought*. New York: New Press, 1995.

Hanson, Kimberly, and Christine A. Gidycz. "Evolution of a Sexual Assault Prevention Program." *Journal of Consulting and Clinical Psychology* 1, no. 6 (1993): 1046–52.

Hart, Lynda. *Fatal Women: Lesbian Sexuality and the Mark of Aggression*. Princeton, N.J.: Princeton University Press, 1994.

Hemphill, Essex. *Ceremonies*. New York: Penguin, 1992.

Herman, Judith Lewis. *Trauma and Recovery*. New York: Basic Books, 1992.

Higgins, Gina O'Connell. *Resilient Adults*. San Francisco: Jossey-Bass, 1994.

Hull, Gloria T., Patricia Bell-Scott, and Barbara Smith, eds. *All the Women Are White, All the Blacks Are Men, But Some of Us Are Brave: Black Women's Studies*. New York: Feminist Press, 1992.

Janoff-Bulman, Ronnie. *Shattered Assumptions*. New York: Free Press, 1992.

Kalven, Harry, Jr., and Hans Zeisel. *The American Jury*. Boston: Little, Brown, 1966.

Kelly, et al. "Beyond Victim or Survivor: Sexual Violence, Identity, and Feminist Theory and Practice." In *Sexualizing the Social*, ed. Lisa Adkins and Vicki Merchant. New York: St. Martin's Press, 1996.

Kelly, Liz. *Surviving Sexual Violence*. Minneapolis: University of Minnesota Press, 1988.

Kimmel, Michael. *Men Confront Pornography*. New York: Meridian Books, 1991.

Kimmel, Michael, and Michael A. Messner, eds. *Men's Lives*. Needham Heights, Mass.: Allyn and Bacon, 1998.

Kimmel, Michael, and Thomas E. Mosmiller, ed. *Against the Tide: Profeminist Men in the United States, 1776–1990, A Documentary History*. Boston: Beacon Press, 1992.

Koss, Mary. *Hidden Rape on a University Campus*. National Institute of Mental Health, Final Report for Grant Ro1MH31618, 1981.

———. "Hidden Rape: Sexual Aggression and Victimization in a National Sample of Students in Higher Education." In *Rape and Sexual Assault II*, ed. Ann Wolbert Burgess. New York: Garland, 1988.

Koss, Mary P., Christine A. Gidycz, and Nadine Wisniewski. "The Scope of Rape: Incidence and Prevalence of Sexual Aggression and Victimization in a National Sample of Higher Education Students." *Journal of Consulting and Clinical Psychology* 55 (1987): 162–70.

Landerman, Donna. "Breaking the Racism Barrier: White Anti-Racism Work." In *Revealing the Web of Life: Feminism And Nonviolence*, ed. Pam McAllister. Philadelphia: New Society, 1982.

Langelan, Martha. *Back Off: How to Confront and Stop Sexual Harassment and Harassers*. New York: Fireside, 1993.

Largen, Mary Ann. "History of Women's Movement in Changing Attitudes, Laws, and Treatment toward Rape Victims." In *Sexual Assault*, ed. Marcia J. Walker and Stanley L. Brodsky. Lexington, Mass.: Lexington Books, 1976.

Liedholdt, Dorchen, and Janice G. Raymond, eds. *The Sexual Liberals and the Attack on Feminism*. New York: Pergamon Press, 1990.

Levine, Arthur. "A New Generation of Student Protesters Arise." *Chronicle of Higher Education*, February 26, 1999, A52.

Loeb, Paul Rogat. *Generations at the Crossroads: Apathy and Action on the American Campus*. New Brunswick, N.J.: Rutgers University Press, 1994.

Lorde, Audre. *Sister Outsider: Essays and Speeches*. Trumansberg, N.Y.: Crossing Press, 1984.

———. *A Burst of Light*. Ithaca, N.Y.: Firebrand Books, 1988.

MacKinnon, Catharine. *Feminism Unmodified: Discourses on Life and Law*. Cambridge, Mass.: Harvard University Press, 1987.

———. *Only Words*. Cambridge, Mass.: Harvard University Press, 1993.

McCaughey, Martha. *Real Knockouts: The Physical Feminism of Women's Self Defense*. New York: New York University Press, 1997.

Marcus, Sharon. "Fighting Words: A Theory and Politics of Rape Prevention." In *Feminists Theorize the Political*, ed. Judith Butler and Joan W. Scott. New York: Routledge, 1992.

Matthews, Nancy. *Confronting Rape: The Feminist Anti-Rape Movement and the State*. New York: Routledge, 1994.

Millett, Kate. *Sexual Politics*. New York: Ballantine, 1969.

Morga, Cherrie, and Gloria Anzaldua, eds. *This Bridge Called My Back: Writings by Radical Women of Color*. New York: Kitchen Table Women of Color Press, 1983.

Morgan, Robin, ed. *Sisterhood Is Powerful: An Anthology of Writings from the Women's Liberation Movement*. New York: Random House, 1970.

Morrison, Toni, ed. *Race-ing Justice, En-gendering Power: Essays on Anita Hill, Clarence Thomas and the Construction of Social Reality*. New York: Pantheon Books, 1992.

Muehlenhard, Charlene L., Irene G. Powch, Joi L. Phelps, and Laura M. Giusti. "Definitions of Rape: Scientific and Political Implications," *Journal of Social Issues* 48, no. 1 (1992): 23–44.

O'Toole, Laura T., and Jessica R. Schiffman, eds. *Gender Violence: Interdisciplinary Perspectives*. New York: New York University Press, 1997.

Pharr, Suzanne. *Homophobia: A Weapon of Sexism*. Little Rock, Ark.: Chardon Press, 1998.

Pierce-Baker, Charlotte. *Surviving the Silence: Black Women's Stories of Rape*. New York: W. W. Norton, 1998.

Richie, Beth. "Facing Contradictions: Challenge for Black Feminists." *Ageis* 37 (1983): 14–20.

———. *Compelled to Crime: The Gender Entrapment of Battered Black Women*. New York: Routledge, 1996.

Russell, Diana E. H. *The Politics of Rape: The Victim's Perspective.* New York: Stein and Day, 1984.

———. *Sexual Exploitation: Rape, Child Sexual Abuse and Workplace Harassment.* Newbury Park, Calif.: Sage, 1984.

———. *Against Pornography: The Evidence of Harm.* Berkeley, Calif.: Russell, 1993.

Sanday, Peegy Reeves. *Fraternity Gang Rape: Sex, Brotherhood and Privilege on Campus.* New York: New York University Press, 1990.

———. *A Women Scorned: Acquaintance Rape on Trial.* New York: Doubleday, 1996.

Sandler, Bernice R., and Robert J. Shoop, eds. *Sexual Harassment on Campus: A Guide for Administrators, Faculty and Students.* Needham Heights, Mass.: Allyn and Bacon, 1997.

Scarce, Michael. *Male on Male Rape: Hidden Toll of Stigma and Shame.* New York: Plenum, 1997.

Scully, Diana. *Understanding Sexual Violence: A Study of Convicted Rapists.* Boston: Unwin Hyman, 1990.

Smith, Barbara, ed. *Home Girls: A Black Feminist Anthology.* New York: Kitchen Table Press, 1983.

Stan, Adele, ed. *Debating Sexual Correctness: Pornography, Sexual Harassment, Date Rape, and the Politics of Sexual Equality.* New York: Dell, 1995.

Steenberg, Brett N., and Christine G. Zimmer, eds. "Violence on Campus: The Changing Face of College Health." *Journal of American College Health* 40, no. 4 (1992).

Stoltenberg, John. *Refusing to Be a Man: Essays on Sex and Justice.* New York: Penguin, 1990.

———. *The End of Manhood: A Book for Men of Conscience.* New York: Penguin, 1993.

Turaj, Johanna. "Finding the Kiai: Training at a Women's Karate School and Its Relationship to Self-Esteem." Manuscript, Smith College School for Social Work, 1993.

Warshaw, Robin. *I Never Called It Rape: The Ms. Report on Recognizing Fighting and Surviving Date and Acquaintance Rape.* New York: Harper and Row, 1988.

Watkins, Gloria (bell hooks). *Ain't I a Woman: Black Women and Feminism.* Boston: South End Press, 1981.

———. *Talking Back: Thinking Feminist*Thinking Black.* Boston: South End Press, 1989.

Wiehe, Vernon, and Ann Richards. *Intimate Betrayal: Understanding and Responding to the Trauma of Acquaintance Rape.* Thousand Oaks, Calif.: Sage, 1995.

Yamato, Gloria. "Something about the Subject Makes It Hard to Name." In *Making Face, Making Soul: Creative and Critical Perspectives by Women of Color,* ed. Gloria Anzaldua. San Francisco, Calif.: Aunt Lute, 1990.

Young, Iris Marion. *Throwing Like a Girl and Other Essays in Feminist Philosophy and Social Theory.* Bloomington, Ind.: Indiana University Press, 1990.

INDEX

ℬℭ

ANTHOLOGY CONTRIBUTORS

Andrew Abrams has spent the last few years recovering from his involvement in the media feeding frenzy surrounding Antioch College's Sexual Offense Policy, with which he was closely involved. He has heard all the jokes about consent and even laughed at a few. He graduated from Antioch with a degree in anthropology and worked for the college for two years. He is now a writer living in Los Angeles, working at the American Zoetrope production company. Andrew still believes that sex is fun and consent is sexy.

Nate Daun Barnett is a former student activist, coordinator of the Fourth North American Student Conference on Campus Sexual Violence, and co-founder of SpeakOut: The North American Student Coalition Against Sexual Violence. He is a recent graduate of James Madison University with a master's degree in education and currently a residence hall director for Marquette University.

Jesselyn Brown, motivated by the events in which she was involved at Brown University, decided to go to law school (as did three of the other members of the "Committee of Four"). Following her graduation from Yale Law School in 1995, she joined the Attorney General's Honor Program as a trial attorney at the U.S. Department of Justice. She practices constitutional tort litigation and lives in Washington, D.C., with her husband, Dan Radack, and their son, Jacob. She is expecting her second baby in November 1999 and is still very active on gender issues.

Jodi Gold, M.D., graduated from the University of Pennsylvania in 1992 where she played Division I tennis and first called herself a feminist activist. She was the student coordinator of the First North American Conference on Sexual Violence that currently boasts fifteen conferences.

Jodi was a founding member of Speakout: The North American Student Coalition Against Sexual Violence. Since 1989, she has given multiple presentations, mentored students, and consulted with colleges nationwide. She has also researched extensively the history of the antirape movement. In 1994 Susan Villari and she were the recipients of a Frost Foundation grant to develop a national database of the student movement against sexual violence. That database grew out of control and ended up as *Just Sex*.

Jodi graduated from medical school at the University of Tennessee in 1999 and is currently pursuing a career in child and adolescent psychiatry. She is looking forward to a life after *Just Sex*.

Kristine Herman graduated from Antioch College in 1994, received her master's in social work from Tulane in 1995, and graduated from Northeastern University Law School in 1999. Kristine has continued to work on advocacy and policy issues related to domestic violence and sexual assault.

Elizabethe Holland received her bachelor's degree from the University of Illinois in 1989 and a master's degree from Ohio State University in 1995. At Ohio State she was a Kiplinger Fellow and spent much of her fellowship working on a master's project on the Campus Security Act. Her research was summed up in an article she wrote for the *New York Times* education supplement. Before Holland attended Ohio State, she was a crime reporter for the Florida Daily News from 1989 to 1992 and a reporter, editor, and columnist for the *Las Vegas Sun* from 1992 to 1994. She won several journalism awards in Florida and Nevada, among them first-place honors from the Florida Society of Newspaper Editors for her series on two rape victims. Currently, Holland is a sports writer at the *St. Louis Post-Dispatch*, where she covers women's sports and the NFL.

Selden Holt has worked in the field of sexual violence prevention and response for over six years as a volunteer and as a coordinator of Sexual Assault Support Services at Duke University. Most recently she worked for the Governor's Crime Commission in her home state of North Carolina. Currently she is pursuing her master's degree in social work from the University of North Carolina at Chapel Hill. Outside of work, she enjoys singing made-up songs to her daughter Maura and their dogs, hiking, reading novels, and hanging out with friends, including her honey of ten years (husband of five), Michael.

Luoluo Hong received a B.A. in psychology from Amherst College in 1990, a master's in public health from Yale University in 1992, and a Ph.D. in educational leadership and research from LSU in 1998. She is the director of the Wellness Education and Outreach Services and serves as a faculty member in the Department of Kinesiology at LSU. She travels to campuses across the country as an educational consultant for CAMPUSPEAK, an agency based in Denver, Colorado.

Luoluo sits on the board of directors for the American College Health Association and is past chair of the association's Campus Violence Task Force. She has developed a national reputation for her innovative work with the campus peer leadership organization, Men against Violence, and has published her dissertation entitled *Rethinking Babes, Booze, and Brawls: Toward a New Masculinity—Men against Violence.* Recently married, she resides in Baton Rouge with husband Christopher Aamodt, their dog, Toby, and six cats: Mozart, Whitney, Aiwa, Bacchus, Athena, and Puck.

Krista K. Jacob received her master's of science in women's studies from Minnesota State University, Mankato. She has worked as a rape victim advocate and as an antirape educator for the past seven years, and she has presented antirape educational programming for audiences of all ages, especially adolescents. At present she works as a consultant for rape crisis centers and domestic violence shelters providing training and victim advocacy. In addition, she works part-time as an abortion counselor at a clinic in Minneapolis, Minnesota. She is coeditor for the forthcoming anthology *Choices and Voices: Writings about Abortion.*

Katie Koestner landed on the cover of *Time* magazine in 1991 for speaking out about her sexual assault. Since her graduation from the College of William and Mary in 1994, she has presented programs to thousands of students at nearly seven hundred colleges, high schools, and military institutions. In 1994 she founded the organization Campus Outreach Services, Inc., which specializes in educational programs, policy development, and risk management services for schools.

Martha McCaughey is a third-wave feminist active in anti-sexual-assault education since 1989. As assistant professor of women's studies in the Center for Interdisciplinary Studies at Virginia Tech, she teaches courses in the areas of feminist thought, science and technology studies, popular culture, and the body. She is the author of *Real Knockouts: The Physical Feminism of Women's Self-Defense* (1997, New York University Press).

Kathy Miriam is a radical feminist writer and educator. She has worked in the battered women's movement and as an antipornography activist. She recently completed her dissertation for the History of Consciousness Program entitled *Rethinking Radical Feminism: Opposition, Utopianism, and the Moral Imagination of Feminist Thought* (University of California, Santa Cruz). Her publications include *All the Rage*, a critique of queer S/M culture (in *Unleashing Feminism*, Herbooks, 1993) and an essay entitled "The Future of Lesbian Feminism" for *Women at the Millennium* (Gynergy Books, 1998.)

Stephen Montagna is an East Coast native who now calls Madison, Wisconsin, home. Stephen joined Men Stopping Rape, Inc. (MSR), in the fall of 1991 when he moved to Madison to pursue his graduate degree in theater. After receiving his M.F.A. in acting at the UW, he worked as the coordinator of MSR. The organization has since divested itself of university funds, and Stephen now volunteers along with a handful of other men committed to keeping MSR alive. He has presented numerous workshops in both men-only and coed spaces, and served on the planning committees for Sexual Assault Awareness Week and the Madison Clothesline Project in Dane County.

Michael Scarce is coordinator of the Lesbian, Gay, Bisexual and Transgender Resource Center at the University of California, San Francisco, and the former coordinator of Ohio State University's Rape Education and Prevention Program. As a rape survivor, activist, and scholar, Michael has sought to increase visibility and awareness of same-sex rape as a community issue, while fostering a more sensitive and competent response to the needs of adult male survivors of sexual violence. He is the author of two books: *Male on Male Rape: The Hidden Toll of Stigma* and *Shame* and *Smearing the Queer: Gay Male Sexual Health and Medical Science.*

Jason Schultz is a third-year law student at the University of California at Berkeley (Boalt Hall). He graduated from Duke University in 1993 with a degree in public policy studies and honors in women's studies. While at Duke, he volunteered at the Durham County Rape Crisis Center and helped organize Men Acting for Change, a profeminist men's activist group committed to ending violence against women.

Aishah Shahidah Simmons is an award-winning Black feminist lesbian independent filmmaker, writer, and activist who creates work and lectures on issues from her newly defined Afrolesfemcentric perspective. She is presently producing, writing, and directing *NO!*, a ninety-minute experiential documentary that will expose the collective silence of the Black community when Black women or girls are raped or sexually assaulted, physically or verbally, by Black men and boys. For her cultural work and media activism, Ms. Simmons has received the 1994 Philadelphia Gay Pride Grand Marshall Award, the 1995 Atlantic City Black Film Festival Filmmaker's Award, and the 1998 Audre Lorde Legacy Award of the Union Institute Center for Women.

Brett Sokolow founded Men Acting for Change as a student at the College of William and Mary and is now a specialist in sexual assault policy and law. He is the president and director of Risk Management Programs for Campus Outreach Services, Inc. COS provides sexual assault risk management consultation, educational programs, and lobbying efforts for sexual assault legislation.

John Stoltenberg (M.Div., M.F.A.) is the radical feminist author of *Refusing to Be a Man: Essays on Sex and Justice, The End of Manhood: A Book for Men of Conscience,* and *What Makes Pornography "Sexy"?* John is cofounder of Men against Pornography (www.geocities.com/CapitalHill/1139) and a frequent speaker and workshop leader at colleges and conferences (www.speakerspca.com). John and Andrea Dworkin began their life together in 1974, when she was twenty-seven and he was twenty-nine. Their home is in New York City.

Susan Villari, M.P.H. Susan is the director of Health Education at the University of Pennsylvania. Since 1989, she has organized student educators and activists including STAAR, Students Together Against Acquaintance Rape, which hosted the First North American Student Conference on Campus Sexual Violence. She has worked in the women's health movement for twenty years. Susan is a founding member of SpeakOut: The North American Student Coalition Against Sexual Violence. She has presented at numerous local, national, and international health and social justice conferences and consults with universities nationwide. Currently, she lives outside of Philadelphia with her daughter, Alivia.

Janelle L. White is the director of recruitment and training at San Francisco Women against Rape (SFWAR). SFWAR is a community-based organization (composed primarily of women of color) committed to addressing sexual violence. Janelle relocated to San Francisco in January 1997 from Ann Arbor, Michigan, where she worked for over two years as the coordinator of the Peer Education Program at the University of Michigan's Sexual Assault Prevention and Awareness Center. Janelle is a University of Michigan Ph.D. candidate in sociology, and her dissertation focuses on the experience of Black women working in the antirape and battered women's movement. During her time in Michigan she designed and taught a number of courses offered through the departments of sociology, African and African American studies, and women's studies, including a course titled "Our Silence Will Not Protect Us: Black Women Confront Sexual and Domestic Violence." Janelle's writing, research, and community activism are rooted in recognizing how race, class, and gender operate as interconnected systems of oppression.